The Educational Book Division of Prentice-Hall, Inc., is committed to the publication of outstanding textbooks. One important measure of a book's excellence is how well it communicates with its readers. To assure a highly readable book, the content for this text was selected, organized, and written at a level appropriate for the intended audience. The Dale-Chall readability formula was used to control readability level. An inviting and meaningful design was created to enhance the book's visual appeal as well as to facilitate the reading process. We are confident that the students for whom this book is intended will read it, comprehend it, and learn from it.

The following features were incorporated in the content and design of this text.

- The Table of Contents lists all major section heads within each chapter.

- For easy reference for teachers and students, all student activities are listed by title as well as number, on pages 12 to 15.

- Each chapter opens with an illustration that relates to the particular form of writing presented in that chapter.

- Student-written compositions and carefully selected professional models illustrate each of the various forms of writing.

- Marginal glosses for student composition models are set off in color, as are the Major Writing Assignments.

- The chapter "Polishing and Perfecting" includes rough drafts of student compositions with marginal glosses to indicate editorial comments. A second draft (page 48) demonstrates for the student the actual process of revision. A chart of proofreader's marks is provided.

- The chapter "Writing Letters, Memos, and Reports" provides the students with a skeleton letter and line drawings to guide them in the writing of business letters.

- A Style Sheet on pages 398 to 410 helps the students check capitalization and punctuation as they undertake the various writing activities.

- A comprehensive index begins on page 414.

Developing
Writing Skills

Communication **Analysis**

Paragraphing **Argument**

Narrative Exposition **Opinion**

Persuasion **Résumés** Editing

Memos Reports Research Paper

Criticism Letters

Third Edition

Developing
Writing Skills

William W. West

University of South Florida, Tampa, Florida

PRENTICE-HALL, INC., Englewood Cliffs, New Jersey

SUPPLEMENTARY MATERIAL
Teacher's Guide

The **photographs** and **illustrations** in this book appear courtesy of the following:

Royal Asiatic Society, London, England, page 18   Culver Pictures, Inc., page 23   The Granger Collection, pages 30, 32, 34, 71, 86, 93, 108, 170, 206, 227, 232, 262, 275, 285, 317, 330, 357, 362, 388   Mimi Forsyth from Monkmeyer Press, page 52   Shelton from Monkmeyer Press, page 119   Editorial Photocolor Archives, page 134   Dr. Philip S. Callahan, page 149   Liaison Agency, page 154   Dick Huffman from Monkmeyer Press, page 182   Western Ways Photo—Leo DeWys, Inc., page 308

The author and editors have made every effort to trace the ownership of all copyrighted selections found in this book and to make full acknowledgment of their use. Student compositions have, in some instances, been slightly adapted.

Acknowledgments appear at the back of the book.

Developing Writing Skills, Third Edition, by William W. West

©1980, 1973, 1966 by Prentice-Hall, Inc., Englewood Cliffs, New Jersey 07632.

ISBN 0-13-205369-1   10 9 8 7 6 5 4 3 2 1

PRENTICE-HALL INTERNATIONAL, INC., *London*
PRENTICE-HALL OF AUSTRALIA, PTY. LTD., *Sydney*
PRENTICE-HALL OF CANADA, LTD., *Toronto*
PRENTICE-HALL OF INDIA PRIVATE LTD., *New Delhi*
PRENTICE-HALL OF JAPAN, INC., *Tokyo*
PRENTICE-HALL OF SOUTHEAST ASIA PTE. LTD., *Singapore*
WHITEHALL BOOKS LIMITED, Wellington, *New Zealand*

Contents

9 WRITING LETTERS, MEMOS, AND REPORTS 2O7

10 THE LIBRARY RESOURCE PAPER 233

11 NARRATION 263

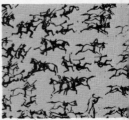

12 THE CHARACTER SKETCH 307

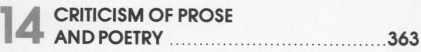

Appendix

Student Activities

Preface

To create a work of art is to impose meaningful form upon significant subject matter. Composers usually confine their creative expressions within the conventional musical forms accepted in their culture. Painters ordinarily give their myriad perceptions visual expression through the accepted style of a current school. Writers customarily choose subjects and treat them within the relatively narrow limits of the traditional genres.

But then, of course, there are the rare geniuses who throw aside all the established patterns and create new and personal forms.

This book is not for those geniuses. No matter how sympathetic progressive educators may be to the idiosyncratic expression of genius, many will attest that the traditional artistic forms of Western civilization should serve as a prelude to original creation. This textbook offers such traditional forms, both as useful structures for the usual student of writing and as preparatory study for the **poiētēs**, or creator, in the Greek sense.

The ideas that form the basis of **Developing Writing Skills** were originally conceived as a way of teaching writing more effectively while, at the same time, alleviating the laborious and often unproductive task of correcting, returning, and reviewing innumerable student themes.

In 1966, after ten years of use and experimentation and a full year of comparative evaluation, this system of developing writing skills became a book. The second edition of 1973 was improved as a result of the recommendations, activities, and models provided by a "generation" of users. The current edition of **Developing Writing Skills** owes much to the previous editions, but it owes more to the current revival of the teaching of writing. The Bay Area Writing Project has been tremendously helpful in guiding the current edition into interesting, stimulating, and productive channels.

Although in any valuable expression there must be both (1) significant subject matter and (2) meaningful form, the basic emphasis of this book is on the latter. Each major chapter examines and teaches a different useful form. The many student-written and professional models in **Developing Writing Skills** were carefully selected to help students master each of these forms. The models are also intended to assist in the discovery of subject matter that is both significant and appealing to student and reader alike.

This third edition of **Developing Writing Skills** continues to stress the chapter content that has been successful in the preceding editions. By following the prescribed sequence, the student gets the necessary practice in expression, and the teacher avoids the enervating and onerous duty of correcting more papers than necessary. The general plan of the chapters is as follows:

1) Professional examples of the particular form being studied (By reading and discussing these models, the student not only begins to understand the form and its possibilities but also begins to explore possible subjects for personal expression.)

2) An explanation of the form and motivation for that particular kind of writing

3) One or more student models with marginal glosses to guide understanding

4) A series of preparatory activities—writing, study, and discussion—focusing on skills and concepts needed for a major writing assignment

5) Specific instructions for the major assignment

Following this sequence, the teacher guides the student through the first four elements of each chapter by encouraging much oral and written expression. Instead of correcting each paper, however, the teacher may capitalize on the self-rewarding features and immediate feedback of the activities and restrict corrections to the final major writing assignments. Because the student is carefully prepared for the major writing assignment, he or she can write more effectively and the teacher's correction load is less burdensome.

The first two chapters purposefully vary from the general plan. Chapter One ("Writing for Effective Communication") is designed to arouse the interest of the student in the range and value of writing in the contemporary world. Chapter Two ("Polishing and Perfecting") familiarizes the student with the steps necessary to all forms of writing. By learning at the outset to apply the basic skills of editing and proofreading to each of the major writing assignments, the student begins to accept revision as an integral part of the writing process.

Chapters Three to Ten cover the different forms of expository writing. Chapters Eleven to Fourteen cover those forms commonly labeled creative writing. New to this edition of **Developing Writing Skills** are the chapters "Paragraphing," "Writing Letters, Memos, and Reports," and "The Library Resource Paper." In addition, a Style Sheet has been included to help the student check capitalization and punctuation during the editing and proofreading steps of the major assignments.

The author wishes to thank the many students who have contributed models; the teachers who have made suggestions for improving the text, especially Lawrence Biener of Locust Valley High School, Locust Valley, New York; and the editors and designers who have worked diligently to shape the raw material and present it in an attractive form. Certainly the project editor at Prentice-Hall, Kathleen Janson, could be recognized as a full collaborator, were there any way to measure her total contribution to this new edition.

William W. West

Chapter 1

Writing for Effective Communication

What is the biggest single industry in the United States today?

Did you answer, "General Motors" or "International Business Machines" or "The Bell Telephone System"? Those are all good guesses, but the biggest single industry in the United States today is *printing and publishing*. It's bigger than the whole automotive industry, not just GM. It's bigger than the whole business machines and computer industry, not just IBM. It's bigger than the whole electronic communications industry, not just the Bell System.

The reason, of course, is that the printing and publishing industry is a very important part of every one of these organizations. All facets of modern life—government, education, industry, commerce, health care, to name just a few—depend not just on communication but on *written* communication.

Even essentially visual enterprises, such as the movies and television, begin with writing. In the words of Robert Spencer Carr, a former Hollywood script writer, "Until the writer writes, the director has no job, the studios stand dark, the technicians are unemployed, and actors are 'at liberty'—meaning hungry."

Writing is involved not only in the finished product of many industries but also all along the way in the production process.

19

It's easy to see the newspapers, books, magazines, periodicals, and advertisements all around you. In addition to these examples of printing and publishing that you see every day, there are many other kinds of writing: memos, letters, proposals, reports, inquiries, directions, cost estimates, contracts, agreements, and so on. All of these kinds of written communication make modern society possible.

Why Writing Matters

As a member of society, you are necessarily involved in written communication, at least as a reader. However, there are at least five good reasons why just knowing how to read is not enough.

1. Writing helps you understand! Your teachers will tell you that the best way to learn something is to teach it. In some kinds of writing, you are explaining your ideas to a reader. This is one way of learning the material yourself.

2. Writing helps you participate! The number of new ideas in the modern world is growing at an amazing rate. In 1976, American inventors were granted 33,181 patents by other nations, and the United States granted 18,744 patents to foreign inventors. These patents on "things" represent a fraction of the new ideas blossoming in every area of the world around you. Almost all ideas either originate in writing or are distributed in written form. How much better for you to participate in and influence this avalanche of new ideas, than to sit by and be buried by it.

3. Writing helps you think! As you prepare to write, you sort out and organize your ideas in order to express them clearly. That process of observing and organizing helps you perceive and understand. These are the initial steps in the thinking process, and as you write, you gain control of many additional parts of the process. You make connections, you see differences and likenesses, you experiment with varying arrangements and patterns, you make inferences (logical guesses) about what things are and mean, you draw conclusions, and you make judgments. All these writing experiences give you new and clearer thinking habits for processing information and for conveying it orally and in writing.

4. Writing helps you enjoy! Everyone can experience the thrill of watching a touchdown in the Superbowl, listening to the Metropolitan Opera, looking at a masterpiece, or reading a bestseller. What some students don't realize, is that everyone

can also enjoy the satisfaction of writing well. The fun of a football game is obvious, but the fun of writing is the personal thrill of expressing your own thoughts and feelings on paper. In fact, all the things mentioned above, from a Superbowl game to the Metropolitan Opera, can be enjoyed again and again through writing. Learning to write provides you with one more source of delight in your life.

5. Writing helps you lead! Whether in school, on the job, or in social situations, each of us comes in contact with people— equals or superiors in authority—whose ideas and principles may be in conflict with our own. In some cases such differences matter little and have little effect on the quality of our lives. In other situations it may be important to reveal and discuss such conflicts in order to resolve the differences, remedy injustices, or otherwise improve our lifestyles. The ability to write helps you to cooperate with people at a distance or to prepare ideas for future use. To influence others, to guide and help them, you need to be able to write.

Although these are the main reasons for learning to write well, there are two additional reasons, which are related to the world you live in:

1. When you can write well you can communicate more fully to others the ideas, insights, emotions, and attitudes that you alone possess. People around you, your nation, and your culture need these from you. In the words of one writer, George Riemer, "Nobody remembers a nation for its readers."

2. When you can write well you can more easily realize your potential. You command the respect of those around you and thereby earn greater opportunity for self-realization.

ACTIVITY 1A

Considering the Role of Writing in Modern Life

Select one of the following tasks, complete it, and report to the class.

1. Select some major undertaking, such as constructing a ten-story building, building a bridge, starting a business, managing a political campaign, or manufacturing a mass-produced product. If possible, talk to someone actually involved in such an enterprise. Make a list of all the kinds of writing likely to be involved in this project. Include the preliminary and plan-

ning stages, such as raising money, getting contractors to submit bids on portions of the construction, attracting renters, drawing up leases, and so on.

2. Consider what the world would be like if learning to read and write in school were made voluntary and elective, as music and art are in many schools. Compare or contrast the roles, lifestyles, prestige, and self-respect of members of the literate and the nonliterate groups. Compare a day in the life of a member of each group.

3. Project yourselves into the future and imagine Phonovision (a system that enables you to see the person with whom you are speaking on the telephone); wristwatch-type television sets; computer access in every home to major world libraries; and other similar advances in communication, either real or imaginary. List all the inventions you can think of, and then prepare a presentation describing communication in the future. (Be sure to include the roles reading and writing play in communication.)

4. Interview five to ten people in various kinds of jobs. Include people who work at relatively unskilled jobs as well as people in management positions. Ask them how important the ability to write well is in their work. List all the different kinds of job-related writing each person does.

5. The country of Nepal in south-central Asia is typical of many underdeveloped nations with a low level of literacy. Only one out of ten adults can read and write. Imagine that, suddenly, literacy in the United States dropped to that level. List the changes that would take place. How would this affect such common things as street signs, telephone books, and labels on foods and medicines? How would employers cope with a newly illiterate work force?

Limitations of Writing

No one knows exactly when or where writing was invented. Many cultures say that it was a gift of the gods. The Mayans of Central America, the ancient Egyptians, and the Japanese all have myths describing how writing came from divine sources.

The legend from the ancient Greeks about the origin of writing is especially interesting because it includes a warning about the limitations of writing and about problems that may arise.

ANCIENT EGYPTIAN		PHŒNICIAN	ANCIENT GREEK	LATIN	MŒSO GOTHIC		CHEROKEE.	
MONUMENTAL	CURSIVE				FORM	SOUND		

Latin column: A, B, C, D, E, F̶, Z, H, —, I, K, L, M, N, —, O, P, —, Q, R, S, T

Mœso Gothic (sound): A, B, G, D, E, F, G or J, H, I, K, L, M, N, O, P, HW, R, S, T, TH, U, CW, W, CH, Z

Cherokee:

Symbol	Sound	Symbol	Sound
D	a	Ꮋ	o
S	ga Ꮹ ka	A	go
oᏤ	ha	Ꮆ	ho
W	la	G	lo
Ꮨ	ma	Ꮽ	mo
θ	na Ꮦ hna Gnah	Z	no
Ꮳ	qua	Ꮴ	quo
Ꭿ	s Ᏸ sa	Ꮌ	so
Ꮟ	da W ta	V	to
Ꮬ	dla Ꮮ tla	Ꮿ	tlo
G	tsa	K	tso
Ꮖ	wa	Ꮼ	wo
Ꮓ	ya	Ꭵ	yo
R	e	Ꭴ	u
Ꭸ	ge	J	gu
Ꭾ	he	Γ	hu
Ꮭ	le	M	lu
Ꭼ	me	Ᏹ	mu
Ꮑ	ne	Ꮒ	nu
Ꮄ	que	Ꮙ	quu
Ꮞ	se	Ꮧ	su
Ꮥ	de Ꮦ te	S	du
Ꮍ	tle	Ꮰ	tlu
Ꮴ	tse	Ꮰ	tsu
Ꮍ	we	Ꮗ	wu
Ꮿ	ye	Ꮆ	yu
T	i	Ꭵ	v
Ꭹ	gi	E	gv
Ꭽ	hi	Ꮂ	hv
Ꮅ	li	Ꮇ	lv
H	mi	Ꮕ	nv
Ꮒ	ni	Ꮚ	quv
Ꮗ	qui	R	sv
Ꮝ	si	Ꮝ	dv
Ꮑ	di Ꮧ ti	P	tlv
C	tli	Ꮵ	tsv
Ꮏ	tsi	Ꮹ	wv
θ	wi	B	yv
Ꮿ	yi		

Written words are combinations of symbols that communicate meaning.

THE MYTH OF CADMUS

Agenor, the king of Phoenicia, sent his son Cadmus to look for his sister Europa, telling him not to return until he found her. Zeus, the king of the gods, had carried her off. Cadmus consulted the oracle (a kind of prophet) of Apollo to ask for advice. The oracle told him to forget his mission and build a city of his own at the spot where he saw a young cow lying in the grass.

Cadmus set out as he was told, found the cow, and sent his companions off to a nearby grove for water. However, the grove was guarded by a dragon that devoured the men. When Cadmus came looking for his friends and discovered what had happened, he attacked and killed the dragon. Alone he could not have built his city, but the goddess Athena appeared and told Cadmus to sow the dragon's teeth in the ground. He obeyed her and, immediately, a small army of men sprang from the earth. Cadmus was frightened and quickly threw a stone into their midst to divert them. The men began to fight among themselves until only five men remained, and these five helped Cadmus build the city of Thebes.

Scholars interpret the story of Cadmus and the dragon's teeth symbolically. The stone represents the alphabet. As soon as it was cast among the people, they began to fight among themselves. In other words, when people have the tools to read and judge for themselves, dissension and death result. Is this a natural result of learning to read and write? To what degree is conflict the inevitable result of learning to read and write?

There is another kind of problem built into written communication. Any experience you have is multidirectional (coming from all sides at once), multisensory (involving several senses), and simultaneous (happening all at once). When you try to communicate an experience, you must translate this multidirectional, multisensory, simultaneous happening into words— which march slowly, one at a time, across a page. Instead of being multidirectional, words come at a reader from one direction; instead of being multisensory, sights, smells, and other sensory impressions must be translated into words to be read one at a time; instead of being simultaneous, the total experience is broken into pieces and put into a sequence expressed in words on a page. The *whole* experience is never communicated by writing. It is rare for a written communication to recapture a multidirectional, multisensory, simultaneous event.

Some writers, mostly poets and novelists, do amazingly well in recapturing events in the written word, but more and more people are turning to other kinds of communication to transmit and experience multidirectional, multisensory, and simultaneous events. The most obvious substitutes for the written word are motion pictures and television. Certainly, a well-executed film can enable you to come closer to experiencing the action of a storm and shipwreck, a trip to outer space, or even a moment of tender affection than most writing can.

Movies and television are not the only means of communicating multidirectional, multisensory, and simultaneous events. Music, dance, drama, painting, sculpture, and architecture extend the methods people have of communicating ideas and emotions. By appealing directly and immediately to one or more senses, they attempt to go beyond what can be expressed in writing and to transmit as much as possible the complete, original happening and all the attitudes, emotions, and feelings that accompany it! From chiseled writing on Mayan temples and stylized dances to mathematically ordered radio waves, people have used many forms to try to communicate sensory impressions, ideas, and emotions to other thinking creatures.

The Range of Writing

Jerome Martin, an educator, once described his own mind as similar to a "butterfly with hiccups." Can you see the image of the butterfly floating, settling down on an idea, and then suddenly, unexpectedly, hiccuping off in a different direction? Actually, the minds of many people function in this unpredictable, flitting manner. This kind of thinking does not lend itself to effective communicaton.

Readers and listeners need to have some idea of where you are coming from, what your purposes are, and where you are going. They need to be able to understand the background of what you say, to make connections between elements, and even to predict what you will say or do next. One writer is so cynical and doubtful about peoples' ability to communicate that he insists, "The only things you can communicate to other people are what they already know!" The statement, of course, is ridiculous because someone can tell you new ideas about atoms, astronomy, Russia, rice, and thousands of other things. Nonetheless, to comprehend these ideas you must understand the language, the vocabulary, the examples, the comparisons—even the patterns and structure of the words, phrases, and ideas. If the communicator's mind flits like a "butterfly with hiccups," you won't get much from the explanation.

For successful communication, you need order and arrangement, or structure. Fortunately, there is a wide range in the kinds and amount of structure necessary for successful communication. For example, one of the greatest American astronomers, Annie Jump Cannon, spent almost forty-five years at the Harvard

Observatory scanning the heavens. During that time, she analyzed 286,000 stars, discovered 300 variable stars, 5 new stars, and a double star. Astronomers all over the world now look to her records, and astronomers hundreds of years in the future will read her descriptions. Annie Cannon could permit no inaccuracies in her work, for fear someone might confuse one of those 286,000 stars with some other one. Consequently, she "wrote" almost completely in mathematics and structured her work carefully. No room here for hiccuping butterflies!

Annie Cannon's work, as an example of structure, accuracy, and precision in scientific writing, can be placed at one end of a line of structure. At the other end of the line of structure might be the work of an experimental, creative writer such as Gertrude Stein. She tried to achieve, in her own words, ". . . exactitude in the description of inner and outer reality." Her work was also highly structured and organized. However, whereas Annie Cannon was describing the stars "out there," which can be located and checked for accuracy, Gertrude Stein was attempting to describe the "inner and outer" reality, which was uniquely her own. Although her work was highly organized and patterned, it was her own pattern, and it baffled and confused many readers. Writers at Gertrude Stein's end of the line are "creative" not just because they are producing new and original works, but because they are developing new and original patterns and structures.

Now look at where various kinds of writing fall on the line of structure:

LINE OF STRUCTURE

Writing which must correspond precisely to objective reality	Structured, accurate writing in which the world's work is carried on	Free, unstructured writing for self-expression—no audience expected	Structured, creative writing of the traditional kind	Experimental writing using original structures and involving the writer's attitudes and vision of reality
Annie Jump Cannon's scientific writing	Business letters, laws, historical papers	Diaries, journals	Short stories, poetry novels, essays	Gertrude Stein's writing

ACTIVITY 1B

Exploring the Degrees of Structure in Writing

Select one of the following tasks, explore it, and report to the class.

1. When you are ready, have someone give you one word. Without consciously thinking, write down the first word that comes into your mind as a result of the word you were given. Continue to list words, not pausing to think, as each new word suggests an additional word. Stop at the end of two minutes. Go back over your list, reconstructing how you got from one word to the next and trying to explain the connections among them. First, explain each connection; then write out explanations for the entire sequence. To what extent is your mind a "butterfly with hiccups"? How easily would a reader be able to follow a presentation that moved as your list moved, unless you reorganized and provided transitions and explanations?

2. An "ineffable" experience is an experience which cannot be expressed in words. Think of some time when you could not express in words the emotion you felt. It may have been anguish or joy or pride or elation or despair. Describe the setting, the event, and the situation which caused you to feel as you did. Then in a separate paragraph try to express the ineffable.

3. Find several examples of the kinds of writing in which the world's work is carried on. Analyze the structure or organization of each of the examples. Discuss the extent to which the structure or pattern limits the writer. Discuss the reader's need for structure.

4. One writer compared the organizing of ideas to the process of going shopping. She would walk hither and yon in a department store, going from one counter to another, retracing her steps and skipping whole areas as she pleased. That was the exploring, selecting part. Next she took her purchases, arranged them in what was, to her, the most interesting and exciting order. This was the organizing, arranging part. Then she shared her shopping trip with her invalid son at home, showing him one package at a time. She rarely told him about the items she put back or about the steps she retraced or about changing the order in which she bought things. (She always saved for last the toy she had bought him.)

Choose a subject, such as discipline, homework, part-time jobs, or dating. With a group, bring up ideas on that subject. (Walk through the department store of ideas in your mind.) Jot down the ideas that you might put into a paper. It might help you in your selection of ideas to have in mind the main idea (the thesis statement). Arrange the ideas in logical order. Discuss to what extent the shopping trip and the composing process are similar.

5. Do you sometimes have trouble getting started writing a paper? Does your mind suddenly go blank? Try this technique. Look out the window or around the room. Think about how you felt when you got up this morning. What did you do yesterday? What are you looking forward to—or dreading—today? Write down whatever comes into your mind. Write freely for twenty minutes. Don't think about punctuation, grammar, spelling, or about the reaction of anyone else to what you are writing. At the end of twenty minutes, read what you have written.

Discuss the results of this activity with a group or with the class as a whole. Share your paper with the others, or not, as you prefer. In your discussion, touch on these points:

a. Did your mind behave like a "butterfly with hiccups"?

b. Did you notice that, as the minutes passed, you began to write more quickly, more easily?

c. Were your thoughts beginning to zero in on a central idea or theme?

d. For what kinds of papers do you think this technique of free writing would be most helpful?

e. Where, on the Line of Structure, would you place your paper?

Save your paper so you can compare it with another paper you will do when you reach Chapter 3.

Special Values of Writing

Near the end of World War II, the United States, England, and Russia issued the Potsdam Declaration calling for "unconditional surrender" by Japan. When Japanese Premier Suzuki was asked by the press on July 28, 1945, what his government planned to do, he declared that the cabinet was holding to a policy of *mokusatsu*. Since the Japanese word *moku* means "silence" and the word *satsu* means "kill," the literal meaning of *mokusatsu* is to "kill with silence." However, the word *mokusatsu* has come to mean two things: either "to withhold comment" or "to ignore." No one knows which meaning Suzuki had in mind. Did the cabinet intend "to withhold comment" until it received more information, or did it intend "to ignore" the declaration? The Domei News Agency chose the translation "to ignore." Nine days later, America dropped an atomic bomb on Hiroshima. Over 100,000 people died, possibly because of a misunderstanding.

The problem with oral communication is that it is lightning fast—zip—and you've said something that cannot be retracted. If Premier Suzuki had written his reply, he would have had time to plan first and polish afterwards. He might have used a different Japanese word—perhaps *mokushi*, which means "to observe silence" and can be interpreted only one way.

This is one special value of writing: Because you can plan first and polish afterwards, you can be sure that you are expressing what you mean.

Another special value of writing is that you can record thoughts, impressions, and results and build on them over a long period of time. Speaking is like quicksilver: you say something, and the words vanish. Because the spoken word is so temporary, it's hard to have any complex, involved, and evolving structure in oral expression. Scientists, on the other hand, keep copious notes and use them to build their hypotheses and explanations and theories. Social scientists, literary scholars, and inventors all use written language to preserve their ideas. The writer Anaïs Nin kept a total of 150 manuscript volumes of her thoughts and impressions so that she built, over a period of many years, a wonderful storehouse of ideas.

Although it is not an intrinsic value of writing, a spirit of cooperation can be a by-product of certain writing experiences. The most obvious example is a newspaper editorial, which is the official, institutional position of the newspaper regarding issues of concern to its readers. The editorial is the cooperative product of hours of dicussion by the officials of the paper; of searching for examples and anecdotes to support the position; and of rewriting and editing one or more drafts. Even the magnificent translation of the Bible published in 1611, which we know as the King James version, was the result of years of cooperation by forty classical scholars. The book you have in your hands is the result of the cooperation of the author with his students, fellow teachers, editors, and proofreaders. Although a single writer is often given credit for a book, most will freely acknowledge that, as the book grew over several years, a number of people contributed to its final form.

ACTIVITY 1C

Discussing the Special Values of Writing

Each of the following activities emphasizes one of the special values of writing.

1. Explain why the following are true:

   a. Why are most legal documents and real estate transactions recorded in writing and registered with county clerks?

   b. Why was the enactment by Hammurabi of a code of written laws considered a great step forward?

   c. Why do modern literary critics admire the "popular" poetry of some coffeehouse poets, who present their work orally, but reserve their highest praise for works which have been presented to the public in published form?

A written record often lasts longer than the people who made it. This Assyrian tablet, that tells of the Flood in Noah's time, is 2600 years old.

2. The next time you watch a television special, take five minutes immediately after the show to jot down some notes on the program's content. Put your notes away carefully. One week later, mentally review all you can remember about the show. Then look at your notes. How many details had faded from your memory? How much would you remember a year from now? Which of the values of writing does this experiment illustrate?

3. Cooperation on a piece of writing can mean assigning to different people the necessary tasks—originating the ideas, expressing them in written form, reorganizing and editing, proofreading. Discuss in what ways this method is helpful for a person learning to write.

A Declaration by the Representatives of the UNITED STATES OF AMERICA. in General Congress assembled.

When in the course of human events it becomes necessary for one people to dissolve the political bands which have connected them with another, and to assume among the powers of the earth the separate and equal station to which the laws of nature & of nature's god entitle them, a decent respect to the opinions of mankind requires that they should declare the causes which impel them to the separation.

We hold these truths to be self-evident; that all men are created equal, that they are endowed by their creator with equal rights, that among these are life, liberty, & the pursuit of happiness; that to secure these rights, governments are instituted among men, deriving their just powers from the consent of the governed; that whenever any form of government becomes destructive of these ends, it is the right of the people to alter or to abolish it, & to institute new government, laying it's foundation on such principles & organising it's powers in such form, as to them shall seem most likely to effect their safety & happiness. prudence indeed will dictate that governments long established should not be changed for light & transient causes: and accordingly all experience hath shewn that mankind are more disposed to suffer while evils are sufferable than to right themselves by abolishing the forms to which they are accustomed. but when a long train of abuses & usurpations [begun at a distinguished period &] pursuing invariably the same object, evinces a design to reduce them under absolute Despotism, it is their right, it is their duty, to throw off such government & to provide new guards for their future security. such has been the patient sufferance of these colonies; & such is now the necessity which constrains them to expunge their former systems of government. the history of the present king of Great Britain is a history of unremitting injuries and usurpations, [among which appears no solitary fact to contradict the uniform tenor of the rest [all of which have] in direct object the establishment of an absolute tyranny over these states. to prove this let facts be submitted to a candid world. [for the truth of which we pledge a faith yet unsullied by falsehood]

Chapter 2

Polishing and Perfecting

In 466 B.C. at Syracuse on the island of Sicily, south of Italy, there was a revolution that has had an influence on the way people have studied speaking and writing ever since! This book as well as many other textbooks you have used gets some of its ideas from this revolution.

Several tyrants had seized control of Syracuse, confiscated the property of many citizens, and exiled a large number of them. Finally, in 466, the people revolted, overthrew the tyrants, and invited the exiles to come home. Immediately, there were problems in the law courts. The exiles wanted their old lands and property back, but many records had been destroyed, the claims were often many years old, and the people had no deeds. The courts were flooded with claimants, and there simply were not enough lawyers to handle the business.

Into this confusion came Corax, a Sicilian Greek, and his pupil Tisias. They developed a little book called a *techne*, which was a kind of do-it-yourself manual on "How to Win Friends and Influence Juries." In short, Corax wrote the first book on how to make a speech and how to organize a paper. For over 2,000 years scholars have used the ideas of Corax, and you have learned some of them in various forms.

In 64 B.C., Cicero used rhetoric effectively to expose a plot by Catiline to overthrow the Senate of Rome.

Later, in the first century B.C., the Roman orator Cicero built an outline of rhetoric, the art of using words effectively in speaking and writing. See if you think the elements of Cicero's outline cover what you have to learn in order to prepare papers.

1. Invention—the analysis of the communication situation and the audience, finding ideas to write and speak about, locating and selecting materials.

2. Disposition—the arrangement of ideas and arguments for maximum effect.

3. Style—the choice and arrangement of words to express ideas clearly, precisely, and vividly.

4. Memory—the ways of memorizing the material in order to present it exactly.

5. Delivery—the techniques needed for presenting the material orally.

Obviously, the last two points in the outline, Memory and Delivery, are useful in speaking but not in writing. Instead of these, let's substitute one that applies to writing:

Mechanics—observing the conventions of manuscript form: spelling, capitalization, punctuation, paragraphing, and sentence structure.

Indeed, there is a good reason to focus on the four areas of Invention, Disposition, Style, and Mechanics as you learn to write. Several years ago, Educational Testing Service asked a number of successful people in various fields to rate three hundred freshman compositions. These businss executives, scientists, attorneys, and writers were asked to rank the papers on a scale of one to nine with no fewer than four percent in any one category. They were to mark the papers and make extensive comments on them. ETS discovered much variation in the way the papers were judged. One reader might rank a paper "one" and another might rank the same paper "nine." No paper was in fewer than five of the nine categories and ninety-four percent were in seven, eight, or all nine. Then the written comments were analyzed by a computer to determine why the judges' evaluations differed so much. The computer revealed that each person was looking for different qualities:

1. Some were stressing content, ideas, and originality (Invention).

2. Some were stressing arrangement, patterning, and structure (Disposition).

3. Some were stressing word choice, sentence arrangement, and vivid imagery (Style).

4. Some were stressing capitalization, punctuation, spelling, handwriting, manuscript form, and paragraphing (Mechanics).

Educational Testing Service concluded from this research that, since no one knows what a particular reader will be looking for, a writer should develop skills in all four areas.

ACTIVITY 2A

Discussing the Divisions of the Writing Process

Consider each of the following questions.

1. Do the four elements, Invention, Disposition, Style, and Mechanics cover all aspects of learning to write? What others would you add?

2. From your personal experiences with writing and having your writing evaluated, which of the four elements do you think most people stress? Do you agree that this is the most important element? Defend your answer.

Five Steps in the Writing Process

You've just been reading and talking about how people judge writing. Now you're going to look at the five steps in the actual writing process. The two are related to each other; and by using the five steps, you can be sure that your writing will have the qualities people look for.

Every time you write a paper—whether you have a message to communicate, or an assignment to fulfill—it is necessary to go through five steps. Some of these steps may be unconscious, but you can probably do a better job if you are aware of the process.

Step One—Prewriting. Before you begin to write, you think about what you want to communicate or about the assignment you've been given. You consider the situation, the readers, the time you have, the format you will use, what ideas you have and what research will be necessary, and how you will organize your paper. Obviously, before you even begin to write, you have a lot to do. Part of this step corresponds to Invention in Cicero's outline; that is, analyzing the audience and discovering ideas. Part of it corresponds to Disposition; that is, arranging ideas for the most effective presentation. Perhaps you haven't thought about how important this step is, how much time it takes, how interacting with others can help you, and how in-class time may be used effectively for prewriting preparation.

Step Two—Composing. Composing means actually writing the rough draft. If you have built an outline during the Prewriting process, you're off to a great start, but not everyone works well from an outline. Instead of using an outline, perhaps you will have made a list of ideas in approximately the order you expect to use them. In any case, you plunge right into your paper, using whatever organizational help you've prepared for yourself, and letting the paper grow and shape itself as you move along. You may think of new ideas that didn't come to you during the Prewriting step. You will reject some ideas that don't seem to fit and reorganize wherever appropriate. You won't worry too much about style and mechanics at this point because you don't want them to slow you down, but you may give them incidental attention as you write.

Most people perform this step alone because they don't want others to interrupt their train of thought. Thoughts flow better for many people when they compose by themselves, on a good Prewriting base.

This step involves you in Invention (finding ideas and checking them to see that they fit the audience and situation), Disposition (organizing), and Style (expressing ideas in appropriate arrangements of words). Therefore, this stage doesn't exactly correspond to any one of the sections of classical rhetoric.

Step Three—Editing. Editing means going over the rough draft, reworking the words, phrases, and sentences, and pulling the writer's ideas into the best and most effective shape possible. This step, in professional writing, is performed both by the writer and by specially trained editors. Sometimes they work separately, and sometimes, for brief periods, they work together. The editing process can involve a dozen revisions by the writer and perhaps even more after consultation with the editor! Editing involves four basic processes:

a. Adding material, such as examples, transitions, definitions, or summaries.

b. Deleting material, such as repetitions, clumsy expressions, or clichés.

c. Rearranging material, such as putting a main idea last for a more effective climax, or subordinating one idea to another.

d. Substituting material, such as finding the most descriptive words ("crept" instead of "walked"), or using more formal words ("informed" instead of "snitched").

It includes doing everything possible to reshape the rough draft into the most effective and artistic communication possible. For you to eliminate the editing process in preparing a school paper would show overconfidence, since even the greatest writers edit and submit their manuscripts to editing all the time.

Step Four—Proofreading. Proofreading comes as the last step in the composing process. When you proofread, you put the final polish on your product by checking for such mechanical errors as capitalization, punctuation, usage, manuscript form, and other conventions. This is a demanding task which publishers often leave to a whole battery of specialists. You don't have the services of a professional proofreader, as does the author of a book, and you have the handicap of working with your own material. It's much harder to find your own errors than those of another writer. Nonetheless, part of becoming an educated person is learning to be reasonably proficient at proofreading. The fact is that for much of what you write throughout life, both in school and out, you will not have someone to polish it for you. However, if it is possible and your teacher (in the case of assigned writing) agrees, you might work out some system of shared or cooperative proofreading in which you help someone else and he or she helps you. In any case, do not let the proofreading task interrupt your thought processes while you are composing. If possible, let a day or two elapse between editing your paper and proofreading.

Step Five—Sharing. The purpose of most writing is communication. In a few cases, as the chart on page 26 indicates, you may write for self-expression without expectation or need of an audience. But in most cases, whether you are expressing ideas, opinions, judgments, inferences, attitudes, or emotions, you will be writing for an audience. One audience is your English teacher, who brings to your writing special background, skills, and experience. Another is a group of your peers; they can react to the content and form of your paper with openness and honesty. Reluctance to expose your paper to an audience may be a sign that you know you could have done a better job.

Your Special Editing and Proofreading Tasks

You've looked briefly at the entire Writing Process: Prewriting, Composing, Editing, Proofreading, and Sharing. Then why, you may ask, is this chapter entitled "Polishing and Perfecting"?

In the chapters that follow, you are going to be looking very closely at the kinds of Prewriting, Composing, and Sharing suitable for different kinds of papers. You will be looking carefully at models for each kind of writing to help you develop your own papers. Despite the fact that the kinds of writing will be different, the editing and proofreading processes will be much the same. Rather than repeat them in each chapter, we devote this chapter specifically to editing and proofreading suggestions. In this way, you will know the procedures when you are ready to work with the various kinds of writing. These procedures have been developed by writers, editors, and publishers over a long period of time, so take advantage of them to produce your best work.

SUGGESTIONS FOR EDITING

1. After you have written your rough draft, lay it aside for a day or two. Leave time to get some "distance" from your paper, so that you can be objective.

2. Read your whole paper aloud, as if someone else had written it. Check to see that it communicates what you had intended to say and that it sounds good to your ear. If it fails either test, try to locate and correct the problem.

3. Check the basic development of your paper: the opening, the thesis statement or main idea, the opening clues (if any) to your paper's organization, the logic in the order of your topics, the transitions, the ideas supporting your main points, and your conclusion. Use the four processes of editing—Addition, Deletion, Rearrangement, and Substitution—to increase your effectiveness.

4. When you're satisfied that your basic structure is good, reread your work and polish the phrases and sentences. Be sure that it reads smoothly, that the tone is appropriate, and that the whole paper produces the effect you desire.

5. After you have done your best to edit your paper, share it with an interested friend. Together, repeat the foregoing process. Talk about any suggestions you have for each other, and seek additional help if you disagree.

After you have edited your paper, you are ready to proofread. If you can proofread your paper before making a final draft, you have saved yourself a step. However, if your rough draft has suffered from erasures, cross-outs, substitutions, writing between the lines, and other changes, you may need to recopy it before proofreading. As you proofread, you may need to make extensive additional corrections on this second draft. In most cases—for the purposes of your English class, for example—you will not need to prepare a third or fourth draft for the final copy. It is not unusual, however, in professional writing, to make a number of preliminary drafts. The standards set in your English class plus your own standards of excellence will help you determine when additional drafts are necessary.

SUGGESTIONS FOR PROOFREADING

1. Read slowly and carefully, sentence by sentence, being careful to let the meaning of each sentence register with you.

2. Pay special attention to natural phrasing of groups of words and the punctuation associated with them and with the ends of thoughts.

3. Use a dictionary to check spellings. Since some dictionaries will not have entries for all proper nouns, consider other sources of information. (Where would you find the following? Is it Fara Fawcet Majors, Farrah Fawcett Majors, Farah Fawcet

Majors, or some other spelling? Is it coca-cola, Coca-cola, or Coca-Cola?)

4. Use the Style Sheet on pages 398-410 to check major mechanical problems.

5. Consult other students and your teacher if you have specific problems.

6. After you have proofread your paper, share it with an interested friend. Repeat the foregoing process with each other's papers. Discuss any changes and be sure that you understand the reasons for them.

7. Make the following proofreader's marks in light pencil in the margin of any paper you work on. To show where a correction goes use an "insert mark" (called a caret) as we have done here∧ and place the correction in the margin.

⸎ Delete	*no* ¶ Do not begin a new paragraph
⸎ Delete and close up	
# Insert a space	∧ Insert comma
tr Transpose (this or)	✓ Insert apostrophe
	✓ Insert quotation marks
¶ Begin paragraph here	—/ Insert dash
∧ Insert material shown in margin	⸌ Insert semicolon
	?/ Insert question mark
stet Let it stand; restore what is ~~crossed~~ out	(Sp) Spell out
	Caps Set in <u>CAPITALS</u>
	lc Set in L̶O̶W̶E̶R̶ C̶A̶S̶E̶

---

8. Recopy your entire paper whenever the number of corrections suggests that you have not done your best. However, a few neat, carefully made corrections are acceptable.

ACTIVITY 2B

Locating and Correcting Errors

Copy the following paragraph on a sheet of paper. Make all necessary corrections, using the proofreader's marks shown on page 40.

> The availability of food plays a key role in detremining peoples eating habits. Certain foods grow well in 1 part of the world but poorly in another. Saltwater fish of seas and oceans differ from freshwater fish of lakes and. Why do you suppose the Chinese people eat rice and the Eskimos eat blubber. People learn to survive on foods that are near at hand, and in doingso they acquire a tatse for the foods that they know. throughout human history our eating patterns - what we eat and when and and how we eat it have been influenced by culture, religion, and geography. In the modern World, a number of other things also affect our eating patterns.

How Two Papers Developed

Roger Stryker received this assignment in English class: "Choose a controversial subject having to do with school. Present the arguments on both sides, and develop a position defending the side you believe is correct. Make your paper informative, persuasive, and interesting."

This is the way Roger developed his paper, following the "Five Steps in the Writing Process" (pages 36-38).

Step One—Prewriting. Roger first considered all the possible topics. He took into account his purpose (as defined in the assignment), his probable audience (teacher and fellow students), his situation (his own available time, the length limitations, the available information, and so on). He did part of this thinking while doing other things—brushing his teeth, walking home from school, eating lunch. Part of it he did at his desk, remembering and putting down what he had thought of previously and thinking up new possibilities. He also casually discussed his assignment with his fellow football players, with his girl friend, and at dinner with his parents. Then he brought this list of possible topics to the small group he was working with in class.

SOME IDEAS FOR MY POSITION PAPER

Eliminate pep assemblies
Maybe have soccer team during football season
Forget the prom and just have an after-midnight post-prom
Not publish rankings, or standings, of graduating seniors
Have a senior workday in which classes are canceled so kids can do something for the school or town (like maybe planting bushes or something)
Work out recycling plan for paper, aluminum, etc., to earn money for clubs and set example
Eliminate dress code
Improve library, esp. back magazine collection for term papers and compositions

Because this was a personal work sheet not intended for anyone else, Roger didn't hesitate to use fragments and abbreviations.

Each member of the prewriting group brought a similar list or a collection of ideas. Most preferred to bring a written list both to help them remember their ideas and to demonstrate to the group and to the teacher that they had made an effort to do their fair share. Only one student had a mental list.

The prewriting group pooled ideas, discarded some as uninteresting, too difficult, out-of-date, or inappropriate for the audience. Then each group member selected a single topic. Finally, the group consulted to help each person develop his or her topic.

Roger, with the group's help, selected "Not publish class rankings, or standings, of graduating seniors" as his topic. The group helped him list these ideas to treat in his paper:

Reasons for publishing the list:	*Reasons for eliminating it:*
Provides incentive to study	Outmoded custom
Develops healthful competition	Too much importance attached to them
Rewards bright and studious kids	Doesn't show intelligence anyway
Important for getting a job	Rewards grinds
Provides self-competition	Not important for getting a job
Rewards effort and perseverance	Not important for most colleges
Important for good colleges	Encourages unhealthy competition
Has social implications	Doesn't take into account all school activities and learning
Students label themselves	Marks people for life
You get ranked for promotion out of school	

Roger took this list, added a few more ideas, discarded some he didn't like, and made the following list of ideas from which to write his paper. Although he knew how to make an outline, he preferred to work from a list.

Reasons for doing it:
1. Gives incentives
2. Important for jobs
3. Important for college
4. Rewards effort

Reasons for not doing it:
1. Hurts people
2. Outmoded custom
3. Encourages unhealthy competition
4. Not important for job or college
5. Encourages lopsided personal development
6. Doesn't take all factors into account

This list is crude and perhaps illogical in some places, but Roger used it only as a guide. He didn't worry about order or arrangement. He is now ready for Step Two.

Step Two—Composing. This is the rough draft Roger wrote from his list of ideas. Some comments regarding suggested changes are shown on the left.

ACTIVITY 2C

Sharing Your Opinions

Read the draft without reading the editorial comments in the margin. As you read, jot down your own suggestions and comments. When you have finished, compare your comments with the marginal notes. Be prepared to discuss and defend your comments and the changes you suggested.

EDITING GROUP REACTIONS

Not a bad introduction. Probably could be more graphic and gripping. Could create more interest and excitement in the subject.

The word "stupid" is too harsh. Also, if any readers like class ranking and you call it "stupid" they'll quit reading.

Good transition question. Oh, oh! The "well" is informal, and you're going to turn off all the "Highland" kids with that comment about the mommas and poppas.

ROUGH DRAFT

TIME FOR A CHANGE

Since Probert High School was built in 1922, every graduation program has devoted the last page to a numbered list of students. The first person listed has the highest grade-point average in the class and is the Valedictorian. The second person listed has the second highest grade-point average and is Salutatorian. The last person listed has the lowest grade-point average in the class and is generally recognized as stupid. Well, it's time for Probert High School to end this stupid custom.

Why publish the class standings? Well, I suppose it's to make a few rich mommas and poppas from Highland feel real swell about how good their daughters have done. Yes, I said daughters. About 8 out of the top ten grade-wise in the last ten years have been girls. Because mostly boys play sports and work after school and maybe have to help out at home which girls don't and don't have time to study. Boys are just as smart as girls and any old I.Q. test will prove it. And boys—that is, men—do more important things out of school than girls. Look at the history books and even science. Most of the people doing things are men, except an occasional Marie Curie. But the list just rewards the girls.

You'll turn off the girls with your comments about them!

You ought to leave out the whole section about boys vs. girls on intelligence and accomplishment. It's off the subject.

They say that publishing class standings helps in getting a good job and into a good school. Well, it sure doesn't help the guy on the bottom of the list. Besides, I don't think it's important anymore. It's just an outmoded custom. Some say it gives an incentive to study, but that isn't so. If you're going to study, you will, and that's all there is to it.

"They" doesn't carry any weight. Can you name somebody? "Guy" is pretty informal.

Using what *you* think as proof is pretty weak. What proof can you offer?

Well, why should we quit listing the class standings? I think the main reason we ought to quit is it makes people feel bad. How would you feel if on graduation night, everybody knew you were 352 out of 352. Or even 351 for that matter? Or 350? Besides, nobody asks you when you go to college or get a job, were you number 351 in your graduating class? Nobody cares. And as for encouraging people to study, what it does is make a few kids into grinds who don't do anything except study. No sports or clubs or anything. And that isn't healthy.

"Well" is informal, but you do provide a good transition to your next main idea. It's not subtle, but it's clear. There's that "I think" again. What can you do to *show* that the ranking makes people feel bad? Since this is your main idea, maybe you could begin or end with it, instead of burying the idea in the middle.

These numbers are ineffective.

You have a jumble of ideas right through here. Can you sort them, take them one at a time, and give some sort of "proof" or example in support of each one?

You're going to turn the studious students off by calling them "grinds."

Besides, it doesn't take into account all your other activities, how many hours a week you work, whether you have a car you have to pay for, or if you're a girl. (Girls like to study better than boys.)

Do you think fragments are acceptable for this audience?

You shifted into the second person (using "you") in these paragraphs. It doesn't seem consistent with the earlier paragraphs.

The girls won't like this section.

Therefore, I think we should stop publishing the class standings of graduating seniors.

—Roger Stryker

Your ending is weak.

Step Three—Editing. The comments placed beside the rough draft came from an editing group that met and shared comments on each other's papers. Roger reread his paper after putting it aside for a day or two. He then used the four editing processes, Adding, Deleting, Rearranging, and Substituting, to prepare an improved version of his paper.

ACTIVITY 2D

Refining Your Opinions

Another student in Roger's class decided to write her position paper on "Our Inefficient Grading System." Like Roger, she began with the prewriting step and then wrote this rough draft. As you read it, jot down your suggestions and comments just as you did with Roger's rough draft. Then compare your comments with the marginal notes.

EDITING GROUP REACTIONS

Wouldn't it be a good idea to begin with a concrete example or story or quotation to interest readers?

Your first sentence expresses what seems to be your thesis, but your paper goes beyond it to try to prove that some other system should be tried. Also, the three parts ("inaccurate," "unproductive," and "unfair") seem to be main divisions of your paper that you ought to prove. You do show that the system is inaccurate and unfair, but you ignore "unproductive." You ought to prove that, too.

The phrase "dogged train of thought" isn't accurate. In the first place, it's not a "train of thought," though the advocates follow it "doggedly." "Untrue" is the wrong word. A belief may be untrue, but a train of thought would have to be "misguided" or something suggesting process.

ROUGH DRAFT

OUR INEFFICIENT GRADING SYSTEM

The present grading system used by most American schools is an inaccurate, unproductive, and often unfair method of evaluating a student's knowledge and progress. However, many advocates of the system persist in maintaining that it is the only realistically feasible grading method available. This dogged train of thought is, in face of many new ideas and facts, so very untrue.

The feasibility of the present grading system has only one point in its favor: simplicity. The calculation and transference of grades is quite simple for teachers and administrators, but so very unfair to the students. Grades are relative to so many things: classmates, quality of the teaching, difference in school grading scales, curves, and etc. How can educators continue to sacrifice the purpose of grades for simplicity? The purpose of grades is to evaluate a student's knowledge and to help pinpoint areas of difficulty so that they may be corrected. The present grading system does neither. How can educators continue to sacrifice these main objectives for the sake of simplicity?

Educators are incorrect when they maintain that the present grading system is the only method of student evaluation feasible. There are many new methods evolving today; many from teachers who are dissatisfied with the present system. For example, the Montessori Method, named after Maria Montessori, is based not upon relation to classmates, not upon tests, but upon achievement and progress. No distinction is made between school year (first grade, second grade, etc.), students' age, or grades (A, B, etc.). Instead, children are given tasks to accomplish and practice. Once the task is completed, the child is given something else to work at. The emphasis in this method is upon teaching children how to learn, instead of teaching them distinct subjects. The method takes advantage of a young child's tremendous ability to learn languages or mathematics at certain "sensitivity periods." Proof of these "sensitivity periods" is the ease with which young children can pick up language as opposed to the difficulty which older children have in doing the

Simplify the first sentence in the second paragraph. You're talking about "the system" not "feasibility." Keep the same subject in the second sentence as in the first. Why?

"So" in "so very unfair" sounds odd here. "Are relative to" could be simplified to "depend on."

"And etc." is redundant. *Etc.* alone means "and other things." Also, etc. should not be used in formal writing.

You really don't prove that the "purpose of grades is to evaluate." It could be a main idea for you to prove. If you use the three-part division in the first sentence, however, you have some overlapping.

The closing sentence of the second paragraph is a needless repetition.

Expletives (It is . . . There are . . . Here are . . .) waste words. Semicolons connect equal parts of sentences. This one doesn't.

You seem to be comparing apples and oranges, because the Montessori system is more than a grading system.

Clarify. Simplify. What you mean is that students are not placed in different classes according to grades, age, or scholastic achievement.

Discussion of a child's language ability seems way off the subject.

How do you "prove a sensitivity period"? What you prove is that "sensitivity periods" exist.

At the end of the third paragraph, what does "this" refer to? Is it the focus on tasks appropriate for sensitivity periods, or is it systems other than the Montessori Method?

The word "another," which begins the fourth paragraph, implies that the idea in the previous paragraph and this new one are parallel. They don't seem to be. "Variance" is the wrong word. "Base" and "based" in the same sentence seem awkward.

The verb "vary" should agree with the subject "way."

Many people today object to letting the word "he" stand for people of both sexes. "Wind up" is too informal. Clarify what difference you are talking about. Also, the word "poorness" is not idiomatic.

"The point is" promises a "point," a statement, not a question. Also it seems a bit informal.

Your first task is to clarify your objective. Which do you want to do:
1) Prove the present grading system is bad?
2) Prove that other, better ones exist? or
3) Prove that the whole educational system is inferior to the Montessori approach?

You must limit your discussion of Montessori to its grading system only.

same thing. This is only one method of many. And it is working all across the country.

Another reason that the present grading is not the best available is the variance in which the final grades are calculated. Some teachers base the final grades on a curve based on the classmates' performance. Other teachers drop a low grade or allow for one grade to be dropped. In fact, the way in which grades are calculated vary with the teacher. The methods are limitless. They are also unfair. One student, under a certain teacher, covering a specified subject might get a high grade. But, if that same student were under another teacher, covering the same materials, he might very easily wind up with a low grade. The difference could be related to the ineptness of one teacher compared to another, or the poorness of one test to a better one. The point is, how can such diverse outcomes be overlooked so easily? There are better methods available and educators have the duty to investigate them.

Surely, such a grading system that misses its objectives by such a wide margin can not be maintained, especially when better methods are available. The educators of today have a serious obligation to society to investigate new methods and to implement improvements as soon as possible.

—Theresa Norton

Step Three—Editing. After Theresa reread her paper in the light of the group's comments and suggestions, she put it aside for a few days. Then she edited it. She added some things, deleted others, rearranged her material, and made some substitutions. Her second draft follows. As you read it, notice where she used each of these editing processes.

SECOND DRAFT WITH ADDITIONAL EDITING AND PROOF-
READING NOTATIONS PRIOR TO TYPING IN FINAL FORM

CHANGES MADE AS A RESULT
OF EDITING GROUP COMMENTS
ON ROUGH DRAFT

OUR INEFFICIENT GRADING SYSTEM

Grace and Beth have been friends for a long time. In fact, all the way through Hawthorne Elementary School and East Junior High School, they *were* ~~have al-~~ *always* ~~ways been~~ in the same classes, and ~~they have al-~~ ~~ways~~ earned the same grades. Suddenly, for the first time, at Washburn High they're *are* in different classes, and, for the first time, they get *quite* ~~wildly~~ differ-ent grades. *Is it because there is a* Difference in ability? *Is it an* Accident? No! They are victims of an inaccurate, *and* unproductive, ~~and un-~~ ~~fair~~ grading system, which ought to be replaced.

Theresa has invented an opening story to attract the interest of readers.

The present grading system has only one point in its favor: it is simple. It enables teachers and administrators to calculate and ~~transfer~~ *record* grades very easily. These grades, however, are ~~so~~ inaccurate, unfair, and unproductive. ~~that~~ *E*ducators should not continue to sacrifice major educational objectives for simplicity.

Theresa has clarified her thinking. She will limit herself to discussing the grading system, but she will prove both *that it's bad and that it should be replaced.*

To disarm the opposition, Theresa begins by giving credit to the present grading system for having at least one value. Notice the simplified first sentence. Then she will take up her three criticisms of the system (It's inaccurate, unproductive, and unfair) one at a time and in order. Notice how the word "however" is sandwiched into the middle of the sentence so it doesn't use up a strong sentence-beginning slot.

What are the purposes of grades? They should *student* evaluate ~~the~~ knowledge and progress ~~of students~~ *students* and show ~~them~~ where they need help. The present grading system, unfortunately, does neither. The experience of Grace and Beth is typical. ~~of thousands~~ ~~of experiences which point out its inadequacies.~~ *e*

This short paragraph puts grading into a context so that Theresa can more easily prove that the present system is inaccurate, unfair, and unproductive.

This reference to the opening story keeps the personal and concrete example alive and gives it additional effectiveness.

The grading system, in many cases, is grossly

Here Theresa attempts to prove the first of the three charges she makes against the present grading system.

inaccurate. Grades ~~can~~ depend on many different factors: ~~the~~ stimulation from classmates, ~~the~~ quality of teaching, ~~the~~ manner of evaluation, and ~~many~~ other influences. It is ~~perfectly~~ possible for ~~two~~ students of equal ability, such as Grace and Beth, to receive such different grades that their marks bear no relationship whatsoever to their learning. If the two girls were to switch places, their grades for the next marking period might well be switched also. Such inaccurate marks couldn't possibly provide information about what ~~students~~ *they* have achieved and where they need help.

A grading system ~~which is~~ so inaccurate is necessarily unfair also. Because ~~each~~ *all* teachers calculate grades in the way ~~he or she~~ *they* prefer, ~~there is great variation among procedures.~~ *procedures vary greatly.* Some teachers ~~base~~ grade on a curve based on student performance. Others have absolute standards. Some ~~teachers~~ figure in all grades. Others let students drop an occasional low grade or make allowance for incompletes. Any system ~~which is~~ so inaccurate and inconsistent ~~in evaluation~~ cannot possibly be fair.

Perhaps the worst thing about the present *grading* system ~~of grading~~ is that it is unproductive: ~~That is,~~ it doesn't encourage either the student ~~who is earning high marks~~ *"A"* or the student ~~who is earning low marks~~ *"D"* to do ~~his or her~~ *their* best. The student *"A"* who is getting ~~high marks~~ thinks, *"I'm* ~~that he is~~ doing fine. ~~and doesn't~~ *I don't*

Here Theresa handles the second charge she makes against the grading system—the charge that it is unfair. Note that she changed the order of her second and third points. Why?

Theresa takes up her third charge against the present grading system. Why does she save this one for last?

have to work any harder." The students ~~who is getting low marks~~ thinks ~~that he~~ "I" can't do any better, ~~so he doesn't~~ *I won't* try." The present grading system doesn't encourage either type ~~of student~~ to reach their own potential. It is unproductive.

Some advocates of the present system maintain, however, that the present grading system is the only realistic~~ally feasible~~ system available. On the contrary, many new grading systems are evolving today, ~~some of them even coming from teachers dissatisfied with the present system~~. One interesting "grading system," ~~which~~ is a small part of ~~a completely different total educational package, is that built into~~ the Montessori Method. Maria Montessori based her grading, not on tests, but on actual observable achievement, ~~and progress.~~ She let students work at specific tasks, ignoring any age, ability, or grade-level differences. As students complete their tasks, they move on to more challenging and more rewarding tasks. There is no "grading" in the traditional sense. Students grade themselves by working at their own individual speeds and reaching their own levels. The Montessori "nongrading" or "selfgrading" system is only one of many ~~other~~ ways of handling the grading problem. Educators owe children and parents a better grading system, so they should seriously investigate some of the new methods, ~~available.~~

This transition prepares the reader psychologically for the "new" system, or systems, which might replace the present one.

Notice how Theresa now limits her discussion only to the grading portion of the Montessori system.

Notice how much of the earlier discussion of the Montessori system is now omitted, since it is not part of the grading system.

By referring to the opening story, Theresa uses the "envelope technique" to round out her paper.

Note how she repeats her main points in an unobtrusive summary.

At the end of their first semester at Washburn High, Grace and Beth discovered that the present grading system is inaccurate, unfair, and unproductive. In spite of the fact that they ~~and their work~~ were treated so differently, *Beth and Grace* ~~they~~ remained good friends and excellent students. Won't it be wonderful when the grading system actually encourages cooperation and friendship and productive scholarship, rather than being something good students must overcome?

—Theresa Norton

Step Four—Proofreading. After writing a second draft following the initial editing, Theresa has given her paper a second editing, as the corrections on the preceding pages indicate. Now, she is ready to make a final copy. Theresa had asked another student to go over her paper with her. Since most professional writers have the benefit of this step, you, as a student learning to write, should have it also.

The one difference between you and a professional writer, however, is that you owe it to yourself to review any corrections to learn the reasons for the changes. To use an editor or a proofreader without learning from the process is both to deprive yourself of the opportunity of learning and to steal an undeserved grade by having someone else do your work.

Chapter 3

Exposition

The second half of the twentieth century has seen an "Information Explosion." As Alvin Toffler has observed in *Future Shock*, a great leap forward in knowledge-acquisition occurred with the invention of movable type in the fifteenth century. Before 1500, about one thousand books a year were printed in Europe. We now produce, world-wide, about that many in a single day. Organizations based entirely on the "information sciences" have been formed specifically to keep business, industry, government, the military, and education up-to-date on the most recent world and national developments. A recent IBM advertisement expresses the current corporate view that "What you don't know *can* hurt you." Many executives and decision makers hesitate to make vital decisions without the latest, perhaps crucial, information.

Television and films have become popular modern sources of information, but for hundreds of years people have depended on exposition to extend and transmit knowledge. Exposition is the kind of writing that communicates information. Basically, it explains and exposes, or "puts forth," information. At one time, writers insisted that exposition should not be concerned with the imagination or the feelings or with convincing a reader to act in a certain way.

Things have changed, however, and modern writers know that presenting information alone is not enough. Good exposition appeals to the imagination and feelings of a reader. In many cases it will also lead the reader to act on the basis of the information given.

Three Samples of Modern Exposition

As you read these samples of exposition, pay special attention to the four qualities people look for in writing: Invention, Disposition, Style, and Mechanics. Look also for appeals to imagination, feelings, and decision making.

I

THE NEW COMPUTER REVOLUTION[1]

The new age of the computer has been called the second Industrial Revolution. Just as machinery amplified and extended the power of human muscles, so computers amplify and extend the power of the human brain. Although computers have definite limitations, there are virtually no areas of activity in the world today that have not been influenced by the computer to some extent. You cannot get through a day without being touched by this influence many times, whether or not you are aware of it.

Let's look at some of the areas in which computers are helping people to do their jobs better, or freeing them for more enjoyable activities.

In the areas of scientific research, engineering, and space science, computers have had the earliest, greatest, and most constant impact. In the world of business and finance, increasingly complex operations are possible only because of the computer's capacity to store and retrieve masses of information. In industry, many of the processes that transform raw material to finished product are controlled by computers.

Schools and universities have felt the impact of the computer age. Administrators use computers for record-keeping and scheduling and other routine tasks. Teachers use them as instructional tools. At the university level, major areas of study from architecture to forestry are making use of computers. Many universities that once made Latin a mandatory entrance requirement now require instead proficiency in at least one computer programming language!

There is still another area where the use of computers is growing rapidly. Since human beings play as well as work, it's not surprising that a major use of the computer is for fun. Chess champions have played exciting games with a computer as a partner. Swimmers touch electronic plates at the finish line. And for spectators, computerized ticket agencies can reserve seats, print tickets, and charge the cost to credit cards.

Perhaps the most important thing to keep in mind as we marvel at this computer revolution is this: Because computers can relieve us of doing routine mental tasks, we find ourselves with more freedom to develop our creativity. While computers carry on the more mundane work of society, we are free to organize, invent, create, and wonder—and put the computer to work producing the inventions and helping to discover the answers.

II

The family gathered round the TV set, but instead of the usual diet of sitcoms and cops 'n' robbers, the program this night was brought to them by their friendly real estate agent. House-hunting is now as easy as watching TV.

Videotaping of homes for sale is one of the newest methods being used by the real estate industry to cut down on the time-consuming visits with prospective buyers to houses frequently spread over wide areas.

"Our tapes are complete productions of color, movement, and sound," said Larry Eulenfeld, who heads Jacksonville-based PHTV—*Preview Homes thru Video.*

The camera slowly pans each room while an announcer gives the dimensions and describes each feature. Classical music plays softly in the background. The tape also includes panoramic views of the outside of the house and the yard, and even a few brief shots of the surrounding neighborhood.

The Jacksonville firm sees its market as lying with small-volume realtors, who might not be able to afford a professional videotape production. "It's a question of educating the realtors to the different uses of videotape," said Chris Ballard, Eulenfeld's partner in PHTV. "Once this catches on, though, it will revolutionize the whole industry."

PHTV also is looking into the possibility of videotaping new homes. The tapes conceivably could show various phases of construction, the kinds of materials used, and other building features.[2]

III

What's a *palimpsest* anyway? The word is not in everyday usage, but it is important to art historians. A palimpsest, by definition, is a canvas or parchment used over and over again: a painting on a painting on a painting. . . . Art thieves use palimpsests. How else could they get the *Mona Lisa* past French customs? Once safely through, the thieves would carefully rub off the top layer of an unremarkable work to reveal the smiling lady. You can find an everyday example of a palimpsest when you chip paint in an old apartment. The tastes of each of the previous tenants are preserved in chronological order with your color on top.

Land is also a palimpsest. A succession of human cultures, each with different priorities, has painted its record on the basic environmental canvas. Today's shopping center was yesterday's orchard and before that a frontier farm and an Indian council ring. Probe back 40,000 years in North America and there is an environment totally unmodified by *Homo sapiens.*

It is good to celebrate places in the world where the crust of civilization is thin and broken. It is important that the palimpsest occasionally part to reveal the Old Master beneath man's paintings. It does not matter that the gaps vary in size. Some of them are relatively large:

(we call these national parks and wilderness areas). Others may be as small and unexpected as a fringe of tall-grass prairie paralleling a railroad in the Midwest or a mossy boulder in New York City's Central Park. Beauty—and meaning—is in the eye of the beholder. What really matters is that the wild not vanish from the world that we have largely repainted. As curators we must be worthy of the delicate palimpsest we have inherited.[3]

—Roderick Nash

The Outside Structure

Every piece of exposition differs from every other piece, and by looking in textbooks, magazines, newspapers, and hobby kits, you can find many different types. Because exposition is the kind of writing that gets the world's work done, it is everywhere and of every type.

For our purposes, then, we'll leave out the instructive "how-to-do-it" type that makes no attempt to interest or to motivate. The kind of exposition you're going to produce is like the preceding models: short, focused, interesting, and purposeful.

This kind of exposition is easy to write because it has two structures: the *outside* structure and the *inside* structure. The outside structure consists of a kind of "wrapper" that goes around the main body of an expository paper. It consists of the introduction and the conclusion. Look at the beginning and end of each of the foregoing selections. (Sometimes the beginning will be just one sentence; sometimes it will be a paragraph or two. The endings vary similarly.)

A good introduction does two and sometimes three tasks as it prepares a reader psychologically for the main body of the paper. An introduction:

1. Arouses interest.
2. States the main idea or purpose of the paper.
3. Gives an overview of the main divisions of the paper (optional).

By the time readers have finished the introduction, they are ready to go on to the body of the paper.

Look at the preceding selections. Read the introductions carefully. Determine where and how each introduction arouses interest and reveals the main idea or purpose of the selection.

None of the examples gives the overview of the main divisions of the paper. You will look at this task of introductions later.

A good conclusion does one task and sometimes two as it wraps up the expository paper. A conclusion:

1. Summarizes the main points (optional).
2. Provides an interesting closure (ending) and a satisfying feeling of completion.

The introduction and the conclusion, which together "wrap up" the body of the paper, are the outside structure.

ACTIVITY 3A

Investigating Outside Structures

A newspaper or magazine must "earn" its audience. If it doesn't, people don't buy it, and the company fails. However, some publications are not required to "earn" their audiences. For example, certain technical reports, laws, directions, and so on, are required reading whether the writer has earned the attention of an audience or not. Students are required to read certain textbooks, interesting or not.

For this assignment, limit yourself to the kind of publications that are required to earn their audiences. Look at the beginnings and endings of selections from them and try to find out how they have used the outside structure of exposition. Be prepared to read in class, or to your group, the introduction and conclusion of one of your selections. Discuss the way the writer caught the interest of the reader, how the main idea was expressed, and how a feeling of closure was provided.

The Inside Structure

The inside structure of an expository composition consists of the material as it is organized in the body of the paper. Look at the different ways the three selections you have just read are organized.

1. The selection called "The New Computer Revolution" divides the material into paragraphs according to the various areas in which computers are being used.
2. The selection on house-hunting defines and explains house-hunting by TV, describes what a production includes, tells how it is currently used, and explores the future possibilities.

3. The selection on the environment defines the word "palimpsest;" then it uses the comparison pattern to show how layers of civilization built on our land are like a palimpsest.

Though each of these "inside structures" is different, each is closely tied to its "outside structure," and each develops the main idea or "thesis statement" set forth in the introduction. The thesis statement gives the main idea or purpose of the composition. Stating this idea is one of the tasks of a good introduction.

Following is a piece of writing that lacks an outside structure. The inside structure, or body, contains interesting historical information, factual information, and anecdotal details and examples. Yet, the lack of an outside structure to support the body results in problems. What do you think the main idea of this paper is?

I

The metric system was first proposed in this country by Thomas Jefferson in 1790. The U.S. has been "officially" a metric nation since 1875. We signed the Treaty of the Meter in Paris in 1875. We received refined meter bars and kilogram weights to use as standards in 1890. However, Congress has kept this nation on a system that, besides ourselves, only Brunei, Burma, and Liberia use.

Let's take a look at our system: We have a short ton, a long ton, a register ton, a measurement ton, and a wheat ton—all different.

We have an avoirdupois ounce, a liquid ounce, and a Troy ounce—all different.

We have at least eighty different standards of measurement in our system, none of which bears any logical relationship to any other.

Let's look at some of these beauties:

Henry I of England decided that the distance from the tip of his nose to his fingertips was a yard; the inch, the span of the knuckle on King Edgar's thumb; the foot was the length of Charlemagne's foot; our gallon was Queen Anne's wine gallon; and our acre was the amount of farm land a yoke of oxen could plow in one day. The only thing that makes sense is our decimal monetary system.

We are already using the metric system in many areas. Vitamins and medicines are weighted in milligrams. Skis are sized in centimeters. Movie or still cameras use 8mm or 16mm or 35mm film. All are metric measurements.

I can teach anyone (with some brains) a working knowledge of the metric system in 15 minutes.[4]

Thesis Statement

A thesis statement is to a longer paper what a topic sentence is to a paragraph, and both thesis statements and topic sentences consist of two parts: a complete subject and a complete predicate. The complete subject identifies a topic and limits that topic to something the writer intends to discuss. The complete predicate presents an attitude toward or an idea about the topic that the writer will demonstrate or prove. A topic sentence, then, names the subject of a paragraph and states what the writer will prove or demonstrate about that subject. A thesis statement does the same for a longer paper. To write a thesis statement or a topic sentence, then, a writer must define the subject (if it needs defining) and present, in the predicate, an attitude toward or an idea about the subject. Here is a diagram of a thesis statement:

The Swiss	have chosen a neutral role in international affairs.
The subject	An idea about the subject

Here are the thesis statements of the first three selections.

COMPLETE SUBJECT	COMPLETE PREDICATE
1. . . . the computer Revolution	is here
2. House-hunting (by means of videotape)	is now as easy as watching TV
3. Land	is also a palimpsest

As you look at the preceding thesis statements, which subjects seem to you to need defining? Has the writer done it? Do any of the predicates seem to need defining or explaining as well as proving? Has the writer done it?

It is not always necessary to express a thesis statement. Sometimes writers imply or suggest a thesis statement. A problem with implied thesis statements, however, is that sometimes readers do not really understand what the writer is trying to prove. Look for the thesis statement in the selection on the opposite page about the metric system. Do you find it expressed anywhere? Is there an implied thesis statement? What is it? How could the selection be improved?

ACTIVITY 3B

Locating and Understanding Thesis Statements

Locate the thesis statement in each of the following passages. It may be stated or implied. Divide the thesis statement into its complete subject and complete predicate. Discuss with the class what tasks the writer must do because of the way the thesis statement is expressed.

The first one has been done for you.

1. The governor runs in place. A film actor works out with weights. And a judge has turned to disco dancing—not for entertainment but for exercise.

When the newspaper, *Florida Accent*, recently asked eleven well-known Floridians in politics, sports, entertainment, and the professional and business worlds what they do to keep in physical shape, their responses generally followed national trends.[5]

—Nash Stublen

Thesis statement:

COMPLETE SUBJECT	COMPLETE PREDICATE
The responses (of eleven well-known Floridians to a question regarding what they do to keep in shape)	generally followed national trends

The thesis statement indicates the writer's task—to name the well-known Floridians, to give their answers to the question, and to show that those answers fit the national trend. Note that the term "national trends" must be defined even though it's in the predicate.

2. You buy, collect, inherit, and hoard. And suddenly there comes a day when you have an irresistible desire to unload the excess baggage.

Whatever it is that you have too much of, you want to eliminate it. This happens to all of us. The question then arises, how to dispose of the goods most advantageously? The answer depends on the types of items and why you want to pass them on.[6]

—Harriet Webster

3. A few years ago, Noel Vietmeyer, a staff director of the National Academy of Sciences, was surprised to find in a collection of reports on tropical plants one with a curious title: "*Psophocarpus tetragonolobus*: Crop with a Future?" Neither Vietmeyer nor any other agriculture scientist would be surprised today. For the plant, better known as "the winged bean" because of the four winglike flanges on its pod, is now regarded as a great green hope among the experts who worry about new food sources for the overpopulated and underdeveloped world.[7]

4. Three years ago, Steve and Jean Bonyun planned their dream house. It was big and luxuriously equipped; but having it built, they soon learned, was far beyond the means of a truck driver with a wife and three children.

So the Bonyuns built a house themselves. It took months of evening courses to learn the fundamentals of homebuilding, then several more months of drawing up plans before they could even begin construction on a lot Steve's family owned in Wiscasset, Maine. But it took very little money—about $18,000 in labor and materials—for a comfortable, one-and-a-half story, pitched-roof home.

The family moved in last winter. "There've been times I thought we'd never get finished," admits Jean Bonyun. "But I'm glad we did. I love it."

With the median cost of a new home climbing by twelve percent each year, and existing houses selling for close to $54,000 at the median, thousands of families are seeking ways to invest more of their labor, and less of their money, in real estate.[8]

—Paula Span

5. Shortly after the 1978 college basketball play-offs, a reporter asked a top official of the National Collegiate Athletic Association how much NBC television had paid for the rights to the games. Without pausing for a moment the official tossed out the startling figure of $4.5 million. "But we don't announce that," he added. "You'll have to say you got it from another source."

The NCAA, a nonprofit organization with a near-monopoly on the brokering of college sports, does not like to advertise that college sports are big business or that the NCAA—with its full-time staff of 65 and gleaming new office building outside Kansas City—is busy minding the store.

In fact, the major college sports are business, and the stakes get higher every year.[9]

—Janice Kaplan

ACTIVITY 3C

Creating Thesis Statements

Working alone or in groups as your teacher designates, go through the following steps to prepare a list of at least ten possible thesis statements on which you might base an expository paper.

1. List subjects on which any teenager ought to be able to speak for three minutes without any preparation. What are subjects that most young adults know something about and have opinions about? (Begin with television, cars, health foods, and go on from there!) This is just a point of departure for building a storehouse of ideas on which you can write. Your life is filled with topics for exposition, and you can get many ideas from television, newspapers, magazines, films, libraries, conversations, experiments, and questionnaires.

2. Of all these topics, select ten that interest you. Narrow each subject. For example, if the topic were cars, you might narrow it to "dune buggies." If the topic were television, you might select one particular program or "science fiction programs."

3. Now take five of the ten topics you chose and narrow them even further. Instead of "dune buggies," narrow your topic to "The plans I bought for a modified dune buggy."

4. When each topic has been narrowed sufficiently, it can serve as the complete subject of a thesis statement. If it's too broad for that, go through more narrowing steps. Now think of an idea you could communicate about each of the subjects you have chosen. Your idea should be something worth saying, something that isn't so obvious as not to need proving or explaining, and something you can handle. These are your thesis statements. For example, "The plans I bought for a modified dune buggy are too complicated for me to use."

5. Keep your original list of topics, your ten narrowed topics, and your thesis statements. Use all of these as your storehouse of raw materials for future writing. Add to your storehouse from time to time, consciously expanding your store of ideas.

Some Warnings About Topic Sentences and Thesis Statements

The suggestions you've just read for developing topic sentences and thesis statements are helpful. But, at times, you may have trouble developing a thesis statement on certain subjects. Some people just don't write effectively if they are forced to develop thesis statements before they write. Here are two warnings.

1. Writing is, in itself, a process of discovery. Sometimes writers really don't know what they want to say before they begin to write, so they can't possibly begin by expressing a thesis statement. In such cases, they begin writing and the process of writing helps them clarify their thoughts and discover what they want to say. When they get to the point at which they know their thesis statement, they then go back over their work and make sure that everything pertains to the subject and supports that main idea.

2. Sometimes, for various reasons, writers do not express a thesis statement directly. For diplomatic reasons, they may not want to offend readers. For aesthetic and artistic reasons, they may prefer a more subtle approach. For psychological reasons, they may feel that the main idea will be more effective and longlasting if the reader has to discover it. These variations from the expository pattern are fine. Indeed, the most outstanding writers are probably the most subtle, seldom using anything as obvious as an overt, direct statement of purpose. However, for direct, simple communication, thesis statements are best for beginning writers.

Preparing Introductions

You've looked at the most important part of an introduction—the thesis statement—but the second part is almost as important. This is the part which arouses the readers' interest, gets them involved, and makes them want to continue reading.

Frank Luther Mott, a famous professor of journalism, developed a formula to explain why people choose to read certain selections rather than others. He calls his formula the "fraction of selection."

$$\text{Fraction of Selection} = \frac{\text{Expectation of Reward}}{\text{Effort Required}}$$

In other words, to get people to read what you write, you must show them that they'll get a high reward for little effort. If your reader is highly motivated because of previous interest in the subject or because the reading is required, motivation is less important. Nonetheless, it's a good idea to arouse interest by having a clear, interesting thesis statement and by writing clearly and sharply.

ACTIVITY 3D

Examining Interesting Openings

The following opening paragraphs show a few of the ways writers arouse interest at the beginning of an expository paper. Read each carefully to see what it contains. Discuss its advantages and disadvantages. Try to devise additional types of interest-arousers.

1. In Ohio, the Southeastern office of the State Department of Health reports with pardonable pride that the most popular course in Appalachian public schools is toothbrushing.[10]

2. The small, brown moths darkened the skies in Maine's mountain country in early July cutting visibility at times to less than 300 yards. Motorists who left the windows of parked cars open near Presque Isle had to beat away the insects to get back behind the wheel. Since then, the moths have dropped eggs in massive quantities, and tiny quarter-inch-long spruce budworms are now eating their way through 150 million acres of forests in Maine and southeastern Canada. Evergreen spruce and fir trees stand brown and naked in the summer sun.

3. Kingston, R.I. That steel-drivin' section hand immortalized in railroad ballads, rhythmically driving spikes with his nine-pound hammer, is about to join the steam engine, the Model T, and the buttonhook.
   To meet its congressional mandate of a quiet, smooth, 120-mile-an-hour service between Washington and Boston by 1981, Amtrak has just

put into service a track-laying system unique in the U.S. that will renew or restore sections along 424 miles of right-of-way.[11]

—Jak Miner

4. Inflation is not going away. It has become a permanent feature of financial life in America in the last third of the twentieth century, and those who wait for it to suddenly disappear might just as well look for the tooth fairy.

For almost all of recorded history, prices were stable. A piece of ground that cost 100 sesterces in 100 B.C. might have cost 98 sesterces in 250 A.D. or perhaps 102 sesterces, but basically the price level did not change. For almost all the time the American Republic—the most formidable claimant in history to an ideal society—has existed, the price level has been stable. Occasionally, as during the Civil War, there would be extreme inflation, and occasionally, as in the Panic of 1907, there would be stupendous drops in the price level, but generally prices rode serenely along on an even keel.[12]

—Benjamin Stein with
Herbert Stein

5. "She's got an indiscreet voice," I remarked. "It's full of . . . I hesitated.

"Her voice is full of money," he said suddenly."[13]

What Gatsby thought he heard in Daisy's voice is what any number of ambitious people sense they are sure to find in perfume, that it is "full of money."

6. What is the single greatest social problem in the United States today? Every day ten thousand human beings die of starvation. And every day millions of thoughtless, overfed people do nothing about it.

7. Modern human beings must develop a universal social conscience. Walk through almost any village and you will discover on at least one edge of town the dirty, neglected, overcrowded tenements or hovels where the poor abide. In leaky-roofed shacks with torn, dingy shreds of wallpaper hanging from water-stained walls, the children huddle with pinched and hungry faces around the evening's scanty offerings. It is ironic that modern people have developed their technology to the point where they could relieve virtually all of such unnecessary suffering, but have not developed social conscience to the point that they are moved to do so.

ACTIVITY 3E

Writing Interesting Openings

Bring to class openings that you have written yourself or some you have found in current expository writing. Following are three activities to provide materials for a class discussion.

1. Look through several current magazines and make notes on the different kinds of openings you find. Bring examples of unusual openings to class. (Do not destroy library magazines.)

2. List on the blackboard various topics suitable for expository compositions. Select one of these and write an interesting opening for it. Discuss it with the class.

3. Choose two subjects from the list you prepared for Activity 3 C (pages 61-62) and write openings for them. Exchange papers with each other in class for suggestions and corrections.

Thesis Statements and Inner Structure

There are many patterns of organization for the internal structure or body of a paper. These patterns are: development by details, arrangement according to space or time (chronology), comparison and contrast, analysis, synthesis, cause and effect, enumeration (listing), classification, definition, and example.

A good thesis statement in the introduction (outer structure) often suggests a way of organizing the body (inner structure). Planning and writing the inner structure will be easier if you are aware of the various patterns available to you.

Patterns of Organization. A brief definition of each of the major patterns of organization follows. You will learn more about these patterns later in this chapter.

Development by details. The presentation of small portions of a whole or of items, often those which appeal to the senses, in order to support a generalization. What details, for example, would support the generalization, "It was a perfect night for a luau!"?

Arrangement according to space. This pattern is similar to development by details, but the details are carefully arranged to move logically from left to right, top to bottom, around in a circle, inside to outside, far to near, or in some other spatial pattern. This pattern is often used in describing a place in order to communicate the same feeling about it as was specified in the thesis statement or topic sentence: "His living room was a shambles."

Arrangement according to time (chronology). This involves arranging a series of events according to time sequence. Flashbacks and other distortions can be used for emphasis and effect, but the usual order is the natural order of time (chronological order).

> After that, everything happened too quickly, but I think the order of events was this—the dog started across the road right in front of the car, and Mr. Calloway yelled, at the dog or the car, I don't know which.

> Anyway the detective swerved—he said later, weakly, that he couldn't run over a dog—and down went Mr. Calloway, in a mess of broken glass and gold rims and silver hair, and blood.[14]
> —Graham Greene

Comparison and contrast. The juxtaposing (placing side by side) of two objects or ideas and showing, point by point, how they are similar or different. There are two basic patterns. Using the first pattern, you would describe the characteristics of one object fully before turning to the other. For example, in a comparison of a Ford and a Chevrolet, you would describe the engine, body, and transmission of a Ford and then the engine, body, and transmission of a Chevrolet. Using the second pattern, you would compare or contrast the engines of the Ford and Chevrolet, the bodies of each, then the transmissions of each.

Analysis. The examination of an object or idea by separating it into its component parts and elements. Since there are always a number of ways to do this, the purpose of the analysis must be determined. A different purpose will demand a different way of separating the elements of the object being examined. For example, a builder might analyze a house in terms of its materials— stone, wood, metal, plastic. But a person renting the house might analyze it in terms of its layout—kitchen, living room, bathroom, bedrooms. A good analysis should divide the item into parts so that no two overlap and nothing is left out. Both of these analyses would be faulty:

> The student body is divided into boys, girls, and redheads. (overlap)
>
> The federal government is divided into legislative and executive branches. (omission)

Synthesis. The opposite of analysis. In this pattern, the various parts or elements are examined and gradually the object or idea is perceived as a whole. Often this pattern is used to create a mood or atmosphere by putting together a number of sensory impressions. It is similar to development by details.

Cause and effect. Presenting the forces which are the causes of an event or reversing the order and presenting an event first and then specifying the causes.

> The explorer dropped a bar of soap into the steaming mouth of the hot spring. The soap lowered the surface tension of the water so that, immediately, a geyser spurted forth.

Enumeration. The listing of parts or elements of a whole. Enumeration is different from analysis in that the parts are simply listed rather than analyzed.

> The Iroquois nation included the Tuscaroras, the Onondagas, the Mohawks, the Senecas, the Oneidas, and the Cayugas.

Classification. The grouping of items or individuals into groups on the basis of similarities. When you ask if something is animal, vegetable, or mineral, you are trying to classify it.

Definition. There are three definition patterns:

a. Nominal definitions—explaining the meaning of an unknown word by linking it with a known word ("Galluses are suspenders.")

b. Extensional definitions—pointing to an actual object to which the word refers ("That plastic disk those people are throwing back and forth is a frisbee.")

c. Formal definitions—naming the word to be defined, placing it in a class with which the reader is familiar, and describing the details that differentiate it from other members of that class.

Example. The description of a single outstanding and dramatic event, situation, or instance that demonstrates or proves the truth of your topic sentence or thesis statement.

ACTIVITY 3F

Determining Patterns of Organization Appropriate to Thesis Statements

Discuss which pattern of organization would be preferable in developing each of the following thesis statements. Skilled writers can sometimes adapt different patterns to the same thesis statement. Therefore, more than one response is possible for most of these items.

1. The government's treatment of Native Americans has evolved slowly as the nation industrialized.

2. Contrary to popular opinion, the genitive form has five uses in addition to showing possession.

3. Edison's laboratory in Ft. Myers, Florida, remains exactly as he left it.

4. A Moped is quite similar to a motor scooter, but there are definite differences.

5. From the foregoing information, you can readily see that Mr. Booth was a regular Jekyll and Hyde.

6. If the Puritan work ethic—the inner compulsion of Americans to work hard—has vanished, a number of forces have killed it.

7. The prevailing attitude toward authority in America during the late 1960's was the product of complex problems during the period.

8. The *Marble Faun* was the most perfect statue I ever saw.

9. Chaucer's work had a profound influence on the English language.

10. The Italian sonnet is quite different from the Shakespearean sonnet.

11. Dante Gabriel Rossetti belonged to a group of artists and writers who called themselves "Pre-Raphaelites."

12. The various instruments in an orchestra belong to different families.

13. The Bucs got worse and worse during the game.

14. Every portion of the scene contributed to the growing feeling of terror.

15. From such varied arguments as those just stated, the committee built the energy bill.

16. The fifty or more subjects taught at East High are grouped into five departments.

17. The mission of the press in American society encompasses six major responsibilities.

18. The cafeteria is arranged for sanitation and efficiency.

19. Your attitude will depend in large part upon your understanding of the word "maturity."

20. The kinds of jobs open to high school students are quite limited.

Some Common Developments of Thesis Statements

Although the thesis statements you have just examined lend themselves to development of a certain kind, many thesis statements can be developed in any of several different ways. The same is true for topic sentences. The following sample paragraphs show how a single topic sentence can be developed in three different ways.

MAIN IDEA (TOPIC SENTENCE OR THESIS STATEMENT):

TEEN-AGERS TODAY ARE GIVEN MUCH RESPONSIBILITY.

Details. Teen-agers today are given much responsibility. Almost all teen-age boys and many teen-age girls have their driver's licenses, and often their own cars. Frequently, they have either a sizable allowance or a part-time job which gives them considerable spending money. Even in school they are given many responsible assignments. Many office-practice classes handle a student-activity fund amounting to over ten thousand dollars, and often the student council plans every school activity, from pep meetings to graduation exercises. It is no wonder that both colleges and employers are pleased with the responsibility of today's young people.

Illustration or example. Teen-agers today are given much responsibility. Sharon Connors, for example, undertakes many important jobs at home, at school, and at work. At home, because her mother works, Sharon must prepare the evening meal and take care of Beth, her younger sister, between the time the sitter leaves and the time Mrs. Connors returns from the second shift at the factory. At school, because she is president of her class and secretary of the pep club, Sharon is always taking on new duties: making arrangements for the Junior-Senior Prom, directing the sale of the pep-club pompoms, or just maintaining the interest of her classmates in the activities she considers important. Her responsibilities at home and at school leave Sharon little time for work, but she manages to babysit on at least one weekend night. At these times, she is completely on her own as she cares for three-year-old Jeffrey and one-year-old Susan. If most teen-agers accept as much responsibility as Sharon does (and informal polls indicate that they do), they will certainly be ready for greater responsibilities at an earlier age than students in the past.

Cause or effect. For a number of different reasons, teen-agers today are given much responsibility. Pessimists say that they get their responsibilities by default. Adults, say the pessimists, are simply too busy (or irresponsible) themselves, so they let teen-agers take over. A few equally cynical people blame the commercial interests for increasing the responsibilities given young people. Certainly it's true that American business now recognizes teen-agers as an important market, and no doubt vested interests have encouraged teen-agers to open their own charge accounts and to assume important jobs for less money than adults could accept. But probably the most important reason that teen-agers have more responsibilities today is that as democracy has matured, Americans have realized that accepting responsibility is an important aspect of the American way. Moreover, educators now realize that the best way to teach responsibility is to delegate responsibility. And, finally, teen-agers have been given more and more responsibility because they have demonstrated their ability to handle it.

Comparison or contrast. Teen-agers today are given more responsibility than were teen-agers a generation ago. Today many students have joined neighborhood action groups, and they are given the tasks of informing adults and even leading them in community programs. A generation ago, such teen-agers would not have been given such tasks and adults would not have followed their leadership. Many students rush from school to work, and some of them have surprisingly large responsibilities on the job. The merchant who now trusts a teen-ager to deposit the day's receipts or to take charge of the store at night shows a confidence in his part-time worker that earlier employers would not have had.

ACTIVITY 3G

Developing Topic Sentences in Several Ways

Working as your teacher directs, plan the development of each of the following topic sentences into different kinds of paragraphs. These may be worked out individually or in groups. They may be shared orally, as brief topic outlines, or completely written out as those on teen-agers and responsibility.

1. The bedroom to which I was assigned was the most unusual I had ever seen.
2. Fewer students are going to college today than went ten years ago.
3. Noah Webster enjoyed his jaunt by horseback along the Boston Post Road.
4. Becoming educated involves growing in many different ways.
5. Hillsborough High offers all the girls' sports offered anywhere.
6. The electronic age began back in the 1900's.
7. Europeans usually want to see five major attractions when they come to America.
8. Discovering why an automobile won't start is quite easy.
9. The second she entered the ballroom, the mood of the moment seized her.
10. When the morning alarm rings, our household springs into action.

Aiding Your Reader with Definitions

Communication is possible only when people can identify experiences or information they all share. If you refer to a *proscenium arch* and your readers have no experience with the theater, they may not know that you are referring to the arch that frames the opening in the wall through which the audience sees the stage. Whenever you are using a word or concept that your readers may not know, it is a good idea to provide either a definition or an example.

Definition patterns. On page 67 you read briefly about three definition patterns. For a nominal definition, you simply identify the unknown word in terms of a word the reader is likely to know (A vireo is a kind of bird.) For an extensional definition, you point to something in the real world. "Do you see Matthew's shirt? That's the color I call cerise."

If you can explain one word adequately by simply giving another, or if you're in a situation in which you can point to an actual object, it may be unnecessary to give a more complicated definition. Your next choice might be descriptive definition—a kind of verbal pointing:

> When I talk about school spirit, I mean the kind of dedication that leads to service, as when the Honor Society sold scrap and raised $2600 for the new p.a. system or when the yearbook staff sells candy at every single football and basketball game to support our yearbook.

The proscenium arch of the old Metropolitan Opera House in New York City.

Occasionally, however, you must use a formal definition. The formal definition follows this pattern:

Term to be defined ➝	Name the word you are defining.	A python
Connector ➝	Usually the word required is *is*.	is
Class ➝	Use a class or category with which your reader is likely to be familiar.	a snake
Differentiating details ➝	Describe the details that make this thing different from other members of the same class.	large, non-poisonous, crushes its prey to death.

Adding differentiating details. In writing a formal definition, first place the referent (the word in question) in a class that the reader or listener already knows. Then give enough differentiating details to separate it from others in the same class: "A beagle is a dog . . . (present as many details as are necessary to distinguish a beagle from other dogs)."

Notice that the definition must be based on the principle of finding an idea or experience that the reader and the writer share. They must both have had experience with the class into which you place the word being defined and, of course, the word must fit that class. Make sure that you never define a word with other words that the reader is not likely to know (An opossum is an omnivorous marsupial.) Ordinarily, the search for shared experience as a basis for a definition means that the definition will be easier to understand than the original word.

ACTIVITY 3H

Working with Formal Definitions

Using a dictionary, prepare definitions for five of the following words. As you write out your definitions, remember to follow the formal definition pattern and to put the referent into a class that your reader is likely to know. Then add as many differentiating details as are necessary to distinguish the word from others in the same class. Be prepared to discuss your definitions in class. Note that the dictionary does not always follow the formal definition pattern and that you may have to select a single definition from among several given.

touchback	radar	moor	pilaster
plagiarism	vassal	phoenix	legume
blurb	sonnet	antivivisectionist	shaman
selvage	caduceus	ecology	haiku
laser	capacitor	vampire	Texas tower

Using Comparison and Contrast in Exposition

On page 66 you read a brief explanation of comparison and contrast. Sometimes you can clarify an item or idea you are explaining by comparing or contrasting it with another item or idea. If your readers are familiar with the second item or idea, they can readily make connections with the first.

Here is an excerpt containing both comparison, which emphasizes similarities, and contrast, which emphasizes differences:

> The words "education" and "training" are often used interchangeably, especially as the liberal arts courses are losing students and professors are tempted to shift their traditional role to preparing students for earning a living. A major difference between "education" and "training" is immediately apparent from looking at the etymologies of the two words. "Education" comes from the Latin words *ex*, meaning "out of" or "from" and *duco*, meaning "to lead." Education, then, attempts to lead out or draw out from within the individual what is already there. "Training" comes from the Latin word *trahere*, meaning "to draw" or "pull." Rather than leading out what is already inside, training seeks to pull the individual along a preconceived, external path.
>
> A second difference emerges from the first: Education benefits the individual, whereas training enables the individual to benefit others. For example, millions of dollars are spent on medical and dental training so that the individual doctors and dentists can use their training to benefit others.
>
> A third difference is that education is general and theoretical, while training is specific and practical. In addition, education involves a kind of lifelong "learning to learn" commitment, whereas training is limited to a definite time period. Continued "in-service training" and updating may be necessary from time to time, but this cannot be compared to "learning how to learn" all kinds of things in all areas for a whole lifetime.
>
> Finally, although liberal arts professors are currently having a hard time convincing potential students of this lifetime value, educators believe that education is its own reward, and they promise nothing more than the joys of competence, adaptability, and self-fulfillment. On the other hand, the rewards of training may include the satisfaction of being a skilled teacher, shoemaker, or physician, but along with that satisfaction come additional rewards—salaries, fees, recognition—from the outside world. Both education and training are necessary in human society, and most experts hope that students will choose to get a good education as a basis for their training, no matter what field they select.

According to the preceding passage, these are the ways in which education differs from training:

EDUCATION	TRAINING
Involves "leading out" what is already in the individual	Involves drawing the student along a preconceived path
Undertaken for the benefit of the individual	Undertaken for what the trainee learns to do or produce for others
General and theoretical	Specific and practical
Lifelong "learning to learn"	Limited period to acquire specific skills
Self-rewarding	Leads to external rewards

Each of the ideas listed above is called a point of comparison. In a formally written comparison, the two items being compared are examined carefully; and for each point of comparison for one item, there is a corresponding point of comparison for the other item.

The formally written comparison can be organized in either of two ways:

FIRST ORGANIZATION

1. All the points of comparison for Item One are treated.
2. All the points of comparison for Item Two are treated.

SECOND ORGANIZATION

1. First point of comparison
   a. The way the first point of comparison appears in Item One.
   b. The way the first point of comparison appears in Item Two.
2. Second point of comparison
   a. The way the second point of comparison appears in Item One.
   b. The way the second point of comparison appears in Item Two.
   Continue with all the other points of comparison.

Although the formally written comparison and contrast paper should be organized around identical points of comparison and the treatment of these points should be in either of two particular orders, the fact is that many fine writers do not organize their work so precisely. Indeed, some feel that they would be inhibited by such precision.

ACTIVITY 3 I

Using Comparison and Contrast

1. Refer to Activity 3C, pages 61-62. From your list of topics, choose one for which the comparison and contrast pattern is appropriate. Write a paragraph or two in which you identify points of comparison and explain their similarities or differences. For practice, try each of the two organization patterns just described.

2. If the comparison and contrast pattern is not appropriate to your subject, think of some subject that lends itself to this pattern. Some suggestions follow. Choose one and write a paragraph or two using comparison and contrast.

   maturity—immaturity   community college—university
   cheap—inexpensive   confident—brash
   educated—uneducated   gifted—intellectual
   radical—liberal   chivalrous—courteous
   candlepins—tenpins   bridge—pinochle
   sports car—dragster   uninterested—unmotivated

Unity and Focus

Sentences and paragraphs rarely stand alone. Usually they are part of a longer unit of writing and must be tied in somehow with what has gone before and what follows. Sentences and paragraphs seem to belong together when:

1. They are on the same subject—giving unity to the material.
2. They are closely related to one another logically—having the quality of coherence.
3. They treat the subject from the same point of view—maintaining a single focus on the material.

The following paragraph consists of sentences on the same subject, but because the subject is treated from a different point of view in almost every sentence, the focus shifts and both unity and coherence are lost.

When my father gets called for National Guard duty, he goes through a complicated procedure getting ready. First, the duty officer lets him know whether he's being called for a flood or tornado or strike or riot. Then the equipment appropriate for that kind of duty is made ready.

At the same time, Mother begins to call platoon leaders in Dad's company. The squad leaders in each squad are then called by the platoon leaders, and the men in each squad are notified by their sergeants. As soon as all the men know the details of assembly and departure, the co-workers in Dad's civilian office must be told how to take care of his work while he is gone. Finally, with all the equipment readied, the men notified, and the job arrangements completed, the executive officer picks Dad up and drives him to the armory.

Focus and Variety. Notice that the focus shifts in this paragraph because the subject changes from sentence to sentence. In the first sentence, the subject is *father*; in the second, it is *duty officer*; in the third, *equipment*; fourth, *Mother*; fifth, *squad leaders* and *men*; sixth, *co-workers*; seventh, *executive officer.*

Some students mistakenly shift focus because they believe that doing so gives variety to their paragraphs. Of course, variety is desirable, but not at the expense of unity, coherence, and focus. In general, avoid shifting unnecessarily from one subject to another. When you do shift, provide links to help the reader change subjects with you. Avoid inserting a passive-voice sentence (e.g., "The squad leaders . . . are then called . . . .") in the middle of a series of active-voice sentences. In the preceding paragraph, notice how the passive-voice sentences cause shifts of focus.

ACTIVITY 3J

Correcting Focus

Rewrite the sample paragraph so that *father* is the subject throughout. Achieve sentence variety by making some sentences long and some short and by combining some related ideas in a single sentence. Avoid using the passive voice.

Coherence

Sentences cohere when they have mechanical or logical connections. Some have both.

Mechanical connections. A mechanical connection is one that results from the use of a connecting word or words ("therefore," "however," "besides," "on the other hand") or from the repetition of a word, phrase, or idea used earlier. Generally, a connecting word signals a logical connection as well; and sometimes the repetition comes when a substitute word, such as a pronoun or synonym, repeats an earlier idea.

Logical connections. A logical connection is a phrase that relates the ideas in two sentences, directing the reader to note cause and effect, sequence of events, idea and example, generalization and detail.

ACTIVITY 3K

Examining Sentences for Coherence

Discuss in class the mechanical and logical connections in each of the following pairs of sentences. Identify the words or phrases that make the connections and describe the relationships (e.g., cause and effect, contrast, sequence, etc.) they signal.

1. The way people stand, sit, or use their heads and arms often communicates a great deal about what they are thinking. As a matter of fact, linguists are making a serious study of "body language" so that people can understand one another better.

2. When Disney World was created in the swamps near Orlando, Florida, a great many people worried about what this huge entertainment business would do to the local ecology. Now, however, ecologists are realizing that Disney's influence on the environment has been better than that of the local residents, and they expect to learn a good deal from the Disney staff about preserving the environment.

3. Some psychologists estimate that most human beings use only one-fifth of their brainpower. Imagine the great things people could accomplish if they could unleash this wasted resource.

4. As machines and inventions are perfected, such machines and inventions become more powerful and less wasteful. The first transatlantic cable, for example, required thousands of tons of pure copper cable to send one telephone message at a time; now, however, a satellite weighing only a few hundred pounds can handle hundreds of such messages.

5. The explorer Thor Heyerdahl warned that we may kill off life in the oceans if we continue polluting the waters of the world. He described how in the middle of the Atlantic he sometimes disliked brushing his teeth in the stained and fouled ocean.

Transitions Between Paragraphs

Just as sentences must be tied together, so paragraphs must be tied together. Indeed, writers use many of the same connecting devices between paragraphs that they use between sentences. In addition, they are likely to use a "principle of transition" which can best be described as *look back and go forward*. In other words, they *look back* at what they have just said, and then *preview what they are going to say*. Some such "look back and go forward" transitions follow:

LOOK BACK (Review)	GO FORWARD (Preview)
So much for the causes:	let's look at the effects.
But Shakespeare's genius does not stem solely from his mother's genteel influence	his education in the local Latin school surely contributed greatly to his preparation.
The preceding explanation is interesting, but inconclusive.	Another frequently-offered explanation is that . . . .
The apparent causes of the war were quite simple	but the real causes are another matter.

ACTIVITY 3L

Examining Transitions

From any expository material that you are currently reading (textbooks, magazine articles, editorials, how-to-do-it books), read six consecutive paragraphs. Pay particular attention to the beginning and ending sentences of each paragraph. Come to class prepared to discuss how the paragraphs are tied together.

Simplifying Your Writing

If you compare sentences written in English at different times over the last four hundred years, you will discover that, although words have grown longer, sentences have grown shorter. The reasons are twofold: First, many people won't read long sentences any more; and, second, good writers have learned to load more meaning into fewer words.

The second reason is important for you. To communicate successfully, you must discipline your mind to think clearly and choose words and structures appropriate to your meaning and subject. You are a little like a gardener who cuts away dead branches and pulls out weeds. If you learn the following techniques you will eliminate the "deadwood" in your writing and not burden your sentences—and your reader—with unnecessary words. The grammatical structures are named in these examples, but if you do not know the terms, you can understand the processes by looking at the examples. You do not need to review your grammar to learn and use these techniques for simplifying your writing.

A. Omit excess words from relative clauses. Change the clauses into either prepositional phrases or simple adjectives.

RELATIVE CLAUSE

He purchased a boat that was made of fiberglass.

PREPOSITIONAL PHRASE

He purchased a boat of fiberglass.

SIMPLE ADJECTIVE

He purchased a fiberglass boat.

B. Omit excess words from relative clauses and change the clauses into participial phrases.

RELATIVE CLAUSE

The boy who was tumbling on the mat looked tired.

PARTICIPIAL PHRASE

The boy tumbling on the mat looked tired.

C. Omit excess words from relative clauses and change the relative clauses into appositives.

RELATIVE CLAUSE

The test, which was our first examination of the year, disappointed me.

APPOSITIVE

The test, our first examination of the year, disappointed me.

D. Omit excess words from subordinate clauses and change the clauses into infinitive phrases.

SUBORDINATE CLAUSE

The annual staff held bake sales at every game in order that they could afford to pay for hard covers on the school yearbook.

INFINITIVE PHRASE

The annual staff held bake sales at every game to pay for hard covers on the school yearbook.

ACTIVITY 3M

Simplifying Sentences

1. Change the relative clause in each of the following sentences first to prepositional phrases and then to simple adjectives.

   a. Richard likes paintings that are in the realistic style.

   b. The singer, who appeared in a red wig, was very funny.

   c. Karen and Bill frequently took a path that went beside the sea.

2. Change the relative clause in each of the following sentences first to participial phrases, then to prepositional phrases, and then, when appropriate, to simple adjectives.

   a. Many students do not especially like books that are written for schools.

   b. Decisions that are made by students ought to be binding.

   c. The girl who is coming with the flowers is very pretty.

   d. The rug that is spread on the floor must be removed for dancing.

3. Change the relative clause in each of the following sentences into appositives.

   a. Kate Federico, who was our National Merit Scholarship winner, was invited to speak at the Rotary Club.

   b. President Kennedy's decision, which was to confront the Russians on the Cuban missiles, was very courageous.

   c. The "Summerhill" idea, which has students choosing their own activities and being responsible for their own learning, is becoming increasingly controversial.

   d. Fred's first trip away from home, which was a visit to Chicago, opened his eyes.

   e. The national concern for ecology, which is a fairly recent development, is opening up new careers.

4. Omit excess words from subordinate clauses in the following sentences and change the clauses into infinitive phrases.

   a. So that he might attract more attention for the forthcoming elections, Sam prepared a skit for the school public address system.

b. The Waterloo *Daily Courier* ran an editorial saying that the firm was happy that it was sponsoring a scholarship for the Newspaper Fund.

c. In order that the class could get the value of writing more compositions, the students voted to ask for corrections on only every third paper.

d. Mary wrote that she hoped that she could come.

5. Look through the compositions you have written so far this year. Locate any clauses that begin with *who, which,* or *that.* These usually signal relative clauses that can be reduced by using the techniques you have just worked with. Try reducing such clauses and see whether or not the sentences are improved. (Not all of them will be.) Share your experiences in your group.

Summary Endings

The final paragraph of a composition is the one that most readers will remember longest. Many writers sum up their main points and repeat their thesis statement in the final paragraph. Though such a summary is not always necessary, it is often effective.

ACTIVITY 3N

Examining Summary Endings

Be prepared to discuss in class how the following final paragraphs restate and emphasize the main ideas of the compositions they end. Working in a group, reconstruct the main paragraphs of the inner structure (the body) from the clues given here.

1. Because of the new masses in motion, the new planes and rapidly changing government policy, the airlines are flying into uncertain skies. Some of the portents are promising. Says Eastern's Borman: "If people start seeing us as a good replacement for the auto, business could go wild. That's the kind of market we're aiming for. We've taken on the ship and the train, but the private auto is the heavyweight championship." Detroit is not worried yet, but the summer of 1978 has proved that the air travel market can grow much bigger, and that the surest means to exploit it is through lower fares.[15]

2. There is little danger that salmon will become extinct. One of the great lessons of salmon conservation is that the fish have a tremendous capacity to increase in number, if given the chance. But unless we use more wisdom than in the past, and learn to control such adverse pressures as pollution, dams, and overfishing, there is no doubt that more and more streams will lose their runs of a handsome and delicious fish— one of mankind's major natural resources.[16]

3. The members of Congress, of course, are aware of the transgressions of morality and the law that occur under the capitol dome. They would do well to remember that an informed public can bring about a change in the ethical standards of Congress by mandating a change in its membership.[17]

4. Both because of "progress" and in spite of it, the sailing ship may well displace many motorized tramp and trade ships, especially in the South Pacific. The higher costs of fuel, the simplified navigation techniques and improved weather prediction, the development of automation to replace crew members in setting sails, and the use of space-age materials in centuries-old sailing devices will all contribute to the return of sails. The square rigger is not dead!

5. Almost all women in the Soviet Union work outside the home, usually at menial jobs. They attend to household chores without help from servants, husbands, or modern appliances. They spend hours in line shopping for hard-to-get items. They are passed over for the elevated, higher-paying, and easier executive positions. Despite emphasis on sexual equality in the Soviet Union, the life of the average woman remains very difficult.

ACTIVITY 3O

Writing a Summary Ending

Read the following incomplete composition carefully, then write a summary ending for it. Be sure to restate the main points in the order in which they appear in the body of the composition. If possible, try to restate them in different, more interesting words than appear in the original.

When you see animated cartoons on television or at the movies, you often think of the huge studios of Walt Disney, Paul Terry, or Hanna and Barbera, but making animated cartoons is becoming increasingly popular in junior and senior high school, and even in some elementary schools. Most of these student-produced films don't have the slickness and professionalism of Terry-Tunes or Yogi Bear, but they're fun to watch and even more fun to make.

The first thing to do in preparing to make an animated cartoon is to forget what you know about commercial cartoons and take a look at some of the simple cartoons. In "Boiled Egg," for example, a real egg is the main character, and as it was moved, photographed, moved, photographed, and so on, it shows very simply the egg's attempts to escape an unknown threatening force. In "Clay," a cartoon made by college students, a lump of clay is photographed, shaped one pinch at a time between photographs, into an animal and then, one pinch at a time, into another, and so on. In the finished cartoon, the lump of clay unexpectedly grows into one thing, swallows itself, and becomes another, and so on. In "American Time Capsule," a long series of still photographs and paintings, each shot separately, gives in a few brief moments a history of the United States.

After you have looked at the kinds of cartoons you can make without drawing hundreds and even thousands of scenes, write out a script of what your film will contain. You might use a pair of paper clips to show one clip falling in love with and chasing another—or you might use a cluster of coat hangers, as Norman McLaren once did, to show an evil force multiplying and growing and eventually overwhelming someone. In any case, choose an idea requiring only a few simple props which you can move easily a little at a time as you show motion and emotion in your shots.

Next, either borrow or build a copy stand. A copy stand is simply a flat board about two feet by three feet with an upright pipe sticking out of it. A sliding bracket that will hold a motion-picture camera sticks out from the pipe and can be adjusted to the right height for focus. Of course, you need some fairly strong lights to illuminate your subject.

The business of actually shooting your film is the most fun. On the foot of your copy stand, Scotch-tape the background—usually a sheet of brightly colored construction paper with some trees or a house drawn on it—before which you will shoot your scenes. Place on the paper your "characters," whatever they are. They might be those paper clips or perhaps a mean eraser that rubs out whatever a gentle pencil tries to write. Then follow your script as you move the characters about an eighth of an inch, trigger your camera for a fraction of a second, move them again, shoot, and tell your whole story in this way.

If you're using color—and you probably will—the dual complications of handling movie film and color will probably make it necessary for you to have your film commercially processed. Meanwhile, you might be searching for mood music to use as background for your film. As soon as the film comes back from the laboratory, view it, put the music on a cassette tape recorder, and get it ready for showing. A professional filmmaker might cut out as much as eighty percent of the footage and splice together the rest to get exactly the effect wanted. For your purposes, however, the less cutting, rearranging, and splicing, the better.

▇▇▇▇▇▇ MAJOR WRITING ASSIGNMENT

AN EXPOSITORY COMPOSITION

To write an expository composition, you must have an idea to communicate. Your first task, then, in writing a patterned expository composition is to choose a general subject you would like to write about. Next, you must narrow that subject to a specific topic. The third logical step is to specify definitely and clearly the main idea you would like to communicate.

Unfortunately, human beings do not always operate logically. Many people must write out a complete rough draft before they can organize their thoughts sufficiently to specify their main idea. But having written a rough draft, having located and stated their main idea, they then rewrite their entire paper in terms of the main idea, or thesis statement. With a thesis statement to guide them, they can easily determine where they need to add more material, where they need to make certain points clearer, and where they should remove unnecessary details.

STEPS IN WRITING EXPOSITION

I. Determining your thesis statement
   A. Choose a general subject (for example, ecology).
   B. Narrow it to a specific topic (preserving marine life).
   C. Write your thesis statement, a clear one-sentence statement of your main idea. (Dredge-and-fill operations must be halted to preserve the spawning grounds of marine species.)

   (If you cannot develop a thesis statement at this point, proceed to II, and return to your thesis statement when it becomes clear to you.)

II. Developing your ideas
   A. Explore and research ideas for your paper (interviews, library research, conversation, experimentation, observation).
   B. List ideas about your specific topic and thesis statement in what seems to be a reasonable order.
   C. Write a rough draft and leave it untouched for a day or two.
   D. Read your rough draft—preferably with an interested partner or listener—and check it against your thesis statement. Either revise your draft or rewrite your thesis statement, if necessary.

III. Preparing your final paper
   A. Rewrite your paper in the light of your critic's comments and your revision of your thesis statement.
   B. Impose the exposition pattern on your paper: insert an interest-arousing beginning, work out an effective ending, check your transitions. (In Chapter 5 you will learn how to provide in your introduction an overview of the main divisions of your paper.)

   C. Revise and recopy.

Your teacher may ask you to submit the following materials together with your completed expository composition:

1. Your preliminary planning sheet, including
   a. General subject
   b. Narrowed subject
   c. Initial thesis statement (if you had one at Step I C)
   d. List of ideas arranged in a reasonable order

2. Rough draft of the paper, followed by your revised thesis statement
3. Rough drafts of opening and closing paragraphs
4. Complete second revision (if you needed to prepare one)

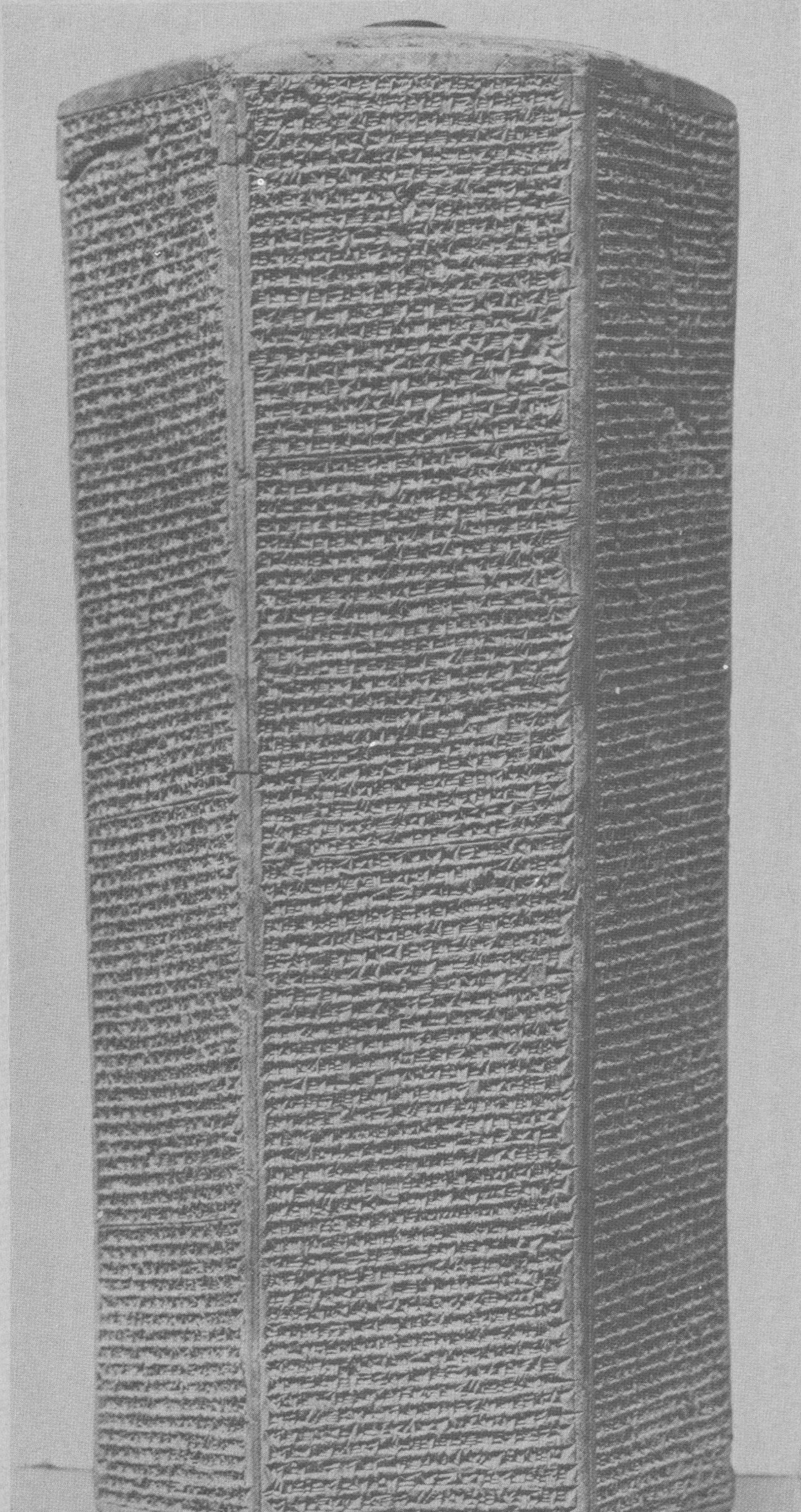

At one time, paragraphing as we know it today did not exist. This clay monument gives an account of King Sennacherib's siege of Jerusalem. Even if you knew cuneiform, do you think it would be easy to read?

Chapter 4

Paragraphing

From the time you were in third or fourth grade, you have been given exercises in the writing of paragraphs, and you have been taught that an expository paragraph usually follows this order:

Topic sentence
Supporting details, examples, comparisons, analogies
Clincher sentence

A writing skills manual used by the United States Army describes a paragraph this way:

"... a paragraph is almost always a collection of sentences that attempts to make a point, to convince the reader of something, or to "sell" an idea. It has an argumentative edge. But the argument a paragraph makes is only as effective as it is clear. To write effective paragraphs, therefore, you will need to use at least three clarifying devices: (1) the topic sentence, (2) the operative term, and (3) the clincher sentence."[1]

This definition adds one more element to your understanding of paragraphing: *the operative term*. The operative term is a word or phrase in the topic sentence which tells or implies the writer's attitude toward the subject of the paragraph. A good topic sentence communicates an *attitude* toward the idea it expresses. What is the operative term, or attitude, in each of these sentences? (Sometimes a phrase or even several separated words will show the attitude.)

a. The opening of the Erie Canal in 1826 gave new life, verve, and optimism to the young country.

b. Mathematician Carl Gauss allowed his keen, restless mind to wander productively in fields far from his calling.

c. Fortunately, Ground Control in Houston was prepared to begin the delicate process of redirecting the satellite.

d. The inventors of the submarine and the airplane both resigned themselves to taking their inventions to other governments.

The inclusion of operative terms, or attitudes, within your topic sentences enables you to write more easily and to communicate more effectively. Because you have stated your attitude toward your material, you can more easily select and control material to communicate that attitude. Because your readers quickly grasp the attitude you are trying to communicate, they can recognize the supporting ideas as they read.

Here are those same topic sentences without operative terms. Obviously, it would be much more difficult to write effective and interesting paragraphs with such neutral topic sentences as these.

a. The Erie Canal opened in 1826.

b. Mathematician Carl Gauss explored many different fields.

c. Ground Control in Houston began the process of redirecting the satellite.

d. The inventors of the submarine and the airplane both took their inventions to other governments.

ACTIVITY 4A

Adding Attitudes to Topic Sentences

Each of the following sentences could be used as the topic sentence of an expository paragraph. Yet each of them would be more effective and interesting if an attitude, or operative term, were included. You can do this by adding an adverb, by adding an adjective, or by changing the verb or noun.

ADDING AN ADVERB:

The phonograph worked the first time Edison tried it.
Surprisingly, the phonograph worked the first time Edison tried it.

ADDING AN ADJECTIVE:

Anthony voted with the majority.
Anthony voted with the misguided and unthinking majority.

CHANGING THE VERB:

The detour went through the Ozark Mountains.
The detour meandered through the Ozark Mountains.

CHANGING THE NOUN:

The Eiffel Tower was the center of the Paris Exposition.
The Eiffel Tower was the miracle of the Paris Exposition.

Rewrite each of these sentences to include an attitude:

1. Few of my fellow students know how they want to spend their lives.
2. Americans have only recently learned that big is not necessarily beautiful.
3. Recent developments in information science will change the way we get our news.
4. Napoleon Bonaparte was selfish.
5. The Pantheon is a famous building in Rome.
6. Some experts indicate that the weather will continue to become colder in the years ahead.
7. Some descendants of the Mayan Indians in Honduras still retain their traditions.
8. American automobiles are becoming smaller.
9. Thomas Jefferson wanted most Americans to live on farms or in very small towns.
10. The federal interstate highway system has added few additional routes in recent years.

Improving Paragraphs

Professor Edwin Peterson of the University of Pittsburgh added two more requirements for good paragraphs. He used the same pattern (Topic Sentence—Support—Clincher Sentence), but his requirements for topic sentences were more demanding. He used the formula SATP by which he meant:

Topic Sentence = **S**ubject plus **A**ttitude plus **T**ime plus **P**lace

The function of this formula is to limit the subject. Look again at the examples given in Activity 4A.

1. The phonograph worked the first time Edison tried it.
   This sentence would be more informative and more interesting if the writer had added a time and place.

   > Time (When) When he wrapped tin foil around a cylinder in 1877 . . .
   > Place (Where) . . . in his laboratory at Menlo Park . . .

2. Anthony voted with the majority.
   Anthony didn't always vote with the majority. The sentence only makes sense if the reader already knows the time and place being written about. It improves the sentence to add:

   > Time (When) During the zoning debates . . .
   > Place (Where) . . . in the City Council meetings . . .

3. The detour went through the Ozark Mountains.
   Without a Time and Place specified, this sentence has very little value for the reader.

   > Time (When) The detour Ella took last summer . . .
   > Place (Where) . . . on her vacation in Arkansas . . .

4. The Eiffel Tower was the center of the Paris Exposition. A place is already specified in this sentence, but the time has been omitted. The sentence is more meaningful when you give the reader the additional information.

   > Time (When) In 1889 . . .

ACTIVITY 4B

Adding a Time and Place to Topic Sentences

1. Look back over the ten topic sentences you expanded with attitudes in Activity 4A. See if you can make these topic sentences more meaningful by expanding them even further with a time and place. Follow the patterns above.

2. Look back in Chapter 3 at the ideas that you listed for possible compositions. Working as your teacher directs, develop five good topic sentences which include all of the SATP requirements: Subject—Attitude—Time—Place.

Discuss your topic sentences in class. After the class has discussed your sentences and improved on them, choose one of them to develop. Write a complete, unified paragraph of from four to ten sentences (up to 250 words). Use the standard expository paragraph pattern: topic sentence, supporting details, clincher sentence.

Different Kinds of Paragraphs

Even though you have learned the basic paragraph pattern, and even though this pattern has been taught for a long time, many people ignore it! Almost every day you can read an article like this:

I

Is Advertising Losing its Creative Touch?

H. E. QUIGG
UPI Senior Editor

New York—Now! New! At Last! Introducing!

Some things never change. You can be cute. Far out, far down. Factual or farcical. Double-dome or dunce.

But does it sell?

The big, soft, loud, insinuating, eager, insis-tent, clever, folksy, blithering, sophisticated sell.

Empires may teeter, skylabs falter, hemlines hesitate and snail dart-ers triumph, but the sell stands firm: look at me! Here I am!

And the ad moves the merchandise.

Morris the cat gets a longer obituary than anybody that day.

Madison Avenue is a juggernaut that starts at 23rd Street in Manhattan, in U.S.A. East, and runs right up Kalakalua Avenue in Honolulu smack into Diamond Head, U.S.A. West.[2]

Obviously, Mr. H. D. Quigg, senior editor for United Press International, is a professional writer. Why, then, does he break all the rules that you have been studying?

The answer, of course, is that Mr. Quigg knows what he is doing and is doing it for a reason. He's not writing the traditional kind of paragraph you have been studying. He's using paragraphing in a different way, for a different reason, for a particular kind of publication. What have these things to do with the rules for paragraphing? Discuss why you think Mr. Quigg paragraphed as he did. (There's no "right" answer and certainly no single answer, other than that he was trying for a "rhetorical effect." He presented his message in this way in order to enable that message to do a specific job. What was the job?)

Actually, the way Mr. Quigg was using paragraphs is probably an "older" way than the way you have been studying. Many of us are inclined to think that the customs or symbols we know best have always been in existence, but that is not always true. For example, Sir Isaac Newton, who invented calculus, would not have known that π equals 3.1416! The symbol π, or Pi, was borrowed from Greek and introduced into mathematics by Sir William Jones after Newton was dead. And William Shakespeare could not have read the number 3.2 because the decimal point was introduced by John Napier in 1617. Shakespeare had died in 1616!

Similarly, the paragraph pattern you are studying would have been a mystery to Shakespeare or Washington Irving or even Edgar Allan Poe! All of these people, as well as the monks in the Middle Ages and the scribes in the Renaissance, would have understood Quigg's method of paragraphing. They would not, however, have understood yours, for it was not introduced into the teaching of writing until 1866 when Alexander Bain first described it.

Until that time, writers indented and began a new paragraph whenever they wanted to, whenever they felt like it, whenever they wanted to signal something to the reader about a change or a break in thought. Monks first started this kind of paragraphing in the Middle Ages when they realized that readers needed warning signals to tell them to read the next section in a differ-

In medieval manuscripts, monks drew highly decorated letters to signal the beginning of a new section. The first three letters here are I N P from the Latin words *In principio* (In the beginning).

ent way. The monks began placing the symbol ¶ to stand for *para graphein* (*para* means "*beside*"; *graphein* means "*the writing.*") They placed the paragraph symbol in the margin beside the writing to indicate to the reader that a new kind of material was coming. Thousands of years before the monks and scribes were copying manuscripts, the people of Mesopotamia were writing on clay tablets and other surfaces made of baked clay. Perhaps because of the difficulty of writing in this fashion and of the need to get as much as possible on a single tablet, little thought was given to paragraphs or margins.

Look at the illustration that opens this Chapter. Baked in clay is the story of the siege of Jerusalem by Sennacherib, the king of Assyria. As you can see, the account was written without any thought of paragraphing to help the reader follow the story.

Alexander Bain's invention of a new kind of paragraph means that now there are two ways to paragraph. Perhaps you have been confused because you studied one kind of paragraph in school (Bain's very formal paragraph with a topic sentence, supporting details, and a clincher sentence), but you saw the other kind of paragraphs in newspapers, magazines, and books.

The author of the following selection used the earlier kind of paragraphs.

II

The next bad thing I remember happening was the lie I told about the cat.

I am sitting at one of the long tables, I think in a reading class. Suddenly I have a fearful urge, a need, to assert myself, and I remark that at home I have a cat who can read and write.

"Oh, Nancy!" says the teacher. "No cat can read or write. Don't tell lies."

But it has become true. I *have* got, privately, at home, a remarkable cat who actually can read and write. In my mind's eye I can see her, the book propped up before her wise and whiskered face.

"I'm not telling a lie," I say. "She really can read and write."

The trouble that came to me after that! I was called, alone, into Miss Cavendish's study, where she sat, a thoroughly terrifying object by now, at her desk, in her robes.

"Nancy, you are telling a lie."

"No, I have a cat who can read and write." I clung to it as if everything—stability itself—depended on it.

My mother was got in touch with, paid a long call shut away with Miss Cavendish in her study, and emerged with red eyes.

"Nancy, you mean you can *imagine* a cat who could read and write," my mother said.

"No, I really have . . ." But here something broke. It was because I was looking at my mother. Watching her handsome, distressed face, I know that in the place where she and I live, there is no cat who can read and write. It is very much of a shock to realize this.

So then there are apologies exacted to Miss Cavendish, to the room teacher—"I'm sorry I told a lie." And after that there is a distinct difference, not only in the way I feel about school but in the way school feels about me, for I am branded as a liar, unreliable, at least for a time.[3]

—Nancy Hale

ACTIVITY 4C

Looking at Reasons for Paragraphs

Notice the paragraphing in the preceding passage and try to determine why the writer wrote as she did. Don't try to fit this kind of paragraphing into the formal pattern. Simply try to understand what it is that the writer is signaling to the reader. Discuss your findings in class.

Two Kinds of Paragraphs

Since 1866, when Alexander Bain introduced the new formal kind of paragraphing, there have been two types of paragraphing. To distinguish them, borrow a symbol from the mathematicians and call them Paragraph₁ and Paragraph₂.

*Paragraph*₁. The older, original kind of paragraphing. The writer indents during the course of writing a longer passage to signal that a change is coming. Paragraphs are set off for many purposes. They can be of any length. They rarely follow the pattern of Paragraph₂, and they are always a part of a longer piece of writing.

*Paragraph*₂. The paragraph invented by Alexander Bain. These paragraphs are actually "miniature compositions," or "minicomps." They have a beginning, a middle, and an end and are always limited to one subject; that is, they have *unity*. The sentences within such a paragraph all "stick together" or cohere. One rarely sets out to write one of these paragraphs the way one would write a letter or an essay or a short story. They occasionally occur in "real" out-of-school writing, but mainly by accident, rather than because someone planned to write one. One researcher found that this kind of paragraph comprised only about twenty-three percent of the paragraphs in contemporary expository writing. They occur much less frequently in such other kinds of writing as narrative, descriptive, and argumentative essays. They are, however, just the right length for a school assignment and, since they give excellent practice in miniature for learning to write full-length papers, the time you devote to writing these paragraphs is well spent.

How to Learn to Paragraph

As you study paragraphing, keep in mind the differences between the two types. Paragraph$_1$ is the kind of paragraph you will most often write outside of school, so learn how skilled writers indent to help their readers. Spend some time noting different uses for this kind of paragraphing. Writers use them to show the following:

1. Change of subject
2. Need for a break in masses of type (common in newspapers and magazines)
3. Change of time
4. Change of viewpoint
5. Change of tone
6. Change of place
7. Change of mood
8. Change of emphasis
9. Change of speaker
10. Emphasis
11. Change of style
12. Subdivision of thought

Outside of school, you will not be called upon very often to write the Paragraph$_2$ type. However, do your best to master this kind of paragraphing because as you select and express a main idea, limit it, support it, and drive it home, you are learning the skills you will use in writing long papers.

ACTIVITY 4D

Examining Reasons for Paragraph Breaks

Select six pages from any one of the following publications. Examine each paragraph break and try to determine why the writers began a new paragraph at each point.

Social studies textbook
Newspaper
Science textbook
Victorian novel
Modern novel

National Geographic
Harper's or *Atlantic Monthly*
Editorial
Newsweek or *Time*
Modern short story from your literature text

Be prepared to report on the average number of words and sentences per paragraph, and the reasons the writer seems to have had for starting each new paragraph. Report also if you find one topic sentence developed in two or more paragraphs, or two or more seeming topic sentences developed in one paragraph.

Report also on any complete, formal Paragraph$_2$ types that you find.

More Kinds of Paragraphs

In Chapter 3, you looked at paragraphs from another point of view. They were classified as:

The Introductory Paragraph. As part of the outer structure of a paper, the introductory paragraph tries to interest the reader, name the subject of the paper, indicate what idea will be expressed about it, and perhaps show how it will be handled.

The Concluding Paragraph. Also part of the outer structure of a paper, the concluding paragraph provides closure and often summarizes the main idea or restates the thesis.

These are called "functional paragraphs" since they do specific jobs, or perform definite functions in a paper. Three additional types of functional paragraphs are:

The Transition Paragraph. Notice how the transition paragraph below creates a kind of bridge between the ideas which have preceded it and the new ideas which will follow. Like a bridge spanning a river, the transition paragraph carries you from one set of ideas across a gap to another set of ideas.

> But, although Descartes had come from an old, noble family and had the best classical and religious training available, he was hardly the reserved, ivory-tower philosopher. After a brief bawdy residence near Paris and a taste of soldiering in Holland, he enlisted under the Elector of Bavaria, who was then waging war against Bohemia.

What has the previous passage treated? What will the next passage treat?

The Parenthetic Paragraph of Explanation or Definition. Writers try to use words and ideas appropriate to their audience. Sometimes, a writer may realize that readers need additional help. At such points, writers pause, put in a paragraph of explanation or definition, and then move forward with their main idea. The parenthetic paragraph of explanation is the second in the following example.

> Some of the best mathematicians today are working in an unusual, Alice-in-Wonderland world in which familiar objects are twisted, pulled, bent, and deformed—always with the provision that the surface not be torn, broken, or perforated. Topology, as it is called, is concerned with such unusual one-sided peculiarities as a *Mobius strip.*
>
> Described by the German astronomer Augustus Mobius in an article published after his death in 1868, the Mobius strip is simply a long

strip of paper with one end given a half-twist and then connected with the other end to make a loop. The unusual half-twist permits you to put a pencil in the center of one side and begin making a line down the center parallel to both edges and to continue until your mark extends down the center of both sides of the strips and you are back where you started, having marked both sides of the strip, without having crossed an edge or having turned the strip over.

The preceding example doesn't quite follow the pattern of Paragraph$_2$, but good exposition is filled with this kind of parenthetical explanation. Because the reader needs the information, and the writer recognizes this need, a paragraph of explanation is used. It is a little side trip, rather than a sprint down the main street.

The Summary Paragraph. The summary paragraph often comes at the end of a paper as part of the concluding paragraph. Occasionally, a writer feels the need to remind readers what has been covered to a certain point. In this way the writer "keeps them together," makes sure of not losing anyone, and gets a fresh start for the next passage.

So far we have looked at the types of communications material the technical writer produces, at the audiences which read this material, and at the group processes used in developing the material. The foregoing analyses clearly indicate the nature of the skills the successful technical writer must have.

ACTIVITY 4E

Discussing Function Paragraphs

Each of the following brief paragraphs ought to be followed by a definition or explanation paragraph, a transition paragraph, or a summary paragraph. Working as your teacher directs, discuss the way you would write such a paragraph. Then prepare at least two of the five you have discussed. If you do not have the knowledge needed to develop the paragraph, go to the school or local library and research the topic.

1. Scientists can see individual atoms with an electron microscope. But most of what is known about atoms has come from studies with other instruments. For example, scientists may direct a beam of X rays at a small crystal of rock salt. Photographs of the X rays reflected from the crystal reveal the regular arrangement of its atoms. The distance between atoms in the crystal can be determined precisely.[4]

(A paragraph of explanation or definition is needed here.)

2. The mathematical theory of probability was formulated in the seventeenth century when a wealthy gambler, Chevalier de Mere, went to

Pascal with a problem. "If one of two dice players must leave before a game is finished, how should the stakes be divided between them?" Pascal, a mathematician, readily recognized that a fair division would be based upon the chances each has of winning the game at that point. In order to figure out the probabilities, Pascal made extensive use of the arithmetical triangle which now bears his name, Pascal's Triangle.

(A paragraph of explanation or definition should follow.)

3. The Reverend William Archibald Spooner is best known for the peculiar quirk of speech that has made his name a common noun. Without intending to, he would shift initial consonants between words, or interchange vowels in others so that his speech was filled with humorous surprises. Once when extolling the virtues of riding a bicycle, he exclaimed that he liked nothing better than to "pedal gently round on a well-boiled icicle." Another time he scolded one of his history students by saying, "You have hissed all of my mystery lessons, and completely tasted two whole worms." One unforgettable sermon on good intentions included the line, "All of us have in our hearts a half-warmed fish to lead a better life. . . . "

(The transition paragraph should be inserted here.)

Spooner served for twenty-one years as warden of New College until his retirement in 1924 and had an astonishing record of continuous residence at New College for sixty-two years. He was an extremely popular minister, serving a number of small parishes near Oxford. Also popular as a teacher, administrator, and counsellor, Spooner established an outstanding record as a professor. He wrote books and articles on subjects taken from literature, history, and geology, as well as religion.

4. Since Arabs believe that only Allah can foresee the future, they consider anyone who tries to plan ahead as somewhat insane. Consequently, farmers refuse to estimate the crops their fields will yield, families are reluctant to plan to send children on for higher education, and insurance salesmen might as well stay home.

(The transition paragraph should be inserted here.)

We have whole "think tanks" full of futurists. The government pays planners and designers to develop various "scenarios" for the future. Every major business has a long-range merchandising and development plan. Families do their best to project their future needs for education, housing, and income. In a sense, the whole banking, investment, and insurance complex is based upon our conviction that we ought to look to the future.

5. The most ancient kind of writing system is the pictographic system, or picture writing, in which the subject under discussion is represented by pictures. Some traces of that system exist today, as when the Chinese or Japanese use symbols to convey the word "man" and to stand for "river" and to represent "rain." These symbols usually become so stylized that they no longer really look like what they "mean." At that point the language moves to a sound-based system, beginning with a *syllabic* system. Again, the Japanese can serve to illustrate this type of writing, for they use not one, but two syllabic systems when writing new words or foreign words for which they do not have a Japanese pictograph. Since every language has more combined sounds than it has unique sounds, the next logical development is the *phonemic*

system in which each written symbol stands for a separate sound, and combinations of symbols are used to represent syllables and words. English has a phonemic writing system. However, no natural language— that is, a language which has not been deliberately created by linguists and scholars—is completely phonemic.

(The summary paragraph should follow here.)

More New Kinds of Paragraphs

You've looked at Paragraph$_1$ types, in which the writer begins a new paragraph any time he or she wants to signal a change to the reader. You've reviewed Paragraph$_2$ types and looked at ways of improving their structure by improving the topic sentence. You've looked at a number of "Function Paragraphs," such as introductory, concluding, transition, definition-explanation, and summary paragraphs.

(What kind of paragraph is the preceding paragraph and why did the author include it?)

But there are longer and more pleasing and more helpful Paragraph$_1$ types than those rather peculiar short ones on pages 91 and 93. In much good modern writing, these kinds of paragraphs are very effective, even if they don't quite follow the older patterns. Look, for example, at this sensitive paragraph. Notice that though it has unity and coherence and profound effect, it doesn't follow the traditional Paragraph$_2$ pattern.

I

At this crucial time my father died, and on the day I lost him, after a long illness that had made him grow remote from me, I found my brother Warren. We sat side by side on the piazza of our house on the strange April morning when we became fatherless. We watched the undertakers coming up the steps into the house, and going busily back and forth between the house and their terrible high black carriage. I felt cruelly little sorrow, considering how very deeply my father had cherished and loved me, perhaps because his cultivating love had helped to create the little girl whom I was now intent on destroying. Instead, his death gave me an exultant happiness because it strengthened and intensified my new awareness and adoration of cosmic things. It made me feel mature and experienced and proud because I could see it in the radiance of the new daybreak that was in my mind. Death was another of the great and ordered mysteries of life, and being so, it could never frighten me any more. In that revelation there was indescribable ecstasy and joy for the young mystic who was beginning to inhabit my mind and look out of my eyes.[5]

—Katherine Butler Hathaway

The opening sentence of this paragraph seems to promise to explain how the little girl found her brother. Actually, it does nothing of the sort. It explains how she grew in sensitivity and awareness as a result of her father's death. Yet, everything in the paragraph fits together: it has unity and coherence; it makes sense; it moves the story forward.

Clearly, some other way of organizing paragraphs is operating.

These kinds of paragraphs have been around for a long time, but until recently no one ever described them or showed people how to develop them.

A New Way of Looking at Paragraphs

Professor Francis Christensen of the University of Southern California was very much frustrated by the paragraph pattern taught in schools. He looked at thousands of paragraphs written by outstanding modern writers. Finally, he developed his own description of the way twentieth-century writers prepare paragraphs.[6] These are some of the things he discovered.

1. Writers usually place their main idea in the first sentence of a paragraph.
2. Later sentences usually explain more concretely the idea of the first sentence.
3. Later sentences may give details about something in the first sentence, attributes or qualities (such as size, color, or feeling), or comparisons with something in the first sentence.
4. The first sentence usually moves forward, but later sentences, as they explain the first sentence, often seem to move backward.
5. The first sentence is usually general and abstract, with later sentences providing a more concrete explanation.
6. The third and later sentences may explain more concretely any earlier sentences, as well as explaining the first sentence.
7. In order to be well-developed, concrete, and interesting, paragraphs must be fairly long.
8. Paragraphs have more interesting "texture" if they are fairly long and have several "layers of generality."
9. Ideas in a paragraph are either on the same level (parallel and equal—coordinate) or on a lower level (explaining, describing, exemplifying—subordinate).

These ideas will become clear to you as you look at the analyses of the following paragraphs.

The following paragraphs are set up to show how the sentences work together. A sentence which modifies, describes, or supports another sentence is indented to show that it belongs under that sentence. Arrows point from the supporting sentences to the topic sentence they describe to show how they relate to one another.

II

This is the main idea of the paragraph.

But New Orleans is more than Mardi Gras.

This sentence explains one way that "New Orleans is more than Mardi Gras."

The rest of the year the city is still home to much of the best jazz and blues music.

This sentence, too, explains another way that "New Orleans is more than Mardi Gras."

It also offers some of the finest dining in the country at landmark restaurants like Antoine's, Brennan's, Galatoire's, The Court of the Two Sisters, and Begue's.

This is another way that "New Orleans is more than Mardi Gras." All of these sentences are at a lower level of generality and are more concrete than the first sentence.

Or for the same French flavor at a fraction of the cost, settle for *cafe au lait* (coffee with milk) and a fresh, warm croissant at the Quarter's refurbished French Market.

This sentence, too, is at a lower level of generality, is more concrete, and explains another way "New Orleans is more than Mardi Gras."

Follow that with a leisurely stroll up St. Ann Street, past the old St. Louis Cathedral and down Bourbon Street.

The first sentence moved "forward." All of the others seem to move backward as they explain more concretely how "New Orleans is more than Mardi Gras."

The sights and sounds of the French Quarter are peculiarly American with a heavy dash of Creole and French influences.[7]

III

This sentence states the main idea of the paragraph.

When I was a lad, I did not serve a term as office boy to an attorney's firm.

This sentence, humorously, comments on the information in the first sentence.

It was one of a number of omissions.

This sentence adds more concrete information to the first sentence.

I did, however, work for a while as a file clerk in a credit agency.

This sentence does not go back to explain the first. Instead, it moves backward to explain the one just before it.

Since I was sixteen years old at the time and had been graduated from high school, I knew a great deal and had opinions on a variety of subjects that I thought anyone else in the office would consider it a privilege to hear.

This sentence is parallel to the one before it, for both refer to and explain more concretely the idea in the third sentence.

I also thought that I discerned flaws in the way the office was run.

This sentence, too, is parallel with the two before it in that it adds to the information in the third sentence.

One fine day I was advised to keep a civil tongue in my head.

This sentence refers to and explains more concretely the one just before it. It is at a lower level of generality, and it moves backward to explain that sentence.

That meant "Be respectful to your elders," or less gently interpreted, "Shut up."

This sentence, in explaining what the writer did, refers to the third sentence once more and explains more concretely and at a lower level of generality the idea "I did . . . work . . . as a file clerk . . . ."

Although I did not know the word at the time (nobody did), I prioritized my interests, even as Jimmy Carter many years later suggested that the Democrats prioritize their platform.

This sentence explains more concretely the idea in the sentence just before it: "The writer prioritized his interests."

Having a job was more highly-prioritized than not having a job.

This sentence is parallel to the one before it in that both explain more concretely what the writer means by "prioritizing his interests."

Shut up I did.[8]

This whole paragraph is more interesting, more concrete, is better developed, and has more interesting "texture" than the paragraph about New Orleans because it is longer and has more levels (layers) of generality.

IV

The house is alive.

This is the main idea of the paragraph.

It's a big creature and I live inside it.

This sentence moves backward to explain more concretely the first sentence.

Sometimes it likes my being inside and sometimes not.

This sentence moves backward to explain more concretely the sentence before it.

It tries to talk to me and tell me stuff but I can't understand a word it says because we speak two different languages, the house and I.

This sentence moves backward to explain more concretely how the house shows the feelings attributed to it in the preceding sentence.

Instead of words I hear gibberish and the gibberish eventually changes into drops of water that run down from the roof like rain, spilling across my window in wide sheets of water.

This sentence refers to the one before it, explaining more concretely the idea that the house and the writer speak different languages.

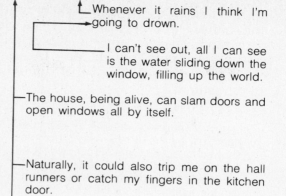

This sentence, too, explains more concretely something in the one before it.	∟Whenever it rains I think I'm going to drown.
This sentence explains the one before it, giving reasons the writer thinks she will drown.	I can't see out, all I can see is the water sliding down the window, filling up the world.
This sentence goes all the way back to the first sentence and explains in more detail and more concretely in what way "the house is alive."	The house, being alive, can slam doors and open windows all by itself.
In explaining another way "the house is alive," this sentence is parallel to the one before it and refers to and supports the first sentence.	Naturally, it could also trip me on the hall runners or catch my fingers in the kitchen door.
This is another parallel sentence referring to the house being alive.	It could possibly lock me up in a closet, but it hasn't tried yet.
Not quite parallel in idea to the sentences before, this sentence is parallel to them in a logical sense because it refers to the first sentence and shows another way the house is alive.	Its works are down in the cellar: the guts, heart, gizzard, intestines, all the things you have inside you to make you function.
This sentence is parallel both in content and logic to the one before it. It also refers to the first sentence and shows another way, in the writer's mind, the house is alive.	I never go up into the attic because I don't want to come across any big fat gray housebrain up there.

This paragraph demonstrates the nine principles listed on page 100. Go back to those principles and trace their operation in this paragraph. If there are some you do not understand, ask your teacher for additional information.

ACTIVITY 4F

Analyzing Paragraphs

Look at the preceding paragraphs. Notice the placement of the broad and general topic sentence. Note that supporting sentences have been indented slightly under the sentences they support. Parallel sentences which refer to and support a preceding sentence are indented the same amount.

Now look at the following paragraphs. Read them carefully and analyze the way each sentence works in contributing to the paragraph. Then recopy the paragraph, indenting to show which sentence supports which idea. Compare your results with those of other students. Discuss those on which you differ and come to an agreement.

1. With profound relief he recognized his father coming around the bend on his horse. He was riding fast and his strong square face showed deep concern. His powerful shoulders were hunched forward against the cold, and strands of his long black hair had come loose from the *chonga* knot on his neck and from the red headband that had given him his name. Despite the cold, the horse was lathered.[9]

2. You just can't win with parents, Taf thought. You go out for a lot of sports, and they say you're neglecting your studies. You get good grades and don't go out for sports, and they say you're a bookworm. You join clubs, and they want to know what are you, a social butterfly or something? You don't join clubs, and they call you a loner or maladjusted. You hang around with a gang, and they say you're getting in with a bad crowd. There's no satisfying them, no matter what you do.[10]

3. Sonia outdid herself that morning. She was wearing a Spanish shawl that looked as if it had come off the top of a piano. It had a fringe and was embroidered in limes and pineapples in living color. She'd wound it around her smooth hair, draped it over one shoulder, and pinned it with a velvet rose. And under it she wore basic black, something like an evening gown, with beads following the seams on the skirt down to high-heeled suede boots. "She's really going too far," Alison said, though she only glanced at Sonia and kept a worried eye on me. Sonia swept past us on a cloud of *Evening in Paris* cologne.[11]

4. The Parkers lived in a modest, white stucco and wood frame house that looked, with minor variations, exactly like every other house in the neighborhood. It was a half-heartedly gabled box into which doors and windows had been cut, a squared-off, man-made mushroom surrounded by look-alikes in a vast anonymous sea of tastelessness. What had originally been intended as a lawn was a thick tangle of crabgrass. Along the outer walls of the house were sparse beds of emaciated petunias, columbines, and lilies of the valley.[12]

5. I shall never forget those first few hours in Paris. Never before or since, have I felt so free and elated. I was in rags, without much money, a countrybred youth in a strange, foreign city, an exile from my own land and, as far as I knew, without a relative in the world, yet I felt like a king setting out on a tour of his domains. Looking back, after nearly two years, I can still partially recapture the mood of that hour, and enjoy once again the vivid sights, sounds and smells of that summer afternoon in the Paris of '92.[13]

ACTIVITY 4G

Following Christensen's Patterns in Paragraphing

The paragraph that follows has been built step-by-step according to the directions below. Note how each sentence is added as the directions suggest. After you have looked at the way this paragraph is built, write your own following the same directions. Then follow the directions for B and C.

You can get additional experience in building paragraphs in this way by coming back again and again to these sets of directions and building new paragraphs on different subjects.

A. 1. Choose the name of a place in which you like to be and tell how it makes you feel.

2. Name something in the place that contributes to that feeling and describe one detail of it.

3. Give additional information about the detail you described in the second sentence.

4. Now name something else on the same level as the second sentence and describe one detail of it.

5. Give additional information about the detail you described in the fourth sentence.

6. Give additional information parallel to sentence five for the detail you described in the fourth sentence.

7. Now go back and state in different words the feeling you described in the first sentence.

Example: (1) The shallow cave in the stone quarry makes me feel that I am back in prehistoric times. (2) Its narrow, jagged mouth shuts out the modern world. (3) The crude initials on the worn, brown limestone rocks look like the scratchings of cave dwellers. (4) The scorched, sooty fire pit at the back could be the home hearth of generations of these people. (5) It smells of wet wood ashes, pine pitch from half-burned logs, and scraps of bread and lunch meat from forgotten picnics. (6) Flat stones are crudely stacked, making a ring that encloses the fire pit. (7) Everything about that cave takes me back to the ancient people who could have lived there.

B. 1. Select one of your good friends and tell what you think of his or her personality.

2. Choose one aspect of that personality and describe it.

3. Choose another aspect of that personality; describe it.
4. Choose a third aspect of that personality; describe it.
5. Choose a detail about the aspect you described in sentence four and give additional information about it.
6. Restate the information from the first sentence in different words.

C. 1. Name one of your favorite possessions and tell why you prize it.
2. Choose one feature of that possession and describe it.
3. Describe in more detail the feature you named in the second sentence.
4. Write a sentence on the same level as the third sentence giving more detail about the feature you named in the second sentence.
5. Choose a second feature of your possession and describe it. This sentence should be on the same level as the second sentence.
6. Describe in more detail the feature you named in the fifth sentence.
7. Write a transition sentence which names the favorite possession you just described and connects it with another favorite possession which you might describe if you were writing a second paragraph.

(For additional practice, follow this same pattern in describing the possession you named in the seventh sentence.)

MAJOR WRITING ASSIGNMENT

AN IMPROMPTU COMPOSITION

Paragraph₁ types are meaningless apart from the passage or selection in which they occur. Therefore, you cannot "practice" writing such paragraphs. However, you can and should practice writing Paragraph₂ types. There are occasions when you are expected to be able to write a clear, concise, well-organized paragraph. Some job and college applications and, indeed, some of your assignments in other subjects require a paragraph rather than a longer paper.

For your major writing assignment you will use your knowledge of paragraphing to write the kind of paper you may have to submit in your first college English class.

At many colleges and universities, the first day in the freshman composition course is a very important, but very frightening, experience. Since almost all new students take the writing course, several hundred students may be herded into an auditorium, a gymnasium, or a lecture hall.

At a given signal, everyone begins writing. Sometimes the topic is assigned; sometimes it is open to choice. At the end of a specified period—usually an hour, but sometimes as long as two hours—time is called and the papers are collected.

Then the instructors plunge into action. Often two different instructors skim each paper, ranking it either "Advanced," "Average," or "Remedial." If they disagree, the paper may be read by a third person. Then they code the ratings, feed them into an IBM machine, and post the results.

Eager students mob the English Department bulletin board. They search desperately among the masses of figures for their individual student numbers and the rating that will launch them into their study of English.

An impromptu composition is a composition written without advance preparation. To prepare yourself to write an impromptu composition on a specified topic, build a fund of general information on a variety of subjects. The best way to do this, of course, is to read widely. You will find that the information you have gathered can often be adapted to suit some aspect of the assigned topic.

For impromptu papers on a subject of your own choosing, the best preparation is to accumulate a list of topics that interest you and about which you have good solid information and definite opinions.

So much for content. The next step is to practice thinking quickly through the inside and outside structures of papers on several different subjects. Here your knowledge of the Paragraph$_2$ pattern will help you. The thesis statement of your paper corresponds to the topic sentence of the paragraph pattern. The body of your paper, the inside structure, corresponds to the supporting details of a paragraph. The conclusion of your composition corresponds to the clincher sentence of a paragraph.

For this assignment you will need at least two full class periods. On the first day, write your impromptu paper. Your teacher may either specify the subject or allow you to choose your own topic. Be sure to time yourself. You may have to shorten the body of your paper in order to allow enough time to write an effective conclusion. On the second day, work as your teacher directs on the finished composition.

C·PESCENNIVS·...

IMP·DOMITIANI·CAESAR·AVG·SVBCVRA
EVTYCHI·ET·PROCVLI·CHYMINVS·CAESAR·SER

IVLIAE·A...

Chapter 5

Process

Throughout your school life you study processes; after you leave school, you use processes constantly, both at work and in your leisure hours. How does something work? How do you make something? How do you organize something else? How can you get a job done? Sometimes you are a "receiver" of instructions, and sometimes you are a "sender" of explanations to other people. Knowing how to write process compositions, those that describe or explain a process, will help you with both activities. Perhaps the simplest kind of exposition, process compositions are generally organized in simple sequential order.

Although basically concerned with how something works or how to make something, process compositions can vary greatly in subject matter and tone. Following are two examples of process compositions written by high school students. One is informal and humorous; the other is serious. As you read them, note the comments in the margin. The suggestions and criticisms may be helpful when you write your process composition.

Student Composition 5A

LEARNING TO WATER-SKI

Learning to water-ski can be quite difficult, but it is also very rewarding. If you have the determination and perseverance to master the fundamentals, you'll move into the great thrill of skipping back and forth across the frothy wake, lifting one ski in salute to the spectators, and perhaps even building a pyramid at twenty miles an hour.

But the first thing is learning to put the skis on correctly. Sometimes just getting into the rubber shoes fastened to the skis is pretty difficult. They wobble back and forth, jump out of the water (because of their buoyancy), and point the beginner in the wrong direction. It's a real problem, trying to hold the animals down, getting them stuck in the soft sand, and falling over backward during the process.

After you finally get your skis in place, you must be able to hold the skis upright until the boat can bring the ski rope to you. When the wooden handle drifts anywhere within grasp, you lurch desperately, lose your balance, and nine times out of ten must go back to Step One. Finally you get to the point where you have your skis pointed almost in the right direction, your feet almost in the shoes, and the tow rope marginally in your grasp. Now you're ready to make your first attempt at actually skiing.

Gritting your teeth, tensing your leg muscles, and waiting for the sudden shock, you yell to the driver, "Hit it!" As the boat accelerates, you relax your arms and let it pull you partially upright. Then, gently, you pull on the rope, and up you go to the beautiful, confident, soaring position—for the briefest moment before tumbling backward.

You repeat the foregoing steps with varying results and often ludicrous variations for perhaps a whole day. One variation is called the plough. For some reason or other, with the plough, the skier, unable to rise from the water, ploughs a spectacular third wake behind the boat. Another variation is the header, in which the sudden lurch forward of the boat throws the beginning skier head forward in a graceful, shimmering arc before the inevitable splashdown.

Finally, you master the skill, manage to stand upright, shift a little to either side. Then you stabilize, begin to relax, and even pull up on the rope and

---

How interesting do you find this beginning? What technique does the writer use to make you feel her paper will be worth reading?

What is the natural order the writer follows?

How effective is the metaphor here? Is it "correct" as regards tone?

How effective are the phrases in series? Is there anything in the nature of a process composition that would make a writer use them frequently?

How much attention does the writer pay to concrete detail?

Do you approve of the use of the dash in this sentence? What is it supposed to do?

How realistic are these details? Should the writer avoid such interruptions in her main direction?

Are you prepared for the climax of the skier's desire to be a member of the "small and select group" of water-skiers, or has the emphasis been on something else as the reward?

turn your skis to control your direction. Across the wake and back. And still standing. Now you're on the road to many hours of fun and excitement. You feel the satisfaction of having joined a small and select group. You can water-ski.

—Sherrie Aly

Student Composition 5B

HOW THE HEART WORKS

Are you interested by the reference to William Harvey and the date of his work? How might you eliminate the circular second use of the form of *work*?

Until the 1600's, when William Harvey discovered the circulation of the blood and the workings of the heart, no one really knew what the heart did or how it worked. It was believed that it had something to do with the blood, but people generally considered it to be the place in the body where love and courage are felt. Until Harvey's discovery, no one realized that the heart is one of the toughest muscles in the human body, and one of the most amazing pumps in the world. Though its size is like a clenched fist, it does enough work during a single day to lift a person weighing 150 pounds almost 1,000 feet in the air. The heart is really two pumps side by side; one on the right and one on the left. The pump on the right pumps blood from the veins to the lungs. Then it pumps blood through the lungs to the pump on the left, which sends it through the body.

Why does the writer use a simile in this passage? Why does he use an analogy?

Can you provide a more imaginative transition for this paragraph? What is gained in the simple, direct sentence?

Would a picture or diagram aid you in understanding this process?

This is how it works. Each pump consists of two hollow chambers, like balloons in shape, and one above the other. The upper thin-walled chamber is called the auricle. The lower chamber, thick-walled and more powerful, is called the ventricle. The two chambers are separated by door-like valves that allow the blood to flow in only one direction. When blood enters the heart, it flows through the veins into the right auricle. The blood pours into the auricle and down through open valves into the ventricle. The auricle helps this flow slightly by a brief squeezing action just before the ventricle begins its constriction. As the ventricle contracts, the valves between the auricle and the ventricle shut to keep the blood from returning to the auricle. The blood can then go only one way—out the ventricle through other valves that open into the large artery leading to the lung.

On the left side of the heart, the pump has two chambers, exactly as on the right. The blood is pumped from the upper left chamber to the lower left chamber. The lower left chamber sends the blood to the main artery of the body, which is called the aorta. From the aorta, the blood runs on to the different branches of the arteries and is pumped throughout the body. The heartbeat continues involuntarily at a regulated pace and keeps the blood moving even at the farthest corners of the body; even though the right- and left-hand sides of the heart are two different pumps with no direct connection between them, they squeeze and relax in just about the same rhythm.

Would you suggest any change in sentence structure here? What is your reason?

The most wonderful thing about this priceless heart is that it goes on beating throughout life, resting only a fraction of a second after each beat. It seems that the heart must be a very complex muscle, yet the way it keeps alive the entire body is in reality a simple process.

What words weaken this final passage? How might you improve it?

—Bob Burke

ACTIVITY 5A

Discussing the Process Compositions

Although there is no single correct way of writing a process composition, discussing the techniques these students have used will help you understand some techniques you can use later. If you have read and discussed the comments and questions beside the models, you should be able to agree on answers to the following questions.

1. In Chapter 3 you learned about the organization of the "outside" structure of a composition and about the "inside" structure of a composition. To what extent has each writer followed the "outside" structure pattern? To what extent has each alerted the reader to the main idea? To what extent has each tried to interest the reader and to tie the composition together at the end?

2. The usual arrangement of a process composition is sequential. Is each of these models sequential? If not, why not? Do you believe that either might be improved if a different order were used? Why or why not?

3. In process compositions, transitions are especially important. Call attention to any noteworthy transitions. Are any transitions weak?

4. Often in explaining processes, writers must clarify new vocabulary words or explain objects or relationships. Call attention to any such definitions or explanations. What words or concepts do you think should have been defined? How do you explain the writers' choosing not to define them?

Keep these discussion questions in mind as you read the following examples of professional writing. Each one describes a process—how to do something, how something works, even how to avoid something.

I

HOW THE FEDERAL RESERVE SYSTEM EXPANDS THE MONEY SUPPLY[1]

By 1907 the money shortage was so severe that Congress realized it had to do something to provide the country with enough currency. It appointed the National Monetary Commission to study the problem and decide what could be done. The study found that nearly all countries whose currency supply could expand or contract to meet the needs of the people had some kind of central bank. After several years the commission reported back to Congress. It recommended that the United States have a strong central bank that could issue currency as needed.

In 1913, after many hearings and much debate, Congress passed the Federal Reserve Act, which provided for the type of central banking system recommended by the National Monetary Commission. One important change in the commission's original plan was made to satisfy people living in the South and West, far from New York City, the nation's financial capital. Instead of a single central bank like the Bank of England or the second Bank of the United States, Congress established a Federal Reserve system consisting of twelve Federal Reserve banks—located in Boston, Massachusetts; New York, New York; Philadelphia, Pennsylvania; Cleveland, Ohio; Richmond, Virginia; Atlanta, Georgia; Chicago, Illinois; St. Louis, Missouri; Minneapolis, Minnesota; Kansas City, Missouri; Dallas, Texas; and San Francisco, California—each serving a particular Federal Reserve district. This meant that America's financial plans would be set by bankers who came from every part of the nation rather than from only New York and Washington, D.C., as was the practice.

The organization of the Federal Reserve has not changed significantly over the years. Member banks include all national banks (those that receive their charters from the federal government) and some state banks (those that receive their charters from state governments). Each member bank must have an account with the nearest Federal Reserve bank. This account is called a reserve account. The Federal Reserve bank acts as a bank for its members. In addition, the member banks can use the Federal Reserve bank as a check-clearing and check-collection center for all the banks in its district.

Having as strong a bank as the Federal Reserve behind it, a member bank can create checkbook money with confidence. We shall pretend that you have just visited your bank to deposit $100 in your account. If your bank is a member of the Federal Reserve system, it must deposit a certain percentage of your money in the nearest Federal Reserve bank. We shall also assume that current Federal Reserve regulations call for 15 percent reserves, meaning that 15 percent of $100, or $15, will go into your bank's reserve fund at the Federal Reserve bank. This will leave $85, which your bank is free to lend.

After you have made your deposit, a farmer enters the bank. It just happens that he needs a loan of $85 to have his truck repaired. The lending officer decides the man is a good risk and agrees to lend him your $85 if he signs a note promising to pay the money back with interest within a year. The $85 is then transferred to the farmer's checking account and is known as new money, deposit money, or checkbook money.

What would happen if you needed your $100 back in a hurry? We noted that $15 had to go to the Federal Reserve bank, and all that is left of the remaining $85 is the promissory note that the farmer signed. Since you made a demand deposit, you can request your cash at any time. The bank is able to pay you the $100 because it has enough cash in reserve. Bankers know from experience how much cash they must have on hand, and fortunately, all depositors never ask for all of their money at the same time. Of course, if every depositor should come to the bank and demand his cash at once, there would not be enough on hand. Most of the deposits are out on loan to businessmen, mechanics, farmers, and others who need to borrow. Some depositors mistakenly think that their demand deposits are always in the bank ready for immediate withdrawal. If this were the case, much of our nation's money would be stored in bank vaults and would not be available to those who need to borrow money.

The use of your deposits and those of other bank customers greatly increases our nation's supply of money. When the farmer pays out the $85 to the garage, the money is put back by the garage into the same or another bank as a demand deposit. The $85 is available to be lent out again less 15 percent ($12.75), which must go into the bank's reserve account at the Federal Reserve. The remaining $72.25 goes out as a loan and returns to a bank as a demand deposit to be used—less 15 percent. The cycle is repeated again and again. Your $100 can grow 6 2/3 times—into as must as $666 of deposit money.

When you think of money, you probably think of the currency you carry. Actually, demand deposits make up the greatest part of our money supply. Most men and women keep a few bills and coins for small purchases but write checks to pay for their large expenditures. Americans use checks to pay nine dollars out of every ten dollars they spend. Businesses make almost all of their payments with checks, which later become demand deposits as they are put in banks.

Think what might happen if banks could create all the checkbook money they wished. There might be so much money that it would become practically worthless. Instead of paying ten cents for a candy bar you might have to spend fifty cents or more. Fortunately that is not likely to happen, because the board of governors of the Federal Reserve shares the responsibility for regulating the Nation's money supply with the men who head each of the twelve Federal Reserve Banks.

—Adrian A. Paradis

II

SOMETHING NEW ON THE SEA: S.S. SAVANNAH[2]

The first steamship to cross the Atlantic actually used her boilers only 89 hours out of a 24-day crossing and carried no passengers or cargo. Yet, that 1819 crossing by the S.S. Savannah was as significant in her time as the launching of her namesake 140 years later.

On July 21, 1959, the first successor to the vast brood of coal-and-oil-powered offspring of the original Savannah was launched at Camden,

New Jersey. What was strange about the appearance of Savannah II was the disappearance of the smokestack, which had been the most startling feature of Savannah I. In its place, a little astern of amidships, rises an unobtrusive deck in front of the bridge with an oddly large, square hatch cover. This hatch cover is not designed to be lifted often. Underneath it is a well-secured steel dome. When this is removed, twenty-one round metallic circles come into view. These are the tops of twenty-one rods that control the nuclear "fire" surrounding them.

A nuclear-powered reactor produces heat, which can be used in a variety of ways. Instead of coal, it "burns" a fissionable substance, usually a special form of the heavy-metal uranium, which is composed of atoms that can easily be split in two. As these fly apart at great speed, they generate heat by colliding with surrounding matter. At the same time, neutron particles are released from the centers of the splitting atoms. These may strike other atoms, causing further fission, and so keep the chain reaction going. The heat given off is picked up by a coolant, usually water, which in the process generates steam that is used in the ordinary way to turn turbines.

—Joseph Gies

III

HOT OFF THE PRESS AND INTO THE OVEN[3]

This is the time of year when because of inclement weather and bad pitches by groggy newsboys, your Sunday newspaper may be arriving in a wet or soggy condition. Most people get angry at this state of affairs, maybe because they don't know how to dry and bake a good Sunday paper. Once you know how to do this, you may never fear getting a wet newspaper again.

My recipe for baking a newspaper was handed down in my family from one generation to the next, and even on the rainiest, snowiest, sleetiest days our family always has had the crispiest, tastiest Sunday newspaper on the block.

As a public service, it is my intention to pass on this family recipe to my loyal and devoted readers.

First, pre-heat oven to 300 degrees.

While you're doing that, drain off liquid from the paper and put aside.

Now get a sharp knife and start peeling off the sections of paper: the front section, then the society, sports, comics, etc. Wipe each section lightly with a damp cloth and roll to even out.

By this time your oven should be hot. If it isn't, you can study the wet football scores or the classified advertisements.

Once your oven is hot enough, arrange the sections of the newspaper on the racks of the oven, but make sure they do not touch each other or get in the way of the oven door.

Note: It is always best to put the comics on the lowest shelf so the color does not drip down on the black-and-white pages.

(If your paper is very, very large, you may have to bake it in two roastings. Therefore, select the sections you want to read first. Bake them, and then while you're reading them, stick the other sections in the oven.)

I know that the big question on your minds is how long to bake or roast a Sunday newspaper. This depends strictly on the paper. Give 15 minutes for each pound of wet newsprint. But every five minutes turn over the sections on the rack so that they don't get too brown. Some people prefer to cook their newspapers on a rotisserie which keeps going around in a circle, and this is probably a faster way to do it. But the danger is that if the paper touches the flame, it will go up in smoke and that won't leave you much to do on Sunday morning.

After you've allowed your newspaper first to simmer, then stew, and finally bake, you can test it to see if it's ready to be read. Take out the travel section, or the book review, and hold it in both hands. If the paper seems firm and stays up stiff of its own accord, it's ready. On the other hand, if it sags or falls apart while you're holding it, put the rest of it back in the oven for at least another 10 minutes.

Sometimes people make a mistake and overcook their paper. You'll know your Sunday paper is too well-done if it gets black around the edges and has a funny smell to it.

Your Sunday paper can either be served hot or cold to your family, and can also be sliced very thin or very thick, depending on how they like it.

If you want to read it cold, transfer to a cool, dry place and let stand 15 minutes.

The important thing to remember is that *anyone* can bake a Sunday newspaper. All you need for the ingredients are newsprint, rain, slush or snow, a hot oven and patience.

One more thing: There may be times when the news is so depressing that you're sorry you took the trouble to bake your paper. If this happens, just pour some cognac on it, light it and make it into a *flambé*.

—Art Buchwald

IV

HOW TO AVOID SHARK BITE[4]

Never underestimate the power of the press. Since the release of *Jaws*, shark attack has vaulted from the number thirty-six position in popular fears (just behind ring around the collar) to number eleven. Even the sharks seem to have caught the spirit. Sightings near beaches have doubled in the past year, though many reports are inaccurate. The brave burghers of Miami Beach, for example, bludgeoned to death one ten-foot invader, only to discover the victim was a baby whale.

Still, better safe than sorry. For those who wish to be prepared, here's the latest on how to preserve life and limb.

Elude 'em. Sharks don't have anything particular against humans; they are much too dumb to hold grudges. The going theory, these days, is that aggressive shark species eat everything that is accessible. The more you resemble easy prey, the more likely you are to get eaten. Hence the obvious precautions. Avoid swimming near concentrations of fish—natural bait for sharks. Avoid dead fish in the water—sharks have good noses. Avoid high-contrast clothing—sharks perceive contrast better than color. Don't splash about near sharks—it reminds them of wounded fish.

On the other hand, don't believe the myth that you're safe swimming in cold water. Few shark attacks have been recorded in water below 65 degrees because few people swim in water below 65 degrees. Shallow water offers little protection if it is close to a deep channel.

Repel 'em. Chemical shark repellents don't work very well. The U.S. Navy uses something called Shark Chaser, a mixture of copper acetate and black dye, developed during World War II. The copper acetate supposedly reduces shark appetite, while the dye hides the potential victim. Unfortunately, the combination hasn't proved effective outside the laboratory.

What does work is a simple camouflage device called the Shark Screen. This is nothing more than a dull-colored plastic sack with a flotation collar, big enough for a person to fit inside. Sharks ignore it because it doesn't resemble an ordinary meal. And unlike Shark Chaser, the protection lasts indefinitely.

Kill 'em. The standard anti-shark weapon for divers is the bang stick. It's just a long pole with a shotgun shell and trigger device on the business end. Unfortunately (as everybody who saw the movie knows), the bang stick will stop a big shark only if you nail the beast directly in the brain. Sharks have very small brains.

Other weapons may revolutionize the art. The Shark Dart, carried by Navy divers at Apollo splashdowns, punctures the skin with a hollow steel needle, then fills up the shark's gut with compressed gas. Very deadly. An electric dart, also being tested by the Navy, paralyzes the monster with a thirty-volt shock. Disadvantage: when the battery wears out, so does the paralysis.

Probably the most appealing anti-shark weapon under development, though, is the porpoise. Porpoises defend their young by ramming predators at high velocity with their thick skulls. The Navy hopes to train them to do the same on behalf of divers. A big problem is getting porpoises angry enough to risk their own hides.

Eat 'em. Should you tangle with a shark and win, the following recipe will come in handy:

Shark a la Ross

2 lbs. filet from young, medium-sized shark, preferably a Mako (no dark meat)

2 shallots, chopped

½ cup parsley, chopped

¼ cup fresh basil, chopped

¼ cup dry white wine

¼ cup fish stock

4 tbs. butter

½ lemon

salt and white pepper

Sprinkle the bottom of a buttered baking dish with the shallots, parsley, and basil. Pour in the wine and stock. Rub both sides of the filets with salt and pepper; place in the baking dish. Squeeze lemon juice over the fish and dot with butter.

Cook, uncovered, in a preheated 350-degree oven for 20 minutes, basting a few times with the pan liquid. Then brown under the broiler for a few minutes. Garnish with parsley sprigs and lemon wedges.

Serves 6.

—Peter Passell

ACTIVITY 5B

Discussing the Professional Models

1. Two of the professional models are presented in their entirety. Two are extracted from longer selections. Which ones are which? What cues do you get from the structures of the models? What insights does this give you into the way you should organize your paper?
2. Refer to the discussion questions (page 112) based on the student compositions and apply them to the professional models you have just read.
3. In what respects do the student compositions differ from the professional models? Consider inside and outside structure, logical arrangement, transitions, vocabulary choices.

Suggested Topics for Your Process Composition

Here is a list of possible subjects for your process composition. You may, of course, devise your own topic, dealing with something you are especially interested in. As you work through the activities that follow, keep your chosen topic in mind. The techniques described and the examples given will help you write your own paper.

You will notice that the suggested topics have been divided into five categories. Into which category would you place each of the professional models? The student compositions?

1. How to do something: baby-sit; cook a meal; prepare an assignment; repair a toy or appliance; develop a personal quality; grow a crop; camp out; plan a trip, party, meal, game, visit, or campaign; get along with someone; pass time; learn a language, a trick, a sport, a stunt; run a publicity or public relations campaign; establish a business; improve race relations; keep or make a friend; track an animal; review a book; choose a wardrobe; earn spending money; collect coins; enjoy a vacation; hide embarrassment; study systematically; overhaul your car; tune up your car; show cattle; enjoy music; loaf; caddy; give artificial respiration; become popular.
2. How something works: camera, canal locks, helicopter, motion picture machine, radio, door bell, electric motor, gasoline engine, a political system, steam engine, vacuum bottle, precipitation cycle, fluorescent light, EFT (electronic transfer of funds), automation, binary computer, telephone, telegraph.

How many steps are involved in the process pictured here?

3. How to operate something: coin telephone, combine, mimeograph machine, automobile, automatic coin washer, pinball machine, tractor or end-loader, airplane, calculator, model airplane, outboard motor.
4. How to avoid something: making enemies, airplane crashes, accidents, being chosen for duties, being called on, blind dates, criticism, work.
5. How a process or system operates: passing a bill in Congress; becoming a candidate for office; using the Initiative, Referendum, or Recall; system of checks and balances in government; International Monetary Fund; how a student council operates.

Making Your Inside Structure Clear

In Chapter 3 you looked at the relationship between the inside structure and the outside structure of a paper. You learned that the thesis statement or topic sentence specifies clearly what the paper is about and automatically provides direction and structure for many papers. Although the thesis statement or topic sentence is part of the outside structure, it definitely shapes the inside structure.

In addition to this major way of making the inside structure clear, writers have developed many other techniques you may want to borrow. Here are five of these techniques that are especially useful in organizing process compositions, although they are useful in other kinds of writing as well.

An explanation and examples of each follow.

1. Specify in as few words as possible the major divisions or steps you will discuss.
2. Use topic headings to define and limit sections of your paper.
3. Use a combination of 1 and 2: Open with a list of main ideas and repeat them as topic headings.
4. Use a vivid image to help the reader *see* your subject.
5. Use a series of questions to control brief passages.

As you read the following examples, notice how each writer uses one of these techniques to make the inside structure clear.

1. Specify in as few words as possible the major divisions or steps you will discuss.

Here is a brief passage from a book by General Douglas MacArthur in which he specifies the major tasks he took upon himself as Supreme Commander of the Allied Powers in Occupied Japan after World War II. In the book, each of the short, crisp statements is developed in long, expanded sections explaining the process involved in each.

> From the moment of my appointment as supreme commander, I had formulated the policies I intended to follow, implementing them through the Emperor and the machinery of the imperial government. I was thoroughly familiar with Japanese administration, its weakness and its strengths, and felt the reforms I contemplated were those which would bring Japan abreast of modern progressive thought and action. First destroy the military power. Punish war criminals. Build the structure of representative government. Modernize the constitution. Hold free elections. Enfranchise the women. Release the political prisoners. Liberate the farmers. Establish a free labour movement. Encourage a free economy. Abolish police oppression. Develop a free and responsible press. Liberalize education. Decentralize the political power. Separate church from state.
>
> These tasks were to occupy me for the next five years and more. All were eventually accomplished, some easily, some with difficulty.[5]
>
> —Douglas MacArthur

2. Use topic headings to define and limit sections of your paper.

Some writers have trouble trying to control the ideas in a long, continuous passage. The solution is to break up a long passage into short sections by using topic headings to limit and control the content of the passage. Editors of magazines and newspapers insert topic headings to help readers follow the main ideas of a passage. You can use the same device to help you organize and control your ideas. If you've thought through the main divisions of your paper, you can use those divisions as topic headings on separate sheets of paper. Then you need only write the content for each topic and later provide transitions to link them. If you haven't thought your paper through, you can label each section after you've finished it. Then, as you continue, check to see whether what you have written deserves a new label or fits under the previous one. Some instructors feel that topic headings in a literary paper are too mechanical. If your teacher feels that way, simply pull out the headings and tighten your transitions when you make your final draft.

Here is the way one writer used topic headings to help control the content of a fairly long composition about how scientists are trying to save polluted lakes. The writer divided the body of the composition into five sections. Here are the topic headings for these sections:

1. Reducing the Source of Pollution
2. Increasing the Flow of Fresh Water
3. Using Chemicals to Neutralize the Pollutants
4. Aerating
5. Dredging

3. Use a combination of these techniques. Open with a list of main ideas and repeat them as topic headings.

The introductory paragraph of the following magazine article lists the major oil companies (the "seven sisters") and reveals the main divisions of the article.

THE SEVEN SISTERS STILL RULE[6]

There's no business like oil business.
—C.C. Pocock, Chairman of Shell

A few years ago, such Ethel Mermanesque exuberance would have sounded strange coming from the chief of one of world oil's fabled Seven Sisters—Exxon, Shell, Mobil, Texaco, British Petroleum, Standard Oil of California, and Gulf. Though the sorocracy* had ruled the international oil trade since it began, the upheaval in the business that started with the Arab embargo of 1973 threatened to end this reign. . . .

Instead, five years after the energy crisis hit, the Sisters' power seems unshaken.

*A coined word meaning "rule by a group of sisters."

Then the writer uses the names of each of the major oil companies as topic headings, making it easy to organize the content. This is the way a combination of the first two techniques works. Specify near the beginning of the paper the major divisions or steps you will discuss, and use topic headings to define and limit sections throughout the paper.

4. Use a vivid image to help the reader *see* your subject.

In writing about the growth of a small town, this writer uses the image of Rip Van Winkle to help readers visualize a sudden "awakening" and change.

> Like Rip Van Winkle, Pasco County dozed in the sun for decades, awakening to find that it had grown a long silver beard of retirees, was wearing the ragged clothes of "too little too late" in the business of government services, and was in bad need of a drink of water.
>
> The process of finding new clothes, tending to the beard and working the kinks out of long-dormant governmental muscles has been a lengthy one, but one in which government and business are, finally, further ahead than behind.[7]
>
> —Jan Glidewell

If you were writing the article on Pasco County, what would you use as your four topic headings?

5. Use a series of questions to control brief passages.

By asking a question, you set for yourself the task of answering it. If your questions are carefully organized, you can take your reader—and yourself—right through a long paper and be sure that no one gets off the track. Here is the way one writer used questions to guide an explanation of the way a gasoline engine works.

> How does the gasoline get from the tank to the engine?
> What does the carburetor do?
> What pulls the vapor into the cylinder?
> What happens when the piston returns to the top of the cylinder?
> What makes the vapor explode?
> How is the cylinder cleared of burned gases to get ready for more vapor?

If you have trouble handling long passages, you can guide your writing by planning such a series of questions. Whether or not you use the questions as headings in the final paper doesn't matter.

ACTIVITY 5C

Planning Control of the Inner Structure of Your Paper

1. Choose one of the Suggested Topics for Your Process Composition listed on pages 118–119, or another one that your teacher approves. List the main divisions that you will use in your paper. If possible, discuss the paper with one or more of your friends to clarify what you are trying to do. Make sure that they can follow your main divisions. Experiment with one or more of the preceding techniques for revealing the inner structure of your paper.

2. If you are unable to think through your main divisions before you begin to write (and many people cannot), write out a rough draft, trying to be as consistent and logical as possible. Then work with one or more of your friends to see whether or not your sequence of ideas can be improved. Experiment with one or more of the preceding ways of revealing the inner structure.

Combining Your Inner and Outer Structures

In Chapter 3 you looked at the outer structure of exposition and at the ways the inner and outer structures interact. In the activity you have just completed, you looked more closely at the inner structure. Now it is time to look at the way the inner and outer structures work together in the process composition.

Although there are other patterns, this is the basic pattern of the process composition:

(Outer Structure)

I. Introduction

A. Arouse interest. (This may mean naming the subject you are writing about, showing that it's important, and putting it into a context.)

B. State the main idea or purpose of the paper. (If this is clear from your title, this step is optional.)

C. Give some clue as to the main divisions of the paper (optional).

(Inner Structure)

II. Body

Take up the major divisions of the paper in an appropriate and logical order. It will probably be sequential, but it could follow some other pattern. Make the movement from one division to another clear. Use topic headings, images, questions, or some other device.

(Outer Structure)

III. Conclusion

A. Summarize the main divisions (optional).

B. Provide interesting, satisfying *closure* (ending).

ACTIVITY 5D

Planning Your Whole Paper

1. Working as your teacher directs, try to build an outline for your paper following the preceding pattern. If you do not write comfortably from an outline, make a simple list of ideas, put them in an appropriate order, and go ahead to your rough draft. Then work out an outline from what you have written, rearranging the ideas in your rough draft if necessary.

2. Submit your outline to an editing group, a school friend, or an adult to learn whether or not your ideas are clear and you are ready to write (or rewrite).

Flavor in Writing: Avoiding Engfish

One of Ken McCrorie's students jokingly misspelled "English" as *Engfish*. Now Professor McCrorie uses the word *Engfish* to refer to the kind of empty, impersonal, careless writing that may have no errors, but that also has no imagination or soul.

The first way to avoid writing Engfish is to find something you want to say and then write about it in such a way that a reader will understand and enjoy your message. The second way is to let your own personality color your writing. Does the personality of the writer shine through in these passages?

I

The cinema is a ribbon of dreams.

—Orson Welles

II

. . . the true writer both of verse and of prose writes with his ear. . . .

—John Macy

III

High up in the North in the land called Svithjod, there stands a rock. It is a hundred miles high and a hundred miles wide. Once every thousand years a little bird comes to this rock to sharpen its beak.

When the rock has thus been worn away, then a single day of eternity will have gone by.[8]

—Hendrik Van Loon

IV

It's always over so suddenly. We hit the end of summer like a traffic jam on Labor Day and are automatically lined up to go through the toll booth of another year.

Our biorhythms gave way to sociorhythms so long ago that we're now as geared up for the first day of school as any six-year-old. No matter what the calendar says, no matter what the thermostat says, ready or not, fall is here.

From now on, any warm day will be hoarded rather than savored and our summer experience will be reduced to 2 × 3-inch Kodachrome slides and 8 × 11-inch essays of what we did on our vacations.

In a matter of days we will have completely covered up our tans with schedules and put on the layered look of obligations. We will all be carrying fall accessories like dentists' appointments and sign-up sheets for music lessons.

The speed with which we do our fall cleaning—sweeping summer out of our lives as if it were sand—has always amazed me. It looks as if we fear that one more minute or month of ease and we would all become permanently flaccid. Instead, September becomes our national tone-up month.[9]

—Ellen Goodman

ACTIVITY 5E

Considering Flavor in Writing

1. Most American newspapers try to avoid a personal flavor in their news stories. Most business, government, scientific, and military reports aim at an impersonal sameness, as though no one had written them—as though they had somehow bloomed on their own with no human creator behind them. Most students in school are taught to write formally, editing out themselves and their own personalities.

   Working as your teacher tells you, consider the foregoing observations. Are they true or not? Why do you think much writing has become impersonal? What are the values of impersonal writing? What are the dangers? What do you want to aim for in your own writing? Why?

2. Very few textbooks show very much flavor or personality. Go to the nonfiction section of your library and check out a popular book from the applied arts (600's) or the social sciences (300's). Compare the flavor you find in that book with the flavor you find in your textbooks on a similar subject. Be prepared to point out what the differences are and the probable reasons for them.

3. Make a list of the elements which contribute to the flavor of a piece of writing. Try to work some of these elements into your process composition.

Using Analogies to Clarify Explanations

In explaining processes—indeed, in all kinds of exposition—a communicator frequently must use a word or a concept which the reader or listener may not know. Since writers are unable to stop and show readers what they are talking about, often they do the next best thing: they compare the object or concept with something the reader knows. They use an *analogy*.

An analogy can be a comparison of the known and the unknown on the basis of a single similarity, or it can explain something by comparing it point by point with something else.

Many figures of speech involve a basic comparison:

METAPHOR:
Deerslayer *snaked* his way through the forest.

(The scout's movement is compared to the movement of a snake.)

SIMILE:
The announcement came *like* a thunderbolt.

(The effect of the announcement is compared to the effect of thunder and lightning.)

PERSONIFICATION:
Autumn *smiled* benevolently on the land.

(Autumn is compared to a smiling person.)

HYPERBOLE:
The chili sauce *tortured* his tonsils.

(The chili sauce is compared to an instrument of torture.)

ACTIVITY 5F

Examining Analogies

Keeping in mind that an analogy is a comparison of things in some way similar, notice how scientific writers in the following examples have used analogies to clarify their material.

1. Every civilization, born like an animal body, has just so much energy to expend. In its birth throes it chooses a path, the pathway perhaps of a great religion as in the time when Christianity arose. Or an empire of thought as built among the Greeks, or a great power extends its roads and governs as did the Romans. Or again, its wealth is poured out upon science, and science endows the culture with great energy, so that far goals seem attainable and yet grow illusory. Space and time widen to weariness. In the midst of triumph disenchantment sets in among the young. It is as though with the growth of cities an implosion took place, a final unseen structure, a spore-bearing structure towering upward toward its final release.[10]

—Loren Eiseley

2. Not long ago I chanced to fly over a forested section of country which, in my youth, was still an unfrequented wilderness. Across it now suburbia was spreading, Below, like the fungus upon a fruit, I could see the radiating lines of transport gouged through the naked earth. From far up in the wandering air one could see the lines stretching over the horizon. They led to cities clothed in an unmoving haze of smog. From my remote, abstract position in the clouds I could gaze upon all below and watch the incipient illness as it spread with all its slimy tendrils through the watershed.[11]

—Loren Eiseley

3. The normal healthy brain puts out "remarkable mileage." It consumes 1 teaspoon of sugar per hour. Using the terminology of industry, total operating costs are remarkably low. Energy output per hour is equal to that of a 20-watt light bulb. It is remarkable that while the combined brain energy of the group of men who worked on the atomic bomb did not equal the electrical energy consumed by the lights in an average office, nevertheless, they released atomic energy which is now being measured in megatons. Thus the brain is the control organ that directs the power flow of modern industry.[12]

—Robert K. Burns

4. Folklore is the country mouse talking. Taken to the city, cheapened by charlatans and opportunists, folklore became fakelore, as the mass took over from the folk. To some, the sad tale ends here. But wait—there's another mutation. Using the new urban material with its chrome and kitsch, imaginative artists, ad men, and scriptwriters are developing a poplore which is as true to its environment as was folklore to an earlier one. Call it poplore, and ask it if doesn't complete the circle.[13]

—Marshall Fishwick

5. A true perfume consists of a large number of odoriferous chemical compounds mixed in such proportions as to produce a single harmonious effect upon the sense of smell. In a fine brand of perfume may be compounded a dozen or twenty different ingredients and these, if they are natural essences, are complex mixtures of a dozen or so distinct substances. Perfumery is one of the fine arts. The perfumer, like the orchestra leader, must know how to combine and coordinate his instruments to produce the desired sensation. A Wagnerian opera requires 103 musicians. A Strauss opera requires 112. Now if the concert manager wants to economize he will insist upon cutting down on the most expensive musicians and dropping out some of the others, say, the supernumerary violinists and the man who blows a single blast or tinkles a triangle once in the course of the evening. Only the trained ear will detect the difference and the manager can make more money.

Suppose our mercenary impresario were unable to get into the concert hall of his famous rival. He would then listen outside the window and analyze the sound in this fashion: "Fifty per cent of the sound is made by the tuba, 20 per cent by the bass drum, 15 per cent by the 'cello and 10 per cent by the clarinet. There are some other instruments, but they are not loud and I guess if we can leave them out nobody will know the difference." So he makes up his orchestra out of these four alone and many people do not know the difference.

The cheap perfumer goes about it in the same way. He analyzes, for instance, the otto or oil of roses which cost during the war four hundred dollars a pound—if you could get it at any price—and he finds that the chief ingredient is geraniol, costing only five dollars, and next is citronelol, costing twenty dollars; then comes nerol and others. So he makes up a cheap brand of perfumery out of three or four such compounds. But the genuine oil of roses, like other natural essences, contains a dozen or more constituents and to leave many of them out is like reducing an orchestra to a few loud-sounding instruments or a painting to a three-color print.[14]

—Edwin E. Slosson

After you have read the preceding examples in class, be prepared to discuss these questions:

1 In each example, what is the unknown or obscure subject being discussed? What is the analogous object or situation and how does it help make the subject clearer and more interesting?

2 Although figures of speech are most often studied in connection with poetry, is their primary purpose (and likewise the purpose of analogy) only decorative? Do figures of speech and analogies actually help improve communication? How? What might be some dangers in overusing figures of speech and analogies?

3. These examples have all been taken from scientific writing. You have undoubtedly heard that this type of material is plain, straightforward, and unadorned. How do you justify the use of poetic devices in connection with scientific writing?

ACTIVITY 5G

Writing Analogy Paragraphs

Each of the following operations can be compared to one or more common objects or actions. For some, the analogy is so simple that the comparison can be communicated in a single figure of speech; for others, one or more paragraphs of development might be needed. After looking the list over and deciding on one or more appropriate comparisons for each item, discuss the list in class. If your teacher asks you to develop an analogy paragraph on one of the items, be sure to choose very carefully so that you will be able to get a complete paragraph. You may have to do some library work if you do not know these processes.

1. Growth of a stalactite and a stalagmite
2. Leveling action of a glacier
3. Growth of crime in a community
4. Progressively easier task of getting signers to a petition as more and more people sign
5. Chain reaction to a nuclear explosion
6. Precipitation cycle
7. Beginning, rise, and fall of a nation or civilization
8. How a computer works
9. How a three-stage rocket works
10. How a laser beam works
11. How a turbine works
12. Growth of prejudice
13. How a rumor spreads
14. How a stream is polluted
15. Development of a popular movement (ecology, feminism, others)
16. Migrant-worker system
17. Social impact of school selection (how the school "assigns" people to varying roles in life)
18. Nonviolence as a social force
19. The credibility gap
20. The electoral system
21. The American political system
22. Government influence on news media
23. Vocational training
24. The expanding economy
25. The influence of advertising on consumption

Process Transitions

Because the usual order in a process composition is sequential, writers must be especially careful to let readers know how they are progressing in time and, if necessary, in space. Often they use such simple transitions as *first, second, third, fourth;* or *immediately, next, later, finally;* or some other combination of words, so that the relationship of each idea to other ideas is clear.

Transitions, which serve as bridges between ideas, may be placed in five categories:

1. Time signals—*first, then, next, later*
2. Place signals—*on the left, nearby, in the center, beside*
3. Minus signals for contrasting material—*however, but, unfortunately, on the contrary, on the other hand*

4. Plus signals for additional material—*and, in addition, moreover, besides*

5. Result signals for consequences—*consequently, therefore, hence, thus*

ACTIVITY 5H

Examining Transitions

1. Reread the professional selections and the student compositions in this chapter, or the analogy examples in Activity 5F. Be prepared to report on the types of transitions used. Try to classify the transitions in the categories mentioned in the preceding section.

2. After reporting on the transitions you located, investigate transitions in the equivalent of two book pages in one of the following:

Article in an encyclopedia	Cookbook
Popular Mechanics	Newspaper editorial
Home economics textbook	*Atlantic Monthly* article
Social studies textbook	Athletic rulebook
Science textbook	How-to-do-it book

From the various types of writing you have investigated in questions 1 and 2, draw some conclusions about the kinds of transitions used in different kinds of writing.

Varying Tone in Describing a Process

Two speakers can address the same audience and say substantially the same thing, and the audience may jeer at one and cheer loudly for the other. Two writers can send substantially the same message to the same reader, but the reader may reject one and agree with the other.

The difference, often, is in the *tone* the writer uses. A student presiding at a class meeting may be able, because of the formality of the situation, to order a friend: "Sergeant-at-arms, stand at the door and keep out any latecomer who tries to get in." If, however, the same speaker, in any other situation, tried to order that same friend around, the response would probably be an angry refusal.

Similarly, in writing you assume an appropriate tone and a voice (an attitude, a point of view, a position with respect to the reader and your material). Because each situation is different, in half a dozen pieces of writing you will probably shift your tone half a dozen times. If you make the wrong decision in your choice of tone and voice—no matter how accurate your communication is otherwise—you probably won't get through to your reader.

ACTIVITY 5 I

Working on Tone in Process Writing

You can write out the solution to the following problem in about a paragraph. Read the problem in class and then write two separate process paragraphs answering the engineers' plea for help. In each paragraph, deliberately use a different tone and voice. Be prepared to read your paragraphs in class and discuss the different techniques by which you varied your tone.

> Two railroad engineers, each with a train one thousand feet long, one east-bound and one west-bound, meet on the same track at a small town. In the town two small spurs of track, each of which will hold five hundred feet of train, make an equilateral triangle with the main track. Neither engineer can figure out how the two trains can pass and continue each in its separate direction. Finally, they telegraph to the terminal for instructions.

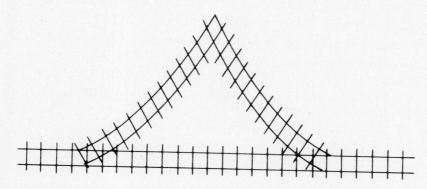

Perhaps in writing your explanations to the engineers you may want to assume one of these tones:

1. An apologetic office boy slightly embarrassed at having to straighten out a superior

2. A disgusted superintendent angry at being bothered

3. A dispassionate, unconcerned official, simply doing a job
4. A frightened yardmaster anxious to clear both trains so an express can use the track
5. An amused buddy of one of the engineers

Improving Continuity by Improving Structure

As you explain your process, you must select grammatical structures that help clarify your ideas and improve your style. They must show the exact order and relationship of ideas, and they must make your writing easy to understand and pleasing to read.

The ability to make such choices of structure can be developed through much reading and much writing. Be aware of examples of sound structure in your reading and practice them in your writing. Then you will become sensitive to the flow of sentences and the movement of ideas.

▰▰▰ MAJOR WRITING ASSIGNMENT

A PROCESS COMPOSITION

You have gone through these steps in preparing to write your process composition:

1. Examined and discussed student and professional models.
2. Considered a list of possible subjects.
3. Examined ways of making your inside structure clear.
4. Planned an outline combining your inside and outside structures.
5. Looked at ways of giving flavor to your writing and avoiding Engfish.
6. Examined analogies and worked out analogy paragraphs.
7. Examined and worked with process transitions.
8. Worked on tone in process writing.

Now you are ready to begin planning and writing your process composition. Use the following as a checklist.

1. Prewriting—Have you thought (either alone or with a group) about a subject and ways of developing and structuring that subject?
2. Composing—Have you written out your rough draft?

3. Editing—Have you delayed your editing so that you can approach your writing with a fresh eye? Have you added, deleted, rearranged, and substituted portions of your rough draft?

4. Proofreading—Have you proofread both before and after preparing your final draft?

5. Sharing—Have you planned a way of completing the communication process so that you have an audience to react to your work?

y knuls auffi ¶ Contre les pe
tis mennes veus ou venin soiet
fait petit soustanhp de farine
aner les fueilles Ou pou tapse
bourse et soient donez a menger

Terebentine est chaude
et seche cest la gome du
arbre nome sapm ¶ Elle a bon
apetit et si deuaste ventosites elle
nete la marris et si la conforte tar
en vsant aner viandes ou en con
felles sans delle aner faarme come
en faisant fumer ou sinapisme
¶ Pour esprainson en son fiet
fumet sur les charbons la quelle
fumee le pacient feroit par bas
a vne tiel ¶ Pour la marris
qui est chene son faarte teme on
suppositoire aner en son enn ¶ Pe

ce mesmes feronic la feme la su
mee delle come on est de esprain
son mais pour la suffocation en
amontent de la marris la feronic
la feme par amon ¶ Pour to
pre apostime son mesire aner farne
dorent et son mist sur ¶ Len la
nutt auffi en maniere ordonez po
feronrdre et desseuder plants
s nielle que len tan delle distille
est moult excellent a gome et a
paralisie et a toute enfleme ou
ettante de nerfs et a douleur de
nerfs quant les maladie sont
caufees de froidure et en deseon
endre le lieu malade su

Tribulus marinus est
chardon marin et est vne
herbe qui croist en terre sablonense
et es partie de la mer et appe
per terre ¶ Len la teme en tere

Chapter 6

Analysis

One of the most serious decisions you will ever make is only a few years away: How will you spend your life? What will you do for a living?

The following selection suggests that in order to answer these questions well you should *analyze* yourself and your personality.

The word "analysis" comes from two Greek words, *ana*, which means "throughout," and *lysis*, which means "a loosening." Analysis, then, means a loosening of the parts throughout, an examination of all of the separate elements making up a larger unit. Analysis is a very important skill and a very important pattern of modern communication.

The following article suggests a way to analyze yourself to determine the type of work for which you are best suited.

I

GETTING TO KNOW YOU[1]

What you do for a living should depend a lot on who you are and who you want to become. Sounds obvious, perhaps—but considerable numbers of people miss the boat on this important issue of choosing a career.

In our society, work tends to be a major piece of your identity. We label each other by our jobs and ask, "What do you do?" within minutes of meeting someone new. Work will probably influence your material comfort, your circle of friends and your feelings of self-worth and satisfaction with life. You can avoid joining the ranks of people who are dissatisfied with their work by making a conscious effort *now* to explore your own needs, talents and interests. Start by looking back on your personal history and applying this checklist:

1. Review all projects, awards, hobbies and other things that called upon your skills and abilities within the past three to five years. Which activities gave you the most personal satisfaction? Can you notice any pattern of areas in which you excel?

2. Now look at your past work experiences and extracurricular or academic activities. Which of these continue to interest you? Why?

3. Next list all of these favorite activities or involvements in order of preference. What specific skills did you use in each (such as managing money, working with people, organizing a system or taking responsibility)? Do you seem to prefer one type of environment over another?

4. Now start adding things up in terms of your past history and current feelings. Do you enjoy working with concrete, physical things, or abstract ideas such as time and space? Do you like to have assignments spelled out in detail or do you prefer to work independently? Are you an indoors or outdoors person? Do you work well under deadline pressure? Are you most comfortable spending time in a large group, with just a few people, or by yourself? Do you like to be in charge?

All of these personality traits help determine the type of work that fits you best. Try taking this checklist or a similar outline of your wants and needs to your career counseling office. With a rough sketch of the real you in hand, it's much easier to locate your specific options in the job market.

Like many analyses (note the way the plural of this word is formed), the one you have just read is informal and incomplete. It does not mention every one of the factors a person should examine before making a career decision. If you were analyzing a closed system, that is, one with a definite number of fixed parts, you would be able to make a definite, complete, and permanent analysis. Unfortunately (or perhaps, fortunately), human beings are much too complex for such a definite, complete, and permanent analysis. In analyzing yourself and many other aspects of the real world, you will have to be satisfied with a tentative and partial analysis.

Kinds of Analyses

As an essential skill, analyses of different types can be found all around us. Analyses can be descriptive, functional, or causal. In a later chapter you will be working with literary criticism, which is another form of analysis.

Descriptive analysis. A descriptive analysis examines the parts of an object and shows how they appear. Usually the writer proceeds in some logical, spatial pattern, and usually in this type of simple analysis, the analysis is complete.

> The *Atlantic* was a huge, beautiful machine believed to be capable of crossing the Atlantic—hence its name. John Lamountane, one of the crew, had been in charge of its construction. It was fifty feet in diameter and sixty perpendicular, and was made of lacquered silk covered by a woven hemp net. At the bottom of the net was an iron load ring, below which was suspended a wicker basket. A special lifeboat, capable of carrying a thousand pounds, was suspended fifteen feet below the basket. The boat was encased in a heavy canvas jacket which acted as a sling and protective cover. A rope ladder enabled the crew to climb between boat and basket.[2]
>
> from *The Greatest Air Voyage Ever Made*
> —Jack R. Hunt

Functional analysis. A functional analysis describes how something works or functions. It is more complex than a descriptive analysis, for it must do two things: 1. describe the parts (though often less vividly than a descriptive analysis does), and 2. show how they work together. Again, the writer helps the reader by moving from one part to another in logical order. In the following selection, the writer uses chronological order (the order of time), rather than a spatial pattern. Sometimes, when describing parts which all work together at once, the writer arbitrarily specifies an order that the reader can understand— even though that order may not really exist! Functional analysis is very similar to the kind of writing you did in your process composition in Chapter 5.

> An electric bell must have a power source (either a battery or a transformer connected to house current), a wire to a push button, another wire from the push button to the electromagnet of the bell itself, an armature which the electromagnet can pull down with a spring that will return the armature to its original position, a clapper attached so that it will move when the armature moves, a bell, or gong, for the clapper to strike, and another wire from the electromagnet back to the power source.
>
> The power source feeds energy along the wire to the push button, but until the push button is pressed, it cannot get to the second wire and travel to the bell. As soon as the push button is pressed, however, electricity travels down the second wire and causes the electromagnet to pull the armature to itself. The movement of the armature to the electromagnet causes the clapper to strike the bell, but the same movement pulls the armature away from the current-carrying wire, stopping the flow of electricity. When the current stops, the electromagnet is deactivated so that it no longer attracts the armature, and the armature is pulled by a spring back to its normal position. In that position, it again makes contact so that current activates the electromagnet, and the process is repeated.

As long as someone pushes the push button, the process continues, with the armature and clapper alternately being pulled to the electromagnet and the bell and then released.

Causal analysis. A causal analysis presents, individually, the various forces which *cause* something. Often, there are many different forces that combine to make something happen. In such cases, causal analysis can be only tentative and incomplete. Can you imagine a writer determining all of the forces that caused World War II—or the decline of the space program?

II

When we were kids, it was the cow that jumped over the moon. Now it's the cost of the cow that's sky high.

But blaming the cow isn't going to bring meat prices back to earth. No matter how much you beef about cost, you can't change a simple fact of life: the biology of the cow.

In large part, the price of beef has to do with the production cycle of cattle. It simply can't be any faster than it is. One cow can only give birth to one calf each year. And once that calf is born, it takes time to fatten it up for market. That may be as long as two years. Then there's another delay: If the farmers want to expand the herd, they have to keep the first offspring for further breeding. This postpones slaughtering another three years.

Five years have now passed from birth of the first heifers to slaughter. Next add to the supply cycle the fickle consumer. When supply is low, prices are high. Consumers buy less beef than usual. When supply is high, prices tumble, and consumers eat lots of meat.

But the farmers suffer. The low prices mean there's a large supply of cattle on the range. And cattle are expensive to produce. Low consumer prices don't give the farmers a sufficient return on their investment. So they sell off for slaughter a large number of stock. That makes things worse down on the farm. The large supply further depresses the market, prolonging the period of falling prices.

As the herd is cut back, consumer demand eventually exceeds supply. Prices start rising. The farmers experience good times, but not the consumers. In reaction to the high prices, shoppers switch to other protein sources. Demand drops off, discouraging the farmers from rebuilding their herds. Once demand picks up again, the entire cycle starts over. Generally it lasts 10 to 12 years.

Related to all this is inflation. Costs for transportation, feed, retailing and packing, and labor are increased.

Another factor is rising consumer incomes. When consumers have extra spending money, demand for beef is high. That, in turn, helps trigger even higher prices.

Today's high beef prices puts us near the middle of the current cycle. Supply is low, so it's continuing high prices for the shopper.[3]

Each of the foregoing passages is one kind of simple analysis. Yet, each is different from the others. Sometimes an entire work follows the analysis pattern but at other times, as in the examples you have just read, just a part of a longer selection follows the analysis pattern.

In this chapter you will look at a formal procedure for using the analysis pattern. Later, as you gain confidence and security, you will move away from the formal pattern to a freer and more exciting style of your own. You will, however, use the same underlying thought process.

The Analysis Pattern

The analyses you have just read reveal a regular pattern. First, the writer begins by clearly stating the subject to be "taken apart." Next, the writer takes the parts one at a time and describes them. In the functional analysis (page 137), the writer goes to a third step and uses a kind of chronological order to show how each of the parts works. Go back to the examples now and locate in each of them the statement of the subject to be analyzed, and determine the various parts to be examined.

There is one more element in the analysis pattern of thought. To analyze something effectively, you must do so in terms of some principle or purpose. This element differentiates the process pattern of writing from the analysis pattern. In your process composition (Chapter 5), you simply wrote an explanation of how something worked or of how to do something. In an analysis, you must first establish your point of view. For example, you could write an analysis of your family's car in at least a dozen different ways, depending on your purpose. Writing your analysis from the point of view of a safety specialist, you might consider the positive safety features (padded dashboard, collapsible steering column, seatbelts, safety glass) and the negative features (excessive engine power, single braking system, worn tires, faulty windshield wiper). Writing from the point of view of a mechanic, you might base your analysis on internal parts (engine, spark plugs, transmission, differential). Analyzing the car from the point of view of a used-car buyer you might write about the good points (late model, good paint job, good tires, low mileage) and the bad points (worn upholstery, dented fender, engine knock, no air conditioner).

Other people looking at your family car might analyze it according to other criteria: a junk dealer deciding which parts could be salvaged, an artist deciding whether or not it would be interesting as the subject of a painting, or even a thief deciding whether or not it would be worth stealing! (Think of what the thief might consider in addition to what the used-car buyer would list!)

Look around your classroom for a few minutes. Think of the various ways different people would analyze it in terms of their own purposes. Use your imagination to decide what each of the following persons would be looking for.

janitor	teacher
good student	student wishing to avoid work
principal	lighting expert
librarian	interior decorator
psychologist	blind student
taxpayer	parent

Analysis, then, involves these steps:

1. Defining the subject to be examined.
2. Specifying the purpose, or principle, of the examination.
3. Examining the various parts.

The second step is particularly important, for by changing the principle of the analysis, you change the way you separate the subject into parts.

ACTIVITY 6A

Writing an Analysis

Write a short descriptive analysis of a classroom in your school. Analyze it from the point of view of one of the persons listed above. Follow the three steps recommended in planning your analysis.

Analysis of Simultaneous Processes

In many very complex processes, everything happens at once. Think, for example, of the process of building an automobile. Various parts are built in various plants or factories. Workers in Detroit may be building the engine at the same time that workers in Lansing are building the transmission. Brake linings are being manufactured somewhere else. Eventually, all the component parts are shipped to an assembly plant where they are put together to make a car. The analysis of this process could begin with any one of these parts, or at any factory, but to help the reader understand the process, some kind of order must be imposed.

The writer considers the various simultaneous operations, examines them carefully, and then determines the order in which to present each step or event. Presenting the steps or events in order helps the reader follow the operation even though the processes are really simultaneous rather than sequential. This kind of analysis is clearly related to the "functional" analysis in example two, but it is more complicated. In many "simultaneous process" analyses, the various parts may be abstractions, and the order they are placed in is an arbitrary order based on the writer's guess as to what will be helpful for the reader.

Here is an outline for such a simultaneous process analysis.

I. Subject to be analyzed: The Industrial Revolution

II. Purpose of the examination: To understand what contemporary situations and events promoted the Industrial Revolution

III. Parts to be examined:

    A. General agricultural and handicraft conditions in the eighteenth century

    B. Scientific progress

    C. Changing political institutions

    D. New agricultural methods

    E. Expansion of commerce

IV. Operation of the various parts in bringing about the Industrial Revolution (in order in which they will be handled):

    A. Social and political conditions at the beginning of the eighteenth century tended to keep economic conditions static.

    B. Scientific progress caused new examination of all customs, processes, and institutions.

    C. New political organizations came into prominence and the middle class began to have more power.

    D. Application of the scientific method caused the introduction of new methods in agriculture and production.

    E. Increased production caused expansion of commerce for new markets, removal of many peasants from the land to the cities, chronic unemployment, social unrest.

Clearly, in the foregoing example, all of the operations in Step IV took place simultaneously rather than one after the other. The writer chose to impose on them, however, an order that would be simple, efficient, and easy to follow.

Student Composition 6A

SIMPLE ANALYSIS

I. Subject to be analyzed: The character of Cape Cod
II. Purpose of the examination: To determine the effect of various periods on the character of Cape Cod
III. Parts to be examined:
    A. Pre-Columbian Cape Cod
    B. Settlement Period
    C. Colonial Period
    D. Early National Period
    E. Subsistence Period
    F. Modern Period

TIME AND A CHANGING CAPE COD

Several hundred years ago, before European civilization was brought to Cape Cod, the peninsula was wild and untouched by progress. The only inhabitants of this vast domain were Indians. The land was rich in natural resources. The forests were large and the ponds were clean and sparkling. Wildlife abounded all along the peninsula. The sea, the most obvious resource of all, was teeming with all the sealife agreeable to that environment. The balance of nature had been untouched by anything but nature herself. The sea, the wind, and all of the other elements worked together to build the strength of the land.

> What is the subject of each of these sentences? How would you improve the coherence of the passage?
>
> How effective in a description is a brief history of the location?

    This natural beauty and bountifulness was not, however, to continue. The arrival of the Pilgrims marked the beginning of a new era. Arriving on the Cape in their hopes of finding a new way of life, they were soon to begin the long and ceaseless process of changing the land to suit their needs. The forests offered the wood needed to build and supply their homes and villages. The land was cleared to permit farming, and the sea supplied much of their daily diet. These things in themselves did little to harm the land because in those days it was abundant in every way. However, these same things, if not controlled in the future, would tear down the environment. But the Pilgrims knew very little about long-range conservation and no one expects that they should have even understood the term. At that time, America symbolized the New World, abundant in every way, beckoning all to come and make a new life from its richness and chance for opportunity.

> Would "bounty" fulfill the task of the longer word? Comment on which is preferable.
>
> What makes this passage seem stilted? How can you make it more simple and direct?
>
> Would you repeat "abundant in every way" here? Should the writer have used another expression here?

    Later, as the New World was becoming settled and Cape Cod became a part of Massachusetts and one of the thirteen colonies, a new breed of people came to inhabit the great peninsula. These were the early breed, the tough, hardy ancestors of an era of well-respected people known as Cape Cod Folks. These people were makers of the Cape Cod tradition. They were the fishers, the shipbuilders, the lobstermen, and that hardy bunch of whalers. There are many legends of these folks and their adventures at sea and ashore and all of these in some way or another show their pride in the land. Although the forests had now been considerably reduced, there was still no thought in the Cape Codders' minds that the land was being abused. They used the land and sea for their own personal existence and did not needlessly exploit its resources, so how could it be in danger?

As the years progressed and those great mariners became part of the colorful history of the past, the newer generations no longer followed in the professions of their ancestors because it was, quite simply, impossible to earn a living in that way. As time went by, the people realized that the Cape was not suited for manufacturing or mass production on any large scale because transportation to and from the peninsula would be costly and time-consuming. This led the inhabitants to turn to the trades of commercial fishing of all sorts, to the crafts of the individual artisans, and to the pursuits of those few who enjoyed the quiet life of the artist or writer. However, by this time the beauty of the Cape was becoming well-known and more and more people wanted to visit or live on the peninsula. This was not economically practical in view of the few jobs available, so that the most obvious and profitable thing that the inhabitants could do was to start capitalizing on that notorious pastime, tourism. It took no time at all for this business to start booming. Cottages, campgrounds, and souvenir shops sprang up everywhere and the tourist business skyrocketed.

This newest breed of inhabitants used the Cape Cod heritage not as a symbol of a proud and traditional past, but as the symbol of a dollar bill! However, in their haste to earn a quick buck, the land and overall environment were greatly suffering. Hotels, motels, and overnight cabins now took the place of marshes and forests. Beaches were marked off as belonging to the "Captain's Rest" Hotel or the "Smith's Seaside Cottages" and that wild, free beauty that once marked the appeal of Cape Cod was gone. The population increased to the point of overcrowding the land available, and much of the wildlife disappeared. The loss of the forests and the lack of careful planning caused the erosion of the coastline in most places. The fresh water was polluted by the carelessness of too many people. The natural resources were being tapped to their utmost.

Cape Cod may still survive. The beauty is still

What is the referent for "its" and "it"? Would you change these pronouns?

What more descriptive approach might communicate the same information?

Why would many readers object to the use of "This" in this sentence?

Is it clear whether the writer is referring here to the tourists or to the merchants exploiting them? How would you clarify the meaning?

Do you feel the expression "earn a quick buck" is appropriate here? Is colloquial language desirable in formal writing?

What is the effect of the frequent changes of subject in these sentences?

What legislation should the writer have mentioned in this connection?

there in the few spots that have somehow been skipped over. Behind it all there are still the efforts of those who are concerned with the land. Measures are being taken to protect the environment and to conserve its resources and hopefully the results of these efforts will be seen in the near future. Despite the hotels, despite the souvenir shops, despite the commercialism, when a lone person stands on the shore of the Atlantic seacoast, the beauty of the sea itself is still there, and the hope for the future is still there.

—Rebecca Marean

Though you may not be able to visualize Cape Cod today, what makes this paper a kind of description?

Is the word "hopefully" used correctly here?

How might a symbolic object be used at the end of this paper?

Student Composition 6B

I have an extra-special feeling for those angelfish in the aquarium at the end of the hall. I doubt that it's the feeling that a lot of people would have. I think that most people are under the impression that angelfish are colorful little splashes of fins and scales, that they are beautiful, delicate creatures. These people are wrong. Angelfish are shiny, conniving little cannibals obsessed with the desire to eat.

The shiny beasts float lazily in circles, their beady eyes swivelling about, silently scanning the plastic seaweed for signs of food. Their fleshy pink lips are always puckering and unpuckering, their jaws chomping steadily as if the wanted food is there. The milk-colored bodies look almost paper-thin, and I often wonder how so much food can fit into such a tiny animal.

Surprisingly enough, I haven't always had this hatred for those fish. It developed slowly, over a period of weeks. When I'd lift open the top of the aquarium at feeding time, the angels would always be there to greet me. I'd sprinkle the food on top of the water; the angels would float up and down underneath it like carousel horses, snapping at the frozen shrimp and making horrible popping noises that could be heard throughout the house.

I'll never forget the morning I forgot to feed them. When they realized that feeding time had passed, the ordinarily independent angels acted as one, singling out a smaller, weaker brother. Together they attacked and killed their victim, then divided the spoils, leaving only the cleaned skeleton sinking slowly to the Kolorbrite gravel below.

The irony, of course, is the name of the ugly beasts—angelfish. Devil fish would be much more appropriate.

—Cynthia D. Graham

This student composition is untitled. After reading it, suggest a title.

Do you think the subject of this paper is angelfish or an analysis of the writer's attitude toward angelfish? How do you know?

What technique does the writer use to make her description effective?

Why does she wait until now to define her "extra-special feeling" as "hatred"? Were you surprised? Find the words in the first paragraph that gave you a clue.

Notice how the writer uses imagery to make her descriptions vivid.

How would you rewrite this sentence to avoid the repetition of "forget" and "forgot"?

What device does the writer use for the conclusion?

I

BUYING A TYPEWRITER IS ALMOST LIKE BUYING A CAR: COMPLICATED AND COSTLY[4]

Typewriters, like early Fords, used to be easy to buy. With only one color and one style available, the choice was simple: Take it or leave it.

Not so today. The marvels of modern technology have finally found their way to the once-lowly typewriter, making that instrument a complex piece of hardware. For business consumers especially, the range of available units now on the market is confusing, to say the least. More important, some of the latest models can perform functions never even dreamed of by the typewriter's principal inventor C. L. Sholes.

The truth is, typewriter purchases can represent significant capital expenditures for small companies. Whether the firm requires top-of-the-line units at the $1,000 level or several less-sophisticated units at $500 each, the investment is one owner-managers will not want to make by the seat of the pants.

"Some typewriters are so poorly made that they cannot be relied on to perform for a month without trouble," says Ted Wirth, president of Buyers Lab, an independent testing company specializing in office equipment. "Others will last for ten years and be reliable throughout. Companies that fail to study the market before buying typewriters can wind up wasting thousands of dollars."

Few laymen have kept up with the introduction of new typewriter technology in recent years. The types and categories of commercial typewriters now available include:

Portables: Experts warn against using portables for business use. Most are not durable, and they do not produce high-quality work.

"Trying to cheap out with a portable for business uses is bound to cost more money in the long run," adds Wirth, whose New Jersey-based company tests the typewriters of 38 manufacturers and publishes the findings in a booklet that sells for $55. "They are meant for term papers or letters to grandma, not business use. We recommend that business owners buy only those machines rated by manufacturers as office typewriters."

Intermediates: Lighter and less expensive than full-size office machines, intermediates are recommended for use in very small offices or remote locations. Priced from $350 to $475, they can perform well in such minor applications as occasional memo writing, shipping documents, and credit applications. Intermediates are not suitable for day-in, day-out use by a full-time typist.

Standard Type-Bar Machines: These are full-size office machines specially designed for use by professional typists. High quality standard type-bar units are durable and are capable of producing clear and attractive business documents. Prices range from $500 to $700.

Single-Element Models: The most advanced of the modern typewriters, single-element models have all of the type characters on a ball or cylinder rather than on individual keys. The beauty of the system is that changing from one type style to another is simply a matter of changing the ball, or element, and this is the major justification for purchasing single-element models. They are the most expensive units, priced from approximately $650 to $1,000, and are recommended only for those companies requiring the use of different type faces.

When purchasing typewriters, small firms should be aware that sometimes "less is more." Although most business machines are now electric, companies in remote locations and those that don't need sophisticated units may be better off with manual typewriters. The main reason for this is that service may be hard to get in remote areas, and manuals need fewer repairs.

The typewriter business is a highly competitive one, and there is a tremendous array of machines in each major category. Although a few manufacturers have come to dominate certain ends of the business—like IBM in the single-element field—independent consultants and distributors insist that other makes may be equally good and may cost less, to boot.

Prospective buyers are advised to compare several models, to test them out in the showroom and to make certain that repair and maintenance services are available. If full-time typists will be using the machines, it is also a good idea to involve them in the prepurchase testing. A typist's comfort with a unit has a major impact on efficiency. As a final precaution, Buyers Lab recommends checking with businesses that already use the machines to verify manufacturers' claims and statements.

—Mark Stevens

II

WHAT'S ON THE LABEL TELLS A LOT ABOUT WHAT'S INSIDE

Oil can labels can tell you almost anything you need to know about today's motor oils.

What in this opening appeals to a reader? Why would anyone want to read on?

There are two motor oil classification systems—SAE and API. The SAE grading system, developed by the Society of Automotive Engineers, rates oil by its viscosity (resistance to flow). The API system, developed by the American Petroleum Institute, in cooperation with SAE and the American Society for Testing and Materials, classifies oils on how well they perform and how they should be used.

What does this paragraph do for a reader?

Under the SAE system, oils are divided into eight grades (weights). Four of these are low temperature grades for winter use and include the letter "W", hence, SAE 5W, 10W, 15W, and 20W. The other four grades indicate high temperature viscosity: SAE 20, 30, 40, and 50. *The higher the grade number the heavier the oil.*

Why should this paragraph be separated from the previous one?

The development of additives called *viscosity index improvers* made multigrade oils possible. Two of the most widely used multigrade oils—SAE 10W-30 and SAE 10W-40—are thin enough for easy

The original article used two topic headings to help the reader keep the main divisions of the article clear. Where would you put such headings? What would they be?

How does this paragraph prepare you for the discussion that follows?

You can see that this paper has been very carefully analyzed into main divisions and subdivisions. Because it is so carefully thought out and organized, it is very easy to outline. What would you place at each point on this outline?

I. Introduction
   A. Why subject is important
   B. Division of content
II. Body
   A.
      1.
      2.
   B. (Digression)
   C.
      1.
      2. (Named—but a discussion is omitted.)

In the outline there would be several subpoints under A.1, A.2, C.1, and C.2. What would they be?

Why did the writer omit a discussion of C.2 in the body? Why does a reader not feel cheated?

One of the claims of the advertising industry is that good ads keep the public informed of new products and of ways of deciding which purchases are in their best interests. How would you rate this advertisement on its value to the consumer?

Why do you think the article omits the traditional conclusion?

If you wanted to end this article effectively and drive home its message what kind of a conclusion might you provide? How do you rate this article as to outside structure? Inside structure?

cranking at low winter temperatures and thick enough to lubricate an engine effectively at hotter summer temperatures.

API service classifications, which are identified by two letters, describe the all-around performance of an oil in lubricating an engine and protecting it against sludge, varnish, rust, and wear. The API system includes nine classes of service. Five of these—SA, SB, SC, SD, and SE—are for service station oils. The other four—CA, CB, CC, and CD—are for commercial oils.

Classifications beginning with the letter "S" for "Service" describe passenger car oils used generally in automobiles and light trucks. Those beginning with the letter "C" for "Commercial" designate oils for truck fleets, heavy equipment, farm vehicles, and the like.

SA, a straight mineral oil with no additives, and SB, which contains only a small amount of anti-oxidant and anti-wear additives, but which is non-detergent, are now largely obsolete. They have been superseded by oils of more recent API classifications.

SC, a detergent oil which provides some control of high and low-temperature deposits, wear, rust, and corrosion, met car manufacturers' warranty requirements for 1964-1967 models.

SD, with higher detergency and anti-wear characteristics, provides greater engine protection than SC oil. It can be used when SC is recommended. SD oils met warranty requirements for 1968-1971 models.

SE oils provide the highest current quality and are recommended for all cars, vans, and light trucks, including older models, which formerly used SC or SD oils.

Certain SC oils are recommended for older cars which burn large amounts of oil because of poor mechanical condition.

Lawnmowers and other 4-stroke cycle engines now use detergent oils of SC, SD, and SE quality, whereas manufacturers used to specify straight mineral oils.

III

PESKY UFOs[5]

They ran outside in time to see a large object, flat on the bottom with a dome on top, hovering over the house . . . They heard a humming noise, and lights around the bottom edge of the object were blinking on and off, giving a predominantly red impression but also appearing at times to be green and yellow.

This incident, related in the 1974 book *The Utah UFO Display*, was just one of 80 sightings of unidentified flying objects reported near the small northeastern Utah town of Roosevelt from 1965 to 1968. The book, carefully researched and written by Frank B. Salisbury, a plant physiologist at Utah State University, was seized upon by UFO buffs as still more evidence of the reality of flying saucers and visitations from extraterrestrial beings.

Now comes word that should really bug the True Believers. In a report in the journal *Applied Optics*, two U.S. Department of Agriculture scientists offer an earthly explanation not only for the Utah UFOs but possibly for many others as well. Reading Salisbury's book, entomologist Philip S. Callahan and his associate, R.W. Mankin, were struck by the similarity between the movements of the UFOs and the actions of insect swarms. Their conclusion, after some painstaking research: the Utah objects were probably moths known as spruce budworms, illuminated by a common atmospheric phenomenon known as St. Elmo's fire.

Long observed as glowing halos around the yardarms of sailing ships, in the vicinity of church steeples and near the wing and propeller tips of aircraft, St. Elmo's fire occurs when strong electrical fields are created in the atmosphere. If atmospheric voltage rises high enough, as under a thunderhead, the electrical resistance of the air breaks down and electrons flow from such pointed objects as a ship's mast, agitating nearby air molecules to produce a strong coronal light.

To test whether insects could also be set aglow, Callahan and Mankin in their lab generated electric fields comparable to those produced during storms. They then confined within the fields several species of insects, including predatory stinkbugs and spruce budworms. The results were invariably the same: the bugs, consisting, as the scientists note, of an excellent dielectric (the exoskeleton) surrounding an electrolyte (the body fluids), displayed brilliantly colored flares from such external points as their antennae, leg joints and jaws. Write Callahan

---

Does the title give you a clue as to the point-of-view of the writer?

Why does the writer begin the article with a quotation from *The Utah UFO Display*?

What is the subject to be examined?

How do you explain the use of the slang word "bug" here?

Is this the conclusion of the article? Do you want to read on? Why?

"Coronal" means like a halo or a ring of colored light.

Notice the parenthetical explanations of the scientific terms. For what kind of audience do you think this article was written?

Seventeen words can be deleted from this sentence without destroying the meaning. What are they?

Predatory stinkbug glowing UFO-like in a lab-created electrical field.

and Mankin: "There is absolutely no doubt that, given the right weather conditions, nature can produce a high enough electric field to light up flying insects."

Strong supporting evidence came from U.S. Forest Service records, which showed that there were in fact several severe spruce budworm infestations in forests near Roosevelt just before the UFO outbreaks. Thus, the budworm moths, having feasted on the trees and flying in well-defined swarms that may have measured miles across, could have been on nocturnal migrations when the people of Roosevelt began seeing those strange, dancing lights. Indeed, as the moths hovered and blinked overhead, while trying to escape atmospheric electric fields on certain stormy nights, they might well have resembled what the scientists call a great "free-floating discothèque in the sky."

Why is this a good conclusion?

Discussing the Analysis Papers

1. To what extent have the writers of these papers written "off the tops of their heads" and to what extent have they done library work, personal research, and interviewing in preparing

the articles? What is the danger in using reference material? What are the relative merits of basing your writing upon library research and basing it upon general personal background?

2. What comments can you make on the organization of each paper? Do you think each writer was conscious of an outline such as that on page 142?

3. How concrete are the papers? Do you find any particularly good comparisons, figures of speech, appeals to the senses, examples, or supporting details?

4. In what ways do the papers differ from each other? Can they all legitimately be considered analysis papers?

5. Could the student compositions in Chapter 3 have been classified as analysis compositions? What are the distinguishing marks of an analysis composition?

ACTIVITY 6B

Outlining an Analysis Paper

Refer to the outline that precedes Student Composition 6A on page 142. Choose one of the professional writing samples and build a similar outline for it.

Faulty Analysis

If someone promised you an apple pie but gave you one with a big slice removed, you'd probably be quite disappointed. And if someone promised you a new motor but gave you a box of miscellaneous parts, some from a Ford and some from a Chevrolet, again you'd be disappointed.

The reader of faulty analysis may feel a similar let down. The introduction to an analytical composition promises the reader, in effect, to take a given subject apart and to examine *all* the necessary parts.

Sometimes a writer does not produce the neat, complete analysis the reader expects. Usually such a flawed analysis errs in one of three ways:

1. It leaves out some of the parts.

2. It includes some parts that don't belong.

3. It treats some of the same parts twice, often using different names for the same things or looking at them in a different way.

Acknowledging incomplete analysis. If you are analyzing a mechanism or a closed system, you can list all of the parts and treat them separately. However, there are many things that do not lend themselves to a neat, tidy, complete analysis. As you examine natural processes, complicated ideas, and many aspects of social studies and literature, you can't be sure that you have located all pertinent parts. In these cases, make your reader aware that there are other aspects of the subject you are analyzing which you will not be dealing with. There are a number of ways to do this. You may use a phrase like "Among the contributing causes are . . . ," "A partial examination reveals . . . ," or "There are many facets of this complex subject; however, I shall discuss just four." Avoid the use of *etc.*, an abbreviation for the Latin words *et cetera* (and others). Most people feel that this suggests incomplete thought or a hasty analysis.

ACTIVITY 6C

Examining Faulty Analyses

Examine the following outlines for analysis papers. Be prepared to discuss each one and explain how you would improve it.

OUR SCHOOL

I. Administration
  A. Faculty
  B. Maintenance
II. Students
  A. Clerical aides
  B. Cheerleaders

BENEFITS OF ATHLETICS

I. Conditioning
II. Friendship
III. Sportsmanship
IV. Status
V. Team spirit
VI. Impossibility of part-time work

LEISURE TIME ACTIVITIES

I. Quiet things
  A. Read
  B. Watch TV
  C. Dream
II. Active things
  A. Swim
  B. Ski
  C. Bowl
  D. Play tennis
III. Community things
  A. Help at recycling station
  B. Volunteer at hospital
  C. Join youth organization

▮▮▮▮▮▮▮▮▮ MAJOR WRITING ASSIGNMENT

AN ANALYSIS COMPOSITION

Reread the articles and compositions at the beginning of this chapter and note that most of them require some research. Choose one of the subjects listed here or another one approved by your teacher, and write an analysis composition.

Whether or not you do your best work writing from an outline, think through your analysis before you begin to write. Use the three-part process explained near the beginning of this chapter:

1. Subject to be analyzed.
2. Purpose, or principle, of the examination.
3. Parts to be examined.

If you work well from an outline, or if you and your teacher think that you need experience in outlining, develop an outline that follows this form:

I. Introduction

   A. Arouse the reader's interest.

   B. Introduce the subject. Define or explain it, if necessary.

   C. Suggest the purpose or principle you are going to use and indicate why this analysis is important, interesting, or worth doing.

   D. List, in the order you have decided on, the main parts you will examine. Be sure that, in the body of the composition, you treat these parts in the same order as you list them here. (This step is optional.)

II. Body

(For Descriptive and Causal Analysis)

Take up and describe or explain each part (in the order you listed them if you had Part D in your Introduction).

(For Functional Analysis)

   A. Take up and describe or explain each part (in the order you listed them if you had Part D in your Introduction).

   B. Show how each part works or functions. Use either chronological or spatial order or work out an arbitrary order the reader can easily understand.

III. Conclusion

A. Review for the reader what you have analyzed and why you did so. Vary your wording so that this reminder is not too obvious.

B. End your composition with an application of what you have presented, an indication of something in the future connected with your subject, a mention of a related subject. You might want to refer to the limitations of your analysis and suggest the possibility of further study.

Be sure to use what you learned in this chapter. The following are some possible analysis subjects from which to select your topic:

Causes of an historical event

An organization (team, class, government, army unit, scout troop, club)

Aspects of an institution (church, school, college, department)

A work of art (painting, mural, statue)

Factors causing a social change (integration, pollution control, inflation)

Manufacture of an item

A job or profession

Issue in a current election

Operation of a community organization

Values of a particular activity (group, philosophy, tradition, idea)

A concept or idea (mercantilism, ethics, scientific method, morality, or other idea to be handled analytically)

A scientific experiment or process

A hobby

Chapter 7

Opinion

All people have personal opinions about and reactions to events in the world around them. An opinion is based not on absolute certainty but on what seems to be true or probable. Pressure is often very strong to make individuals give up their personal opinions and reactions and accept those of a group. Consider this story from World War II.

A sailor on a submarine became very ill. The captain surfaced near a tiny South Pacific island and radioed for a helicopter to come and take the sailor to a hospital.

Two islanders, who had never seen modern machines, watched the transfer of the sailor to the helicopter. Then they rushed back to their village to report the wonder they had seen: A great fish had burst from the water, and two men had climbed out of an opening on its back. Then an enormous bird came from the sky and hovered near the fish. The two men lifted a third man from the great fish and stuffed him into the belly of the bird. Finally, the bird flew away, the men climbed back into the fish, and the fish sank into the sea.

The village elders scoffed at the story. Fish have no openings on their backs, and no bird is big enough to swallow a man. After much discussion, the two islanders agreed with the elders. They admitted that they could not possibly have seen what they had seen. They agreed that the event had never happened.[1]

It is hard to believe that the islanders could have been persuaded to reject the evidence of their own eyes. You probably cannot imagine anyone persuading you to deny something that you have actually seen. It might be much easier, however, to persuade you to deny a belief or an opinion which, of course, you can neither see nor touch. Maintaining an opinion, a belief, or an idea in the face of opposition is difficult because each is an abstraction that you cannot verify with your senses.

Individual opinions are important in helping people discover truths and adapt themselves and their institutions to changes in the world. In some countries, people are denied the right to express their opinions. Even in an open, free society it often takes courage to express an opinion that is unpopular, and the right to express oneself freely must be carefully guarded. As the French philosopher Voltaire said, "I disapprove of what you say, but I will defend to the death your right to say it." In the seventeenth century, the English poet John Milton put it this way: " . . . he who destroys a good book kills reason itself." The same thought was expressed by Benjamin Franklin: " . . . when Men differ in Opinion, both Sides ought equally to have the Advantage of being heard by the Publick; and . . . when Truth and Error have fair Play, the former is always an overmatch for the latter. . . ."

An instance of people exchanging ideas and defending their opinions has been taking place in the little town of Eastport, Maine. A large oil company has been interested in using Eastport's deep-water port to bring in and unload its huge oil tankers. The townspeople have been strongly divided in their opinions and have expressed them everywhere—in their homes, in chance encounters, in town meetings, and in the newspapers. Those in favor of the plan argue that it would provide jobs in an area that has suffered with the decline of the fishing industry. Another point they have made is that it would give them access to cheaper oil. Those opposed question the extent of these economic advantages. They feel the benefits, if any, are far outweighed by the threat to the environment. Because of Eastport's proximity to the Bay of Fundy, famous for its high tides and strong currents, tankers entering the harbor could be in great danger. A damaged tanker could result in a massive oil spill or even in an explosion. According to a local newspaper, ". . . the combination of cold, nutrient-rich waters in the surrounding coastal estuaries provides an ecosystem unique on the East Coast supporting finfish, shellfish, and birds, as well as food for endangered species of whales . . . . a major spill in the area could affect the viability of marine life in Cobscook Bay, Passamaquoddy Bay, and parts of the Bay of Fundy and the Gulf of Maine."[2]

The important point to be made here is that the debate *can* take place and that the people of Eastport have taken advantage of the rights guaranteed to all Americans by the Bill of Rights. For this reason, it is important for you, too, to learn to express your opinions intelligently and effectively.

Opinion papers are similar to both the expository papers you worked with in Chapter 3 and the persuasion papers you will read in Chapter 8. All three are organized in much the same way, opening, as a rule, with a thesis statement (implied or clearly stated) followed by supporting information and arguments. The differences are these:

1. An expository paper attempts to communicate information.

2. An opinion paper attempts to convince readers of the validity of an opinion.

3. A persuasion paper attempts to motivate readers to act in some manner.

Here are some examples of opinion papers.

I

STATE CORRUPTS WITH GAMBLING[3]

Hartford, Conn.—On the outskirts of this city of insurance companies, there is another, less useful business based on an understanding of probabilities. It is a jai alai fronton, a cavernous court where athletes play a fast game for the entertainment of gamblers and the benefit of, among others, the state treasury.

Half the states have legal betting in casinos, at horse or dog tracks, off-track betting parlors, jai alai frontons or in state-run lotteries. Only Connecticut has four (the last four) kinds of gambling, and there is talk of promoting the other two.

Not coincidentally, Connecticut is one of just seven states still fiercely determined not to have an income tax. Gambling taxes yielded $76.4 million last year, which is not a large slice of Connecticut's $2.1 billion budget, but it would be missed, and is growing.

Last year Americans legally wagered $15 billion, up 8 percent over 1976. Lotteries took in 24 percent more. Stiffening resistance to taxes is encouraging states to seek revenues from gambling, and thus to encourage gambling. There are three rationalizations for this:

State-run gambling controls illegal gambling.

Gambling is a painless way to raise revenues.

Gambling is a "victimless" recreation, and thus is a matter of moral indifference.

Actually, there is evidence that legal gambling increases the respectability of gambling, and increases public interest in gambling. This creates new gamblers, some of whom move on to illegal gambling, which generally offers better odds. And as a revenue-raising device, gambling is severely regressive.

Gamblers are drawn disproportionately from minority and poor populations that can ill-afford to gamble, that are especially susceptible to the lure of gambling, and that especially need a government that will not collaborate with gambling entrepreneurs, as in jai alai, and that will not become a gambling entrepreneur through a state lottery.

A depressing number of gamblers have no margin for economic losses and little understanding of the probability of losses. Between 1975 and 1977 there was a 140 percent increase in spending to advertise lotteries—lotteries in which more than 99.9 percent of all players are losers. Such advertising is apt to be especially effective, and cruel, among people whose tribulations make them susceptible to dreams of sudden relief.

Grocery money is risked for such relief. Some grocers in Hartford's poorer neighborhoods report that receipts decline during jai alai season. Aside from the injury gamblers do to their dependents, there is a more subtle but more comprehensive injury done by gambling. It is the injury done to society's sense of elemental equities. Gambling blurs the distinction between well-earned and "ill-gotten" gains.

Gambling is debased speculation, a lust for sudden wealth that is not connected with the process of making society more productive of goods and services. Government support of gambling gives a legitimating imprimatur to the pursuit of wealth without work.

"It is," said Jefferson, "the manners and spirit of a people which preserves a republic in vigor." Jefferson believed in the virtue-instilling effects of agricultural labor. Andrew Jackson denounced the Bank of the United States as a "monster" because increased credit creation meant increased speculation. Martin Van Buren warned against "a craven desire . . . for sudden wealth." The early nineteenth century belief was that citizens could be distinguished by the moral worth of the way they acquired wealth; and physical labor was considered the most ennobling labor.

It is perhaps a bit late to worry about all this: The United States is a developed capitalist society of a sort Jefferson would have feared if he had been able to imagine it. But those who cherish capitalism should note that the moral weakness of capitalism derives, in part, from the belief that too much wealth is allocated in "speculative" ways, capriciously, to people who earn their bread neither by the sweat of their brows nor by wrinkling their brows for socially useful purposes.

Of course, any economy produces windfalls. As a town grows, some land values soar. And some investors (like many non-investors) regard stock trading as a form of roulette.

But state-sanctioned gambling institutionalizes windfalls, whets the public appetite for them, and encourages the delusion that they are more frequent than they really are. Thus do states simultaneously cheat and corrupt their citizens.

—George Will

II

AFTER I, THE DELUGE[4]

When I was a lad, I did not serve a term as office boy to an attorney's firm. It was one of a number of omissions. I did, however, work for a while as a file clerk in a credit agency. Since I was sixteen years old at the time and had been graduated from high school, I knew a great deal and had opinions on a variety of subjects that I thought anyone else in the office would consider it a privilege to hear. I also thought that I discerned flaws in the way the office was run. One fine day I was advised to keep a civil tongue in my head. That meant "Be respectful to your elders," or less gently interpreted, "Shut up." Although I did not know the word at the time (nobody did), I prioritized my interests, even as Jimmy Carter many years later suggested that the Democrats prioritize their platform. Having a job was more highly prioritized than not having a job. Shut up I did.

I now take a civil tongue to mean much more than that. Mere politeness is part of it, though the temptation to place *mere* before politeness ought to be resisted. The alternative to a code of conduct is, if not chaos, certainly confusion and embarrassment, and language is conduct. Not that I am arguing for freezing the language. I would hate to take American English out of a cryogenic compartment in a hundred years and find, after the ice is chipped away and the language has thawed, that it sounds as it does now. I think I would put it back in.

How *does* it sound now? It does not sound civil.

- A scholar writes, "Our children currently have no viable role models to emulate." Heroes they would have been called not long ago. And heroines. But that is too straightforward:

"Father, I cannot tell a lie. With my little hatchet, I chopped down the cherry tree."

"I'm proud of you, George. I was saying to your mother only last week that one day our son will be a role model for generations of Americans yet unborn."

- A New York specialty shop advertises items "for all the giftees on your June list." I hope it spreads to Scotland:

"Wha hae ye there, lass?"

"Tis a wee giftie for the giftee."

"Aye, would some power the giftee gie us . . ."

- "Scientists, investigating spontaneous glucagon secretion in the immediate postnatal period, study groups of infants cross-sectionally and longitudinally." Cross-sectionally should not alarm anyone: it means at the same age. Longitudinally means as they grow older.

- A man is put in jail in Dubuque, Iowa. It isn't called the jail any longer; it's the law enforcement center. Time is served there longitudinally.

- When the soil-collecting scoop on Viking I on Mars fails to function, an anomaly team goes to work to set it right. No hits, no runs, no anomalies.

- Washington churns out its usual nonsense. The chief of the United States Capitol Police posts a notice: "Vehicles will be parked chronologically as they enter the lot" (1975 models in this corner and 1973 models over there). The Undersecretary of the Treasury, Edwin H. Yeo III, is asked about additional loans to New York City: "If we find the reasonable probability of repayment is slipping away from us, then we'll have to respond in terms of extension of future credit." If they don't pay what they owe, we won't lend them any more.

- A weather broadcaster in Marlboro, Massachusetts, calls small storms stormettes. Massachusetts come from a large Massachus.

- In Kansas City, Missouri, television viewers are told about "the heavy storm system that performed over our area last night." Music by Rossini.

- An airline stewardess urges her passengers to "have a nice day in Cincinnati or wherever your final destination may be taking you," and an investment company writes: "We have exceptional game plan capabilities together with strict concerns for programming successful situations." My final destination is taking me far away from game plans, capabilities, programming, and situations, there to have a nice day.

■ A professor, Sam Schoenbaum of Northwestern, explains on ABC television why William Shakespeare was so eminent a playwright: "He had a tremendous commitment to his own medium, the stage." All the world's a medium, but the professor appears to believe that Shakespeare could have left the theater for television or Hollywood.

That is how the language sounds now. A civil tongue, on the other hand, means to me a language that is not bogged down in jargon, not puffed up with false dignity, not studded with trick phrases that have lost their meaning. It is not falsely exciting, is not patronizing, does not conceal the smallness and triteness of ideas by clothing them in language ever more grandiose, does not seek out increasingly complicated constructions, does not weigh us down with the gelatinous verbiage of Washington and the social sciences. It treats errors in spelling and usage with a decent tolerance but does not take them lightly. It does not consider "We're there because that's where it's at" the height of cleverness. It is not merely a stream of sound that disk jockeys produce, in which what is said does not matter so long as it is said without pause. It is direct, specific, concrete, vigorous, colorful, subtle, and imaginative when it should be, and as lucid and eloquent as we are able to make it. It is something to revel in and enjoy.

—Edwin Newman

Student Composition 7A

OUR AMERICAN FUTURE

In the 1830's when Alexis De Tocqueville toured the United States and published his famous observations on the rough, crude, growing nation, he wrote, "America is a land of wonders, in which everything is in constant motion and every change seems an improvement. . . . They [The Americans] have all a lively faith in the perfectibility of man . . . they all consider society as a body in a state of improvement . . . and they admit that what appears to them today to be good, may be superseded by something better tomorrow."*

That was the spirit of frontier America over 150 years ago. The spirit and the reality in declining America today is somewhat different. The fact is that life in the United States isn't getting better, and it will be even worse in the future. It would be easy to look at any number of aspects of life in the United States to show that the country is in a decline, but three aspects alone are enough: the new competition from the Third World, the trade deficit, and the aging population.

Rose had learned in her history class about De Tocqueville's opinions of the United States. How would she use *Bartlett's Familiar Quotations* to find her introduction? What volumes does your library have to help you with this kind of problem?

What do the brackets [ ] mean?

What do quotations and research add to opinion papers?

A fallacy called "begging the question" appears here. Can you find it?

This thesis statement is probably distasteful to many people. How does Rose understate it?

How helpful is this overview of the structure of the paper? What will each section take up? What order will they appear in?

Would some actual facts, examples, or statistics be useful here? Where could Rose find such information? Why may she have omitted it?

This is the kind of surprising or controversial information that Rose ought to document with a footnote. How do you react to such an unsupported assertion? Even though this is a minor point, what does it do to the credibility of all of Rose's argument? If she doesn't know her source, what is an alternative solution?

If you were in favor of this movement, how would you word this sentence? What "loaded" words does Rose use?

Rose has indicated sources, but has not included any direct quotations. In what way might direct quotations be helpful here?

How might Rose support her assertion that Third World nations "have much of the power of the United Nations"? How do you react when she doesn't do so?

Often huge figures are hard to comprehend, so writers use graphic images to make them concrete. What kinds of images might you use to give this passage more power?

Where might Rose mention that problems other than the oil problem exist? How would a listing of additional problems affect the organization of her paper?

Why does Rose repeat exact words she has used previously? Do you think these appeared "naturally" as she was writing or that she went back and inserted them as she was editing?

Americans have always believed in sharing with people less fortunate than themselves. Our history is filled with our generosity to other nations during floods, famines, earthquakes, and other disasters. After World War I, Herbert Hoover led a massive effort to feed the world's poor, and after World War II, the United States sent thousands of ships around the world to help other nations. (It is a little-known fact, however, that Americans are not so generous as they think they are. All during the 1960's, for example, France was spending a larger proportionate share of its gross national product for foreign aid than America was.)

Now, however, it's not a question of sending aid as we please. The Third World, or underdeveloped nations, have banded together and are demanding a much larger share of the world's wealth for themselves. The "Lima Target" set in 1976 declared that the developing countries want one-fourth of the world's manufacturing output in their hands by 2000. To get that wealth, those nations must either stimulate a miraculous and impossible growth rate of 11 percent annually in the world's industrial output—or it must change the world's political and economic arrangement so as to take from us the goods we have considered ours.** According to some people, those nations have already made considerable progress toward the latter. They have much of the power of the United Nations, they are increasing their diplomatic power through "Technical Cooperation Among Developing Nations," and they are taking steps to control the raw materials on which we depend.

An example of the control of raw materials leads to the second reason that the country is in a decline: The OPEC oil cartel has caused us to roll up a huge balance of trade deficit that has terrible implications for our future. In 1967, the United States had an international trade balance of four billion dollars. After the boycott in 1973 and 1974 by the Oil Production Exporting Nations (OPEC) and the subsequent quadrupling of prices, the United States balance of trade plummeted until, in 1977, America had almost a $28,000,000,000 deficit. Moreover, our appetite for energy keeps growing: in 1973 we used 17.3 million barrels of oil. In 1978, we used 19 million barrels and paid $47 billion for oil alone.

This trade deficit has caused our dollar to go down in value, the cost of imports to rise, inflation to soar, and our prestige and power in international life to drop. Perhaps the Third World is on its way to creating a new political or economic arrangement that will get them one-fourth of the world's manufacturing output.

But there is a third reason life in the United States is going to get worse. Americans are getting older. Right after World War II, there was a baby boom which peaked in 1957. Then the situation changed. Fewer women had fewer babies and population growth stopped. At the present time, taxes take about one third of the Gross National Product, and of those taxes, 37 percent go for retirement and medical benefits for the elderly.† Now, there are three people working for every beneficiary, but when people from the Baby Boom must be supported by the smaller generation that followed them, there will be only two workers and the Social Security tax will have to be $7,160 for each worker. Not only that, if the Third World takes more of our products while we pay more and more and earn less and less in international trade, life will be pretty bleak for both the worker and the retiree.

It would be nice to go back to the growth and optimism of De Tocqueville's time. Unfortunately, that world is gone, and an older, poorer, and less optimistic America is at hand.

—Rose Booth

How might this passage be "slowed down" to make the figures easier to follow?

How effective is this passage as a summary of the main points of the paper?

Why does Rose refer to De Tocqueville here? What would you suggest to improve this ending?

How valid do you think Rose's reasoning is? Do you agree with her?

---

*Alexis De Tocqueville, *Democracy in America* (New York: Oxford University Press, 1945), Part I, Chapter 18.

**Charles Horner, "Redistributing Technology," *Commentary*, Vol. 67, No. 1 (January 1979), p. 52.

†"Trying to Slow Social Security," *Time*, Vol. 113, No. 4 (January 22, 1979), p. 53.

Student Composition 7B
TOMORROW WILL BE BETTER

" . . . If the last 50,000 years of man's existence were divided into lifetimes of approximately 62 years each, there have been 800 such lifetimes. Of these 800, fully 650 were spent in caves.

"Only during the last seventy lifetimes has it been possible to communicate effectively from one lifetime to another—as writing made it possible to do. Only during the last 6 lifetimes did masses of men ever see a printed word. Only during the last four has it been possible to measure time with any precision. Only in the last 2 has anyone anywhere used an electric motor. And the overwhelming majority of all the material goods we use in daily life today have been developed within the present, the 800th lifetime."*

How do you feel as you read this long introductory quote without knowing why the writer used it and what it's supposed to prove? What might be better?

The writer has been inconsistent in the spelling out of numbers. What would you suggest as policy for a passage with lots of numbers in it?

Now you know what the quotation is supposed to prove. What better organization might the writer have used?

How effective is the thesis statement? Are you clear on what the writer will try to show?

How do you feel about such cliches as "waiting in the wings"? What other image might be more appropriate here? Why is this one not appropriate?

The writer did not give clues to the structure of the paper, or an overview. What are the main divisions?

Why does the writer not offer proof, authority, or other justification for this idea?

How effective is the change at this point to the second section of the paper? How would you label this section?

Point out some informal phrases and constructions here and elsewhere. How do you feel about them in this kind of paper?

What kind of image does "works in a Think Tank" evoke? How would you rewrite this sentence?

If the writer has not acquired this kind of information from general reading, where might he or she find it?

By beginning with this quotation from Alvin Toffler's *Future Shock*, I want to emphasize how far human beings have come in such a short time and to show that the whole trend of human life has been upward. During their long history, people have constantly progressed, and I believe that Americans are no different from others. People will continue to progress, and life in the future is going to get better, especially in the United States.

The first way that life will be better is in material things. Scientists have already developed thousands of new products that are waiting in the wings for us to call them. Already computers can provide hundreds of services to every household and do chores ranging from paying bills to helping the children with their homework. Optical fibers offer new, cheaper, and more durable ways of communicating. New building materials promise longlasting, carefree luxury at less cost. New engines and transportation systems should make our old, heavy, dirty, and inefficient cars, trains, and buses obsolete in short order. I don't think anyone questions the ability of scientists and inventors to make our lives better if we can afford what they offer.

Some people are worried about whether or not the American political and economic system can provide the kind of structure that will make it possible for us to use the new inventions. They say that science is at least twenty years ahead of social science, and it's in the realm of social science that Americans will fall down. I don't agree with that either. Americans have always been imaginative, creative, and flexible and above all adaptable. But in addition to that, they are beginning to look to experts and planners in social science just as they have looked for years to scientific experts. When John Gardner left public office, he founded "Common Cause," a citizens' lobby with over a million members that works out solutions to problems and then works within the political system to get them into action. Herman Kahn, the director of the Hudson Institute, works in a "Think Tank" with dozens of scientists and social scientists on problems ranging from disarmament to foreign aid to new sources of energy. Similar "Think Tanks" exist at Harvard, M.I.T., Berkeley, and other universities, and both elected officials and bureaucrats consult them and such private companies as the Rand Corporation to help work on problems. I don't believe any problem is too great when we really go after it.

Some people are worried that America will go downhill because of the energy crisis and its dependence on foreign energy. I don't think this is a major problem. In fact, I think the only reason it's a problem even now is that we are too humane to use the substitute power we could easily get in a few years. Think what would happen to all the oil-producing countries if we suddenly stopped buying oil! And if we went all out on solar energy, kinetic energy from windmills, tidal energy from ocean installations, gasahol, woodburning conversions, and atomic power plants, and coal conversions, not to mention oil shale and even methane from manure, we could leave OPEC in the lurch right now, or at least within ten years.

What justification, or proof, does the writer offer for this belief?

Should the writer define any of these terms?

Of course, the new demands of the emerging nations are a problem, especially when they control raw materials we need and when our money has gone down in value. The United States is working, though, through the International Monetary Fund, to give those countries both political and economic stability and to help them build industries of their own, so they won't demand that we continue giving them handouts.** The White House has proposed a "Foundation for International Technical Cooperation" funded initially at fifty million dollars to help some of these countries get together and work cooperatively on their development.

What do you think of the writer's use of "though" and "through" in this sentence?

Why do you think the writer used a "loaded" word here?

Contrast the points of view in this paper with those in the previous paper.

One thing other people worry about is that Americans won't face the challenge of the future. Admiral Hyman Rickover was interviewed by CBS in September 1978 on "Face the Nation," and he said that Americans "have a pretty good life" and have become lackadaisical. He thinks that because everybody is taken care of, Americans are uninterested in important things and lack incentive and education.†

How could this be made concrete and lively? How could the writer make you *see* an American refusing to face the future?

If there's one thing I'm sure of, it's the fact that Americans will rise to any challenge put to them. When the going gets tough, the tough get going, and Americans will do just that. They can tighten their belts if they have to, use less energy if they must, and get along without some of the luxuries they took for granted. I think, however, that science will keep providing more ideas and products, the political and economic systems will change and adjust, the energy crisis will go away, the emerging nations will—with our help—begin to build for themselves, rather than trying to steal from us.

What proof would be desirable here?

How do you react to this slogan?

Here are the main divisions of the paper used as a summary. How does the writer justify not using them in an overview?

All of these forces will make life in the United States better in the future, even if there's a lag for a few years. I don't think any of these forces will fail in the long run, but if they do, I'll fall back on the American citizen to meet the challenge. If necessary, we can start all over, and that might give us a better life, too.

Here is a new idea not treated earlier. How do you feel about its insertion so near the end of the paper?

Here is another new idea. How has the writer helped or hindered the paper with these assertions?

—Vernon Marks

*Alvin Toffler, *Future Shock* (New York: Random House, 1970), p. 15.

**Ron Chernow, "The IMF, Roughest Bank in Town, *Saturday Review*, February 3, 1979, p. 17.

†Admiral Hyman Rickover, "Face the Nation," CBS Television Program, September 3, 1978.

Another Kind of Opinion Paper—Satire

III

EN ROUTE TO NOWHERE[5]

The number of jobs people can perform for themselves grows smaller every year. This is a result of the famous increasing complexity of twentieth century society. Not too long ago, for example, ordinary people could repair their own automobiles, a task which now requires three appointments with a garage, consultations with a service manager and the ministrations of sundry specialists in automotive geriatrics, carburetor cardiology and front end orthopedics.

To file any but the simplest income tax form now requires the services of an accountant. If a lot of the income is unsalaried, you probably need a firm of tax lawyers, since the tax code has become so Byzantine in its complexity that no two persons, including the experts, can agree how much tax is due from a given income, and you are, consequently, always in danger of winding up in the law courts.

The rule is that the simple becomes complex, the complex becomes unintelligible, and the unintelligible becomes litigation. Already in many states, it is possible to end up in a court brawl over auto repair, in which the outcome hinges on the interpretation of the validity of estimate vouchers, issued by your garage for replacing the ash tray.

One result of all this is a radical increase in the number of experts needed to accomplish simple tasks. And the result of this, of course, is a sharp rise in the cost of doing jobs that could once be done at no cost whatever.

Consider the once-simple business of buying an airline ticket to Europe. A woman I know decided to do this very thing last spring, and almost did.

She had done it several times in the old days and began to do it the old way. She phoned an airline, ordered a seat for a given date and told the clerk she would come around in a few days to pay for the ticket.

Fortunately, she told friends first, and they asked her which plan she was flying under. She was startled. She did not know there was a choice of plans beyond the basic Orville and Wilbur Wright plan.

Her friends lifted the scales from her eyes. One did not simply fly to Europe any more without sifting through the astounding variety of money-saving plans available.

Did she not know that if she flew on a Tuesday night flight which originated in St. Louis, agreed to spend three days in Bessarabia, make a side trip to Tunis, attend the church of her choice on Sundays, Wednesdays, and Fridays while abroad and return to the United States, agreeing to land at Waukegan on a day when the temperature did not exceed 78 degrees Fahrenheit, she could get a special fare?

She did not want to visit either Bessarabia or Tunis, but she asked if there were alternatives. There was nothing but alternatives. By joining a sect of snake handlers, she could profit from a fantastic charter rate, which would go even lower if the Dow Jones stock market average rose more than three points on the third day after the first full moon of her European visit.

If she chose to fly crated in a wooden box strapped to the wing of a 747 and agreed not to eat the airline meal. . . .

"Stop!" she cried. "I need expert advice."

—Russell Baker

ACTIVITY 7A

Discussing the Opinion Papers

The entire process of supporting opinions is so complex that Daniel Webster once said when complimented on a speech of opinion, "I have been preparing for that speech all of my life." Your opinions and your thinking processes have indeed grown throughout your life, but a look at how to support an opinion may help you think and write more clearly.

1. The purpose or thesis statement of an opinion paper must clearly state the opinion that is to be supported. What is the thesis statement, or opinion, of each of these papers?

2. Although opinion papers are based on opinions, they must include concrete and specific examples and facts. Have the professional writing samples and the student samples all used concrete, specific examples and facts?

3. The introduction to this chapter suggests that many opinions are controversial and that sometimes a person with a strong opinion encounters opposition. How controversial are the subjects in the model papers? Under what circumstances might any of the foregoing papers encounter opposition?

4. Working with a partner or small group, take one of the thesis statements of the two student samples and make a list of the kinds of concrete specifics and facts you might use to support such an idea. Jot down the outline you might develop if you were writing the paper.

5. Satire is one of the most interesting and readable ways writers communicate their opinions. Discuss some opinions you have about life in the United States and think of how you might present one of these opinions satirically. Use some of the techniques the writer used in the last model.

Selecting Valid Opinions to Support

Perhaps you've heard someone end an argument by saying, "Well, everyone is entitled to an opinion." Yes, in some cases a person is entitled to an opinion. In matters of taste, for which there are no "right" or "wrong" answers, everyone is entitled to decide such questions as "who has the best personality" or "what is the most enjoyable sport." But an argument on a matter of taste is silly; people should discuss such an issue to reveal why they think as they do, rather than to convince anyone that theirs is the "correct" opinion.

Matters of fact. On matters of fact, such as whether Maine or Minnesota reaches farther north, no one can have an opinion. To support, discuss, or argue a matter of fact is a waste of time. Look up the information and set the record straight. Minnesota reaches father north than Maine, and that's all there is to it.

Matters of judgment. One can legitimately argue and write about matters of judgment. Although people may not agree on a matter of judgment, as they must on matters of fact, a person can prove that an opinion is reasonable or believable. But even in this area, some people are not entitled to an opinion. Those who have little background on a subject or who have not taken the trouble to become informed are not entitled to discuss it. To support an opinion one must investigate the facts and then make a judgment.

Three kinds of opinions. As you prepare to select a subject for your opinion paper, consider the major areas in which you have had experience. Then think in terms of three kinds of judgments:

1. *Generalization*—What conclusion or generalization can you draw from a series of facts or events? For example, few students come to see the senior play, *Macbeth*; no one tries out for the oratory contest; the debate team is defeated in the sectional. What do these facts mean? Perhaps "Our students are no longer interested in cultural activities," or "Interest in speech is declining," or "Homework no longer leaves time for extracurricular activities," or "Our speech department isn't very good." Whatever your opinion, you must prove that you have made a valid generalization from the facts. The more supporting facts you can provide, the more believable your generalization.

2. *Evaluation*—What is it worth? Football requires a player to practice at least fifteen hours a week for three months each year. Are its values worth the time? What is football worth? Or, for another example, you've just read *Lord of the Flies*. How much time did you invest? Was it worth it?

3. *Interpretation*—What does it mean? The residents in your town have just voted down an appropriation for a new library. What does this vote mean in terms of inflation, the prevailing goals and values, voter turn-out, the future development of the town, and the other needs of the town? Or, the senior class valedictorian, a top-seeded tennis player with an outstanding personality, was just turned down by Harvard. What does it mean in terms of college admissions generally, Harvard, your school, and the student?

ACTIVITY 7B

Recognizing Different Kinds of Opinions

1. Read the editorials in your daily newspaper for three days. Copy the title and the thesis statement of each. Come to class prepared to discuss the kind of opinion (generalization, evaluation, or interpretation) that each represents. See whether the newspaper has based any editorials on matters of taste or matters of fact. (Remember that the opinion expressed in an editorial is the opinion of a group—the group of editors who set the paper's policy—rather than the opinion of any one person. For example, an Ohio editor lived across from a large field and hoped desperately that a school would not be built across from her home. As an employee of the newspaper she was responsible for promoting the good of the entire community and for carrying out the paper's policy; she wrote an editorial commending the decision to build.)

2. Bring to class three carefully worded opinions you would like to base a paper on. Be sure they do not concern matters of taste or matters of fact. With your teacher's help, determine the best one to use as a basis for the Major Writing Assignment for this chapter.

Patterns of Reasoning

The two basic kinds of reasoning are *induction* and *deduction*. Writing an opinion paper is, in a sense, an exercise in reasoning. You may decide to present specific evidence to support your opinion and lead the reader to draw certain conclusions. This process is called inductive reasoning. Or, you may begin by stating your opinion and, by a pattern of deductive reasoning, examine specific instances in the light of that statement.

Inductive reasoning. Induction can be visualized as a triangle sitting on its base with the vertex, or point, up.

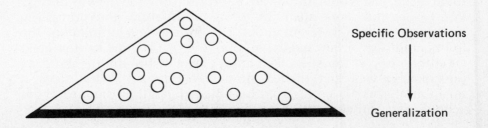

The movement of thought is from the top down. In using induction, you begin with individual observations (the point of the triangle) from which you draw a conclusion or generalization (the base line). The following sample demonstrates one of the pitfalls of inductive reasoning:

> There was once upon a time a census officer who had to record the names of all householders in a certain Welsh village. The first that he questioned was called William Williams; so were the second, third, fourth. . . . At last he said to himself: "This is tedious; evidently they are all called William Williams. I shall put them down so and take a holiday." But he was wrong; there was just one whose name was John Jones.[6]
> —Bertrand Russell

The census officer begins with separate observations (the four people whose names he checked personally) and then makes an "inductive leap" to what is called a "hasty generalization"—"They are all called William Williams." You recognize at once the weakness of that generalization, but do you recognize the nature of your inductive leap when you say, "Those Northsiders are really poor sports. We played them last year and they hissed when we won"? This is called stereotyping, and it is another example of an error in inductive reasoning.

Deductive reasoning. Deduction can be visualized as a triangle with its base up and the vertex down.

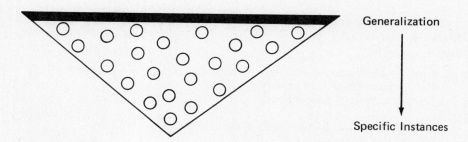

Generalization

Specific Instances

The movement of thought, again, is from the top down. In using deduction, you begin with a broad generalization (the top side) and apply it to a specific instance (the vertex). The following sample demonstrates some of the pitfalls of deductive reasoning:

At their first meeting, Sherlock Holmes said to Dr. Watson, "You have been in Afghanistan, I perceive." Later he explained how he knew:

> "From long habit the train of thoughts ran so swiftly through my mind that I arrived at the conclusion without being conscious of interme-

diate steps. There were such steps, however. The train of reasoning ran, 'Here is a gentleman of a medical type, but with the air of a military man. Clearly an army doctor, then. He has just come from the tropics, for his face is dark, and that is not the natural tint of his skin, for his wrists are fair. He has undergone hardship and sickness, as his haggard face says clearly. His left arm has been injured. He holds it in a stiff and unnatural manner. Where in the tropics could an English army doctor have seen such hardship and got his arm wounded? Clearly in Afghanistan.' "[7]

—Arthur Conan Doyle

Holmes' reasoning *seems* to be very good and it's great fun to read, but would you be willing to accept his generalizations and his logic?

Anyone with the air of a military man is or has been a soldier.
Watson has the air of a military man.
Therefore, Watson was a soldier.

Anyone with a suntan has been in the tropics.
Watson has a suntan.
Therefore, Watson has been in the tropics.

Anyone who holds his arm in a stiff and unnatural manner has been wounded.
Watson holds his arm in a stiff and unnatural manner.
Therefore, Watson has been wounded.

And finally:

Any English army doctor with a tanned and haggard face and a wounded arm must have been wounded in Afghanistan.
Watson is an English army doctor, has such a face and such an arm.
Therefore, Watson was wounded in Afghanistan.

Reasoning Patterns in Student Compositions

The student compositions make use of both inductive and deductive reasoning, but because the patterns of thought are embedded in the paragraphs, they are a little difficult to see. In the first composition, for example, one of the ideas follows this pattern:

> The rise in oil prices caused a trade deficit.
> The OPEC nations are responsible for the rise in oil prices.
> Therefore, the OPEC nations caused a trade deficit.

This is an example from the second student composition:

> Common Cause tries to solve the problems facing our society.
> Ordinary citizens are members of Common Cause.
> Therefore, ordinary citizens can try to solve the problems facing our society.

Again, the reasoning seems logical, but are you willing to accept the conclusion in both of these examples?

ACTIVITY 7C

Locating the Reasoning Patterns

The following sentences are from material in this chapter. Some have been rephrased. Read each carefully, locate the idea in the selection, and determine whether it is part of an inductive or a deductive reasoning process. Write any sentences necessary to complete the thought pattern, as in the examples in the preceding section. Be prepared to discuss in class whether or not the reasoning is logical and acceptable.

1. Fish have no openings on their backs, and no bird is big enough to swallow a man. Therefore, you could not have seen what you have reported you saw.

2. When truth and error have fair play, truth always wins. In order to have fair play for truth, you must play fair with error. Therefore, when people who promote false ideas are permitted to present their opinions, truth will win out in the end.

3. The need for jobs is Eastport's biggest problem. The oil company's project will provide jobs. Therefore, Eastport should allow the oil company to use its harbor.

4. Because the strong currents of the Bay of Fundy affect the harbor at Eastport, oil tankers should not be allowed to use the harbor.

5. Freedom of speech and freedom of the press are very important in democratic life. In order to be sure you do not suppress good ideas, you must accept the expression of all ideas. Therefore, people must be allowed to speak even when their ideas are unpopular.

6. Many states need new sources of money. Half of the states find gambling a profitable source of income. Therefore, the rest of the states should institute gambling.

7. State-sponsored gambling increases the respectability of gambling. When gambling is made more respectable, more people gamble. Therefore, in sponsoring gambling, states may be harming their citizens.

8. The idea of wealth without work is nonproductive and harmful. State-approved gambling promotes the idea that wealth without work is possible. Therefore, the states should not approve gambling.

9. The people least likely to be able to afford gambling are most likely to gamble. These people, then, will contribute from their gambling the most money to the state. Taxing the poor more than the well-to-do is bad. Therefore, states should not legalize gambling.

10. The alternative to a code of conduct is, if not chaos, certainly confusion and embarrassment. Language is conduct. Therefore, it is important to have a pretty strict standard for acceptable language.

11. If you add -ettes to the word "storm," to mean "small storms" then probably any word that ends in -etts or -ettes has been made from another word in the same way. Therefore, Massachusetts means "small Massachus."

12. Because of our complex twentieth century society, it costs more to have our cars fixed.

13. Because everybody is taken care of, Americans are uninterested in important things and lack incentive.

BASIC FALLACIES

Fallacies of inductive thinking. From examining the examples in Activity 7C, you must have become aware of how often and how subtly you use "logical" reasoning and how difficult it is to keep from becoming illogical. Errors in reasoning are called fallacies. The following sections describe briefly several of the basic fallacies of inductive thinking.

"Inductive leap" leading to a false generalization. The basic pattern of induction is to observe a large number of specific cases and then "leap" to a general conclusion. Thus a scientist may have burned several hundred pieces of copper and then generalized, "Copper burns with a green flame." But because he has not tested every piece of copper in the universe, he cannot be absolutely certain that all copper everywhere burns with a green flame. He has made an inductive leap because he is *reasonably* sure. The Welsh census taker in the story on page 169 made an error because he based his generalization on too few observations. How many times do people generalize from too few cases: "Vans are no good. Ours got no mileage at all."

Stereotyping. This is a common fallacy of inductive reasoning. It is similar to hasty generalization. It is the mistake you make when you assign a certain quality to all members of a group, ignoring their individual differences. "I wouldn't bother with anyone who lives up on the hill. They're all snobs" is an example of stereotyping. Try to be aware of this fallacy in your everyday life—in conversations with friends, in judgments you make yourself, in the newspapers and books you read. Prejudice results from the error of thinking in stereotypes. Every time you say, or hear someone else say, "Oh, what can you expect. They're all alike!" one of you is making a statement about an entire group without considering individual differences among the members of that group.

Post hoc, ergo propter hoc. Translated into English, this phrase means "After this, therefore because of this." Another name for this fallacy is "mistaken causal relationship." It designates the fallacy of assuming that, because event B followed event A, B must have been caused by A. "A black cat ran in front of my car. A little later I had an accident. All on account of that cat!" "This firm incorporated while the Democrats were in office. It has become a multimillion-dollar operation. The only reason it succeeded was because the Democrats were in office." "I wore my T-shirt wrong side out for the Upton game, and we won. From now on, I'm going to wear my T-shirt wrong side out for a game."

Ignoring the question. There are many different ways to ignore a question. One way is to change the subject: "I don't care whether good grades help on college admissions or not; a fellow gets an awful lot out of athletics." Another way is to shift from the issue to the character or personality of an opponent: "Here I am discussing the values of athletics with Smiley, and he's never even made first team. How would he know anything about it?" Or, you can use an emotional appeal that may have nothing to do with the argument: "The value of athletics? Why, it's the American way! It's the very lifeblood of the free enterprise system. Competition. That's it!"

Fallacies of deductive reasoning. As was explained on page 169, in deductive reasoning you begin with a generalization and apply it to a specific instance. This kind of reasoning takes the form of a syllogism in which two statements (the major premise and the minor premise) are made and a conclusion is drawn from them. See page 170 for examples of the syllogisms Sherlock Holmes may have used to arrive at his conclusions. The following sections describe some common fallacies in deductive thinking.

False syllogism. To understand the basic pattern of the syllogism, think of the major premise as setting up a large circle. (All human beings are mortal.) Then think of the minor premise as setting up a smaller circle inside the larger circle. (Socrates is a human being.) Finally, think of the conclusion as indicating that the statement in the larger circle must apply to whatever is in the smaller circle. (Therefore, Socrates is mortal.) But what happens if the major premise is false?

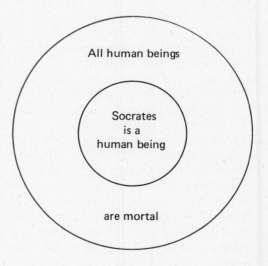

Everything in the paper is true.
I read the story in the paper.
Therefore, the story is true.

And what happens if the conclusion is not stated so that something inside the smaller circle also falls within the larger circle?

Gold is very heavy.
This rock is very heavy.
Therefore, this rock is gold.

The conclusion, of course, is false because the minor premise is weak: something other than gold may be very heavy; consequently the rock may fall outside of the "gold" circle.

Either-or. Probably the most famous example of the either-or fallacy is Patrick Henry's "Give me liberty or give me death." The famous patriot was suggesting that only these two alternatives existed. This assumption, that in a given situation only two alternatives exist, is called the "either-or" fallacy. "If she's not a Republican, she must be a Democrat." "It's either good or bad." But there are many political stands other than Democrat and Republican and many things in life that may be good in some cases and bad in others.

Words with changing meanings. Words often change meanings depending upon the context in which they are used; if you are not alert, you may be caught in a semantic trap. "Anna is very *smooth*. We need a *smoothly* operating student council. We should elect Anna president." In its first use, *smooth* means "diplomatic, gracious—perhaps sophisticated or tricky." In the second use, it means "efficient." The reasoning is illogical.

Begging the question. In this fallacy, the arguer assumes as true something that must be proven. "Our unwieldy constitution should be changed." (Is it really unwieldy? Prove it!) "The least valuable course in our high-school curriculum, health, should be cut to one day a week." (Is it really least valuable? Prove it!) "Shakespeare's sonnets are great literature because Shakespeare was a great writer and he wrote them." (The arguer assumes that a great writer must always write great literature. That the sonnets themselves are great must be proven.)

Non sequitur. A sequel is a book or an event that follows another. A *non sequitur* is simply a statement that doesn't follow from what has gone before. "Sally Cinema is gorgeous, and she recommends Cruncho cereal so it must be great." (Cruncho cereal may have little to do with her looks.) "Charley McKinney is a great quarterback. I'm going to vote for him for class president." (The last sentence implies that greatness on the football field signifies greatness as a class officer. It doesn't necessarily follow.)

A knowledge of these basic fallacies of reasoning will be very helpful to you now and when you are working with Chapter 8, Argumentation and Persuasion. As you read the articles and the student compositions, watch for patterns of reasoning and be alert for any fallacies in the arguments presented.

ACTIVITY 7D

Finding Obvious Fallacies

Locate and list the fallacies in the following statement. Bring your list to class and be prepared to discuss it.

"You want to know what I think about fraternities and sororities in high school? Well, I think they're wonderful. Yes, I think they're very beneficial. I've been in one for two years, and I've had a wonderful time. Certainly, that proves they're very beneficial.

"Let me give you an example: I went out for Alpha Delta and only three weeks later I was elected prom queen. I certainly think fraternities and sororities are very important.

"I see you're quoting Sandy Barron in your article, too. Why, she doesn't know anything about sororities. She's just a little grind who studies all the time. Well, I look at it this way: either you're a grind and study all the time or else you're a normal, well-balanced person interested in sororities. You're either one way or the other—and who wants to be like Sandy?

"Why, I even heard that she's so interested in study that she's going to go to summer school when she doesn't have to. That proves she's crazy, doesn't it?

"This is the way I look at it: school is supposed to produce a well-rounded individual. In order to be well-rounded, you've got to be in extracurricular things, so I like all kinds of extracurricular things, especially sororities. Besides, who likes to study anyway? Ask anybody. Go ahead: ask all of my friends. (But don't ask Sandy; she wouldn't know.)"

Qualifying Your Statements

A broad, general statement can be a sign of fuzzy thinking or of an intent to deceive. However, careful use of the English language enables you to say exactly what you mean. You can make a statement more precise, even more truthful, by qualifying it in some way. You do this by adding to the statement a word, phrase, or clause. In this way, you change the statement enough to make it convey a more exact meaning.

GENERAL STATEMENT

Orland High is the best school in this state.

QUALIFIED BY ADDING

A *word*: Orland High is the best private school in this state.
A *phrase*: According to its principal, Orland High is the best school in this state.
A *clause*: Orland High is the best school in the state if you happen to be a straight-A student.

The next time you are tempted to make a broad, general statement ask yourself, "What is it that I really want to say?" Then qualify your statement so that you cannot be easily misunderstood.

ACTIVITY 7E

Qualifying Opinions for Exactness

Take each of the following "opinions" and qualify it in such a way as to make it more precise. Without naming the grammatical structures you used, just record the qualifying words and notice the difference they make.

1. The older and younger generations will never get together.
2. The government hurts poor people by destroying their homes and building roads for people who can afford automobiles.
3. Life is harder in American cities today than it was fifty years ago.
4. Police officers are treated unfairly.
5. United States conservation policies are failures.
6. Every day in every way we're getting better and better.
7. The government is not responsive to the changing needs of people.

8. Adults don't like the music of young people.

9. Some fashions are flattering.

10. Science will solve all our problems.

11. Cable television is the hope of the future.

12. Political figures are highly honored today.

13. The American image is improving all over the world.

14. No one favors an increase in taxes.

15. Insurance laws are unfair to teenage drivers.

Good English in an Opinion Paper

One definition of "good" English is that it is the language which, in a given situation, communicates best. A message may be grammatically perfect and rhetorically eloquent, but if it is not understood by readers or listeners, then it hasn't done the job the writer or speaker intended, and it's not "good" English. The opposite is also true. A message may be phrased in broken, almost illiterate language, but if it does the job the writer or speaker intended, in that sense it's good. Of course, from other points of view—for example, from the standpoint of permanent literary value—it might be poor. Some people, such as the writer of the sample you read on pages 158–160, insist that language cannot be effective if it is "bogged down" in jargon, or "puffed up" with inflated words.

Some linguists say that if the thought is clear, the language will be clear and, because of its clarity, effective. Therefore, the most significant step in writing an opinion paper is getting your thinking clear. You may be able to think through your idea before you begin to write or you may want to explore the idea by writing about it.

A second element in presenting an opinion effectively is that of selecting the language which is acceptable to your audience for your specific situation and purpose. For example, your friends accept one kind of language when you are chatting informally. They expect another kind of language when you write to them. There's also a difference between what they expect in an informal, friendly note in which you make plans for a party and a more formal plan for several sessions of your church youth group. And, of course, if your minister and the youth leaders are to read the plans, you will use language that is even more formal.

ACTIVITY 7F

Exploring the Nature of Acceptable Language

1. There are a number of language items or expressions that at one time were not considered acceptable as standard English. Some of these have gradually come to be accepted; others are still considered nonstandard.[8]

   Discuss the following sentences from the point of view of a speaker of standard English. Are there any language items in these sentences that you would not accept? Are some of them appropriate under certain circumstances? Are there some that may be considered standard usage in the future?

   a. We're back so far I can't hardly see the stage.

   b. It seems like we've been here for hours.

   c. Jason insists that he didn't break the window but I seen him.

   d. I would of gone if I'da known the Knicks were playing.

   e. Liz won't buy a chance on the raffle. She says she never has no luck.

   f. Carol, my little sister, wants to go to the movies with you and I.

   g. I asked him why he was so late and he goes, "Well, I ran out of gas."

   h. Would you bring them books to the library, please?

   i. My dog he deserves a medal for saving that baby.

   j. You can loan Jerry the money if you want to, but you may not get it back.

2. The standards of acceptable language differ from one community to the next. In small groups, either in or out of class, make lists of about ten language items per group and then ask some people in your community how they feel about certain items. For example, would it bother one of your neighbors to hear someone use "ain't" repeatedly? Would it make a difference if the word were written or printed? How about "It's me." or "They invited she and I" or "I didn't like *him* calling me that"? Report to the class the results of your investigation.

MAJOR WRITING ASSIGNMENT

AN OPINION PAPER

By now, you have chosen one of the three carefully worded opinions you brought to class for Activity 7B. You will now use it as the thesis statement of your opinion paper.

To formulate your thesis statement, complete this sentence:

I believe strongly that _____.

Then cross out the first four words. What remains will be your thesis statement. Remember that to make your opinion acceptable, you must support it with facts, opinions of authorities, logical reasoning, and, above all, specific examples.

Outlines for opinion papers differ. If you choose to write a satire like that of Russell Baker, for example, you must develop your own order. If you wish to follow a fairly standard pattern, however, you might look closely at this outline of George Will's article on gambling.

TITLE: STATE CORRUPTS WITH GAMBLING

Thesis Statement: (Held until the final paragraph) States that sanction gambling simultaneously cheat and corrupt their citizens.

I. Introduction
   A. Arouse interest—Describe Hartford's jai-alai fronton
   B. Indicate subject and suggest its importance—List kinds of gambling in American states, indicate extent of the kinds of gambling in various states, give statistics about the amount of gambling
   C. State thesis—RESERVE THESIS STATEMENT UNTIL LAST PARAGRAPH WHEN READERS ARE PREPARED

II. Body
   A. List general arguments for state-sanctioned gambling
   B. Refute each argument
      1. Legal gambling increases public interest in gambling
      2. As a revenue-raising device, it is regressive
      3. It is damaging to the poor families who indulge
         It is not victimless and it blurs the distinction between well-earned and "ill-gotten" gains
   C. Develop historical theory on which American values are based—quote Jefferson, Van Buren . . .

III. Conclusion
   A. Acknowledge that some "wealth without work" is possible since any economy produces windfalls
   B. End with main idea (thesis statement)—Thus do gambling states simultaneously cheat and corrupt their citizens

Because it is *against* rather than *for* something, this article places the emphasis on refuting an idea rather than on supporting it. Nonetheless, the overall pattern is clear, and it is one which you may be able to use as you work.

Chapter 8

Argumentation and Persuasion

In a series of advertisements published in national magazines, the Caterpillar Tractor Company presented both sides of a number of issues facing the United States: Should the nation build new dams or preserve rivers in their natural state? Should the nation build massive new highways or leave the land untouched? Should certain resources be developed—oil and coal and other minerals—or should the wilderness be saved? It ended each advertisement with the slogan: "There are no simple solutions. Only intelligent choices." One of those advertisements appears on the next page.

At one time, decision makers were less concerned than they are now about making long-range, intelligent choices. They were even less concerned about the right of the people to be involved in those choices. When leaders had decided on a course of action, they did everything possible—sometimes without regard to accuracy and integrity—to implement that decision. Even Benjamin Franklin was not above dishonest tactics. He wrote a false letter to stir up anger against England during the Revolutionary War. In the letter, he pretended to be "James Craufurd" writing to say that he was sending eight large bundles of American scalps to Colonel Haldimand, English governor of Canada, at the governor's request.

Today, at least in a democracy, people have more respect for each other's ideas and they often try to work together to make intelligent choices. This approach has changed the meaning of the words "argumentation" and "persuasion." Argumentation has come to mean presenting the one course of action or judgment that, in a given situation, is preferable to all others. Persuasion goes one step further. It refers to the fair, logical, and reasoned ways one motivates others to act on or believe in what has been set forth as the best or the most intelligent choice.

Your Moral Responsibility

Argumentation and persuasion, then, no longer mean a contest in which one side loses and the other wins by any means possible but rather, a cooperative search for truth based on logic and the most complete set of facts possible. Your responsibility to other people and to truth is to search for all the facts that you can find on an issue, work with others to determine the intelligent choice, and then support this position by evidence and reason. You may, of course, organize your material to make your position attractive to certain audiences, but as an ethical persuader in search of truth for the good of all, you should be willing to change your position as new information emerges, and you should never think of others as "things" which you can manipulate for your own purposes.

You use argumentation and persuasion every day. Think back over last week and try to remember how many times you've argued such unstated propositions as "Resolved, Mom and Dad should let me have the car on Saturday night," or "Resolved, I should get a little extra allowance to go to the concert next week."

Argumentation and persuasion are all around you, and it is not at all surprising that different people and different groups come to different conclusions. Here are two examples of attempts at persuasion in which different courses of action are suggested.

I

There Are Answers

Energy shortages don't have to become a way of life. Gas lines, brownouts, curtailed power supplies: The warnings continue to mount, signalling that our nation's energy problem is today's, not tomorrow's. Tough and realistic decisions are demanded. Now.

First, we've got to make a strong determination to develop and fully utilize every feasible energy source—whether it's coal, nuclear, natural gas, oil, water power, or likely alternatives such as solar, geothermal, and wind. We need them all and we must use them wisely. But despite our best efforts at conservation and increasing fuel supplies, we may still face an energy gap of two or more decades.

One way to avoid it is by recognizing the enormous potential of nuclear power. A third of a century ago, nuclear energy was seen as the wave of the future, promising great benefits to humankind. That's still its promise. This past winter, when coal was hard to burn or hard to get, it was nuclear power that kept factories and vital services operating in community after community.

Nuclear power meets the tests of economy and abundance. With aggressive national effort, safe processing and waste disposal techniques can be developed. Moreover, our reserves of nuclear fuel if used efficiently in breeder reactors would equal many times the combined oil resources of all OPEC nations. In sum, this means savings of billions of dollars for consumers.

Energy shortages don't have to be a way of life. We have the know-how and the resources to prevent them.

There *are* answers.[2]

II

A CALL TO PROCEED WITH CAUTION . . .[3]

The commercial nuclear power plant program planned for the next 25 years in this country represents a serious threat to your health and safety and to the health and safety of the American people. Yet—despite the hazards, despite the growing danger of sabotage from terrorists, despite the unresolved problem of disposing of lethal nuclear wastes safely—you are asked to accept this program as necessary to solve this nation's energy problems.

The Wall Street Journal labeled these nuclear plants "atomic lemons," pointing out that "their unreliability is becoming one of their most dependable features." Yet, you are asked to accept the program as the mainstay of the nation's future electric power supply.

The MITRE Corporation, a Virginia think tank, warns that nuclear materials in the hands of a terrorist group "would give it a power of blackmail over the world at large and the U.S. in particular without precedent in history." (Between 1969 and 1975, ninety-nine threats of violence were directed against commercial nuclear facilities.) Yet, you are asked to accept the program as safe.

Insurance companies have refused to provide the public with full coverage against nuclear accidents because the risk is too great. Yet, you are asked to accept the program as safe.

Consumer advocate Ralph Nader warns " . . . there is no practical solution for protecting our generation, much less our children's and grandchildren's, from the immense accumulation of lethal wastes that are inevitable in the nuclear power industry." Yet, you are asked to accept the program as safe.

According to a report by the Atomic Energy Commission's Regulatory Staff, U.S. nuclear plants are "besieged" by serious safety problems arising from faulty design and construction. Yet, you are asked to accept the program as safe.

The U.S. Geological Survey has found that there aren't enough known uranium reserves in the United States to fuel proposed nuclear power plants. Yet, you are asked to accept nuclear power as the answer to the oil crisis.

This is to enlighten you about how electricity is generated through nuclear power so that you might understand more precisely why the problems involved are so threatening.

This is also to advise you that there is an important step you can take to help control the nuclear risks. That step is your becoming a Sponsor of the Union of Concerned Scientists, the organization dedicated to preventing such a disaster.

The advertisement headed "There Are Answers" is an example of "institutional advertising" in mass magazines. With ordinary advertising, a company attempts to influence readers to buy either a specific product or group of products. Institutional advertising simply buys good will for the company or organization. In this way, the company attempts to influence the opinions, attitudes, and decisions of the public. By promoting or seeming to promote some generally accepted value, it makes the reader feel secure and that feeling transfers to the company. The advertisement you have just read, is an attempt to influence public attitudes concerning the energy problem. The advertisers are not attempting to sell a particular product; they are attempting to promote an attitude or create a climate which will help them operate in what they believe is the most effective or profitable way.

The example of persuasion headed "A Call to Proceed with Caution . . . " is from a brochure mailed by the Union of Concerned Scientists to thousands of Americans. Its purpose is twofold: to provide information and to promote action.

Reread the advertisement that opened this chapter (page 184). What were your thoughts as you read the advertisement? Did you find yourself being led to agree with the choice that had already been made? Do you agree that it was the intelligent choice? Can you think of any other intelligent choices that could have been made?

You can readily see that the subject of these messages—the energy crisis—is a very tangled and complex problem. You can see also that the media in which these messages are communicated (advertisements and a brochure) do not permit a detailed examination of the facts. Such methods of persuasion require you to dig deeper into the issue if you are to make your own intelligent choice. Look back over the discussion of reasoning in Chapter 7 (pages 154–181). Then reread the advertisements and the letter. Examine the reasoning closely. Look for fallacies. Whenever you read anything that attempts to persuade you to think or act in a certain way, subject it to this kind of critical, careful reading.

ACTIVITY 8A

Discussing the Examples

Consider the following questions.

1. What motivates each of the messages? What does each writer expect to achieve by getting this message to the public?

2. What is the "voice" each of the writers uses? Who seems to be speaking to you in each of the selections? How does that voice influence your attitude toward and your acceptance of the messages? Is writing in a "voice" other than your own dishonest? (Remember Benjamin Franklin's use of the voice of "James Craufurd" during the Revolutionary War.)

3. What techniques do the writers use to draw you into their arguments, to make you *feel* something about the energy crisis?

4. Which of the messages seems to offer the most information and the most logically-supported argument? What difference might the "medium" in which the material appears make? How does each of the arguments attempt to provide for the different "levels of audience," which range from the superficial "skimmer" to the more intelligent and concerned student of the problem?

5. Consider the use of such devices as: sentence fragments, one-word "sentences," one-sentence paragraphs, lists, repetition of phrases, quotations, reference to well-known people and organizations. What is the purpose and effect of each of these devices as used by professional writers? To what extent should you use these devices in your writing?

Following are three examples of relatively good arguments—papers in which truth is sought through the use of logic and facts. Two of these are student compositions and one is a professional writing sample. Read them carefully in class and note the comments to the right of the student compositions. When you write your next major composition, you will be preparing this kind of paper.

Student Composition 8A
WE ARE NOT ALONE

We have been taking our first feeble steps toward venturing out into the solar system and eventually beyond. Yet we are not alone in the universe. Mass evidence, supporting the belief that Unidentified Flying Objects (UFOs) do exist and have appeared on earth, includes: UFO sighting reports by credible observers, physical evidence, and the censorship of UFO information by the government.

Can you suggest a more gripping and dramatic beginning for this paper?

Do these structural clues indicate interesting and substantial proofs for the writer's thesis? What is her thesis?

First of all, the UFO sightings serve as their own supportive evidence. A Gallup Poll reported that five million people in the nation were willing to admit that they had seen strange objects which they felt were UFOs. In fact, since the UFOs first appeared in number, in 1946, they have been reported by every nation on earth. Obviously, a high percentage of the reports are false. Yet this still leaves a substantial number of cases where competent witnesses (including astronomers, airline pilots and local police, and military and civilian radar operators) report objects which cannot be identified as either manufactured or conventional in terms of natural space bodies. One such incident took place at Fort Knox, Kentucky, on January 7, 1948. This is the classic case of Captain Thomas Mantell, a veteran fighter pilot, who lost his life while in pursuit of a huge spherical object which was crossing the state of Kentucky.

How forceful is this argument? Do you object to the mechanical transition?

How would you rewrite the sentence beginning "Yet this still leaves . . . ." to make it clearer?

Secondly, there is physical evidence that UFOs have been present in a given location. This evidence includes markings on the ground and fragments of debris discharged from the UFOs. In many cases, the debris is confiscated by the government. However, some UFO evidence has slipped out of the government's hands, and reports that leading

What other transition than the mechanical "Secondly" would you suggest here?

Will you accept this undocumented report from "leading scientists"?

Would you insert a qualifying adjective between the words "several" and "UFOs"?

Is this a case of "begging the question"? What proof must you demand before you will accept the generalization presented here?

How can one argue against this kind of reasoning?

What should the writer do to make the statement on government censorship believable?

How would you rewrite this topic sentence?

What error in reasoning do you detect in this summary?

scientists have often been unable to identify the substances have followed. Other physical evidence includes thousands of photographs of UFOs. In Taormina, Sicily, in 1954, a United Press photographer filmed several UFOs. A crowd of thousands watched these UFOs until an Italian jet arrived and chased them all away. Still other UFO effects include: unexplained stoppage of car motors, interference with radio and TV, and electrical power failure. Many claim that the great New York-New England blackout on November 9, 1965, was directly connected with the UFO that was observed earlier that day.

Thirdly, support of UFOs' existence is based on the fact that the government is deceiving the people by hiding known factual information on UFOs. Attempting to protect the public from panic (as the obvious reason for the Air Force's traditional policy of identifying flying objects as weather balloons, etc.) is something that cannot be indefinitely sustained, particularly when the source of presumed potential panic is a mass of peculiar things that persist in flying around where large numbers of people can see them. An excellent example of government censorship of UFO reports is the still undisclosed information of the numerous sightings by the astronauts. The motives of the government must be questioned. Why would both the voice messages and the television broadcasts from the Apollo be censored to be released, when and as the government sees fit, if there were nothing that was being concealed?

UFOs exist as something unknown to our present understanding and are visiting earth. For one must realize that only people with immature minds quickly reject as impossible or alarming all that which lies outside their own physical experience or beyond the understanding of their limited imagination.

—Ellen Francis

Student Composition 8B
THE MAPLE CREST REFERENDUM

The city council's step was dramatic. Does it make a dramatic beginning?

Why does the writer refer to "luxurious lawns"? Does she have an ulterior motive?

Last week the city council took an unexpected and widely publicized step. In the middle of the day it ordered the water commissioner to shut off all the water to our nearest suburb, Maple Crest. The twenty thousand Maple Cresters became almost panic-stricken; restaurants in the shopping plaza couldn't do dishes, parents were unable to prepare formula for their infants, and the whirling sprinklers saturating the luxurious lawns suddenly stopped.

After two hours, the water came on again, but the city council had made its point. Our town provides many services to our nearby suburbs, and the city council feels that the suburbs should now assume their fair share of the cost of these services. The council wants Maple Crest to merge with the city.

One can understand, however, the suburbanites' reluctance to join the city. In the first place, many of them moved to Maple Crest to escape the high taxes in the city, and it's true that whereas their real estate assessment is about thirty-eight dollars per thousand, ours is up to fifty-eight dollars. Moreover, because they are a relatively homogeneous "upper-middle-class" group in a new development, they don't have many problems with crime, with sewer repairs, or even with fires. Why, then, should they have to pay for a jail, sewer-line replacement, or a fire department? "We pay our fair share," they insist. "We pay for our water; we pay for each time the ambulance or fire engine comes into our area; we have our own elementary school, and we pay tuition to send our students to your high school. What more do you want?"

The Maple Crest dwellers do indeed have some points on their side. They are paying for the services actually provided in Maple Crest. But in another sense, they are not doing their full duty by all of the citizens in the core city. Because the Maple Crest people are "outside the city," they can't run for city offices and thus give us the benefit of their readily recognizable leadership ability. Because we wouldn't want to keep them out if we could, people from Maple Crest use our parks, our pools, our streets, and our municipal auditorium. All of these are supported by city taxes to which the suburbanites contribute nothing. Because the suburbanites pay only the contracted cost—which often doesn't include depreciation on such things as one-hundred-year-old water mains—we can't rebuild and renew the core city as we should.

Maple Crest is scheduled to have a referendum next November 21 to determine whether or not they will join us. Mayor Raisch feels very strongly that, as he puts it, "The well-to-do suburbanites are riding to work on streets paid for by the taxes of the slum dweller." He would permanently cut off from the suburbs all city services: "Why should we," he demands, "give them the belt to strangle us with?"

I don't feel as strongly as Mayor Raisch, but I do feel the injustice of the situation. Though it means an increase in suburban taxes, it could mean a better core city. Therefore, I urge Maple Cresters to vote for the merger.

—Carolyn Stryk

Here the writer reveals her main point. What is the position that she is taking? She does not, however, attempt to motivate her readers until the very end of her paper. Is she wise to have waited?

Why, since she does not agree with them, does the writer present the Maple Cresters' point of view?

Has the writer had to do research for this information? Has she talked to Maple Crest people?

Although the writer disagrees with the speaker here, does she attempt to make fun of or to ridicule the point of view? Although she might have made the speaker seem selfish, why doesn't she do so?

The writer places first an argument which will appeal to the Maple Cresters' pride and ability. Why doesn't she begin by saying, in effect, "We need the tax money they will bring in"?

Here the writer's main attempt at motivation begins.

Mayor Raisch is very outspoken and his quotes, though crude, are graphic and memorable. Why has the writer chosen to put them last rather than first?

In comparison with Mayor Raisch's tone, how does the writer's tone seem? Which will appeal more to the Maple Crest residents?

The Whale Protection Fund

1925 K Street, N.W., Washington, D.C., 20006

Dear Friend,

I am writing to you today to ask for your immediate help in saving the whales from certain extinction.

This year, more than 24,000 highly intelligent warm-blooded whales will be killed - needlessly - by explosive harpoons from the whaling vessels of only a handful of nations.

Who <u>are</u> the whale killers?

By far, the largest whaling operations are carried out by Japan and the Soviet Union. Their floating factory ships, complete with helicopters and accompanied by sonar-equipped catcher boats, methodically hunt, chase and slaughter more than 75% of the whales killed world-wide.

In addition, smaller but equally deadly and unnecessary whaling operations are tolerated by the governments of Denmark, Norway, Iceland, Peru, Chile, South Korea, Spain, Taiwan and Cyprus.

While responsible nations have given up the dead-end whaling industry, eleven nations continue to ignore the 10-year whaling moratorium unanimously recommended by the United Nations Conference on the Human Environment, and are killing whales at a frightening pace.

Unless we halt the needless slaughter immediately, we will, within a few years, succeed in killing off these magnificent creatures which took millions of years to evolve.

To prevent this short-sighted destruction of marine life, the Whale Protection Fund has been working tirelessly to help stop the whale killing and, as I mentioned earlier, we need your immediate help.

Within the next few months, we must convince the whaling nations that continued endorsement of whaling is an international disgrace, and must be stopped.

To achieve our objective, we have planned a well-thought-out, coordinated program and you can help, specifically, by doing the following today:

The Whale Protection Fund is a project of the Center for Environmental Education.

1. <u>Send</u> the enclosed postcard to Mr. Thordor Asgeirsson, Chairman of the International Whaling Commission. We must let Mr. Asgeirsson and the other commissioners know of the wide-spread support which exists for a ten-year moratorium on commercial whaling. The more public support we can demonstrate, the greater our chances are for having the moratorium adopted as soon as possible.

2. <u>Sign</u> the petition directed to the governments of Japan, the Soviet Union and the other whaling nations to stop the whale killing. I have enclosed a petition form which I need for you to sign and return to me today. These petitions will be used to show the press, radio and TV the growing public sentiment against commercial whaling.

3. <u>Help us</u> reach our goal by sending a generous tax-deductible donation with your signed petition. A $15 contribution will help us reach 100 other concerned people like yourself; any contribution—whether $1,000 or $5—will be put to immediate use in reaching our petition goal and putting an end to the whale slaughter.

Our campaign has already had a substantial impact by focusing public attention on the needless slaughtering of whales. But, to achieve our goal of a total halt to commercial whaling, we must maintain the momentum we have begun by reaching more people with this crucial message.

To do this, we must raise $50,000 to pay for printing and mailing expenses during the next few months and we urgently need your support now.

Please send us your check in the enclosed reply envelope and be as generous as you can; we <u>need</u> your financial support and your petition today. We're counting on you.

Sincerely,

William J. Kardash
Campaign Coordinator

P. S.   <u>Public pressure works!</u> Because of the active public education campaign which we were able to wage in Australia, whaling operations will cease there in just a few months. We know public pressure works. . . but we need your help to make it happen. Please help us.[4]

Discussing the Persuasion Papers

1. What is the tone of each of the student compositions and of the professional writing sample? Do the writers seem to recognize a "moral obligation to support their arguments by adequate evidence and reason"?
2. Do the writers somewhere "state a proposition"? That is, do they clearly state what they are trying to persuade the reader to do?
3. Do the papers show evidence of research? Have the writers looked up facts and figures? Have they looked up *enough* facts and figures?
4. How interesting is the writing? Do the issues (the questions being argued) seem important?

Topics for Persuasion Papers

For your Major Writing Assignment for this chapter you may choose a subject important in your school, your community, your state, or the nation. To be worth writing about, the subject must be of interest and concern to readers. To be appropriate for an argumentation and persuasion paper, it must be a subject about which there are at least two points of view. It must also be a subject you know enough about (or can find out enough about) to be able to take an intelligent position.

ACTIVITY 8B

Choosing a Persuasion Topic

Either in class or outside of school with your friends and family, make a list of subjects that are being discussed in your school, your community, your state, or the nation at large.

In the preliminary stages, do not criticize any of the topics as being too broad, too narrow, too difficult, or too controversial. Instead, focus on getting as many ideas as possible. Then go through the list and judge each topic as to its suitability for a persuasion paper.

Common Cause is a large national organization which works for legislation to improve the quality of life in the United States. Following is a list of major issues that it prepared for prospective members. They were to rank them in order of importance.

Perhaps this list will help you select a national problem as a subject for your paper.

1. Establish an equitable tax system, eliminating tax preferences and loopholes.
2. Eliminate wasteful federal programs and subsidies gained by special-interest groups.
3. End unemployment by creating public service and public works jobs.
4. Legislate public financing for congressional election campaigns.
5. Develop enforceable programs for energy conservation.
6. Curb excessive military spending caused by unjustified new weapon systems, ineffective procurement, and just plain waste.
7. Strengthen conflict-of-interest and open meeting requirements.
8. Overhaul laws concerning the power of multi-national corporations.
9. Protect our physical health and natural resources by defending environmental standards.
10. Establish a federal consumer protection agency.
11. Enact legislation to ensure congressional review of intelligence operations such as the CIA and FBI.
12. Review the office of the Presidency, from the way we nominate and elect our chief executive to how we may guard against possible abuses of power to prevent future "Watergates."
13. Intensify action against discrimination based on sex, race, or ethnic background.
14. Organize citizen action to monitor Executive Branch decisions regarding placement of government contracts, subsidy programs, etc.
15. Enact federal no-fault automobile insurance legislation.
16. Create an independent office to prosecute cases of political corruption.
17. Protect the free press that exposed "Watergate" by guaranteeing the newsman's right to confidentiality of news sources.
18. Reform our outmoded welfare system.
19. Develop a workable program of health insurance.[5]

After you have done your data collecting, either by interviewing people, reading, performing an experiment, distributing a questionnaire, or any other way, you should come to the point where you can make a statement similar to this: "I believe strongly that _____ ." Then, after you have filled in the blank with the position you believe in, you can simply cross out the first four words and what is left is the thesis statement you will support.

The Structure of Persuasion

By looking at the examples of persuasion given in this chapter, you can see that persuasion comes in as many patterns as there are people writing. Not only do the writers differ, but their subjects require different presentations, and their audiences must be approached in different ways. Nonetheless, many writers use a kind of general pattern which they adapt as they write. Knowing this pattern may help you.

A PATTERN FOR PERSUASION

I. Introduction
   A. Begin by arousing interest, identifying the subject, and indicating its importance.
   B. State or imply your position on the subject.
II. Body
   A. Indicate one or two of the more important arguments *against* your position.
   B. Refute the positions you have just stated.
   C. Present additional arguments in support of your position.
III. Conclusion
   A. Restate your position on the issue.
   B. Present an emotional appeal for your position, perhaps warning what might happen if your position is not accepted.

Here is a very simple example of a persuasion paper written to promote interest in providing day-care centers in the United States. Notice how the writer follows the pattern for a persuasion paper. Do you agree with the arguments? Perhaps you might be interested in taking the opposite point of view for your persuasion paper.

DAY-CARE CENTERS FOR AMERICA'S YOUNG CHILDREN?

When Professor Yuri Bronfenbrenner of Cornell University compared the educational practices of the United States, the Soviet Union, and Red China, he found many interesting differences. One of the most disturbing differences he found, however, was that both the Soviet Union and China have well-developed and carefully regulated educational day-care arrangements for young children. Bronfenbrenner's conclusion about day-care arrangements in the United States can be summed up in his question, "Who cares for America's children?" and his answer to that question, "No one!"*

Actually, Bronfenbrenner is not being quite fair, for statistics for October 1977 showed that of the 9.2 million children in the United States between the ages of three and five, 88%, or 8.2 million, were in some kind of day-care arrangement outside of their own homes. Someone other than the mother has been caring for all but 12% of American preschool children, but the tragedy is that the care has ranged from superb to miserable, from licensed to illegal, from creative to sadistic.

These children were in day-care centers for two reasons: 1) In most cases their mothers had jobs (in 1978, almost 40% of mothers of children under 3 had jobs), and 2) American parents believe that pre-school attendance is good for children, and many choose it for their children, even when the mother is not working. Since so many American children, then, are in day-care situations, the United States owes its future citizens the protection and education that only a universal, voluntary, tax-supported day-care system can provide.

Some people insist that the United States cannot afford to pay for a system of universal day-care, and it is certainly true that certified teachers in a system like that of the public school would (and should) receive more than the minimum wage paid by many private, profit-making day-care centers. Moreover, these teachers should receive the health, retirement, and vacation benefits of professional workers.

The question is really not whether or not we can afford professional workers in the day-care centers. The question is really, "How can we afford not to protect our children?" Untrained workers who work for minimum wages cannot be expected to have a knowledge of child development, child psychology, psycho-motor coordination, or the other things required in caring for groups of children.**

A second objection to a system of universal day-care is that it interferes with American freedoms. Only dictatorships, so the argument goes, insist that children be placed with the state for indoctrination. However, 88% of American mothers of children between 3 and 5 have already chosen to place their children outside the home. Satisfactory safeguards regarding creeds, varieties of choice, and alternatives can certainly be worked out.

Some positive reasons for providing a universal system of tax-supported, voluntary day-care centers include the following. The United States is the only advanced, industrialized nation which does not now have such a system. Emerging lifestyles permit women to choose both careers and motherhood. And, finally, American democracy and social justice require that the children of mothers who must work from economic necessity be given an advantageous start in life.

For the last twenty years, the United Nations has conducted a continuing study of childrearing and educational practices throughout the world. Many of the published statistics have come as a shock to authorities in the United States. Guaranteed levels of minimal health care and nutrition for infants and mothers in the United States are shockingly low. The percentage of infant mortalities is shockingly high. Even as the nation tries to make provision so that all able-bodied welfare recipients can take jobs, it does little to provide for the children whose mothers must work. A civilized, advanced, industrialized society can surely provide the finances to care for its children.

A second reason to provide a universal system of voluntary, tax-supported day-care centers is that many women choose both motherhood and careers. Some women, of course, will continue to choose one role or the other, and that is as it should be, but others, even as they become mothers, plan to return to work, either because of economic necessity or because of their personal desire—and right—to have a career. For many women, the role of housewife and mother is fulfilling; for others, the role is limiting. It has been estimated that, by 1986, over half of the mothers with children under three will be working—and even a greater percentage of those with older children! The children of these working mothers must be provided for.

Finally, democracy and social justice require that all children be given the same opportunities and that the children of poor families, minority parents, and one-parent homes not be shunted off to inadequate, makeshift, and unlicensed day-care arrangements. Only when the same certified, high-level care is made available—on a voluntary basis—to all people, can we be certain that we are not violating our own democratic ideas.†

As more and more early childhood studies reveal the importance of the early years in forming a child's language, intellectual development, social attitudes, and behavioral predispositions, we shall have additional reasons for supporting universal, tax-supported, voluntary day-care centers. The care of our children is too important to be left to chance.

---

*Yuri Bronfenbrenner. *Three Worlds of Childhood*, Cornell University Videotape.

**William L. Pierce, "Who's Watching the Children," *American Educator*, Vol. 3, No. 1 (Spring 1979), pp. 10-13.

†Marilyn Rauth, "Day Care and the Public Schools," Ibid. pp. 14-15.

ACTIVITY 8C

Experimenting with the Structure of Persuasion

1. Select one of the topics you listed for Activity 8B. Then build an outline for an argument supporting a position regarding that topic. Follow the outline on page 195.

2. After you have worked through an outline, select one of the other topics you have listed and work out a rough outline to support a position on that subject. Remember that you cannot do a satisfactory job on such an outline unless you either already know something about the topic or do some research to get information. Choose a topic suitable for your Major Writing Assignment in this chapter. Working out the outline now will help you later.

3. After you have finished working out your outline, either in class or outside of school, talk through the outline with another person. Discuss the sequence of your ideas and the support you have provided for each point. Talk also about whether or not making such an outline is effective for you before you begin writing your paper. People differ, and some students find it hard to think through a paper in advance of writing it. Others believe that thinking a paper through and developing an outline saves time and effort later.

Tone

The following jingle emphasizes some people's attitude on argumentation:

In matters controversial
My perception's rather fine.
I always see both points of view:
The one that's wrong, and mine.

Whenever you attempt to convince or to persuade, you are, in a sense, asking your listener or reader to abandon a "safe, secure position" and emerge into a world of conflicting ideas and values. You must use a tone that will convince readers that you respect them and their point of view and that if they come to agree with you, you will not feel, or make them feel, that you have triumphed and they have lost. Above all, you must convince them that they will be "safe and secure" in the new position. By using a calm, reasoned, confidence-inspiring tone you can convey this assurance. You achieve such a tone by being logical, fair, and open, and by choosing appropriate words and sentences.

The consequences of using the wrong tone can be very costly. Socrates, one of the greatest philosophers of all time, once used the wrong tone—with fatal consequences. He had been charged with undermining the beliefs of his city and with "corrupting the youth" by encouraging them to ask questions. He was called before the Senate, tried, and convicted. No one really took these trials very seriously. They were looked upon as a warning when someone had stepped out of bounds. Most people, when warned in this way, apologized, received a light punishment, and were careful to conform more closely to the city's customs.

But even though Socrates had been convicted by 281 to 275 votes, and even though the charges were severe enough to deserve death, the great philosopher remained as firm, as haughty, and as confident as ever—a tone that the Senate resented. When the members asked him to suggest his punishment, he suggested that he be fined twenty-five drachmas, a very small sum, and also suggested that he be given a pension for life! When the judges voted on his punishment, 361 of them—80 more than had voted him guilty—voted for his death!

According to *Anthon's Classical Dictionary*, "... he would not have been condemned to death if he had not provoked the anger of the court by a deportment [a tone] which must have been interpreted as a sign of profound contempt or of insolent defiance."[6] Most people believe that Socrates deliberately used this tone because he believed that his death would broaden his influence and increase the impact of his ideas. Choose the tone which will best accomplish your purpose.

ACTIVITY 8D

Examining Passages for Tone

Read each of the following selections carefully and then write a generalization about the tone and about a reader's probable reaction to the tone. Be concrete as you support your generalization. Develop each generalization into a short paper.

> 1. Some Carrollwood residents can be as obstinate as they are rich.
>
> They proved that Monday night when an overflow crowd at the Carrollwood Recreation Center hooted, interrupted, jeered and generally made the evening miserable for the political candidates they had invited to speak.
>
> The confrontation provoked arguments not just between voters of the plush subdivision and candidates but between the residents themselves, some of whom called for at least a show of courtesy to their guests.
>
> But even that suggestion was hooted down.
>
> The jeering began as soon as the first speaker, County Commission Chairman Fran Davin began to speak and reached its crescendo several speakers later during District 3 Commissioner Charles Bean's turn.
>
> Bean brought forth a barrage of incredulous guffaws when he told his constituents—who are steaming over increases of up to 76 percent on 1978 real property taxes—that even though they don't know it yet they would "realize a savings" in their personal property taxes.[7]
>
> —Kim I. Eisler

(In this selection, consider both the tone of the meeting described and the tone of the writer's report.)

> 2. **Dear Ann Landers:** So you think today's teen-agers are just great? You must be living in an air-tight capsule, completely isolated from the real world.
>
> I'm enclosing a clipping from the *Denver Post*, but I'll bet this incident could have happened in any of 200 other cities in the United States.
>
> I quote: "A 15-year-old girl was arrested about 2:30 p.m. Wednesday on suspicion of damaging seats aboard a bus on which an off-duty policeman was riding.
>
> "Police said Det. Edward Roy was working off duty for the transit system and riding a bus in East Denver. A group of youths began tearing up a rear seat, pulling out pieces of foam rubber padding and throwing them around. One youth tried to ignite the foam rubber with a cigarette lighter.

"The bus driver was instructed to drive to the East Denver police station, where the girl was arrested. Four other suspects, all boys, escaped through the back door and windows of the bus."

What do you have to say for American teen-agers, now, stupid?

— Tip of The Iceberg

3. **Dear Ice:** Do you think it's fair to put all teen-agers in the same bag with those Denver hooligans? At the very moment those kooks were tearing up the bus, thousands of teens were riding public transportation and behaving themselves—some even offering their seats to the aged and the infirm, although many people insist such things don't happen anymore.

Unfortunately, it's the troublemakers who make news. Who wants to read that a half million kids rode buses today in 200 cities and not one of them tried to set fire to the seats? Decent conduct gets very little press because it's not exciting. Sorry, but those are the facts, friend.[8]

4. . . . [An] example of cop-out "realism" is the way some communities are dealing with cigarette-smoking by teenagers and pre-teenagers. Special rooms are now being set aside for students who want to smoke. No age restrictions are set; freshmen have the same lighting-up privileges as seniors.

The thinking behind the new school policy is similar to the "realism" behind New York's decision to legalize off-track betting and the numbers game. It is felt that since the youngsters are going to smoke anyway, the school might just as well make it possible for them to do it in the open rather than feel compelled to do it furtively in back corridors and washrooms.

Parents and teachers may pride themselves on their "realism" in such approaches. What they are actually doing is finding a convenient rationalization for failing to uphold their responsibility. The effect of their supposedly "realistic" policy is to convert a ban into a benediction. By sanctioning that which they deplore, they become part of the problem they had the obligation to meet. What they regard as common sense turns out to be capitulation. . . .

The school has no right to jettison standards just because of difficulties in enforcing them. The school's proper response is not to abdicate but to extend its efforts in other directions. It ought to require regular lung examinations for its youngsters. It ought to schedule regular sessions with parents and youngsters at which reports on these examinations can be considered. It ought to bring in cancer researchers who can run films for students showing the difference between the brackish, pulpy lungs caused by cigarette smoking and the smooth pink tissue of healthy lungs. The schools should schedule visits to hospital wards for lung cancer patients. In short, educators should take the U.S. Surgeon-General's report on cigarettes seriously.[9]

—Norman Cousins

5. I am certain that my fellow Americans expect that on my induction into the Presidency I will address them with a candor and a decision which the present situation of our Nation impels. This is preeminently the time to speak the truth, the whole truth, frankly and boldly. Nor need we

shrink from honestly facing conditions in our country today. This great Nation will endure as it has endured, will revive and will prosper. So, first of all, let me assert my firm belief that the only thing we have to fear is fear itself—nameless, unreasoning, unjustified terror which paralyzes needed efforts to convert retreat into advance. In every dark hour of our national life a leadership of frankness and vigor has met with that understanding and support of the people themselves which is essential to victory. I am convinced that you will again give this support to leadership in these critical days.

—from the First Inaugural Address of
President Franklin D. Roosevelt

6. Yossarian looked at him soberly and tried another approach. "Is Orr crazy?"

"He sure is," Doc Daneeka said.

"Can you ground him?"

"I sure can. But first he has to ask me to. That's part of the rule."

"Then why doesn't he ask you to?"

"Because he's crazy," Doc Daneeka said. "He has to be crazy to keep flying combat missions after all the close calls he's had. Sure, I can ground Orr. But first he has to ask me to."

"That's all he has to do to be grounded?"

"That's all. Let him ask me."

"And then you can ground him?" Yossarian asked.

"No. Then I can't ground him."

"You mean there's a catch?"

"Sure, there's a catch," Doc Daneeka replied. "Catch-22. Anyone who wants to get out of combat duty isn't really crazy."

There was only one catch and that was Catch-22, which specified that a concern for one's own safety in the face of dangers that were real and immediate was the process of a rational mind. Orr was crazy and could be grounded. All he had to do was ask; and as soon as he did, he would no longer be crazy and would have to fly more missions. Orr would be crazy to fly more missions and sane if he didn't, but if he was sane he had to fly them, if he flew them he was crazy and didn't have to; but if he didn't want to he was sane and had to. Yossarian was moved very deeply by the absolute simplicity of this clause of Catch-22 and let out a respectful whistle.[10]

—Joseph Heller

Exposition Within Argumentation

Most of the techniques used in writing good exposition are also used in writing argumentation and persuasion. Most argumentation or persuasion papers make an attempt to interest the reader, explain their intention in a thesis statement near the beginning, and support generalizations with specific, concrete details.

In addition, they provide helps for a reader (transitions, definitions, summaries) and they present information in an order that is both understandable and effective. These expository techniques are used in other modes of writing, including analysis, process papers, opinion papers as well as argumentation and persuasion.

ACTIVITY 8E

Recognizing Expository Techniques

Look for at least two examples of argumentation or persuasion articles and prepare a one-page report on the expository techniques you find in them. The preceding section may help you identify them, but you may wish to look over the activities in the preceding chapters for more specific techniques, such as those used in analysis, process, or opinion papers.

You can find brief articles of argumentation or persuasion in many places. Try the editorials in your newspaper or such magazines as *Saturday Review*, *Harper's*, or *Time*. Look at published speeches in your newspaper (if it provides complete texts of speeches). Examine "Letters to the Editor," which appear in your local newspaper when an important issue is pending.

End your analysis with a comment on the writer's tone. Does he or she indicate a respect for the opposition and a note of honest inquiry?

Sentence Length

High-school freshmen average about 17.3 words per sentence. University freshmen average 19.9 words per sentence. Professional writers average 20.9 words per sentence (depending upon their subject, their audience, and their purpose). These figures are based on a recent study.

Average sentence length alone, however, does not tell the whole story. Mature writers may *average* about twenty words per sentence, but to get variety in their work, they consciously try to write sentences of different lengths. One study reveals that out of every ten sentences, six were of about average length (eighteen to twenty-two words), two were extra long (more than twenty-five words), and two were short (fewer than twelve words).

ACTIVITY 8F

Checking Sentence Length

1. Take three of the compositions you have written this year and determine the following:

   A. What is the average length of your sentences in each paper?

   B. What percentage of the sentences in each paper have under twelve words? What percentage of sentences are over twenty-five words?

2. Choose a relatively long paragraph (about 250 words) and revise it. Try to get the 2-6-2 ratio for long, average, and short sentences. Try to include one or two questions, imperatives, or inversions.

3. After you have analyzed your own sentences, choose two modern writers whose work you have enjoyed, and analyze a number of sentences from their writing. Note to what extent variations in sentence length differ for each. Try to come to some conclusions regarding the effect of sentence length on style.

   You might wish to look at paragraphs from such writers as Ernest Hemingway, William Faulkner, John O'Hara, Thomas Wolfe, F. Scott Fitzgerald, John Updike, Winston Churchill, Richard Wright, Ray Bradbury, Shirley Jackson, Kurt Vonnegut, Ralph Ellison, Gordon Parks, Lorraine Hansberry, Saul Bellow, Langston Hughes, Bernard Malamud, or John Steinbeck.

Supporting Your Position

Before attempting to persuade an audience or a reader to adopt your point of view, it is essential to gather your facts. They are the ammunition in your campaign. For example, a concerned woman recently conducted a three-week campaign against welfare spending, during which the charge was made that a woman and two children on welfare would receive $10,000 annually. In response, another private citizen, who is a social worker, revealed the actual facts:

"Given such a hypothetical client, the maximum she could receive would be $166 monthly or $1,992 annually. From that amount a person on welfare would have to pay rent, utilities, cost of food stamps, clothing, as well as any household items not covered by food stamps. The maximum stamp benefits such a person could receive would be $144 a month or $1,728 annually. The other major benefit provided by aid to Families with Dependent Children is Medicaid eligibility. Unless a family member has a catastrophic illness, requiring extensive hospitalization, these benefits along with other "special free programs" could not possibly total $6,280, the amount necessary to make the $10,000 my opponent says such a person would receive."[11]

—Clyde A. Benedix

This is an instance where a person with a legitimate interest in tax reform used the time and energy to make her position known to the public. However, her argument was severely damaged when a person with an opposing viewpoint showed that her statements were "unsubstantiated or misleading" and backed up his claim with statistics.

If you fail to support your position with facts that can be verified, you give your opponent a golden opportunity to destroy your credibility.

Dealing with Controversial Issues

It is important to remember that in argumentation and persuasion the purpose is not to "win" at all costs, but to present facts and opinions in a sincere effort to arrive at truth. In presenting one side in a discussion, writers must give due consideration to opposing points of view and practice diplomacy in presenting their own.

Often writers of argumentation or persuasion are aware that they are taking positions that are unpopular. They must offer facts and opinions in a calm, reasonable manner—otherwise they will alienate those in opposition and fail to persuade any who might be neutral. In order both to be fair to those who hold other opinions and to get a hearing themselves, they must proceed diplomatically. Often writers acknowledge the value of the alternative ideas and, sometimes, borrow them and build on them.

ACTIVITY 8G

Practicing Diplomacy on Controversial Issues

1. Choose some current issue in your school and prepare a very brief talk in support of what you believe is the *unpopular*

side. Concentrate on the introduction and on your manner of revealing your position.

2. Appoint a class secretary to list some of the techniques that different students use to present their material diplomatically.

Students in other classes have spoken on such ideas as the following:

Why the number of required book reports should be doubled

Why football should be changed to an intramural sport

Why a dress code is necessary

Why school dances should be opened to dropouts and to students from neighboring high schools

Why censorship in school publications is desirable

■ MAJOR WRITING ASSIGNMENT

A PERSUASION PAPER

Reread the examples of persuasion papers in this chapter and note the organization of each. Choose a real subject. You may use one of those you listed for Activity 8B or one of those you outlined in Activity 8C. For that topic complete this sentence:

I believe strongly that _____.

Then, if you have not already done so, work through a possible outline following the pattern in Activity 8C.

As you begin writing your paper, keep in mind your moral responsibility to use evidence and logic and your practical need to maintain an acceptable tone.

As you develop your argument, work on variety of sentence structure by using different sentence patterns and by varying your sentence length.

Feel free to depart from the "Structure of Persuasion" outline given to you on page 195, but be sure that you have a valid reason for doing so.

Be sure to allow enough time in writing your paper to take advantage of the techniques described in Chapter 2, Polishing and Perfecting.

Chapter 9
Writing Letters, Memos, and Reports

Before 1900, letter writing was a very important part of most businesses. Men wearing green eyeshades and black pull-on sleeves to protect their white shirts sat on rows of high stools and wrote endlessly. Charles Dickens' Bob Cratchit in "A Christmas Carol" was such a copyist, and so was Bartleby in Herman Melville's "Bartleby the Scrivener."

Personal letter writing was also important at that time. Many people kept personal secretaries to prepare and file their correspondence. In the United States today, over fifteen hundred collections of letters are available. Many of these are letters written by people who are outstanding for some reason. The letters that survive of Lord Byron, for example, number over three thousand and fill ten volumes; they provide a vivid insight into the character of this famous poet. Other collections of letters are simply interesting for their descriptions of the life and times of various people.

Some people say that letter writing has declined in importance, in grace and precision, and in volume. It's true that many people depend on the telephone and on greeting cards to communicate with friends and relatives, and that businesses often have their own Telex machines and special discounted long-distance telephone arrangements.

Nonetheless, letter writing remains important. From 1963 to 1978, the volume of letters mailed has increased by thirty-five percent. Because of this volume, the Post Office is considering making a system of microfilming available. During the Second World War, over one billion letters were reduced to one-quarter inch square microfilmed pictures, flown to their destinations, and then printed full-size once more. Instead of weighing fifty pounds, a bag of eighteen hundred letters on microfilm would weigh only seven ounces. This would save a great deal of cost and labor.

Soon you will be writing some of the most important letters of your life. Here are two letters similar to those you may be writing.

6516 Walton Way
Tampa, Florida 33612
October 14, 1980

Director of Admissions
Pembroke State University
Pembroke, North Carolina 28372

Dear Director:

I am a senior at King High School in Tampa, and I plan to enter college in the fall of 1981. I am a good student with a grade point average of 3.2 on a 4-point scale and a current standing of about 56 in a class of 523 students.

I would be very grateful if you would send me a copy of your current catalog, together with admissions information and application forms.

Because I shall require financial assistance, I would also like information about scholarships, assistantships, work programs, or other student aid that is available.

Sincerely yours,

Nancy Dee West

Nancy Dee West

Nancy does not have personal stationery with a letterhead. Note that she provides her home address and the date in her typewritten heading.

How does Nancy avoid the problem of not knowing whether she is writing to a man or a woman?

Nancy has chosen to use *block style* for her letter. That is, all lines are "flush left"—beginning at the left-hand margin. She doublespaces between elements of the letter (heading, inside address, salutation, body, and complimentary close) as well as between paragraphs. Notice that Nancy has allowed enough space between the complimentary close and her typed name to write her signature.

Note, in the model on the opposite page, the "indented form" which you may use in handwritten letters.

Not too long ago, the heading, complimentary close, and signature began two-thirds of the way across the page. The electric typewriter influenced the more modern placement. Why?

Roy Williams answered this advertisement from the classified section of his local newspaper.

Handwritten letters are usually written in *indented style* (slanted) because it is very hard to get the neat, accurate block of the typewriter in handwriting.

Roy uses as his inside address the exact address given in the advertisement. Note that he "runs over" the name of the company to the second line when the extended name would be awkward on one line.

Although the masculine "Gentlemen" is still common in writing to a company, many people object to the fact that it ignores the increasing number of women in the work force.

Notice that Roy specifies how he knows about the job and immediately tells why he is writing.

Roy must prove that he has had experience, can work with minimum supervision, is accurate with figures, can prepare readable reports, and can accept responsibility.

Which of these does he do well? Which might he improve on? How?

Would including the exact address of the school be an additional courtesy? Why or why not?

Roy can assume that the company will know it can reach him at his home address or through the school. What else might he have included to enable an official to reach him more easily?

Why does Roy mention that he doesn't intend to go to college? Why will this not count against him?

INVENTORY CONTROL CLERK. High School grad. Some experience helpful. Able to work with minimum supervision. Accurate with figures, able to prepare readable reports and accept responsibility. Good starting salary, company benefits. Apply in own handwriting to Safety Equipment Co. of Idaho, 324 20th St., Boise, 83701.

3314 Kelsey Street
Boise, Idaho 83701
May 23, 1980

Safety Equipment Company
Of Idaho
324-20th Street
Boise, Idaho 83701

Gentlemen:

I have just read your advertisement for an Inventory Control Clerk in the *Boise Advertiser* for May 22, and I should like to apply for the job.

I am a graduating senior at Boise East High School, and I will be available to start work after June 7. Actually, if you need me sooner, my counselor has informed me that the school will make arrangements for my early release these last few days.

I have taken a vocational program in school, concentrating on metal working. For the last two years I have served part of the time as tool-room manager and part of the time as assistant foreman for Mr. Phelps.

You can request information about me from

Mr. Lynn Phelps
Shop Instructor
Boise East High School

and

Mr. Elwood Peterson
Principal
Boise East High School

I will be happy to send you any additional information you would like and to authorize release of my school records to you. I can come for an interview at your convenience.

I do not plan to attend college, and I am looking for the kind of position you are offering — a permanent job with responsibility, satisfaction, and an opportunity for growth.

Sincerely yours,
Roy Williams

This is the letter Nancy received from Pembroke State.

PEMBROKE STATE UNIVERSITY
PEMBROKE, NORTH CAROLINA 28372

October 21, 1980

Nancy Dee West
6516 Walton Way
Tampa, Florida 33610

Dear Ms. West:

Thank you very much for your letter of October 14 and your indication
of an interest in Pembroke State University. Our campus located in
beautiful southeastern North Carolina, our wide range of liberal arts
offerings, and our small intimate student body (2,000) are proving increasingly attractive to students like you.

I am enclosing, as you requested, a copy of our catalog, information and
forms for admission, and several brochures regarding social and academic
opportunities on campus.

I have referred your question regarding financial aid to Mrs. Esther Jacobs
of our Student Financial Aid Office. You will be hearing from her within
the very near future.

If you have any additional questions, please feel free to write or call.
If you and your parents are near Pembroke some time during this academic
year, we would be delighted to have you stop for a tour of the campus.

Very truly yours,

Warren Baker

Warren Baker
Director of Admissions

WB/sd

Enclosures

A CAMPUS OF THE UNIVERSITY OF NORTH CAROLINA

Notice how the letterhead makes it unnecessary for the writer to provide anything except the date of the letter.

This is the usual placement for the inside address. Some writers place the inside address at the end of the letter for two reasons: 1. It puts first things first—that is, the message at the beginning; and 2. It makes the inside address easier to find for filing and retrieval purposes.

Note that this writer double-spaces between paragraphs and uses block style. What are some advantages of block style?

These initials remind the reader (and the writers, too, in case it is necessary to fix responsibility for a decision or an error) that Warren Baker (WB) wrote the letter and that a secretary with the initials "sd" typed it.

The word "Enclosure" reminds the secretary to be sure to include enclosure as promised and it enables Nancy to be sure that she received everything that Mr. Baker intended to send.

ACTIVITY 9A

Exploring Various Kinds of Business Letters

Job application letters and college-entrance application letters are two kinds of letters that you are going to find most important in the near future. However, there are dozens of other kinds of letters. Working either alone or with a group, try to collect from your family, friends, and relatives a number of different kinds of letters. Write examples of different types of letters if you can't find real letters.

This is the letter Roy received from the employment manager of Safety Equipment Company of Idaho.

This form of inside address is relatively new, but think how much time it saves a secretary.

Many people think business letters are cold, detached, objective, and formal. Nonsense! They *can* be, but they can also project an image of friendliness, cordiality, and interest. What are the signs in this letter that Mr. Swenson wanted to project such an image?

The cc: indicates that a carbon copy has gone to the person indicated; in this case, the partner.

SAFETY EQUIPMENT COMPANY OF IDAHO
324—20TH STREET
BOISE, IDAHO 83701

YOUR SAFETY—OUR CONCERN
208 832-3821

May 25, 1980

Mr. Roy Williams, 3314 Kelsey Street, Boise, Idaho 83701

Dear Roy:

Ordinarily, my partner and I would prefer to have someone older and more experienced as our Inventory Control Clerk, but both Mr. Phelps and Mr. Peterson gave you the highest recommendations when we called them.

We would like to have you come to our main office at 324 - 20th Street on Friday, June 6 at 4:00 p.m. so that we can both take a look at you.

We're both pleased with the way you express yourself and with the record you've made in school, so we're looking forward to meeting you.

Cordially,

Ben Swenson

Ben Swenson

BS/nc
cc: Bennett

Try to include these types:

Letters of complaint
Letters of inquiry
Sales letters
Letters of application for jobs
Letters requesting adjustments or explanations
Letters of application for college
Letters of application for membership
Letter to a radio or television program requesting air time to present a point of view

Letter to college indicating acceptance or rejection of a place in the freshman class
Letter to an editor explaining a point of view
Letter to an editor challenging a statement
Letter to an elected official
Letter to a government agency requesting information or service
Letter to an organization requesting a speaker or program

After each example or model letter, list some situations in which you or other people in your age group might want to write such letters.

ACTIVITY 9B

Exploring Opportunities for Letters of Application

1. If you are planning on working after high school, skim the want ads of your local newspaper and find several jobs which you think you would like and which would require letters of application. (Some firms discourage letters. They require the person to appear for an interview.) Discuss with your friends or a small group the information you would give and how you would organize such a letter. Actually write one or more such letters and submit them to the group for editing, proofreading, and judging.

2. If you are planning on going to college, discuss with your parents, teachers, and guidance counselors the kinds of schools in which your interests and talents could be best developed. Get the addresses of such schools from the Guidance Office, the library, or from the list in the back of the latest college edition of *Webster's New World Dictionary*. Your library will also have such books as the following:

> Brown, Judy, and Donald Grossfield. *I Wish I'd Known That Before I Went to College.* New York: Simon and Schuster, 1966.
>
> Gummere, Richard M., Jr. *How to Survive Education: Before, During, and After College.* New York: Harcourt, Brace, Jovanovich, 1971.
>
> Kesselman, Judi R. *Stopping Out: A Guide to Leaving College and Getting Back In.* Philadelphia: M. Evans & Co., Inc., 1976.

Write and mail your letter to the one or two colleges in which you are truly interested. It is not fair to ask a college to send you an expensive catalog if you do not plan to apply.

Form and Content in Business Letters

At one time, most schools taught a single form—or at most, two forms—for the business letter. Even at that time, however, individuals and businesses used several different forms. The important consideration is that the letter be neat, clear, and functional. The four model letters at the beginning of this chapter indicate some of the variety you can find in modern business letters. Your scrapbook collections will indicate additional varieties.

Your teacher may let you experiment with various forms. However, many businesses and almost all publishing houses develop a *style sheet* to ensure that their correspondence projects a consistent image. The skeleton letter pictured here shows the six parts of a conventional business letter—heading, inside address, salutation, body, closing, and signature. Notice their placement and how they are punctuated.

```
58 Murdoch Avenue
Oak Hill, Michigan  48015
January 27, 1980
```
··········· Heading:
your street address,
city, state, zip code, and the
date

··· Inside address:
name of person to whom you
are writing
name of firm or organization
street address (if any),
city, state, and zip code

```
Mr. John Mattoon
Office of Public Affairs
U.S. Fish and Wildlife Service
Washington, D.C.  20210
```

```
Dear Mr. Mattoon:
```
··· Salutation:
if you do not know the person's
name or title, you may use
Dear Sir or Madam

··· Body

```
Sincerely,
```
····· Closing: you may use
Very truly yours,
Yours truly,
Sincerely yours, or
Sincerely

Eunice Barker

```
Eunice Barker (Ms.)
```
Signature:
···· your name in your own
handwriting
········ your name typed, showing how
you wish to be addressed

```
Ms. Eunice Barker
58 Murdoch Avenue
Oak Hill, Michigan  48015
```

```
                Mr. John Mattoon
                Office of Public Affairs
                U.S. Fish and Wildlife Service
                Washington, D.C.  20210
```

Stamp

Return address:
your name and address

Name and address of person
to whom you are writing.
Include proper title—Miss,
Mr., Mrs., Ms., Dr., Professor,
etc.

Guidelines for Writing Business Letters

Unless your teacher specifies a certain form, refer to the models at the beginning of this chapter and to the skeleton business letter on page 213. Observe the following guidelines for writing business letters.

1. Use appropriate stationery. In most cases you will choose standard, white, 8½ × 11-inch sheets. Brightly colored stationery attracts attention, but it makes a poor impression on some people. Small or over-sized sheets are easy to lose and hard to file.

2. Type, if possible; if not, use blue or black ink. Use one side of the page only.

3. Center your letter horizontally on the page, leaving at least one-inch margins on each side. Estimate the probable length of your letter and begin far enough from the top of the page so that the letter will also be centered vertically on the page. If you must use more than one page, allow at least an inch and a half at the bottom of the first page. Plan ahead, so that several lines of the body of your letter can be written on the second page.

4. Use one style—either block or indented (slanted)—throughout the letter. Block is more often used in typed letters; indented, in handwritten letters.

5. Using one of the patterns in the models, include this information:

   a. Your address (including the ZIP code).

   b. The date.

   c. The exact name and address (including the ZIP code) of the person to whom you are writing.

d. Your signature. Below your handwritten signature, type your name, showing how you wish to be addressed in a return letter.

6. Double-space between elements in the letter (heading, inside address, salutation, complimentary close, and signature) and either double-space between paragraphs or indicate their beginning by indenting.

7. For a letter written on 8½ × 11 - inch stationery, use a long envelope. Place the return address in the upper left and the main address in the lower center of the envelope.

8. Fold the letter up from the bottom about a third of the way, then down from the top. Place the letter in the envelope so that it will be right side up when taken from the envelope and unfolded.

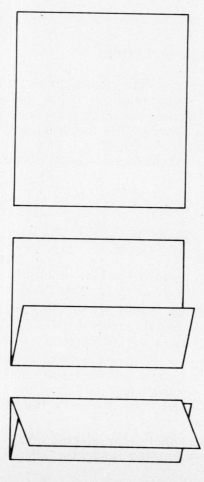

In planning the content of your business letter, follow these suggestions:

1. Be clear.
2. Be accurate.
3. Be brief.

Organize your material in such a way that you answer these three questions:

1. Why am I writing?
2. What will the reader need to know in order to understand and be willing to act on my request?
3. What is my request? What do I want the reader to do?

ACTIVITY 9C

Planning Business Letters

Consult this list of possible places to write to, and think of situations in which you might write to such places. Plan the contents for the letter, answering in a separate paragraph each of the three questions above. Write the letter and follow the procedures for editing and proofreading.

If your letter performs a real function, prepare a final draft and mail it.

ORGANIZATIONS YOU CAN WRITE TO

Here are some places to which you can write a business letter and expect a reply.

1. Write to the American Council of Life Insurance, Dept. SR, 277 Park Avenue, New York, New York 10017, asking for a copy of the Social Report for the current year.
2. Write to the National Archives (NEPS), Washington, D. C. 20408, asking for a list of currently available illustrations and postcards.
3. Write to the Consumer Information Center, Pueblo, Colorado 81009, asking for the latest edition of the Consumer Information Catalog, which includes more than two hundred items of interest, many free.
4. Write to the National Solar Heating and Cooling Information Center, P. O. Box 1607, Rockville, Maryland 20850, for free

information about solar heating and cooling and additional sources of information.

5. Write to the Tire Industry Safety Council, Box 1801, Washington, D. C. 20013, asking for free information on how to choose and care for tires.

6. If you have a question about money, investments, the economy, or costs, write to Moneywise, Box 353, Astor Station, Boston, Massachusetts 02123.

7. If you find a television commercial especially irritating, write a letter to ADmonitor, Hearthside Studio, Box 425, Pleasantville, New Jersey 08232, which will transmit your complaint to advertising executives with the power to act on it.

8. If you have doubts about a charity or other organization which is collecting money, write to the Division of Licensing, Office of the Secretary of State, your State Capitol, and ask whether or not the group is registered.

9. Write a letter of request for information, complaint, or suggestion to one of the major automobile manufacturers:
American Motors Corporation, Owner Relations, 14250 Plymouth Road, Detroit, Michigan 48232.
Ford Motor Company, The American Road, Dearborn, Michigan 48121.
Chevrolet Motor Division, 3044 W. Grand Blvd., Detroit, Michigan 48202.
Chrysler Corporation, 12000 Lynn Townsend, Highland Park, Michigan 48203.
Toyota Motor Sales, 2055 W. 190 Street, Torrance, California 90504.
Volkswagen Motors, Customer Relations, 3737 Lake Cook Road, Deerfield, Illinois 60015.

10. Write to Greetings Office, The White House, Washington, D. C. 20500 giving the birthdate of a person over eighty or the wedding anniversary of a couple married fifty years in order to get an official greeting card from the President of the United States. Be sure to allow four to five weeks for delivery.

11. Write to the U.S. Department of Energy, Washington, D. C. 20585, requesting Fact Sheet No. 91 (Home Insulation Safety) and Fact Sheet DOE/CS-0017 (Insulation) to learn how to conserve home heating fuel safely.

12. Write to Public Relations Department, New York Stock Exchange, 11 Wall Street, New York, New York 10005, requesting information on how the stock market works.

Writing a Résumé

Sometimes you need to tell more about yourself than you can conveniently include in the body of a letter of application. Refresh your memory by rereading the letter of application on page

```
Resume of                                          445 Columbia Street
                                                   Waterloo, Iowa 50701
Marilyn Harris                                     Telephone: 515 - 932-3091

                              Personal Background


                                  Education

1977-1980      East Waterloo Senior High School (Graduation pending)
1975-1977      John Logan Junior High School, Logan Avenue, Waterloo
1968-1974      Hawthorne Elementary School, Franklin Street, Waterloo

Honors:        National Honor Society
               Letters in three sports
               Sports editor for Orange and Black (Student Newspaper)

School Clubs:  Girls' Athletic Association
               Y-Teens
               Science Club
               Writer's Inc. (Creative Writing Club)

                                 Employment

1980           Big "T" Food Mart, West Parker Street
               Checker (Part-time: 15 hours per week)
1979           Waterloo Public Library, East Side Branch
               Page (Shelving and checking out books)
               (Part-time: 10 hours per week)
1978           Friedl's Cafe, 484 Fourth Street, Waterloo
               Waitress (Part-time: 15 hours per week)

Travel:        Trips to Chicago, Minneapolis, Des Moines with school groups
               Family vacation to Washington, D. C. and New York City
               American Institute for Foreign Study program in London,
                   England (two weeks)

Hobbies:       Sports (Volleyball, basketball, softball)
               Reading
               Hiking and Camping

                                 Career Goal

               1. B.A. in Sociology
               2. Employment in social work or other service agency

                                 References

                             Available on request
```

209. After all, such letters should be brief, and by the time you explain why you're writing, give a little background, and make your request, there's little room for a lengthy discussion of yourself. Instead of including such material in the body of the letter, enclose a résumé.

A résumé is a summary of facts about yourself. These facts include your personal situation, your education, your work experience, and any appropriate information about events in your life, your interests, and ambitions. Opposite is such a résumé.

The contents of a résumé can be organized and presented in different ways. Depending upon your purpose in preparing it, you may include different information or stress different ideas.

The required elements of a résumé are these:

1. It should present you in the best possible light. Avoid errors in grammar and spelling.
2. It should be concise and direct.
3. It should be organized so that the nature of the information in each section is clear.
4. It should be neat and attractive. Usually résumés are typed, with headings underlined or in capital letters, and with lots of white space.
5. It should be factual and honest.

Events which occur over a period of time, such as schooling and employment, are usually listed in reverse chronological order, with the most recent experience listed first and working backward to the earliest.

Usually, the information most relevant to the purpose for which you are sending a résumé is listed at the beginning. For example, if you are applying for college, you would probably place your educational background and school honors first. If you are applying for a job, you would probably place your work experience first.

You can list people who will recommend you, together with their addresses, but if you do so, be sure that you have obtained their permission first.

ACTIVITY 9D

Writing a Personal Résumé

Collect the information necessary to write a résumé. Discuss your material with someone who knows your background, and then write the résumé, varying the form, if necessary, to suit your purpose. Before submitting your finished résumé for editing and proofreading, prepare a cover letter that tells why you are submitting the résumé and what you are requesting.

Preparing Memos

Memos, or memoranda, are simple notes, usually on a single subject, to be circulated *within* an organization, rather than between organizations. They are used to communicate information, to summarize oral agreements so that all participants are certain of exactly what was decided, and to record decisions so that at some later time there will be a notation of exactly who was responsible for a particular action. Notice the differences and similarities between memos and business letters.

MEMO

October 21, 1980

To: Everyone Concerned with "The Tiger's Cry"

From: Wilma Schuerer, Student Director *W.S.*

Subject: Dress Rehearsal Schedule

1. At a meeting with Dr. Smith in her office on Tuesday, October 20, the Board of Advisors agreed on a rehearsal schedule limited to 2 1/2 hours per night, three nights a week (Monday, Wednesday, and Friday) from 7-9:30 p.m. The band room has been reserved for these rehearsals beginning October 27 through November 12.

2. Because we need to set up and practice in the gymnasium but cannot do so after school when the basketball team is practicing, Dr. Smith has agreed to excuse everyone in the production from 12:30 p.m. to 3:00 p.m. for dress rehearsals on Thursday, November 13, and Friday, November 14. The homecoming performance will be on Saturday, November 15.

3. Band Director Schubert and Coach Rice have accepted this arrangement.

Here, for example, is a memo, or memorandum (note the plural form in the first sentence above and the singular form in this sentence). As the director of the school talent show, Wilma talked with Dr. Smith, her principal, about the rehearsal schedule. When Dr. Smith gave her permission to have dress rehearsal on school time, Wilma wrote a memo, duplicated it, and sent it to everyone involved. Her memo satisfied all three reasons that memos are written:

1. It communicated information.
2. It summarized the oral agreements of the conference so that everyone would know exactly what was agreed upon.
3. It fixed the responsibility on Dr. Smith for releasing students from class. (Obviously, Wilma wouldn't want to be held responsible for that decision.)

Note that Wilma simply initialed the line on which her name appears, rather than signing the memo formally. Note also that a memo is much simpler than a business letter. What elements of the business letter does it leave out? How does the form differ? Why can a memo, which is prepared for *internal* circulation (circulation *within* an organization) afford to take short cuts forbidden to a letter, which is usually prepared for *external* circulation (circulation *between* organizations or between organizations and individuals)?

ACTIVITY 9E

Listing Situations Calling for Memos

You probably belong to several different school, church, or community organizations. List several situations in which a memo to one or more members in one of these organizations would be an appropriate communication. Write one or more memos. Submit your memos for editing and proofreading. Here are some examples to get you started:

1. The science club circulates information about a trip to a local planetarium.
2. The Sunshine Club arranges a special gift and recognition for Mrs. Herrick, the adviser.
3. The Girls' Athletic Association must change the date of the faculty-alumnae game.

4. The Creative Writing Club agrees on a method of choosing the judges for the annual contest.
5. The Service Club plans the annual canned goods collection for Thanksgiving.

Writing Reports

At times, people refuse to accept and believe what they see with their own eyes. According to Vesalius, a famous doctor in the 1500s, another doctor in an anatomy class once told his students as he dissected a body, "The great teacher Hippocrates said that there is a vein in this spot right here." But as he dissected the body, he found no vein. However, instead of challenging the statement of Hippocrates, he said, "Unfortunately, this body, too, is wrong. In thirty years of teaching, I have never found a body which has the vein where it is supposed to be." Because people ignored their own observations and depended upon the pronouncements of ancient authorities, many incorrect and harmful beliefs continued for centuries. Fortunately, Vesalius was willing to challenge the scientific assumptions of his day.

Consider the accountant trying to improve efficiency in a business office, the industrial engineer working to solve a problem in the design of a machine, or the agricultural scientist studying ways to increase a crop's yield. In almost every field, observing carefully and reporting those observations are very important in trying to make a present situation better.

Critic Karl E. Meyer was bothered because he felt that television is not treated as seriously as it should be by modern magazines. He said, "An off-Broadway play, seen at most by thousands of people, is taken more seriously than a TV miniseries that will be viewed by tens of millions."[1]

Was Meyer correct in his opinion? Was he right in being disturbed? The only way to know would be to do some research and find out. He devised a very simple little study to find out whether or not he was correct. He took thirteen consecutive issues of *Time* magazine and recorded the number of columns devoted to books, cinema, music, art, theater, show business, and television. Then he could say for certain that he was right. In thirteen issues, *Time* devoted one hundred and two columns to books, fifty-two columns to movies, forty-two and a half columns to music, thirty-nine columns to art, twenty-five to theater, twenty-seven to show business in general, and only six to television.

If Meyer had been writing a report for business, industry, or science, he would have organized his paper in this way:

Part I—Why this question occurred to me and why I thought it important enough to research.

Part II—What I did to reach a conclusion.

Part III—What I specifically observed (that is, how many columns were devoted to each medium).

Part IV—What I concluded as a result of what I observed (that *Time* magazine, at least, devotes much more space to media which have less influence than television).

Part V—What I recommend as a result of what I observed and what I concluded. (Mr. Meyer is probably not in a position to make recommendations that will result in action, but someone writing a report to stimulate action might recommend: 1. That readers demand a more balanced allocation of space for reviews; 2. That editors increase the amount of space for television reviews and reduce that for less influential media.)

The report pattern just presented is useful in science, industry, business, education, and every other field in which people benefit by observing and reporting accurately. Chances are you will someday be called upon in your career to prepare some sort of report.

Here is an example of a report by Benjamin Franklin of an experiment he conducted in England in 1765. He knew that the ancient Greeks had learned that oil spread on water would calm waves.

Part I—Why I wanted to find out something

Recollecting what I had formerly read in Pliny, I resolved to make some experiments of the effect of oil on water, when I should have the opportunity. . . .

Part II—What I did

At length, being at Clapham (London), where there is, on the common, a large pond, which I observed one day to be very rough with the wind, I fetched out a cruet of oil, and dropped a little of it on the water. . . . I went to the side where they [the waves] began to form. . . .

Part III—What I observed

I saw it [the oil] spread itself with surprising swiftness upon the surface. . . . and there the oil, though not more than a teaspoonful, produced an instant calm over a space several yards square, which spread amazingly, and extended itself gradually till it reached the lee side, making all that quarter of the pond, perhaps half an acre, as smooth as a looking-glass.[2]

Franklin did not finish his report with Part IV—What I Concluded and Part V—What I Recommend. It is easy, however, to imagine what he might have said:

Part IV—What I concluded

I concluded that Pliny and the ancients were indeed correct and that a minute quantity of certain kinds of oil will calm the waves.

Part V—What I recommend

I therefore recommend that all American naval vessels be required in the future to carry at bow and stern, port and starboard, four barrels of specially prepared oil to jettison into the sea in case of bad weather threatening to sink the ship. I further recommend that shore installations, such as lighthouses, ports, and gun emplacements likely to be threatened by severe storms likewise store barrels of oil for discharge into the water.

Here is a student's report of a simple investigation.

After Mr. Carruthers explained Gresham's Law and showed how "Bad money drives good money out of circulation," I saw what he meant and how people would hoard their "good" money—gold and respected currency—and spend their "bad" money, which might lose its value. When he casually said that the same thing applies to television and that bad programs drive out good, I disagreed with him.	Part I—Why I Wanted to Find Out Something
To see whether or not he was right, I had Miss Lane and Mr. Barrett, two English teachers, rate the six different programs that came on our local channels last night at 9:00 p.m. as either "good," "bad," or "indifferent." The Public Broadcasting System movie on Channel 3 and the Masterpiece Theatre play on Channel 16 rated "good." The PG-rated movie on Channel 8 rated "bad," as did the Channel 10 sit-com. The CBS Special on Channel 13 rated "indifferent," as did the ancient movie on Channel 44.	Part II—What I Did
Then I asked 46 students in two of my classes what they watched. This is what I found:	Part III—What I Observed

Channel		Number watching
3	(good)	0
16	(good)	2
8	(bad)	24
10	(bad)	0
13	(indifferent)	1
44	(indifferent)	0

(19 students were not watching TV)

Part IV—What I Concluded

If this little poll is any indication, students from this school who watch television are overwhelmingly interested in "bad," rather than in "good" or "indifferent" programs. And with television programs depending on ratings for their existence, I guess I would have to agree that bad programs drive out good ones.

Part V—What I Recommend

Although it seems to be an insurmountable problem, I think English and social studies teachers should keep on trying to get their students to watch quality programs, rather than bad ones. Perhaps there ought to be some way to reward producers of good programs and the stations that keep them on the air, in spite of ratings. Maybe we could have a subsidy for good programs, or just more support for public broadcasting. Maybe, too, we could try to turn the networks and the advertisers away from the ratings race.

—Matthew Burke

ACTIVITY 9F

Gathering Ideas for Research Reports

Working as your teacher directs, use each of the following headings as ideas for possible research and report projects. After you get a list of at least five projects, spend some time devising an investigation or experiment to help you learn about each subject.

1. What the people in our town (school, club, neighborhood, church, other) think about a current issue.

2. How certain people act when confronted with a certain kind of situation.

3. How people value different things, programs, ideas, activities.

4. Who supports a certain program.

5. What kinds of career objectives certain student groups hold.

6. Where our high school draws its teachers from.

7. What books, films, magazines, and programs are most popular among certain groups.

8. What characterizes a certain author's style.

9. How people feel about certain highly emotional words, such as Commie, scab, cheat, and so on.

When you have worked out a possible experiment or observation for a number of different subjects, choose one, carry it out as thoroughly as possible, and prepare a written report following the form you have learned. In actual business and industry, the headings used are usually

1. Backgrond
2. Procedure
3. Results (or Observations)
4. Conclusions
5. Recommendations.

For short reports, the headings need not be used. Do as your teacher directs.

Social Notes and Gracious Communication

Up until now, you have been concentrating on business letters of various kinds, résumés, memos, and reports. There will be many occasions in your life when you will find it useful to know these business forms. There will also be occasions that will call for another kind of letter, a friendly letter or social note.

Whole volumes have been written about how to plan and write various kinds of social notes. It is rather unfortunate that modern technology has now simplified life to such an extent that few of these are necessary any more. At one time, almost every-one was very careful to send personally written notes concerning:

Invitations of various kinds (lunch, dinner, special occasions, weekend visits, and so on)

Acceptance or refusal of invitations

Birth announcements

Christening announcements

Engagement announcements

Wedding announcements

Thank-you notes for gifts

Apologies for broken appointments

Congratulations on various events (graduation, promotion, new job, new home)

Birthday greetings

Get-well notes

Letters of introduction (presenting one of your friends to another)

Sympathy for a death

King Edward VI of England was not quite ten years old when he wrote this letter to his uncle, the Duke of Somerset. In this letter, Edward congratulated the Duke on his "good courage and wise foresight" in a battle against the Scots.

Many people solve most of these communication problems by sending commercial cards that express the appropriate sentiment. Although these are quite acceptable, a simple personal note conveying your own sincere sentiments is both less expensive and usually more highly regarded. Rather than memorizing a set form, just express your own thoughts in your own way. If you feel the need for guidance, you can find it in "The Correspondence Guide" in the back of many dictionaries, such as *The Reader's Digest Great Encyclopedic Dictionary*, in such books as *Amy Vanderbilt's Guide to Modern Etiquette*, and in many library reference sources. Various suppliers of services (florists, stationers, wedding shops) will also provide expert, but somewhat expensive, guidelines. It is probably better to visit your library reference room, ask the librarian for help, and prepare your own social note, using the sentiments and form that you are most comfortable with.

Personal Letters

One of the most famous letters of all time was written by Lord Chesterfield to his son, telling him how to write a personal letter.

I

My dear Boy,

When you read my letters, I hope you pay attention as well to the spelling as you do to the histories. You must likewise take notice of the manner in which they are written: which sets out to be easy and natural, not strained and florid. For instance, when you are thinking about sending a billet-doux, or love letter, to Miss Pinkerton, you must only think of what you would say to her if you were both together, and then write it; that renders the style easy and natural; though some people imagine the writing of a letter to be a great undertaking, and think they must write abundantly better than they talk, which is not at all necessary. . . .

Nothing is more requisite than to write a good letter. Nothing in fact is more easy. Most persons who write ill, do so because they aim at writing better than they can, by which means they acquire a formal and unnatural style. For instance, if you want to write a letter to me, you should only consider what you would say if you were with me, and then write it in plain terms, just as if you were conversing.

Affectionately,

(Lord Chesterfield, 1789)

Lord Chesterfield's ideas are excellent. This is the order in which he presents them. Rearrange them in what you consider to be the order of importance:

1. Pay attention to spelling.
2. Pay attention to the ideas (histories).
3. Write in an easy, natural manner.
4. Write as you would speak personally to the one to whom you are writing.
5. Avoid a formal and unnatural style.

At the present time, the United States is far more relaxed and informal than England was in the time of Lord Chesterfield. Personal correspondence is similarly relaxed and informal. In writing to a close friend you may be as informal as you wish. When writing a friendly letter to a person whom you do not know or do not know well, you should use the standard form as in the letter that follows.

The usual form of a friendly letter is identical with that of a business letter with one exception: It has no inside address. There are two reasons for putting an inside address on a business letter: 1. It assures the sender that the letter will reach the proper person within the company; 2. It assures the sender that the letter will be filed properly for retrieval. Since a friendly letter goes directly to an individual, it needs no inside address.

Whether your letter is casual or a bit more formal, you owe it to yourself and your reader to write interestingly and correctly.

Besides the message of its content, every letter carries another message. It tells a lot about the character of the writer. A careless, messy, ungrammatical letter is not only hard to read, it creates a negative impression about the writer. A neatly written letter that is dull and uninteresting creates an impression too. Think about what kind of person you are and make your letters reflect that person.

A Model Letter

In 79 A. D., just south of Naples by the Sarno River, Mt. Vesuvius suddenly erupted, burying Pompeii and some of its people under thirty feet of ashes and mud. In the book, *Letters from Pompeii*, a professor from the University of Maryland and his wife tell, in a series of letters to nieces and nephews, about several visits to Pompeii almost nineteen hundred years after the disaster. No heading was given for this letter. Can you supply one that would be suitable?

II

Dearest Sally, Jimmy, Ruth, and Kathy,

Yesterday was another exciting day. Something happens every day that I know you would like to hear about—but it seems there is little time for writing letters.

"Come with us to the new excavations near the south wall," we were told yesterday morning when we stopped at the *Scavi* office. We knew what that meant! Several days ago we had been shown some mounds of hardened volcanic dust that had been left untouched during the excavation of a large garden. When we examined the mounds, we saw two skulls partly exposed in one of them. The archaeologists knew there would be cavities in the mounds, just the shape of the human bodies that perished there.

The workmen were almost ready to make the casts. We watched them mix plaster of Paris and water and carefully pour it into the cavities. Soon it began to harden. Finally they were ready to pull away the volcanic dust that had smothered these people. It was a dramatic moment.

They began to scrape away the ashes very carefully, for, of course, they didn't know just where the plaster casts would be, and they didn't want to injure them. First the head and back of an adult came out—next a hand, then a foot—finally the second foot. It was obvious that this unfortunate person had fallen on his stomach, turning his face sidewise as he fell.

They continued to remove the rest of the volcanic dust—first at one place and then at another. Finally, they located a second cast. Gently they pulled away more of the covering of earth-like volcanic dust. We watched for nearly three hours. It gave us a queer feeling when we saw a small foot come into view. "A *bambino*," we said. They continued to uncover the little body. "How old?" I asked.

"Seven years," one of the experts estimated.

All at once it became clear. A parent fleeing with a child had not been able to make it to safety as so many did.

Nearby are two other mounds in which we can see cavities and human bones. Who else perished here? Perhaps the rest of the family? Do you suppose they will find other children? We will tell you when they pour the casts.

Love to you all,

Aunt Mina and Uncle Stanley

P. S. You can see in the picture, under the temporary roofs, the exact spot in the garden where the bodies were found! Apparently these people did not try to escape until the ashes began to cover the second story of their home. Then they fled out of the upstairs window, but they did not get far.[3]

ACTIVITY 9G

Discussing the Model

Either in small groups or with the entire class, discuss the following questions.

1. What are the elements of the form of this friendly letter?
2. Why is the letter interesting?
3. Since few people are able to visit a buried city in order to write an interesting letter, what kinds of things that happen to high school students might be worth writing about?
4. How does the letter communicate the personality of the writers?
5. What narrative and descriptive techniques in the model can you use in your own letter writing?
6. Discuss the extent to which a letter should cover many subjects as opposed to focusing on one event or a very few.
7. Make a list of recent school and community events interesting or important enough to include in a friendly letter.

ACTIVITY 9H

Fleshing Out an Empty Letter

Sometimes letter writers simply list ideas without developing them. The following letter is an empty letter. Using its content as a starter, flesh out the details by using your imagination. For example, specify where the writer visited Charlie, who his friends were, and what kinds of things they did together.

175 Warren Street
Newton Centre, Massachusetts
January 8, 1980

Dear Charlie,

It seems a lifetime since I visited you last summer, and yet it's only been seven months. Didn't we have a great time, though? I haven't had such a good time for years, and I certainly enjoyed meeting all of your friends. You certainly have a fine bunch of friends, Charlie. I don't know when I have met such a great group. I'll never forget them, and I'll never forget what we did together.

In the seven months since I saw you, though, I haven't been letting any grass grow under my feet. I've been doing lots of interesting things. I've really been living it up, and I can't wait to tell you about it.

I guess about the most important thing is that I'm going steady again. You remember that I went steady once before, but I stopped. Now I'm going steady again and you should see my girl. You would really like her.

I'm planning a great summer next summer. You know it's only six months until school is out. I can't wait. I've really decided to do a lot of interesting things. It's going to be the best summer of my life. I hope you can join me part of the time.

I hate to break off a letter to a friend, but duty calls. One of my teachers just gave me a big assignment, so I'd better get at it.

I hope I'll see you soon.

Yours truly,
Al

MAJOR WRITING ASSIGNMENT

A FRIENDLY LETTER

Write a letter to a friend or relative, which communicates both your personality and your interests to your correspondent. Follow these suggestions:

1. Follow the form of the models just presented.
2. Write as if you were speaking to the person.
3. Focus on a few ideas and develop them with description, details, and figures of speech.
4. Include events and your reactions to those events.
5. Edit and proofread your work before you submit it.

Chapter 10

The Library Resource Paper

Sometime near the middle of the semester, your English teacher, your history teacher, or your science teacher may say, "Now, your term paper will be due on . . . ."

In your school such a major paper may be called something else—research paper, semester report, major thesis, or senior research project—but the results of the announcement are the same: Panic!

Actually, you shouldn't be as disturbed as the regular student ritual encourages you to be. Prepare yourself for writing such a paper by 1. making sure you understand the assignment, 2. proceeding systematically, and 3. allowing yourself sufficient time. In this chapter, you will be given insights into what a library resource paper is and you will be shown how to proceed. It will be up to you to proceed systematically and to allow sufficient time to do your best work.

What a Library Resource Paper Is

Of all the terms used to describe the major paper some courses require, perhaps the best name is "library resource paper." Very simply, in writing such a paper, you take some subject you know

233

about and are interested in and make a statement about it. Then you try to convince or persuade a reader that your statement is correct. As one of your techniques for convincing or persuading your reader, you frequently refer to what other writers or speakers have said on the subject. In short, you borrow—always using the regularly accepted, customary procedures—the ideas, statistics, reasoning, research, history, and so on that other writers have previously presented. By adding this material to your own ideas, you increase the chances that the reader will accept your thesis. He or she is bound to be impressed with the information you've collected, with the prestige of the people who agree with you, and with the work you've done in supporting your idea.

Reasons for Learning to Write Library Resource Papers

The ability to write a library resource paper is both a "school skill" and a "life skill." Most students are assigned a library resource paper at some time during their high school careers, and all those who go on to college—no matter what field they choose to major in—must, at some time or other, write a paper in which they use the standard customary procedures in citing the works of other writers to support their own ideas on a particular subject. This is, obviously, an important "school skill."

But how is the ability to write a library resource paper a "life skill"? Will students who do not go to college ever use such a skill after graduating from high school? Actually, they may never use all of the formal techniques of arranging footnotes and preparing the bibliographies that list sources of information. However, they will use the skills of finding, arranging, and presenting material to convince or persuade someone that they are right about a certain idea. They may, for example, become active in local politics. In that case, they may need to get information to convince the town council or the voters that city planning pays off, that privately-owned utilities are (or are not) cheaper than city-owned power and water plants, that parking meters are worthwhile, or that closing a street to make a pedestrian mall will help the merchants. If they become active in a service club or a P.T.A., they may need to find material to prove that a certain kind of fund-raising drive is (or is not) a good idea. If they work in a church group or a neighborhood improvement association, they may need to convince others, by finding, arranging, and presenting information, that certain kinds of businesses should be banned from an area, that groups in other

places have found certain procedures successful, or that tax re-
ductions (or raises) will benefit the residents. If they run their
own businesses, they may find themselves using these skills
frequently.

Some college professors have said to high school teachers,
"Don't bother teaching the library resource paper in high school.
Just teach your students to write paragraphs, and we'll teach
them to write library resource papers in college." The Pennsylvania English Association, for example, has taken such a stand.
But these professors explain that they are not really opposed to
teaching library resource papers in high school. What they are
really afraid of is 1. You will spend so much time doing library
papers that you won't have time to do any other writing; 2. You
will copy huge chunks of material from encyclopedias and other
books and produce long, formless papers instead of selecting and
organizing materials to support your own position; 3. You will
worry more about the formal conventions (customary practices)
of title pages, footnotes, and bibliographies than about choosing
an important, interesting, and believable idea and using good
logic and intelligently selected library material to support it.

However, most people believe that high school graduates
should know how to write library resource papers for these
reasons:

1. The skill is both a school skill and a life skill.
2. You learn other important English skills, including library research procedures, paragraphing, and logic, as
   you do the library resource paper.
3. The skill is important for success in high school.
4. Many college professors—both of English and of other
   subjects—simply assume that beginning college students
   have the skill and assign resource papers without teaching the procedures.

Library Resource Paper Procedures

Writing a library resource paper involves these steps:
1. Deciding on a subject, an area, or a field
2. Acquiring general information, background, or experience
3. Narrowing the subject to a specific topic and making a statement you believe in about the topic (stating your thesis)

4. Searching for information to support your thesis statement
5. Recording your sources of information
6. Recording *usable* material to support your thesis statement
7. Ordering your ideas as a guide for your rough draft
8. Writing your rough draft to fit your thesis statement and revising where necessary
9. Revising your thesis statement and your rough draft
10. Preparing your final draft, complete with footnotes and bibliography
11. Preparing your front matter (title page, outline or table of contents, and possibly an introduction)

The following sections will explain each of these steps. Each of the next eleven sections is a separate activity for you to do as you prepare your library resource paper. Because you can combine some of the steps and handle others in different ways, they are not listed for you as "Activity 10A," "Activity 10B," and so on. Nonetheless, you should consider them as helpful and necessary as you prepare your paper.

Before you begin this section, work out with your teacher both a schedule of when you will be undertaking each step and an indication of how much time, both in and out of class, you ought to be spending on each one. For example, for Step 2, your teacher will probably advise you that to write a good paper you will probably need to browse in the library at this point for three or four hours.

To write a well-developed paper, you should probably allow from three to five weeks, but, of course, you will be doing other kinds of writing assignments at the same time.

1. Deciding on a Subject

The most important step in writing a library resource paper is the first: choosing a subject that is interesting to you, important enough to be worth your time, limited enough for you to handle, significant enough to capture a reader's attention, and impressive enough to earn you a good grade.

You must, of course, observe any limitations your teacher imposes. An English teacher may insist that you write about literature. A history teacher may limit you to a specific country and period of time. A science teacher may restrict you to contemporary problems, rather than to ancient experiments. But within whatever limits you are given, you still have a universe of choices. The first step is to find out what that universe consists of. Discuss the assignment with a group of your friends outside of class. If necessary, ask the teacher who made the assignment for help. Discuss the assignment with your parents, other teachers, or experts in the field. Skim the topic headings and main ideas of books in the subject area. Review appropriate encyclopedia entries. Browse among the library books in the field of the assignment.

Be sure to go through this step immediately after you receive the assignment. Even if you postpone your serious research until later, you can get your subconscious mind working on your problem, and sooner or later you will arrive at an appropriate subject. Be sure that it's something you're interested in, that it's important enough to be worth your time, that it's limited enough for you to handle, and that it's right for your audience and your teacher.

2. Acquiring General Information, Background, or Experience

Often, even after you've decided on a broad general subject, you still don't know enough about the area either to limit it to an appropriate topic or to specify an idea about it which you believe in. For example, a high school student named Julia Martin knew, after going through the first step, that she wanted to write about "energy," but until she moved to this step, she had no idea of the possibilities of this huge subject. Julia's paper will be used as a model for this chapter and you will follow her procedure step by step. By talking to other students and to friends outside of school, by asking her teacher for some direction, by skimming some books on energy, reading encyclopedia entries, and browsing both in the library and in the *Readers' Guide to Periodical Literature*, she began to narrow the field. She discarded such aspects of energy as "synthetic natural gas," "petroleum imports," "geothermal energy"—none of which she had even known about before this survey—and limited herself to "solar energy." Sometimes, as you browse and explore, some special subdivision will attract you. At other times, facing a deadline and realizing you need to move ahead will compel you to make an arbitrary choice.

3. Making a Thesis Statement

Even after Julia limited herself to the topic "solar energy," she still found the subject much too broad. As she continued her explorations in the library and elsewhere, she learned that under the heading "solar energy" she could have written lengthy papers on such subtopics as "Wind Chargers" (because wind comes from solar energy), "Solar Furnaces," "Solar Energy for Houses," "The Economics of Solar Energy," "Early Uses of Solar Energy," "Promising Research in Solar Energy," "The Future of Solar Energy," or "Laws to Stimulate the Use of Solar Energy." Even with a subtopic, however, Julia would not have a suitable place to begin writing a library resource paper until she determined what her thesis statement would be.

The reason a topic or subtopic alone is not enough for a library resource paper is this: If you have just a topic or subtopic, all you can do is collect facts, statistics, information—as much of these kinds of data as possible—and present them wholesale, similar to the way an encyclopedia presents a lot of ideas on a topic. What results is fine for an encyclopedia, but not for a library resource paper. A library resource paper is not strictly a presentation of information; it is, rather, a persuasion or argumentation paper that tries to get a reader to accept an opinion or point of view. In order to do this, it must have a thesis statement.

In Julia's case, specifying a thesis statement was easy. After reading at length on solar energy, she sat down and tried to complete this statement:

"I believe strongly that solar energy _____ ."

In no time at all, she had listed several ideas that she could support:

I believe strongly that _____

solar energy is about to come into its own.
solar energy is a much neglected resource.
solar energy research deserves more support,
  from the government, universities, scientists.
solar energy cannot fulfill America's immediate
  energy needs.
solar energy is practical on a small scale now.

From among these and other possible thesis statements, she finally specified her tentative choice:

I believe strongly that solar energy is the answer to America's long-range energy problem.

By crossing off the first clause and the relative pronoun "that," Julia produced this thesis statement to guide her further research and writing:

I believe strongly that ſolar energy is the answer to America's long-range energy problem.

Notice that this was Julia's *tentative* thesis statement. The word "tentative" means "not definite," "temporarily held," "subject to change or replacement." If, as Julia learned more about her topic, she had decided that she believed in some other idea more strongly, she would have changed her thesis statement and selected and reorganized her material to fit the new thesis.

If you can select your tentative thesis statement before you begin to write, your task is made easier for you. Sometimes, however, you may have to begin to read, organize, and write in order to find out what you believe about a subject. In that case, you do your best to select information, organize, and write logically, even though you may have to redo some of your work when you formulate your thesis statement.

4. Searching for Information to Support Your Thesis Statement

Your two main tools for finding information in the library are the Card Catalog and the *Readers' Guide to Periodical Literature.* As you work to acquire general information about your subject, you will go to the Card Catalog and find the *subject card* related to your topic. Here is one of the subject cards that Julia used in researching solar energy.

SUBJECT CARD

```
          POWER RESOURCES--Dictionaries

R333.7    McGraw-Hill Encyclopedia of energy.  Daniel
M147m     N. Lapedes, editor in chief.  New York.

          McGraw-Hill, c 1976

              785 p.  il.
          Includes index.


          1.  Power resources--Dictionaries.  2.  Power
          (Mechanics)--Dictionaries.  3.  Power resources
          --Addresses, essays, lectures.  4.  Power (Me-
          chanics)--Addresses, essays, lectures.  I.
          Lapedes, Daniel N.  II. Title:  Encyclopedia of
          Energy.

          TJ 163.2.M3          333.7      76-19026
```

Before this book was ever published, the McGraw-Hill editors gave the information on this card to the Library of Congress. The Library of Congress, in turn, printed this card, indicated recommended call numbers for the book, and made the cards available to schools and libraries much less expensively than they could prepare such cards themselves.

Notice that on the subject card, the Library of Congress suggests, after the Arabic numerals 1, 2, 3, and 4, other subject card headings the book may be listed under in the Card Catalog. This librarian decided that headings 1 and 3 were sufficient and crossed out 2 and 4. The Roman numerals I and II indicate the headings for the *author card* and the *title card*.

Many years ago each library prepared its own cards. In each library, a cataloger wrote or typed each subject card, author card, and title card. Now, most catalogers buy cards prepared by The Library of Congress or by another service and simply type at the top of each card the heading under which it will be filed.

Obviously, then, you can look for any nonfiction book under any of the three kinds of catalog cards: the author card, the title card, and one or more subject cards. The author and title cards for Julia's book look exactly like the subject card, except for the first heading.

AUTHOR CARD

```
                    Lapedes, Daniel N.

        R333.7      McGraw-Hill Encyclopedia of Energy. Daniel
        M147m       N. Lapedes, editor in chief.  New York.

                    McGraw-Hill, c 1976

                        785 p.  il.
                    Includes index.


                    1.  Power resources--Dictionaries.  2. Power
                    (Mechanics) Dictionaries.  3.  Power resources
                    --Addresses, essays, lectures.  4.  Power (Me-
                    chanics)--Addresses, essays, lectures.  I.
                    Lapedes, Daniel N.  II. Title: Encyclopedia of
                    Energy.

                    TJ 163.2.M3              333.7        76-19026
                    ISBN 0-07-045261-X
```

TITLE CARD

```
                    Encyclopedia of Energy

       R333.7       McGraw-Hill Encyclopedia of Energy.  Daniel
       M147m        N. Lapedes, editor in chief.  New York.

                    McGraw-Hill, c 1976

                         785 p.  il.
                    Includes index.

                    1.  Power resources--Dictionaries.  2.  Power
                    (Mechanics)--Dictionaries.  3.  Power resources
                    --Addresses, essays, lectures.  4.  Power (Me-
                    chanics)--Addresses, essays, lectures.  I.
                    Lapedes, Daniel N.  II. Title:  Encyclopedia of
                    Energy.

                    TJ 163.2.M3              333.7          76-19026
                    ISBN 0-07-045261-X
```

The Readers' Guide to Periodical Literature

A *periodical* is a publication which is issued at regular periods of time. The popular word "magazine" comes close to identifying most periodicals.

The Readers' Guide to Periodical Literature is an index to approximately 191 different periodicals. Editors of the H.W. Wilson Company list all of the contents of these periodicals in a single index that comes out twice monthly from September to January and from March to June. In February, July, and August, the index comes out once a month.

If you had to search through each of these indexes to find all the articles published in one year on a given subject, you would have to look through twenty-one separate indexes! Fortunately, the H.W. Wilson Company editors simplify things for you by collecting all of the indexes for a three-month period into a single quarterly index. Then, at the end of the year, they collect all of the indexes for the whole year into a single hardbound volume. Except for recent periodicals, you need to look only in one place in a single volume to find all of the articles published on a single subject in a whole year.

An entry in the *Readers' Guide to Periodical Literature* looks like this:

SOLAR Energy Research Institute
    SERI; Interview, ed by K. Frazier. Sci News 113:255 Ap 22 '78
SOLAR engines
    60-cycle AC from sunshine: solar Stirling engine. E. F. Lindsley. il
      Pop Sci 212:74-7 Je '78
SOLAR flares
    Solar superflare is noisiest on record. il Sci News 113:309 My 13 '78
SOLAR heating
    Revolving barrel banks solar heat. R. Stepler. il Pop Sci 212:91 My
      '78
    Solar lab soaks up sunshine with exotic new materials. R. Stepler. il
      Pop Sci 212:96-8 Je '78
    Solar refractions. W. Greene. il por New Times 10:4-6 My 29 '78
    Something new under the sun. il Redbook 150:206-8+ Ap '78
      See also
    Solar apartment houses
    Solar collectors
SOLAR houses
    Look—no wires! A stand-alone passive solar house. J. Mattill. il
      Tech R 80:61 My '78
    Place in the sun; Canada's first solar-heated housing development.
      D. Thomas. il por Macleans 91:55-6 Ja 23 '78
    Solar plus saves a bundle. J. R. Trull. il Mech Illus 74:64 Je '78
SOLAR power plants. See Solar energy
    See also
    Solar energy
SOLAR reflectors
    More sun for stronger seedlings. il Org Gard & Farm 25:142-4 Ap '78
SOLAR system
    See also
    Planets
SOLAR water heaters
    Different kind of solar collector; heating a campground swimming
      pool. il Mech Ilus 74: 52+ My '78
    Manhattan goes solar. R. R. Knabel. il N Y 11:53-5+ My 8 '78

Julia was able to figure out the meanings of most of the entries. When she was puzzled by an abbreviation, she looked it up in the list near the beginning of the guide. She also found a model entry that explained all the abbreviations. For example, this is the way the entry "Solar reflectors" would be explained:

An illustrated article on the subject of solar reflectors entitled "More sun for stronger seedlings" will be found in Volume 25 of Organic Gardening and Farming, pages 142-144, the April 1978 issue.

From several recent *Readers' Guides*, Julia prepared bibliography cards for the articles most likely to be of value. She avoided frustration by limiting herself to the periodicals the library subscribed to. Their names were posted near the *Readers' Guides*.

5. Recording Your Sources of Information

For each book, magazine, or pamphlet which she thought would be helpful, Julia prepared a separate bibliography card, or "bib card." She chose to use 4" × 6" cards, rather than a larger or smaller size. She could have used separate sheets from a note pad or uniformly cut sheets from notebook paper, but like most students she found cards easier to handle and less likely to be lost.

On each "bib card," Julia listed all of the information she would need to find that book or magazine in the library and also to record the book properly in footnotes and bibliography. Two of the bib cards looked like this:

```
                                                          1

"Bruce Anderson; Total Environmental Action, Inc.;"
interview, ed. by K. Thomas. Mother Earth
News  52:16-23 July 1978.

      (About solar houses)
```

```
                                                          3

697.78  Hudson Home Guides. Practical Guide to
H886p. Solar Homes, New York: Bantam/Hudson
        Idea Books, 1978
```

After preparing a separate card for each book or magazine she might use, Julia alphabetized them according to the last name of the author or editor and then placed a number in the upper-right-hand corner of each. As she prepared note cards while reading or skimming each source, she would be able to write on each note card simply the *number* for that source. Such a number would save her time and writer's cramp by making it unnecessary to copy publication information on each note card.

6. Recording Usable Material to Support Your Thesis Statement

After preparing her bib cards—even though she was prepared at any time to add more sources—Julia began her in-depth research. Beginning with the most promising sources first, she skimmed rapidly, slowing down only when she noticed something important she might be able to use.

When she began taking notes, she tried to limit herself to several different kinds:

1. Direct quotations of statistics, details, or even stylistically satisfying sentences she might want to quote directly. (These she *always* indicated with quotation marks.)

2. Brief notations (often abbreviated), paraphrases of ideas and passages too long to quote, key phrases to remind her of entire ideas.

3. Short outlines of complicated thought processes.

Two of Julia's note cards looked like this:

9

Political pressure for solar energy

"... the military construction bill requires ... that all new military housing use solar energy if it is cost-effective, and that at least 25% of all other military construction do the same, on structures started after Dec. 8. [1978]"

12

Different kinds of solar energy

Six dif. kinds solar energy:
1. Photovoltaic - photons enter semi-conductor, activate electrons
2. Photogalvanic - don't understand this. Check again.
3. Photothermic - selective coatings, one accepting lower wave lengths and one limited to higher wave lengths set up differential elec. charges
4. Photosynthetic - grow plants, algae, etc. Burn them to get energy

5. Ocean thermal gradients — warm surface water vaporizes high-boiling-point fluid, which drives "steam"-type generator; vapor then pumped down to cold ocean floor to condense and up again to become steam
6. Wind-driven generators

The "topic heading" on the top left of each card identifies the content of each card, and Julia limits each card to one topic, or subject, to make it easier to sort the cards and arrange them in the order she might want to use them. The number on the right identifies the "bib card," which names the source from which the material came.

The first card has quotation marks around the material that is quoted exactly as it appears in the original source. The three dots called ellipses (. . .) indicate that words are omitted, and the brackets ([ ]) enclose material that Julia has added to clarify the original.

Julia actually found that she wasted time in preparing the second card. Although the nice, neat summary of the major kinds of solar energy looked like something she might be able to use, when she went back to the source a second time and still couldn't understand "photogalvanic" solar energy, she threw the card away.

7. Ordering Your Ideas as a Guide for Your Rough Draft

After reading from several sources—especially when guided by a thesis statement—many people are able simply to take the note cards they have prepared, arrange them in what seems to be a logical order, and begin to write a rough draft. Whenever it seems appropriate, they indicate with a blank and a topic heading from a card exactly where they will copy the information from that card in the final paper.

Other people at this stage are able to work out a complete outline, either a topic outline or a sentence outline, to guide them as they write. Since most term papers include an outline as a kind of "Table of Contents," being able to prepare the outline in advance saves a lot of time.

Julia was not able to depend either on the cards or on an outline. The best she could do was to make a tentative (temporary, subject-to-change) list of ideas in the order she thought she would treat them. At this stage people work in many different ways, depending upon their background, experience, training, and personal thought processes.

Julia's list of ideas—in the approximate order she would take them up—looked like this. Note that she placed her thesis statement at the top of the work sheet as a way of controlling the material.

Solar energy is the answer to America's long-range energy problem.

1. Modern need for energy
2. American dependence on oil
3. Dependence on oil from other countries
4. Arab boycott and effect
5. Realization that fossil fuels can't last
6. Turn to other sources
7. Oil shale
8. Coal
9. Nuclear fission and fusion
10. Geothermal
11. Wind-tide (actually solar)
12. Potential of solar energy
13. Saudi's use of solar energy
14. Different kinds
15. Pre-war Florida uses
16. Making solar energy cheap
17. California laws
18. 1978 tax credits
19. Research for the future
20. Big companies in solar energy

8. Writing Your Rough Draft to Fit Your Thesis Statement

Writing has often been considered a lonely craft. Actually, much of the writing for modern publication involves group work, as you learned in Chapter 1. At this point, however, in the actual preparation of the rough draft, it does become lonely. It is up to you to follow or modify your list of ideas and to create the core of your paper.

This is the way Julia Martin's rough draft looked. To make it easy for you to see the connection between Julia's list of ideas and her rough draft, the ideas are placed in the margin next to the paragraphs developing them. The numbers in parentheses refer to her bib cards.

Modern need for energy.

All over the world, people are either using, or are dreaming of using, enormous amounts of energy. In advanced nations, people depend on energy for heating, cooling, transportation, for providing fertilizer for farm products, for manufacturing products for daily use, and for a million other things. In undeveloped nations, people are beginning to demand their share of the world's energy so that they, too, can live the good life that abundant energy makes possible.

American dependence on oil.

Unfortunately, the United States has shifted from most other sources of energy to oil. According to *The World Book Encyclopedia* (1) the United States produces 609 gallons of oil a year for each person in the country, but even this amount isn't enough, for Americans are among the 6% of the world's population (2) that uses a third of the world's energy. Although Americans furnish only one-third of the total world output of oil, they use over two-fifths of that total.

Dependence on oil from other nations.

Obviously, the United States is dependent upon importing energy from other nations. Saudi Arabia, Iran, Venezuela, Mexico, Iraq, Kuwait, Canada, and even Great Britain now furnish oil to the United States. Indeed, _____ of America's oil comes from other nations.(3)

Effect of Arab boycott.

Perhaps Americans would not worry so much about both their dependence on foreign oil and about the possibility that world supplies of oil are vanishing, if the OPEC (oil producing and exporting) nations of the world had not placed an embargo on exports to the United States in 1973 and 1974 and doubled the price of oil. The brief period of the oil shortage taught Americans what it could be like to be cold and to be without transportation, and the sudden increased price changed the United States from a wealthy nation constantly earning more from its exports than its imports to a nation constantly spending more than it earns. (4)

Realization that fossil fuels can't last.

Perhaps the worst shock for Americans was to realize that their own oil reserves had been overestimated by as much as 80% (5) and that oil would be in short supply worldwide by 1985 and all but unavailable for fuel by 2000 A.D. (6) In addition, oil shale which at first promised to provide more oil would force the destruction by strip mining of vast areas of farm and forest and would be only a temporary solution. Also, increased use of coal would harm the environment, cause pollution problems, and still be a short-term solution. Admittedly, coal reserves might last another hundred years, but at terrible human and environmental cost. The possibility of unlimited cheap energy from either nuclear fusion or nuclear fission might eventually be realized, but, at the present time, neither is completely practical. Fuel for reactors is both rare and expensive, and the problems of safety and the disposal of wastes have not yet been overcome. Besides, there is no certainty that the fuel for reactors will last much longer than the fossil fuels of coal and oil. (7)

Turn to other sources
Oil shale
Coal
Nuclear energy

Much has been written about the use of geothermal power, that is, the use of heat from the inside of the earth. Actually, such power is in use in Newfoundland and New Zealand, (8) and could probably be developed wherever volcanoes exist, or hot springs or lava come from the earth. Unfortunately, these places are few and far between and scientists are reluctant to spend billions of dollars elsewhere to penetrate the earth's mantle for fear they will release forces they can't control. (9)

Geothermal power

Solar energy alone offers the possibility of unlimited, clean, safe, inexpensive power for the whole world. "The amount of energy falling on the earth's surface each year is equal to that supplied by 250 million million tons of coal, or about 100,000 tons of coal for each person on earth." (10) Stated another way, "At 10% efficiency, the United States could supply all of its energy needs from the sunshine which falls on about 50,000 square miles of land, which is about 3% of the total arable land of the country." (11)

Potential of solar energy

Among the people who recognize the potential for solar power is the leading Arab oil-producing country. The Saudis know that the solar energy falling on the Arabian desert alone is equivalent each year "to the world's entire proved reserves of coal, oil, and gas." (12) They are now planning to harvest that energy for their own use and in the future to save their oil for chemicals and other nonfuel uses. Already, they have in operation the world's largest solar heating system, which services a 14-building education complex. (13)

Saudi's use of solar energy

In the United States, before World War II, between 30,000 and 60,000 solar water heaters were installed in the state of Florida. (14) This use of solar energy in Florida was the result of a number of forces. Florida was a poor state at that time, and electricity was slow in coming to many areas. Labor was cheap and the solar heaters required few expensive materials at that time. Unfortunately, the situation has changed, and the use of solar heaters in

Pre-war Florida uses solar energy

Florida has declined. The basic problem now is to make solar energy as cheap as it once was in comparison to energy from gas and oil.

"The problem remains in making the costs of solar equipment for residential use competitive through mass production so that solar energy becomes an attractive alternative to fossil fuel sources. The equipment to power an American home cost, in 1975, between $5,000 and $8,000 and costs more today. However, with the present high cost of oil, gas, and coal, the investment pays for itself within five years. But the initial outlay is still beyond the reach of most homeowners." (15)

One way of making solar energy competitive with fossil fuels is by granting tax credits for the installation of expensive equipment. At the present time, 37 states offer incentives to encourage solar power, (16), but California offers the greatest tax credit. A large builder, for example, can earn a tax credit equal to 25% of the cost of a solar installation in an apartment complex, and a home owner can deduct 55% of the cost of buying and installing a solar energy system, up to a maximum writeoff of $3,000. "California's energy commission estimates that the law might encourage as many as 170,000 solar units of all types by 1980." (17)

As part of President Carter's national energy proposal, the tax credit that was written into the 1978 Federal Income Tax is a little less generous. (It will allow individual tax credit of 30% of the first $2,000 spent on home solar equipment plus 20% of further costs up to a total of $8,000. According to a Senate Budget Committee estimate, that incentive will push solar sales to more than $1.5 billion each year until the credit expires in 1985.) (19)

Increased emphasis on research and development should also help decrease the cost of solar energy in the future. According to Energy Secretary James R. Schlesinger, he will ask the Office of Management and Budget to nearly double for fiscal 1980 the $500 million that his agency will spend on solar research and development in fiscal 1979. (2)

Business Week for October 9, 1978, predicted "The Coming Boom in Solar Energy." (21) It called solar energy "inefficient and expensive compared with most other means of generating power" and it predicted that "No single, big technological breakthrough is on the horizon. . . ." Nevertheless, it continued ". . . for all these drawbacks, solar power is on the threshold of a boom that may well transform it into a key energy source by the turn of the century." (22)

As the American need for energy continues to grow; as the world supply of energy decreases and as other nations compete with us to use the energy

Making solar energy cheap

California laws

1978 tax credits

Research for the future

that is theirs, rather than ours; as we find alternative sources of energy expensive, dangerous, polluting, and increasingly scarce, it is certain that we shall turn to solar power. Already both state and federal governments are providing the tax incentives for Americans to gear up to use solar energy and the funds to stimulate research and development. Already such companies as Aluminum company of America, American Smelting and Refining, Exxon, General Electric, General Motors, Honeywell, and many others are committing themselves heavily to solar energy production. (23)

Big companies in solar energy

Surely, solar energy will be the answer to America's long-range energy problem.

9. Revising Your Thesis Statement and Your Rough Draft

Although she had produced a good rough draft with numbers indicating where to document or footnote the ideas, Julia was dissatisfied with the direction the paper had taken. True, the thesis statement had guided the list of topics and the list of topics had guided the rough draft, but somehow the thesis statement and the rough draft didn't quite come together. The last page and a half were the most powerful portion of the paper, and they were devoted almost exclusively to government policies and tax credits as ways of shaping and promoting solar energy. The reader comes away from the paper feeling not that "Solar energy is the answer to America's long-range energy problem," but that "Governmental policies and tax credits can make solar energy the answer to America's long-range energy problem."

Julia decided to revise her thesis statement because she discovered in the actual act of writing what it was that she really meant to say. Of course, this meant more work, for she then had to go back and revise her rough draft. She cut out some of the introductory material about the American dependence on oil and some of the information about other energy sources in order to focus more on the role of government in promoting solar energy.

10. Preparing Your Final Draft, Complete with Footnotes and Bibliography

A library resource paper should go through the same cooperative editing and proofreading procedures that were described in Chapter 2. Just as a professional writer uses the insights of others in making a publication as nearly perfect as possible, you should take advantage of the insights of other students and adults. The difference is that the professional writer is usually aiming only at improving the selection. You are aiming both at improving your paper and at learning something yourself. Julia met with a group of four students, and each person contributed his or her insights to improve the work of all the others.

Then Julia began to prepare her footnotes and bibliography. Because she had kept careful bib cards and note cards, the task was easy. Julia wanted to lend authority and credibility to the facts and ideas in her paper and to avoid the charge of plagiarism (the attempt to pass off another person's ideas or words as one's own) so she was conscientious about acknowledging her sources. She knew that she should use footnotes in these situations: 1. to indicate that she had borrowed an idea, judgment, or information from an author even though she had used her own words; and 2. to show that she had borrowed an author's exact words as well as ideas. She put quotation marks around directly borrowed passages. She knew that she did not have to use footnotes for information that is common knowledge.

Julia's bibliography, made with the help of her bib cards and note cards, listed complete information about the sources she used in preparing the paper. Each item in the bibliography included the author, if given, the title of the article or book, the place of publication, the publishing company, and the year of publication. As Julia made up her footnotes and bibliography, she kept in mind the function of these two parts of her paper.

FOOTNOTES

1. A number slightly above the line in the paper signals a footnote. The number refers the reader to extra information at the bottom of the page. (Or the information may be grouped together at the end of the paper before the bibliography.)
2. A footnote gives the source of a specific idea, fact, quotation, or judgment.
3. Footnotes are always in the order in which they occur in the paper. They are numbered consecutively.

BIBLIOGRAPHY

1. The bibliography always comes at the end of a research paper.

2. The bibliography lists the sources (books, magazines, pamphlets, etc.) used in writing the paper.
3. The sources in the bibliography are listed alphabetically by the last name of the author or by title, if no author is given.

4. Each footnote is begun with the name of the author, first name first.

4. Each entry is begun with the last name of the author first (if the name of the author is given).

As Julia prepared her footnotes and bibliography, she used these models for guidelines.

FOOTNOTE	**BIBLIOGRAPHY**

For a book—one author:

[1]Sam J. Lundwall, *Science Fiction: An Illustrated History* (New York: Grosset & Dunlap, 1977), p. 48.

Lundwall, Sam J. *Science Fiction: An Illustrated History.* New York: Grosset & Dunlap, 1977.

For a book—more than one author:

[2]David Frost and Antony Jay, *The English* (New York: Stein and Day, 1968), pp. 210-214.

Frost, David, and Jay, Antony. *The English.* New York: Stein and Day, 1968.

For a book compiled by an editor:

[3]Ashley Montagu (ed.) *Man and Aggression* (New York: Oxford University Press, 1968), p. 35.

Montagu, Ashley, ed. *Man and Aggression.* New York: Oxford University Press, 1968.

For a book—only one chapter used:

[4]Milbourne Christopher, "Buried Alive," in *Houdini: The Untold Story* (New York: Thomas Y. Crowell Company, 1963), p. 233.

Christopher, Milbourne. "Buried Alive," in *Houdini: The Untold Story.* New York: Thomas Y. Crowell Company, 1963, pp. 230-237.

For a magazine article—author given:

[5]John N. Cole, "It's Not Safe To Be An Eagle," *National Wildlife*, December-January 1979, p. 13.

Cole, John N. "It's Not Safe To Be An Eagle." *National Wildlife,* December-January 1979, pp. 13-17.

For a magazine article—no author given:

[6]"Warning . . . Danger . . . Loaded Words Ahead!" *Senior Scholastic*, March 11, 1966, p. 6.

"Warning . . . Danger . . . Loaded Words Ahead!" *Senior Scholastic*, (March 11, 1966), pp. 6-11.

For an encyclopedia article—signed:

[7]*Funk & Wagnalls Standard Reference Encyclopedia*, 1967 ed., s.v. "Cervantes Saavedra, Miguel de," by E.F.

Funk & Wagnalls Standard Reference Encyclopedia, 1967 ed., s.v. "Cervantes Saavedra, Miguel de," by E.F.

For an encyclopedia article—unsigned:

[8]*Encyclopedia Americana*, 1963 ed., s.v. "Sitting Bull."

Encyclopedia Americana, 1963 ed., s.v. "Sitting Bull."

(Note: *s.v.* means "sub verbo," or "under the word." Encyclopedia articles are cited by the title of the article rather than by volume and page number.)

For a pamphlet—no author given:

[9]*Kindergarten Education*, Washington, D.C., National Education Association, 1968, p. 24.

Kindergarten Education, Washington, D.C., National Education Association, 1968.

For a newspaper article—unsigned:

[10]"Amazing Amazon Region," *New York Times*, 12 January 1969, sec. 4, p. E11.

"Amazing Amazon Region," *New York Times*, 12 January 1969, sec. 4, p. E11.

When Julia was writing her paper and preparing her footnotes, she decided she would use only *reference* footnotes and not *content* footnotes. Content footnotes provide additional information not included in the text; they are rarely used in library resource papers. They may confuse readers, who must jump from the text to the foot of the page and back again. Reference footnotes, on the other hand, merely indicate where the writer found specific facts, opinions, and direct quotations included in the text.

As Julia discovered that she was referring to the same sources in several footnotes, she found the following abbreviations useful in saving time and trouble.

Ibid.—The abbreviation Ibid., which is capitalized, underlined, and followed by a period, means "in the same place." If the third footnote in a paper comes from the same source as the immediately preceding reference, simply put Ibid. and the new page. The entry would look like this:

[3]Ibid., 5.

Do not use <u>Ibid</u>. if some other reference comes between the new reference and the earlier one from the same source.

<u>Op. cit.</u>—The abbreviation <u>Op. cit.</u>, which is also capitalized, underlined, and followed by a period, means "in the work cited." It is used to refer to a source used a second or subsequent times, but which cannot be referred to by <u>Ibid</u>., because another reference comes in between. But to be sure a reader doesn't become confused, the author's name must be repeated. Such a footnote looks like this:
[3]Harper, <u>op. cit.</u>, 295.

SOLAR POWER: AMERICA'S ENERGY SOLUTION

The first recorded account of the use of solar power was at the battle of Syracuse in 212 B. C.[1] According to contemporary accounts, as the Greeks attacked the Roman ships, Archimedes fashioned parabolic reflectors which focused the sun's rays on the Roman sails and set them afire. Whether or not Archimedes really did insure the Greek victory (which most historians doubt), solar power is now ready to become the answer to America's long-range energy problem--but only governmental policies and tax credits can enable it to do so.

At the present time, people all over the world are either using or dreaming of using unlimited amounts of energy. In advanced nations, particularly the United States, people depend on energy for heating, cooling, transportation, cultivation of fields, manufacture of thousands of products, and a million other things. In undeveloped nations, people are beginning to demand their share of the world's energy so that they, too, can live the good life that abundant energy makes possible.

Unfortunately, the United States now uses far more than its fair share of world energy. The 6% of the world's population on the North American continent now use a third of the world's energy,[2] and the previously patient under-developed nations are now beginning

---

[1]<u>The World Book Encyclopedia</u>, 1968 ed., s.v. "Petroleum," by William B. Harper.

[2]William R. Barada (ed.) "Solar Water Heaters a Step Toward Energy Conservation," <u>Enfo Newsletter</u>, I, No. 5, May 1975, p. 3.

In this case, <u>op. cit.</u> is not capitalized, because it does not come at the beginning of the footnote.

The first page of Julia's paper on the opposite page shows the finished appearance of two of Julia's footnotes.

In preparing her bibliography, Julia chose the title "Selected Bibliography" because she knew she had not used all the sources available on her topic. If she had limited her bibliography to works mentioned in footnotes, she would have labelled it "Works Cited." If she wanted to indicate that her bibliography included both works she mentioned in footnotes and works she merely read, she would have used the heading "Sources Consulted." For every source mentioned in a footnote, Julia was careful to have the work listed in her bibliography. She also remembered that a bibliography includes *only* those sources actually read and consulted. When Julia's paper was complete, a part of her selected bibliography looked like this.

SELECTED BIBLIOGRAPHY
Books

Gambs, Gerard C. "Energy Sources," <u>Encyclopedia of Energy</u>, pp. 243-256. Edited by Daniel N. Lapedes. New York: McGraw-Hill, 1976.

Harrah, B. C. and Harrah, D. W. <u>Alternative Sources of Energy</u>. Metuchen, N.J.: The Scarecrow Press, Inc., 1975.

<u>The World Book Encyclopedia</u>, 1968 ed. s.v. "Petroleum," by William B. Harper.

Magazines

Barada, William R. ed. "Solar Water Heaters a Step Toward Energy Conservation," <u>Enfo Newsletter</u>, I, No. 5, (May 1975): 1-9.

The method of preparing footnotes and bibliography explained here is set forth in Kate L. Turabian's *A Manual for Writers of Term Papers, Theses and Dissertations*. As you write more library resource papers for different instructors, you may choose to learn the format for footnotes and bibliography recommended by the Modern Language Association in its style sheet or you may want to use a newer format, called the APA style, specified in the *Publication Manual of the American Psychological Association*. For now, you mainly need to learn the importance of being exact and thorough in your documentation of sources.

11. Preparing Your Front Matter (Title Page, Outline or Table of Contents, and possibly, an Introduction)

A writer always has the responsibility of attracting, interesting, and holding readers' attention. As Julia reread her rough draft, she realized that she could do something both to interest her reader and to emphasize the revised thesis statement. Before she recopied her rough draft in final form, she wrote this opening paragraph. As a good beginning is supposed to do, this one attempts to interest the reader and specify the thesis that the writer will support.

> The first recorded account of the use of solar power was at the battle of Syracuse in 212 B.C. According to contemporary accounts, as the Greeks attacked the Roman ships, Archimedes fashioned parabolic reflectors which focused the sun's rays on the Roman sails and set them afire. Whether or not Archimedes' plot really did insure the Greek victory (which most historians doubt), it was a fine demonstration of solar power. Today, solar power is ready to become the answer to America's long-range energy problem—but only governmental policies and tax credits can enable it to do so.

Julia then typed her title page, which appears on page 257.

She prepared her Table of Contents, which is shown on page 258.

Julia's teacher also asked for an outline to come after the Table of Contents; so Julia decided to provide a new decimal-type outline, rather than the traditional Harvard outline with Roman numerals, Arabic numerals, and letters. Although she wasn't able to prepare an outline before she wrote her paper, Julia found it quite easy afterwards. Julia's outline reflected the changes she made in her final draft.

The outline begins on page 259.

Solar Power: America's Energy Solution

Julia Martin

Submitted in Partial Fulfillment

of the Requirements

of English Composition 2

William Horlick High School

May 19, 1980

Assembled and retyped, the library reserach paper that Julia Martin submitted to her teacher was twelve pages, including title page, table of contents, outline, body of the paper with footnotes at the bottom of the pages, and selected bibliography. Your library research paper may be shorter or longer than Julia Martin's, but like hers it should display these qualities: neat margins, consistent format, sound facts, clear progression of ideas, and thorough documentation of information.

CONTENTS

Solar Power: America's Energy Solution

Thesis Statement: Governmental policies and tax credits can make solar energy the answer to America's long-range energy problem.

1. The world has outstripped its energy supply.

    1.1 The United States uses more than its share of energy.

    1.2 Developing nations are demanding their share of energy.

    1.3 Total resources available are rapidly being depleted.

2. Americans now realize their energy problem.

    2.1 The Arab boycott drove home the problem.

    2.2 The balance of trade and the declining dollar emphasize the American position.

    2.3 The impending depletion threatens the American way of life.

3. Experts have emphasized the weaknesses of alternative energy sources.

4. Solar energy has unlimited potential.

    4.1 It is plentiful, well-distributed, constant, and renewable.

    4.2 The Saudi Arabians already are using it.

    4.3 Americans used it when it was economically competitive.

5.   The United States is moving to make solar energy
cost competitive.

5.1 Costs of regular fuels are now very high.

5.2 California offers tax credits.

5.3 The federal government will soon offer tax credits.

5.4 The federal government will double its research
funding for solar energy.

6.   Entry of big companies into the solar energy field
bodes well for the future.

◾ MAJOR WRITING ASSIGNMENT
AN EVALUATION OF YOUR LIBRARY RESOURCE PAPER

Before you put your paper in final form and submit it to your teacher, ask yourself these questions to see if you have followed through on each stage of writing the library resource paper.

1. Is my topic important to me and others and suitable for the assignment?
2. Have I acquired enough facts and ideas on my topic to qualify me to say something significant about it?
3. Is my thesis focused and stated in terms that make it persuasive, argumentative, easily discussed, and easily supported?
4. Have I consulted the *Readers' Guide to Periodical Literature* and the card catalog in the library in search of a variety of material to support my thesis?
5. Have I prepared my bibliography cards carefully, including all the necessary information, such as the author, title, volume, date, publisher, and call number of each source?
6. Have I done the right amount of in-depth research and have I gathered enough usable material to make a good case for my thesis? Have I been accurate in my recording of direct quotations, in my paraphrases, and in my outlines of thought processes?
7. Have I followed the list of ideas or the outline I prepared before my rough draft, or have I revised this preliminary organization to be more effective and logical?
8. Does my thesis fit the material in my paper? Does every section and idea in the paper derive from the thesis and support the thesis?
9. Have I found and corrected all mistakes in content, structure, grammar, and spelling?
10. Are my footnotes and bibliography neat, accurate, and complete so that anyone could find my facts and information in the sources?
11. Are my title page, outline or table of contents, and introduction in the correct form? Does my introduction capture the reader's interest and prepare for the discussion of my thesis?

Chapter 11

Narration

Everyone loves a story, and that's all a narration, or a narrative, is—a story. It can be a story based on something that actually happened, as in a biography or an autobiography (nonfiction), or it can be a story that the writer has made up (fiction). In both fiction and nonfiction, the writer uses many of the same techniques to make a series of related events come alive for readers.

In learning to write narration, a good place to begin is with your own personal experiences. After all, you were there. You know what happened better than anyone else. You know how warm it was, how the sun felt on your shoulders, and how the conversation went. More than that, you know better than anyone else how you felt as the event was taking place. In addition, personal experience narrations are the stuff of which history and literature are made. They are also the raw material you will use as you go on to write fiction. You can even combine personal narrative and fiction by imagining that you are some other person and then writing a fictional account of events that might have happened to you as that person. You will then narrate the events as in a personal narrative. ("I stepped carefully around the fallen tree.")

During the 1930s the federal government employed six thousand writers to collect over ten thousand interviews from ordinary people. These narratives were published in 1979 under the direction of Benjamin Botkin, and they provide a priceless portrait of American life during the Great Depression. These personal narratives prove that everyone experiences events and emotions worth describing and preserving. It isn't just professional writers who can handle narration; you have within you hundreds of stories worth exploring and writing, if only you take the time to do so. The great short story writer O. Henry named one of his books *The Four Million* because there were that many residents in New York City at the time and he believed that each of them had a story to tell.

Why should anyone want to write narration? One of the best reasons is simply that writing stories is fun, just as reading them is fun. Another reason is that writing narration lets you either relive your own experiences or create a whole new life. Writing personal narratives based on your own experience gives you an opportunity to reexamine, reshape, relive, and interpret your life. Writing fictional narratives gives you an opportunity to create a whole new world with events occurring and characters acting just as you wish them to.

Here are some examples of narratives.

I

I once knew a little boy who spent a million recess periods standing right in the middle of a windswept playground just praying that someone—anyone—would notice him and knowing all the time that nobody would.

I once knew a child who sent Valentine cards to every person in the whole class and received not a single one in return.

I once knew an adolescent who always sat at an empty table in a junior high school cafeteria pretending that he wasn't even aware that he was sitting next to emptiness.

I once knew a teen-ager who spent days waiting for the telephone to ring, but it never did, and who spent Saturday nights alone with his radio pretending he was listening to it.

I once knew a man who was afraid that because he happened not to see, he would be consigned to an eternity of loneliness where there would be nobody who would want to marry him. . . .

But on the evening of November 7, 1970, I sat with Kit at a corner table in the Riviera Room of the Sheraton Boston Hotel, with the assurance that as long as the two of us lived, I would never again know all those lonely people who had once been me.

I leaned way back in my chair and let the soft sounds of the orchestra wash over me. The happiest moment of my life was about to take place, for this was the evening that I was going to ask Kit to be my wife.

The first twenty-five years of my life had been a long uphill struggle to function successfully in the sighted world. I was lucky. I had a family whose faith in God and confidence in me never faltered. Ours was a team effort which had made it possible for me to be in a position now where I could proudly ask Kit to share a very full and exciting life with me. I had already been graduated from Harvard College and Harvard Law School and was about to commence my practice of law at the firm now known as Surrey, Karasik and Morse in Washington, D.C. I had been awarded a Rotary Overseas Fellowship to read for a Diploma in Law at Oxford University for the following year, and I was fortunate enough to have inspired the Broadway hit *Butterflies Are Free*.

But as Kit squeezed my hand, I knew that as far as she was concerned, none of these things made any difference. I was simply the man with whom she was in love. We were a man and a woman, eagerly looking forward to spending a lifetime together. Nothing else mattered, least of all my blindness. . . .

"Okay, Mr. He, let's dance," Kit said.

With a silent prayer to the muse in charge of poetic proposals, I rose and strolled with Kit to the dance floor. The orchestra began to play something slow and romantic. At least I am told it was slow and romantic. All I could hear were chapel bells and voices saying, "'Til death do us part."

I have no recollection of ever popping the question, but apparently I must have mumbled something that resembled a proposal because the next thing I knew Kit and I were dancing our way back to our table.

"Now that the preliminaries are finally taken care of, let's see the ring," Kit kidded.

She stretched out her hand to me as I dipped into my pocket, found the little jewelry box, and removed the ring from it. What a moment this was: I was about to slip the ring, which had taken me hours to pick out, onto the hand of truly the most wonderful woman in the world!

I drew the ring out and very gently reached for Kit's hand. Unfortunately, being unable to find it immediately, I dropped it into her tossed salad.

Then, holding a diamond ring drenched in Thousand Island dressing, I muttered, "Where is your hand?"

"It's right here," she said.

" 'Here' tells me absolutely nothing."

"Listen, Don Quixote," she replied, "this was your idea. Why not just give me the ring, darling?"

"Absolutely not," I replied emphatically.

I rose from my chair, walked around the table, and found her arm. Then, using the logic I had learned in law school, I immediately reasoned that where there is an arm, there is usually a hand. I followed it, finally found her hand, and slid the ring onto her finger. Kit loved the ring, Thousand Island dressing and all.[1]

—Harold Krents

II

I never learned hate at home, or shame. I had to go to school for that. I was about seven years old when I got my first big lesson. I was in love with a little girl named Helene Tucker, a light-complected little girl with pigtails and nice manners. She was always clean and she was smart in school. I think I went to school then mostly to look at her. I brushed my hair and even got me a little old handkerchief. It was a lady's handkerchief, but I didn't want Helene to see me wipe my nose on my hand. The pipes were frozen again, there was no water in the house, but I washed my socks and shirt every night. I'd get a pot, and go over to Mister Ben's grocery store, and stick my pot down into his soda machine. Scoop out some chopped ice. By evening the ice melted to water for washing. I got sick a lot that winter because the fire would go out at night before the clothes were dry. In the morning I'd put them on, wet or dry, because they were the only clothes I had.

Everybody's got a Helene Tucker, a symbol of everything you want. I loved her for her goodness, her cleanness, her popularity. She'd walk down my street and my brothers and sisters would yell, "Here comes Helene," and I'd rub my tennis sneakers on the back of my pants and wish my hair wasn't so nappy and the white folks' shirt fit me better. I'd run out on the street. If I knew my place and didn't come too close, she'd wink at me and say hello. That was a good feeling. Sometimes I'd follow her all the way home, and shovel the snow off her walk and try to make friends with her Momma and her aunts. I'd drop money on her stoop late at night on my way back from shining shoes in the taverns. And she had a Daddy, and he had a good job. He was a paper hanger.

I guess I would have gotten over Helene by summertime, but something happened in that classroom that made her face hang in front of me for the next twenty-two years. When I played the drums in high school it was for Helene and when I broke track records in college it was for Helene and when I started standing behind microphones and heard applause I wished Helene could hear it, too. It wasn't until I was twenty-nine years old and married and making money that I finally got her out of my system. Helene was sitting in that classroom when I learned to be ashamed of myself.

It was on a Thursday. I was sitting in the back of the room, in a seat with a chalk circle drawn around it. The idiot's seat, the troublemaker's seat.

The teacher thought I was stupid. Couldn't spell, couldn't read, couldn't do arithmetic. Just stupid. Teachers were never interested in finding out that you couldn't concentrate because you were so hungry, because you hadn't had any breakfast. All you could think about was noontime, would it ever come? Maybe you could sneak into the cloakroom and steal a bite of some kid's lunch out of a coat pocket. A bite of something. Paste. You can't really make a meal of paste, or put it on bread for a sandwich, but sometimes I'd scoop a few spoonfuls out of the big paste jar in the back of the room. Pregnant people get strange tastes. I was pregnant with poverty. Pregnant with dirt and pregnant with smells that made people turn away, pregnant with cold and pregnant with shoes that were never bought for me, pregnant with five other people in my bed and no Daddy in the next room, and pregnant with hunger. Paste doesn't taste too bad when you're hungry.

The teacher thought I was a troublemaker. All she saw from the front of the room was a little black boy who squirmed in his idiot's seat and made noises and poked the kids around him. I guess she couldn't see a kid who made noises because he wanted someone to know he was there.

It was on Thursday, the day before the Negro payday. The eagle always flew on Friday. The teacher was asking each student how much his father would give to the Community Chest. On Friday night, each kid would get the money from his father, and on Monday he would bring it to the school. I decided I was going to buy me a Daddy right then. I had money in my pocket from shining shoes and selling papers, and whatever Helene Tucker pledged for her Daddy I was going to top it. And I'd hand the money right in. I wasn't going to wait until Monday to buy me a Daddy.

I was shaking, scared to death. The teacher opened her book and started calling out names alphabetically.

"Helene Tucker?"

"My Daddy said he'd give two dollars and fifty cents."

"That's very nice, Helene. Very, very nice indeed."

That made me feel pretty good. It wouldn't take too much to top that. I had almost three dollars in dimes and quarters in my pocket. I stuck my hand in my pocket and held onto the money, waiting for her to call my name. But the teacher closed her book after she called everybody else in the class.

I stood up and raised my hand.

"What is it now?"

"You forgot me."

She turned toward the blackboard. "I don't have time to be playing with you, Richard."

"My Daddy said he'd . . ."

"Sit down, Richard, you're disturbing the class."

"My Daddy said he'd give . . . fifteen dollars."

She turned around and looked mad. "We are collecting this money for you and your kind, Richard Gregory. If your Daddy can give fifteen dollars you have no business being on relief."

"I got it right now, I got it right now, my Daddy gave it to me to turn in today, my Daddy said . . ."

"And furthermore," she said, looking right at me, her nostrils getting big and her lips getting thin and her eyes opening wide. "We know you don't have a Daddy."

Helene Tucker turned around, her eyes full of tears. She felt sorry for me. Then I couldn't see her too well because I was crying, too.

"Sit down, Richard."

And I always thought the teacher kind of liked me. She always picked me to wash the blackboard on Friday after school. That was a big thrill, it made me feel important. If I didn't wash it, come Monday the school might not function right.

"Where are you going, Richard?"

I walked out of school that day, and for a long time I didn't go back very often. There was shame there.[2]

—Dick Gregory

Student Composition 11A
IMPRESSIONS

Which of the 5 W's and an H (Who, What, When, Where, Why, and How) are answered in the first paragraph? If so much is revealed, how does Wendi make you want to read on?

Everything about my grandmother's death seemed quick and abrupt. We found out she had lung cancer on the fourteenth of September, and then, only sixteen days later, it was all over, and she was dead. Just that fast, she was gone.

I didn't realize until weeks later how very bravely Nana died. She knew towards the end that she was about to die, but she never cried or felt sorry for herself or even complained when the pain grew worse. She accepted everything quietly and peacefully and only once said a word about her death. Only a few days before she left us, she suddenly said to my Aunt Sue, "I want to be cremated." And nothing more was said between them about the matter.

When I found out that Nana was to be cremated, it bothered me because I could not understand why she had wanted such a thing. It made her death seem even more final to me. Then our pastor took me aside, and he reminded me that the Bible says, "Out of the ground were you taken; you are dust, and to dust shall you return." He explained that cremation was just a way of speeding up the natural process of returning to the earth from which we come—ashes to ashes and dust to dust, only much faster. Because he took the time to discuss it with me, I began to accept it.

The ashes were stored at the funeral home for three months, not forgotten, just left there because we didn't know what to do with them. It was difficult to get the family all together at one time, and Nana had not instructed just where she wanted her ashes to be scattered. We finally decided upon the woods of my Aunt Sue's ranch. So, on December 31, the last day of 1977, we took my grandmother's ashes to the place where they would mix back into the earth.

We walked to a large clump of tall, ancient oak trees, and they looked like great wooden pillars supporting a roof of boughs and branches and drooping Spanish moss. The open space inside and the upward curving slope of the trunks formed a natural cathedral, and we knew that this sanctuary was the perfect place.

Each of us stood there, silent and deep in our own private thoughts and loving memories as my father said a prayer. Then I watched as Uncle Hunter carefully and lovingly began scattering handfuls of ashes around the trees and into palmetto bushes. The last ashes gracefully floated into powdery clouds before finally settling on the ground, and we burned the plastic bag. Then it was all done.

As we walked away, it began to sprinkle lightly, and I knew that the ashes had begun their journey back into the earth.

—Wendi Jordan

Is this narration basically about Wendi or about her grandmother? Explain your answer. What seems to be the point, or purpose, of the narration?

In much narration, emotions are overstated rather than understated. How would you criticize Wendi's writing in this respect? What does that contribute to the mood and tone of her piece?

What details help you visualize the place the ashes were scattered?

What might the sprinkling of rain in the last paragraph symbolize? Discuss the effectiveness of the very short final paragraph.

Student Composition 11B

MY NEW CAR

Some narratives are made more exciting because the writer begins in the middle of the story— often near the climax. This is really the story of Alice's car, rather than her brother's. Where in the story, then, might she have begun? What would she have included in a *flashback*?

How would you rewrite this long sentence in order to make it more crisp and more interesting?

In formal writing, the word Dad would have an apostrophe and "s" so the phrase would read "Dad's sitting down." What is the rule for the possessive in this case?

How realistic does Dad's speech sound here? What might David say after each sentence?

In writing narration, authors can make time pass as rapidly as they want to, just as long as they make clear the time and sequence of each event. What does Alice do to help give the feeling of passing time?

How adequate is Alice's description of her dream car? What details might you add to make the car of your dreams seem real?

What is the *foreshadowing* here?

On the morning David turned sixteen, Dad laid down the paper, pushed back his breakfast plate, and said, "Davy, I guess it's time for you and me to go out and get you a car!"

"A car, Dad? You mean it? For me? All my own?" David was so excited he could hardly talk, and milk and toast crumbs decorated his lips. I had four years to go before I would be sixteen, and cars didn't really mean much to me then, but I knew that when I became sixteen, it would be my turn, and Dad and I would go out the door together, his arm around my shoulders, just as he and David left home that morning.

They returned about two o'clock that afternoon, with David driving a "new" 1970 Pontiac Firebird. It was green with low, fast lines, and oversized tires. I actually thought it looked a little funny, but David was so excited and happy, and Dad was so pleased with himself, that right then I began to think of when I would get my new car. I remember Dad sitting down with Dave at the kitchen table and saying, "Now, son, this isn't a new car, but it's in good shape, and we'll keep it that way. I've paid the first year's insurance, but after that, you've got to pay it. And I don't ever want to hear of you speeding or burning rubber or doing anything that breaks the law. If you do, that's the end of your car."

"Don't worry, Pop," David grinned. "I'm going to take good care of this car. No way I'm going to lose it."

I knew it would be the same for me. Dad wouldn't buy me a new car, but he'd spend as much as he could afford, and he'd buy my insurance. From that time on I became car-conscious, and as the four years passed, I learned more and more about cars and what kind I wanted. The last six months I could hardly wait.

What I really wanted was a Satellite, one of those nifty little jobs with a lift-back. I knew I might not have a choice of color, but I imagined that it had a metallic gray body with lots of chrome and a bright red interior. I spent hours imagining myself at the driver's seat with girls piled in for rides home after basketball practice. Each day of the month before my birthday seemed like a year.

About a week before my birthday, Dad got me up early one Saturday morning. "Come on, Alice," he said. "We're going to get your car today!" While he scrambled some eggs and I showered, I began to worry. "We're going to *get* your car today!" Not

"We're going to pick out your car today" or "*look for* your car today," but "We're going to *get* your car today."

I didn't say anything at breakfast, but as we drove away from the house, I asked quietly, "Where are we going, Dad?" I think he knew I had a premonition, because he looked at me, and suddenly all his excitement faded. In fact, I think he began to get angry, but he kept it under control, even though he paused before answering and I could see his jaw working.

"We're going to Mrs. Gibson's house, Alice, to get your new car."

"Mrs. Gibson," I wailed. "You don't mean Mrs. Gibson's old Tempo, do you?"

"That's exactly what I mean, Alice. I bought it yesterday. She's decided that she's too old to drive any more, and I got a fantastic deal on it. It's got only 25,000 miles, so it ought to last you another 75,000—at least through your first two years in college."

By this time, we had pulled into Mrs. Gibson's old two-strip concrete driveway right behind her 1974 Tempo. It was a four-door; dirty, faded brown, no chrome, no style, and not a smidgen of personality. It wasn't at all like my Satellite with its style and chrome and pizazz.

"I don't want it, Dad," I said quietly. "Dave got to pick out his car, and I want to pick out mine."

At that instant, Dad blew up. "I can't believe, Alice," he said coldly, "that you're turning down the car I found for you! It was an accident that David got to pick out his car. I simply hadn't found a good one for him. I promised you a car. I didn't promise you could pick out your car, and I didn't promise you any certain car. Nobody ever bought me a car—nobody ever even bought me a bicycle. This car is the best deal for the money. Now, take it or leave it."

My Satellite dreams vanished, and I looked at the ugly old bus that would be my trademark for the next four years. Dad couldn't understand why I was disappointed, and I couldn't understand why he felt so hurt. He still thinks I'm selfish and ungrateful, so we just don't talk about it.

Before Mrs. Gibson sold Dad the Tempo, I used to think how it suited her personality. She was fat, drab, and slow-moving. She never drove over forty, and she always hugged the curb. I'm sorry I hurt my Dad and made him feel that I don't appreciate my new car—but whenever I sit in my Tempo, I feel that I am Mrs. Gibson.

The worst of it is that I'm just a senior. I'll have that feeling for two or three more years.

—Alice Ashton

What word here indicates a change in tone and attitude in the paper? What tone, attitude, or mood do you really expect as a girl gets her first car? What attitude does the father expect?

How well do father and daughter understand each other? To what extent is each justified? How does the writer indicate that she still doesn't quite understand her father?

In what way does the phrase "two-strip concrete driveway" and the description of the Tempo tell you what Alice is feeling? What is Alice objecting to? Is she justified?

What details of Dad's appearance would make this passage more interesting and visual?

How does this passage indicate Alice's purpose in writing this narrative?

How sympathetic would the father be to Alice's feelings about the Tempo and Mrs. Gibson? How would this whole story change if written from his point of view?

Who has your sympathy as you finish this narrative? Why?

Reacting to the Narrative Models

Two of the models were written by professional writers, and two of them were written by students. None of the models is perfect, of course, but you can learn from them. After reading the models, discuss the following questions.

1. Of all the personal experiences the writers must have had, something has caused each one to write about one particular incident. What seems to have influenced each writer's choice? (There may be several influences.) How will recognizing these influences help you select your subjects?

2. Rudyard Kipling, who was a newspaper reporter as well as a writer of stories and novels, once wrote a verse that names the elements of both news stories and narratives:

> I have six faithful serving men
> They taught me all I know.
> Their names are what and where and when
> And why and how and who.

Where does each of these elements occur in the selections? Is any element ever omitted from a narrative? To what extent are most of them included in the introductory paragraphs of these models?

3. How closely do the selections follow natural chronological order? What advantage, if any, results from using out-of-order incidents (flashbacks)? What dangers does using them entail?

4. What are the differences between *showing* an event and *telling about* it? Which is more interesting and exciting? Why? (You will learn about these later in this chapter.)

5. How important are concrete descriptions and appeals to the senses? How can you make the readers smell, taste, touch, hear, and see objects and incidents?

6. How are the various paragraphs connected with each other? What helps the thought flow smoothly from one to the next?

Elements of Narration

In order for a narration to be interesting and meaningful, it must have the following elements:

1. Emotion. Writing is really such hard work that people ought not to bother writing something with which they are not emotionally involved. What emotions are apparent in each selection? How strongly is the narrator involved? What indications are there in the models of strong emotional involvement?

2. Action. Something happens; that is, tension increases and conflict intensifies as various events occur. In simple stories, the action is very often physical—fights, calamities, contests—but in more subtle stories the action may be emotional or intellectual. The action, however, whether it is exterior and visible or interior and invisible, causes the situation to change so that conditions are different at the end of the story from the way they were at the beginning. This movement, or development, is important.

3. Suspense. Each passage suggests that something is going to happen so that the reader eagerly anticipates the outcome of these events. To build suspense, you plant seeds that hint at conflicts, problems, mysteries. You promise the reader that you will show the plants in bloom and all conflicts, problems, and mysteries solved at the end of the story. Suspense is a vital factor in building and retaining the interest of the reader.

4. Structure, or order. Events in real life happen in a definite order—the order of time. But in discovering meaning in the events or in imposing a meaning on them, the writer may need to arrange them differently from the order in which they originally occurred. Whether writers use straight chronological order or determine a new order, they are giving structure to their narrative in order to heighten suspense and make incidents and events more meaningful.

5. Point or purpose. Although everyone loves a story and thousands of narratives are written and read only for entertainment, the best stories have a purpose or meaning of some kind. Indeed, even those written and told for their own sakes, often make some kind of statement on human beings, human values, or some aspect of life. To get the most satisfaction from the effort that goes into writing a narrative, select an incident in which you can discover a meaning or an event on which you can impose meaning. Sometimes the meaning is an overall impression or attitude. At other times it is an idea that can be expressed in a single sentence. What are the meanings of the models?

6. Point of view. In every narrative, someone (or something) tells the story, and this person or animal or thing marks the story with his or her personal imprint. Imagine how much different the story of the "Three Little Pigs" or of "Little Red Riding Hood" would be if, in each case, the wolf told the story! If you write a personal story about one of your own experiences, you will probably use "I" or "we," which is called *first-person narrator.* Occasionally, you may write a first-person narrative when you are relating events in the life of a fictional character, rather than yourself. In those cases, you have "assumed a *persona*," or taken on the role of another person, much as an actor does. You then speak consistently from that person's point of view—seeing things as he or she sees them, reacting as that person would, and even using the language appropriate for the character. Sometimes, when you are reading narratives, it is difficult to separate the author from the persona he or she is "speaking through." For example, Ernest Hemingway really did participate in the Spanish Civil War and go on safaris in Africa. Yet sometimes when one of his characters tells about those experiences, it is a persona, or imagined character, rather than Hemingway who is speaking. Knowing who is speaking is sometimes important in getting the meaning of a narrative. Another point of view often used in narration is *third-person narrator*. When telling a story from that point of view, you relate events as though you were an onlooker, and you use the pronouns "he," "she," "it," or "they." Of course, you already know that when you are telling a story that is really true, you are presenting nonfiction. If, however, you are making up a story, then you are presenting fiction.

7. Effective description. Concrete details create images, or pictures, in the readers' minds and make the events in the narrative come alive.

Preparing to Write

The first step in preparing your narrative is either to recall or invent some situation which excites you emotionally. It is better to recall an actual event if you can, but there is nothing wrong with inventing a situation, provided it is realistic and you can become emotionally involved with the events.

Getting an Idea

Everything you learn comes to you through your senses. You experience life through seeing, touching, tasting, smelling, and hearing. Your senses are the sources of all your ideas.

Of course, you can experience life vicariously—at secondhand—by reading, listening to the radio, and watching television and films. By using these secondary sources well, you can find out about anything you choose, and you can write on thousands of subjects you have never experienced firsthand. But the most vital writing you do will be the writing in which you are emotionally involved with your subject.

Using an emotion to stimulate an idea. Think. Remember. Feel. Go back to your storehouse of personal sensory experiences. Dredge up the details and emotion of some half-forgotten event. Perhaps you can remember the anguish of a moment long ago when others seemed for some reason to forget you. Perhaps you still feel loneliness or fear or pain or delight from some experience you once had. From this memory you can begin to write about the experience.

Of course, as you examine some previous experience in your life, you will see a difference between real life and stories that you read. In life, events are not crisp and clear and precise with a definite meaning and emotion. As one writer declared,

> One thing that makes art different from life is that in art things have a shape; they have beginnings, middles, and endings, whereas in life, things just drift along. In life somebody has a cold, and you treat it as insignificant, and suddenly they die. Or they have a heart attack, and you are sodden with grief until they recover to live for thirty petulant years, demanding you wait on them. . . . In other words, in life one almost never has an emotion appropriate to an event. Either you don't know the event is occurring, or you don't know its significance. . . . Feelings are large and spread over a lifetime. . . . Anyway, that is a thing art does for us: it allows us to fix our emotions on events at the moment they occur, it permits a union of heart and mind and tongue and tear.[3]
>
> —Marilyn French

As you begin to think about your experiences, the chances are that the emotion-laden events will at first have little meaning or importance to you. As you think about them more and more, however, you will be going through an artistic shaping and exploring process. As Alice Ashton began writing "My New Car" (pages 269-270), she probably began with no more than the memory of her disappointment at not being allowed to choose a sporty car. Yet as she examined, explored, and, above all, organized the experience, she found new significance and many additional meanings in the event. Many events without additional insights might not be worth reading about, but with the action sharpened and highlighted and with the meanings explored, they become interesting and important.

ACTIVITY 11A

Exploring Areas of Personal Experience

In anticipation of the Major Writing Assignment for this chapter, be prepared to discuss in class the areas in which you have had important personal experiences. List these areas on the black-

These Egyptian hieroglyphics, carved in stone, gave an account of the career of Thetä, a royal advisor who lived four thousand years ago.

board. Then begin listing under each of these categories possible subjects that you might write on. Does the following list include most of the significant areas of your experience?

Family and home	Mass media	Friends
School	Clubs	Travel
Work	Hobbies	Reading
Church	Boy-girl relationships	People

Creating imaginary events to portray real emotions. Working with someone whom you like, describe to your partner a situation that you remember and an emotion that you still feel.

Then decide whether or not your writing about the situation would cause a reader to feel as you felt. If you decide it would not, discuss what imaginary situation you could create to communicate the feeling you wish to convey. For example, if a favorite uncle promised to take you to a movie and forgot to come for you, your pain and disappointment might be very real to you, but the incident is so slight that a reader might not be moved. What imaginary incident might communicate the same pain and disappointment? Perhaps readers would be touched by the story of a fatherless child who was heart-broken when plans for a rare visit to the circus fell through. Or perhaps they might feel the hurt of a girl who is all dressed up for her first dance and learns that her date is not coming.

ACTIVITY 11B

Writing about Real and Imagined Events

Write a brief description of an event you experienced and of the emotion it generated. Then write a brief description of an imagined event that would convey to a reader the same emotional reactions even more vividly.

Giving Order to Your Narrative

Reading novels and short stories will convince you that there is no single pattern for a narrative. Each writer chooses the organization that seems appropriate to the story. Nonetheless, each narrative must have a beginning, a middle, and an end. As you understand how each part functions, you will be able to develop distinctive patterns for your own narratives.

The beginning. The beginning of any narrative is important for these reasons:

1. It establishes the relationship between writer and reader.
2. It hints at why the narrative is worth reading. It suggests the significance of the events.
3. It reveals the background for the events. It often defines the *who*, *what*, *when*, *where*, and hints at the *why* and *how*.

The middle. The middle section develops the narrative.

1. It narrates selected events, often in the natural order but always in the order best calculated to hold the reader's attention and create suspense.
2. It explains, comments on, and interprets the events when explanation, comment, and interpretation are necessary.
3. It provides guides to time, place, sequence, and significance, so that the reader doesn't get lost.

The end. The end contributes to the final impression left with the reader.

1. It brings the sequence of events to an interesting close.
2. It comments on, reaffirms, or simply clarifies the meaning or significance of the events.

Reread the student compositions to see whether each fits this pattern. This outline of a narrative is so simple that most writers follow it automatically. This chapter should help you gain additional insight into your own most effective means of using such an outline. Even professional writers differ from one another in their use of the standard pattern.

Some outline a story before they begin to write.
Some prepare a simple list of events in the order of occurrence.
Some prepare a simple list and then experiment with different orders of presentation.
Some plunge right into the rough draft, ignoring any kind of standard pattern.
Some plunge right into the rough draft following a kind of standard pattern they have internalized so that they follow it automatically.
Some—usually the ones who have planned ahead most carefully—do little revising.
Some—usually the ones who have plunged ahead most quickly—revise extensively.

How do you work best? With what procedures are you most comfortable and most productive?

Adapting the Inverted-Pyramid Style to Narration

Have you ever heard someone ruin a joke by telling the punchline first? How frustrating it is to be on the verge of hearing a fresh, new joke, only to have it spoiled because the narrator gives you too much too soon. The same is true in writing or telling a story: you want to give your reader or listener just enough of the who, what, where, and when to arouse interest and make the story understandable. Then, with interest aroused, you want to reveal more details, one at a time (especially those about the why and the how of events) to intensify interest and build suspense right to the climax of the story.

Newspaper writers have a different purpose from storytellers. They organize their articles to give a complete summary of their story in the first paragraph. Consequently, they use inverted-pyramid style and include in the opening the who, what, when, where, why, and how of the story. Then they fill in the less important details.

Inverted-pyramid style developed during the Civil War when correspondents on battlefields began using the newly invented telegraph. Because the telegraph was unreliable and might fail at any time, reporters sent their most important information first: the who, what, when, where, why, and how. Busy people seemed to like this order of presentation, possibly because it allowed them to skip the less important details that came at the end of the story. And so, inverted-pyramid style has become standard newspaper form.

You may find it helpful to be aware of the 5 W's and an H as you think through your narrative and plan your beginning. Determine which of them will help arouse interest and make the rest of the story easy to understand. Avoid including information in your opening that will destroy suspense.

ACTIVITY 11C

Studying Introductions

1. Discuss how the writers of the following story openings 1. borrow from journalistic inverted-pyramid style, 2. provide background information, and 3. include a "narrative hook" to get the reader interested.

   a. There was a cheerful atmosphere in the gym the night of the parent-teacher basketball game, and the teachers enjoyed a seven-point lead midway through the second quarter. My dad was playing along with the other parents, and they all seemed to be enjoying the game. Suddenly a big man on the parents' team drove for the basket and missed the shot. He slammed his fist against the protective mat under the basket and snarled like a savage animal.

   b. If you have been blessed with a perfect set of thirty-two teeth, impeccable speech, and a charming smile, you have been luckier than I. I don't remember ever having straight teeth, being able to say the word "statistic" without lisping, or smiling without feeling like a stand-in for Bugs Bunny. And, somehow, when I was in the sixth grade, I realized that my teeth were not going to correct themselves. My mother realized it, too, for she took me to a well-known orthodontist in our area.

2. From the list of subjects you prepared for Activity 11A, choose two or three and write an introductory paragraph for each. Come to class prepared to exchange papers and to evaluate the introductory paragraphs of other students in terms of 1. background provided, 2. interest aroused, 3. concreteness, and 4. suspense.

Giving Meaning or "Point" to an Experience

One day a young mother carefully cleaned the refrigerator, piled seven-year-old Brian into the car, and went grocery shopping. Upon their return, just as she started to put the food away, the telephone rang. After a long conversation, she was delighted to find that the child had continued storing the food in the pantry, cupboard, and refrigerator.

Then she opened the refrigerator to find egg all over the back, sides, and shelves, and all over the food inside as well. She was furious.

Suddenly, she stopped and thought. Why did he do it? Her first reaction was to think that he was angry and frustrated at being left alone. Then she looked at the little oval-shaped compartments for storing eggs on the inside of the refrigerator door. They were full. There was no room for the extra eggs. Brian, wanting to be helpful by keeping like foods together, had piled the six extra eggs on top of the eggs already stored. When he closed the refrigerator door, the six precariously perched eggs were thrown all over the inside of the refrigerator.

What was the mother's interpretation: that her son was careless and stupid, or that he was eager to help but inexperienced?

One of the differences between life and art is that anything that is included in a poem, a painting, or a drama is significant. It's there for a reason. In life, however, some events or objects seem to mean absolutely nothing. Other events or objects might have several different meanings. For example, a star might be interpreted as a symbol for the Soviet Union, the rank of brigadier general, or the brand of a certain cattle ranch. If the writer intends only one meaning, a setting or context must be provided to limit the interpretation to that one meaning. In some cases, events can have several different meanings or interpretations. We know that, especially in poetry and painting, such *ambiguity* (the condition of having more than one meaning) is prized very highly. For example, when A. E. Housman thought of the friends he had in his youth who had since died, he wrote, "With rue my heart is laden." The word "rue" has two meanings: "regret, remorse, unhappiness" and "a strong-scented woody herb whose bitter leaves are used in medicine." Both meanings are appropriate, and the ambiguity enriches the poetry.

As you write narratives, you must not leave things frustratingly ambiguous. You must omit anything that is completely meaningless, you must clarify anything that could have more than the one meaning you intend, and you must be sure that ambiguous objects or events are presented so that all possible meanings are appropriate and enrich your narration.

Here are some simple examples of situations in narratives in which the writer had to guide the reader to the correct interpretation.

1. In Joseph Conrad's novel *Lord Jim*, an officer on a ship full of pilgrims, abandoned them when he thought the ship was sinking. He was the only officer who was eventually tried in court. Later, he left Western society to live in Malaysia. Was he ashamed and afraid to face his people, or was he determined to find his true nature and prove himself in another emergency?

2. Owen Warland, in Nathaniel Hawthorne's story "The Artist of the Beautiful," was so preoccupied with creating a perfect mechanical butterfly that he neglected his watchmaking business and was willing to let himself and his family starve. Was he a lazy, inconsiderate lout, or a brilliant, dedicated artist?

3. In Henry James' novel *The American*, the hero is a self-made millionaire who falls in love with a beautiful, sophisticated daughter of the French nobility. She rejects him. Did she do so because he is ignorant, brash, and of a lower class, or because the members of the ancient nobility are too self-centered to see that the American has qualities superior to their own?

These are examples of situations in which you must impose meaning on a sequence of events. Whenever any event or series of events makes an impact on you, you must analyze, interpret, and impose a meaning or "point" on the events. Can you see how the young mother in the incident on page 279 might spank her child because of one interpretation or hug him because of another?

ACTIVITY 11D

Imposing Meaning on Events

For each of the following briefly described incidents, determine one or more interpretations. Working as your teacher directs, take one of the incidents and flesh it out with real people in a real situation. Use description and conversation, and make clear, either through implication or direct statement, the interpretation you want your readers to make.

1. A respected citizen dresses up in a costume and mask and dumps sewage and motor oil in the office of the president of a company that has been polluting the environment.

2. A new girl at school sits by herself, refuses to speak to anyone, and ignores attempts of others to be friendly.

3. A family with the finest home, the most beautiful lawn, and the best car in town has always been very careful about appearances in all situations. Suddenly, the lawn goes to seed, the house needs painting, the car's fenders, bent in an accident, have not been repaired, and the children go to school in soiled clothes.

4. A brilliant, outgoing foreign exchange student suddenly becomes quiet, sullen, and withdrawn.

5. At an auction, a student bids casually on an oil painting and gets it for practically nothing. Shortly afterwards, a well-dressed, apparently wealthy stranger bursts into the room and declares that he owns the painting.

Point of View

It is most important, as you think about the narrative you will write, to decide from what point of view you will tell your story. When you are reading or writing a narrative, the person who is telling the story makes a difference in how much you believe and how much you will accept. One basic point of view is the first-person narrator, in which the person telling the story says, in effect, "I did this" or "This happened to me." The student composition "Impressions" on pages 267-268 is an example of a story told in the first person.

Sometimes, of course, the I-narrator is an imaginary, or fictional persona who tells the story as though it had happened to him or her, even though the reader recognizes that the events never actually happened and the person never existed.

In Chapter 12 you will read a character sketch (page 316) in which the author, Charlotte Brontë, uses a fictional persona.

Another common point of view is the omniscient author, in which a kind of superhuman all-seeing narrator tells the story.

This point of view allows you to enter the mind of any of your characters. You can shift the focus from one character to another. You can interpret the actions of your characters or explain their innermost thoughts.

There are other variations on these two basic points of view. The narrator may distort the truth, and the reader must decide what to believe and what not to believe. In some stories, the narrator is a character in the story who does not perceive or understand anything beyond his or her own experiences.

ACTIVITY 11E

Experimenting with Point of View

Following is a brief narration from a point of view that is rarely used in storytelling, second-person point of view. (First-person narration uses the pronoun "I;" second person uses the pronoun "you;" third person uses the pronoun "he" or "she.") Working as your teacher directs, discuss which point of view would be most effective for this story. Rewrite this second-person narrative using first-person or third-person point of view.

> You walk from the locker room to the dark, dirty minehead. Overhead and in the distance you can see the tipple and hear the clank, clank, clank of the conveyor belt. You wait with the other men for about two minutes until you hear a sharp, metallic screech, the bar to the elevator lifts, and the lunge of about fifty other miners carries you onto the scarred wooden platform with the steel cage surrounding you. You hear the bell ring, smell the moldy air from the deep shaft, reach to your helmet to flick on your light, and feel the wooden bar once again clunk into place. Then you grip the sides of the cage as the platform drops suddenly from beneath your feet, and you plunge at breakneck speed into the darkness. At intervals, you pass dimly lighted transverse shafts until you are a mile below surface and the cage slows screechingly and stops with a jerk. Now, you're at work level, a mile down, and the hot, moist air wraps around you as you leave the elevator. You're ready to work.

Using Narration to Support Exposition

In writing exposition, a writer will often present a topic sentence or a thesis statement and then tell a story to demonstrate or illustrate the idea. Locate the topic sentence in the following paragraph and notice how the narrative that follows illustrates the idea.

> Electric automobiles may be the answer to the pollution of the internal-combustion engine. Inventor Ray Boeger established Electrodyne, Inc., as a manufacturer of three-wheeled golf carts and electric prams for factory messengers and beach vacationers. Then he got the idea of developing Mark II, a four-wheeled vehicle weighing 940 pounds, able to range forty to fifty miles without recharging, and adding very little to the average family's electric bill. Boeger set up an assembly plant in Garden Grove, California, and established sales offices at Leisure World in Seal Beach, California. He now sells about four Mark II's a week but he believes that with little trouble he could set up to produce ten to fifteen a day. Anyone who purchases a Mark II must be satisfied with traveling silently at twenty-five miles an hour, and he must be prepared to be towed home if the six heavy-duty batteries lose their charge.

ACTIVITY 11F

Using Narratives to Support Expository Ideas

Read the following paragraph and then locate the topic sentence and the supporting narration. Think of some other narrative you could use to support the main idea. It may be fact (an actual instance) or fiction (an imagined instance).

> Sometimes the name given to a group of people is entirely wrong, and its continued existence perpetuates a misconception about them. For example, in the American northwest and the Canadian southwest is a group of Indians commonly known as the "Gros Ventres," which is French for "the big-belly Indians." These people are now, and for many years have been, slim, trim, neat, and attractive. When they were first discovered by the old French voyageurs however, they were in the throes of a long and devastating famine. Suffering from hunger and malnutrition, their bellies had become distended and swollen, and their limbs were shrunken. For this reason the voyageurs called them "the big bellies." This led other explorers for two hundred years to think of them as wastrels and gluttons, when nothing could have been further from the truth.

ACTIVITY 11G

Writing and Developing Topic Sentences

1. Prepare a list of ten sentences that you might use as topic sentences. You will support one of these topic sentences with

a narrative paragraph similar to that in Activity 11F. Work as your teacher directs to develop a list of acceptable ideas. Begin with the following.

a. Noise pollution is one of America's most destructive problems. For example. . . .

b. Open enrollment in colleges (that is, the policy of permitting everyone to enter college regardless of high-school record or achievement test scores) has (or has not) meant great opportunity for minority-group students. Clyde Smith, who would never have had a chance at college. . . .

c. Commercials are (or are not) the best thing on television. My favorite. . . . (The one I hate the most. . . .)

d. The right to bear arms as guaranteed in the Bill of Rights is essential (or is outmoded) in modern America. In any newspaper you can find such reports as. . . .

e. Young people dominate the world of fashion. When _____ began wearing _____, it seemed far out, but now. . . .

2. Take about fifteen to twenty minutes of class time to develop one of the topic sentences by writing a narrative paragraph in support of it. You may need to use your imagination to create a fictional narrative for this purpose. Then work on your rough draft as your teacher directs.

3. Be prepared to spend about half a class period discussing your narrative paragraphs and the ideas that give them purpose. As other students read their work, take notes so that you can react to such questions as these:

a. Is there a meaning or point in the paragraph? Is this hinted at or expressed in the first sentence?

b. Is the rest of the paragraph tied to the topic sentence?

c. Is this a narrative; that is, does it tell of an event or a sequence of events?

d. Is it fairly concrete? Does it present real people in a real situation doing real things? Does the description appeal to your senses?

e. Is each sentence tied to the preceding one so that the thought flows smoothly, without shift of focus?

Enriching Your Narrations

So far in your study of narratives, you have looked at first-person and third-person narratives written by both professional and student writers. In addition, you have examined ways of getting ideas and making use of experiences that evoked emotions. Next, you examined ways of organizing your narrations by emphasizing suspense, by adapting the journalistic inverted-pyramid style to your openings, by finding or imposing meaning on your experiences, by selecting and using consistently an effective point of view, and by shaping your narrative to support an expository idea.

Even with all of these techniques mastered, however, you might find yourself with a carefully organized but lifeless narrative unless you enrich it and flesh it out by describing the sensory experiences which cause real-life incidents to register details on your consciousness. In addition to adding sensory experiences and descriptive details to your writing, you have the

This pictograph was painted on deerskin. It probably tells the story of the creation of the Mixtecs, a people who lived in Mexico before the coming of Columbus.

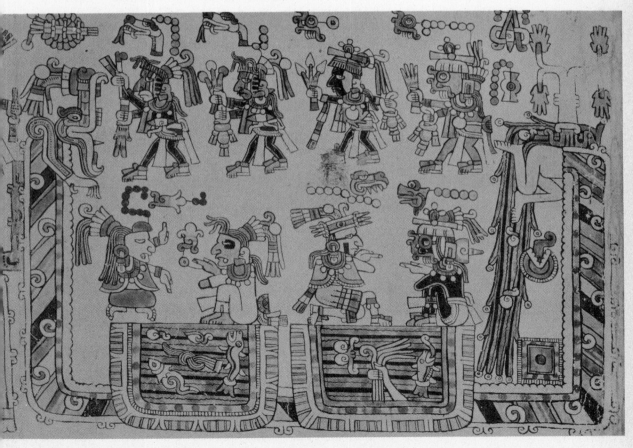

opportunity to select, focus, and organize details that will heighten the impression you want to make. In a real-life situation, your mind may select a few from the thousands of impressions that surround you, but it's a rare person who can focus to the extent that only the details appropriate to one preconceived mood or attitude enter the mind. In art—and writing narration is an art—you can determine in advance the impression you want to create. Then you can select only the sensory details that will reinforce that impression, and focus and organize them for the most powerful effect. No wonder art focuses and heightens experience.

Selecting Details That Convey Meaning and Add Concreteness

Suppose you are sitting in English class when a baseball suddenly shatters a window. Your senses are bombarded. You *hear* the smashing of the glass, the thud of the ball on the floor, the tinkle of the shattered fragments, the gasps of your classmates. You *see* the flash of the ball, the quick, fluttering reflections as the fragments of glass catch the sun, the jagged hole, the skinned horsehide of the ball. At the same time your senses of taste and smell and touch are providing subconscious impressions of the total situation. (You *taste* the remnants of the beef stew the cafeteria served at lunch; you *smell* Janie's perfume, the chalk dust from the blackboard, the burst of fresh outdoor air; you *feel* the desk with your elbows, the floor with your feet.)

Yet, when you tell a friend about the incident, you may say simply, "A ball broke the window in our English class." Just think how much of the complete experience you have left out!

Recreating experiences by selecting details. Anyone who wants to write an interesting narrative tries to include the details of the total experience to reinforce an idea and communicate an experience to the reader. Writing can never communicate the whole experience, but it is important to be aware of all the aspects of the situation so that you can select the details that support the idea or impression you are stressing. Then, by using a specific word instead of a general word, by using modifiers, and by using comparisons, you can come closer to communicating the experience or the idea.

Omitting details. It is just as important to omit some aspects of an experience as it is to stress others. Just as your mind consciously perceives only a small portion of a total experience, so you must transmit only a small portion of your total perception to your reader. To include all the details would result in a fuzzy, confused, purposeless narrative. Choose, instead, the incisive, important details, and make them clear and memorable.

ACTIVITY 11H

Three Ways of Achieving Concreteness

1. *Exact words.* Be prepared to discuss in class why the sentences on the right are better than those on the left.

a. The plant grew higher than the other plants.
b. The clock sounded.

a. The milkweed towered above the tomatoes.
b. Big Ben boomed.

2. *Modification.* Be prepared to discuss in class why the sentences on the right are better than those on the left. Note that in English sentences single-word modifiers ordinarily come before the word they modify (the *heavy* book, the *tired* dog) but that phrasal and clausal modifiers ordinarily follow the word they modify (the book *of Roman myths*, the dog *who was so tired he couldn't move*).

a. The milkweed towered above the tomatoes.

b. Big Ben boomed.

a. The blown milkweed, its pods shivering in the breeze, towered above the young tomato plants.

b. High above the Houses of Parliament, Big Ben boomed over sleeping London.

3. *Comparisons.* Be prepared to discuss in class why the sentences that follow may or may not be better than those on the right above.

a. Looking like a captured queen, the blown milkweed towered haughtily above the young tomato plants.
b. High above the houses of Parliament, Big Ben laboriously hoisted his hands to the hour and boomed noisily above sleeping London.

ACTIVITY 11 I

Expanding Sentences to Achieve Concreteness

1. Prepare a list of simple sentences like those in the first set of examples in Activity 11H. Perhaps these will help you get started.

   a. The thing came into the room.

   b. The group gave the boy a present.

   c. Amy thought the present nice.

   d. The official seemed puzzled.

   e. The message inspired the action.

2. After you have listed fifteen or twenty sentences, be prepared to participate in a class discussion during which your teacher lists on the blackboard the most stimulating sentences of the class. Then you may choose five to rewrite. First, replace general words with exact words. Next, add modifiers. Finally, insert, where appropriate, a figure of speech or a comparison.

3. The following day, bring to class the rewritten sentences, recopied in good form. Working as your teacher directs, note how students have developed the same basic sentences in different ways. Discuss which sentences are particularly well done and which sentences lose effect because they are over-done.

4. The following passage is written in very general terms. In order for it to be effective narration, it would need to be fleshed out with the sensory impressions that can be added by using exact words, modification, and comparison.

   Working as your teacher directs, rewrite this passage to include more sensory impressions. Use the three operations you have examined above: substituting exact words, adding modifiers, and including comparisons.

   The parade is the most exciting event in the town during the whole year. For a while before the date, all the townspeople work as a team. They sew things. They build things. They create things. They practice things. A publication holds an election for the parade couple.

   No one knows the winning couple until the day of the parade. The two winners wear unusual robes with things on their heads. When the people see the winners, they usually make a lot of noise. Next come the men in funny clothes, then the things people have been working together on all year, then the vehicles from the various precincts. Finally the boys and girls from local schools come by with musical instruments. It is a big day for the town.

Linking Narration and Description

Everyone loves a good story, but not many people enjoy long descriptive passages. In the past, when life moved more slowly than it does today, people who read books for pleasure were not distracted by television and other entertainments easily available today. With more time and fewer distractions, readers were happy to read more slowly and to spend more time on savoring description. Today, description is usually presented in the context of various kinds of writing, such as narration, exposition, and argumentation rather than as a separate and distinct kind of writing. Since, however, it is absolutely essential in narration, the art of writing description is presented in this chapter.

Despite some people's preferences for watching television, skimming magazines and newspapers, or simply listening to records, a larger group of people than ever before reads and enjoys good description. Their tastes, however, have been influenced by the activities that compete with reading, and the style of description today reflects those influences. As you read the following examples of descriptive writing notice the techniques used by the writers.

I

A yellow sun always broils Southern Italy in August. But on this morning in the Roman pleasure resort of Pompeii, the earth steams. The heat is almost unbearable. Springs and wells already have dried up mysteriously, and for four days the ground has rumbled and growled. Along the shore, the Bay of Naples sizzles like a massive devil's cauldron. Dogs strain at their leashes and birds fly away.[4]

—M. W. Newman

II

I think the next ten miles were the most exciting I have ever traveled in a train. We were on the coast, moving fast along a spit of land, and on either side of the train—its whistle screaming, its chimney full of smoke—white sand had drifted into magnificent dunes; beyond these dunes were slices of green sea. Sand whipped up by the engine pattered against the carriages behind, and spray from the breakers, whose regular wash dramatized the chugging of the locomotive, was flung up to speckle the windows with crystal bubbles. It was all light and water and sand, flying about the train speeding towards the Rameswaram causeway in a high wind. The palms under the scudding clouds bowed and flashed like fans made of feathers, and here and there, up to their stupas (dome-like mounds containing Buddhist shrines) in sand, were temples flying red flags on their crooked masts. The sand covered the track in places; it had drifted into temple doorways and wrecked the frail palm-frond huts. The wind was terrific, beating on the windows, carrying sand and spray and the whistle's *hooeeee*, and nearly toppling the dhows (single-masted ships) in full sail at the hump of the spangled horizon where Ceylon lay.[5]

—Paul Theroux

III

It was noon before the wind let up a little and the rain slowed to a drizzle. I pushed open the door and leaped out. The wind snatched off my rain cap and sent it whirling across the highway, jerked open my raincoat and spread it like wings, lifting me completely off the ground.

Clasping my hands below my knees, I collapsed the wings, flopped like a wounded turkey and stumbled toward the entrance. Ann Cullen flung the door open, letting in a blast of wind, a gush of rain—and me.

My raincoat looked as if it had been peppered with buckshot; my arms and legs were spotted with blood where pebbles had struck; and the car had a severe case of freckles, bare metal glistening where paint had been chipped by flying debris.[6]

—Gene Plowden

IV

During the seventeenth century, an Indian ruler named Shah Jahan fell in love with and married a beautiful princess. Her title was Mumtaz-i-Mahal which means "pride of the palace." To show his love, he determined to build her the most wonderful building in the world, but before he began the building, the lovely Mumtaz fell ill and died. Shah Jahan then decided to convert the building into a tomb for her. We know it as the Taj Mahal. This is the way one American writer remembered his visit to the Taj Mahal.

I have heard about the Taj, seen pictures of it, but *nothing* can reproduce it. It takes one's breath away. It is so beautiful it hurts. I spent six hours looking at it the first morning. That night the last of a moon was due to rise at 2:30 a.m. Alone I walked three miles and wandered around the inclosure till twelve when I hid. I was determined to see what I had come to see.

Words fail to describe these magic hours—all, all alone with the Taj! A light burned over the graves under the dome, two guards slept outside the doors, two were inside the wall gate—that was all. Only I was awake. The slanting beams gave a mellowness and softness to the marble dream that defied comprehension. The odor of flowers was everywhere, roses and lilies and fragrant shrubs. The park is drenched with water and while the surrounding country is a desert at this season, the trees and grass here are emerald green and make a luxurious setting for the most luxurious building on earth. It's white as snow though 300 years old, in perfect preservation and built with such niceties time will never touch it.

For three hours, I roamed about the garden, on the glittering side, on the black side, where the moonlight gave a glowing edge to the domes and minarets. There is an elevated marble pool halfway down the walk from the entrance gate. I took off my shoes and stockings to bathe my feet. How cool the water was! Then, in the moonlight, I took off my shorts and shirt and dropped into the refreshing lily-padded water. It was too warm to catch cold, just romantic and magic. For half an hour I sat by the pool with my clothes off, dabbling my feet, the moon pouring itself over everything, the garden about me a fairyland, and the Taj above me. I was transported out of this world. It was a taste of paradise.[7]

—Richard Halliburton

V

The building has been turned inside out, with all the intestines, normally hidden from public view, hanging on the outside. What's more, the pipes are in a riot of colors: blue for air conditioning, red for elevators, and green for water. The whole mass is suspended from a giant metal scaffold that displays its bare metal bones, too. Escalators, enclosed in tubes of Plexiglas, make their way up the outside walls like giant, inquisitive caterpillars creeping along.[8]

—Horace Sutton

Here are some characteristics of modern description you can observe in the preceding examples.

1. Single tone, mood, and atmosphere—Everything in a description should add up to one feeling or impression. Anything that would weaken or change that feeling should be omitted.

2. Action—Many of today's readers refuse to spend time reading a description for its own sake. They want movement and action even in descriptive passages.

3. Many sensory impressions—Writers include words and phrases that appeal to all five senses to make the reader feel what they are describing.

Reread the selections and notice the mood and atmosphere of each. In the first writing sample the writer uses several verbs that appeal to your sense of hearing. Can you hear the Bay of Naples sizzling, the ground rumbling? What are the words in sample two that give you a feeling of action and speed? Notice the images in sample three. First you see the narrator flying through the air like a bird then flopping about like a "wounded turkey." Sample five also makes good use of figurative language. The writer speaks of the "intestines" of a building and compares the escalator to "inquisitive caterpillars."

Though you are studying description in connection with narration, good description is important in all kinds of writing, even in the writing of technical and scientific reports. Here is a story to prove it.

Othmar Ammann, the engineer who was hired to build a bridge over the Hudson River near the Palisades, prepared a paper describing the two kinds of bridges that could be constructed there. He described the landscape in vivid detail. Then he described the visual effect of the two kinds of bridges, ending with a plea for the suspension-type bridge. "A cantilever bridge," he wrote, "the nearest other possibility, would, with its dense and massive network of steel members, form a monstrous structure and mar forever the beauty of the natural scenery."[9]

Ammann's fine writing and vivid description were amazingly effective. Although his report asked for one hundred thousand dollars to carry on his planning for the bridge, the New York and New Jersey legislatures pledged him ten million dollars. When you visit New York City, be sure to look at the graceful beauty of the George Washington Bridge stretching over the Hudson between New York and New Jersey. It is there because a great engineer could write description well.

Distinguishing Between Showing and Telling

At the beginning of a silent movie, a printed title might say, "Oliver Hardwick was a stern and heartless man. His greatest joy was to foreclose on the homes of widows and to turn them out." Then Oliver Hardwick would rub his hands in glee.

Today, movie directors avoid *telling* the audience what a character is like. Instead, they *show* the characters in action and let the audience form their own ideas about them. The finished film reveals the character and background of each person by showing details of behavior, mannerisms, actions in relation to other people, and many other revealing features. These are not told by narration.

Comparing methods. Writers can either tell what they want readers to believe about a character or they can show a scene or an incident and let the readers draw their own conclusions. Similarly, in description, a writer can tell that a road is a scarey place after dark or show it through details and mood.

Here are examples of each method, taken from the same short story.

TELLING

"Don't come back till you have him!" the Ticktockman said, very quietly, very sincerely, extremely dangerously.

They used dogs. They used probes. They used cardioplate crossoffs. They used teepers. They used bribery. They used stiktytes. They used intimidation. They used torment. They used torture. They used finks. They used cops. They used search & seizure. They used fallaron. They used betterment incentive. They used fingerprints. They used Bertillon. They used cunning. They used guile. They used treachery. They used Raoul Mitgong, but he didn't help much. They used applied physics. They used techniques of criminology.

And what the hell: they caught him.

SHOWING

Once more, in anticipation, the elfin grin spread, and there was a tooth missing back there on the left side. He dipped, skimmed, and swooped over them; and then, scrunching about on the air-boat, he released the holding pins that fastened shut the ends of the home-made pouring troughs that kept his cargo from dumping prematurely. And as he pulled the trough-pins, the air-boat slid over the factory workers and one hundred and fifty thousand dollars worth of jelly beans cascaded down on the expresstrip.

Jelly beans! Millions and billions of purples and yellows and greens and licorice and grape and raspberry and mint and round and smooth and crunchy outside and soft-mealy inside and sugary and bouncing jouncing tumbling clittering clattering skittering fell on the heads and shoulders and hardhats and carapaces of the Timkin workers, tinkling on the slidewalk and bouncing away and rolling about underfoot and filling the sky on their way down with all the colors of joy and childhood and holidays, coming down in a steady rain, a solid wash, a torrent of color and sweetness out of the sky from above, and entering a universe of sanity and metronomic order and quite-mad coocoo newness. Jelly beans![10]

—Harlan Ellison

In the first example, Harlan Ellison gives a motion-picture montage impression of a rapid-action search for the independent clown who refuses to fit into a timed and scheduled daily world. Because the impression of the rapid-action search is more important than the realistic details that would make it slower, but more real, he simply tells, rather than shows.

In the second example, which appears earlier in the story, Ellison shows the audience the crime of which the Harlequin is guilty: floating on an air-boat, he gummed up the machinery and the time schedule of a modern factory by dropping millions of jelly beans into the moving sidewalk carrying workers to their jobs. This time he shows the event in full detail.

Both showing and telling are legitimate and useful techniques. Each should be used where appropriate.

ACTIVITY 11J

Recognizing Showing and Telling

Number your paper 1 to 10 and (a) write Showing or Telling to indicate which method predominates in each of the following passages; then, (b) if the passage primarily *tells*, write two or three good sentences with some concrete information that would show the same thing. If the passage primarily *shows*, write a single sentence that tells or summarizes what the passage shows. An example follows. (Since the telling-showing distinction applies in forms other than description, many of the passages are not descriptive.)

TELLING

There was something gallant in his carriage and something fearless in his manner.

SHOWING

The soldier swaggered into the room and bowed elaborately. As he looked at the twenty pairs of hostile eyes, he smiled coldly, and his right hand sought the hilt of his sword.

1. Rex Braddock was perhaps five and thirty, thickset and towering, yet no mean figure on the whole. But when one looked in his face, the hideous protuberances seemed to seize the eyes and force them again and again over the grating pustules, like hands tortured by being rasped on a file. And yet the face was not hard nor harsh; indeed, its very softness added to its horror. It was the kind of face President Lincoln must have meant when he turned away an office seeker "because he didn't like the man's face." "Surely," the President insisted, "a man who has lived behind such a face for forty years must have had some power in its development." Rex Braddock had had such power; his had been the diabolical Machiavellian force of pure evil.

2. Although many South Pacific islands are beautiful, perhaps none matches the television picture of paradise.

3. The temperature on the prairie rose as high as 110 degrees, but none of the hunters could be seen to perspire. The thirsty air greedily absorbed the moisture and left only whitened salt stains on the fading homespun. On both sides of the trail lay husks of broken wagons and the bleached bones of oxen. An occasional rude cross, fashioned from the only wood available—a broken singletree, the slats of a barrel, the tortured rocker from a prized chair—marked a human resting-place.

4. At the first whoop of the destroyer's alarm siren, the slender craft knifes to the south and bends its wake into a sudden bow. In less than fifteen gale-tossed minutes it hovers above the suspected shoals, now lighted with blinkers, searchlights, and white parachute flares. Then,

where the huge oil slick ironically traps the rainbow hues of the flares and calms the sullen waves, we see the flotsam of the sunken sub: a mattress, some life preservers, a battered briefcase. A strong smell of diesel oil pervades the atmosphere.

5. A grimy little door at the very top of the stairs stood ajar. A very poor-looking room about ten paces long was lighted by a candle-end; the whole of it was visible from the entrance. It was all in disorder, littered up with rags of all sorts, especially children's garments. Across the furthest corner was stretched a ragged sheet. Behind it probably was the bed. There was nothing in the room except two chairs and a sofa covered with American leather, full of holes, before which stood an old deal kitchen table, unpainted and uncovered. At the edge of the table stood a smouldering tallow-candle in an iron candlestick.[11]

—Fyodor Dostoyevsky

6. Karintha, at twelve, was a wild flash that told the other folks just what it was to live. At sunset, when there was no wind, and the pinesmoke from over by the sawmill hugged the earth, and you couldn't see more than a few feet in front, her sudden darting past you was a bit of vivid color, like a black bird that flashes in light. With the other children one could hear some distance off, their feet flopping in the two-inch dust. Karintha's running was a whir. It had the sound of the red dust that sometimes makes a spiral in the road.[12]

—Jean Toomer

7. Dogs often wander into the classrooms at schools, and always cause an uproar. Kids cannot contain themselves when dogs appear in the midst of Egypt lesson, for what reason no one seems to know. Why couldn't they, the kids, just let the dog be in the class, wandering around, sniffing here and licking a few hands there, quietly, moseying about in the style of dogs while the class continued with the most important part of the lesson about Egypt? But no, they can't. They got to rush the dog, they got to pick him up and drop him, they got to offer the dog candy and pieces of sandwich, they got to yell and scream and act like they never saw any dog before in their whole lives.[13]

—James Herndon

8. Lincoln Park in the center of town may once have been as inviting and pleasant as the square around a rural county courthouse, but all that is changed today. Whether it's because there are too many people for the little space, because people are too careless, or because taxes no longer will support the care that such a park requires, Lincoln Park has changed. It's no longer inviting. It's no longer safe. It's no longer comfortable. It's crowded, dirty, littered, and dangerous.

9. Two great concrete parabolas intersected, seeming to float in the sky a hundred feet above the runway, capturing the billowing of a parachute or perhaps the half-imaginary lines of a Leonardo da Vinci flying machine. On the front of the building, an acre of vertical smoked glass filled the void from ground to roof and showed the visitor the floors, offices, and floating stairs within. The great glass expanse half mirrored the parking lot and highway behind the visitor and made him think himself indeed into the fourth dimension.

10. The Interstate Highway cuts our block in two. Not in two, really, because it takes the whole center out and leaves only two awkward-

looking three-story flats lonesome at each end. When they were attached to the block-long row, they looked all right, but now they look dead and out-of-place, like old snags of teeth, perhaps, or blackened survivors of a forest fire. The chain link fence touches the side of our house and keeps us off the right-of-way. Rick Collins once was my best friend, but he lives across the road, so I only see him once in a while at school.

More Meanings of Point of View

On page 281, you learned that point of view refers to the writer's choice of the narrator to tell the story. The term "viewpoint" may also be used to refer to the concept of what the narrator sees. As you recall, the writer may decide to tell the story with no limitations on what the narrator knows about the characters, about their actions, and about their thoughts. If, however, the writer has chosen a character in the story as narrator, that person will have some restrictions on what he or she can tell. Obviously, if Uncle Jimmy is telling the story and Uncle Jimmy has been isolated in a cabin in Alaska for ten years, he simply cannot narrate what happened in Panama last month. He has no way of knowing about it. Similarly, if Uncle Jimmy is a natural-born optimist who always looks on the bright side of things, it would not be consistent to have him narrating the aches and pains and miseries of the world. We know that most people, depending upon the mood they happen to be in at a given time, will either not perceive or will deliberately ignore details that don't fit that mood. Also, personality is a determinant of a person's response to a situation. Uncle Jimmy can reveal to the reader only what he feels, suspects, or knows.

Choosing your point of view, then, is like deciding which camera to use. Here are additional meanings of point of view. They can be compared to deciding where to place your camera (physical viewpoint) and selecting a filter to put over the lens (psychological viewpoint).

Choosing a physical viewpoint. If photography is your hobby, you know how important it is to focus your camera carefully. You know also, that by changing your position in relation to your subject, you get a completely different picture. For an unusual perspective, you may aim from overhead in a tree or from a prone position on the ground. Similarly, a writer chooses a physical viewpoint for a story. Just as a camera cannot take a picture of anything out of its range, so a writer, once the viewpoint has been established, cannot reveal anything beyond that limited viewpoint. In many stories, the narrator maintains the same physical viewpoint throughout. A writer may, however, decide to allow a shift in the narrator's viewpoint. This is something like shifting from a still camera to a moving-picture camera. In such cases, the writer must let the reader know that this shift is deliberate and there must be some explanation to account for it.

Choosing a psychological viewpoint. Writers may also choose a psychological viewpoint, selecting and emphasizing the details that would be seen if one were in a particular state of mind. Just as a camera lens may be covered with a filter to screen out undesirable lights or shadows, so writers can "cover the lens of perception" by adopting a certain attitude or mood. For example, a narrator might describe the hall of a school immediately after receiving an A in a test. Or, the narrator might describe the same scene after receiving a failing grade. The mood "filters perception" so that different objects might be recorded, different colors emphasized, and different comparisons used. In the first case, the engraved list of valedictorians might be described as "a modest plaque gently reminding students of the accomplishments of their predecessors." In the second case, because of anger, disappointment, and frustration, the plaque might be called "a garish brass tombstone mocking students' aspirations."

Changing a viewpoint. In Ray Bradbury's novel, *Dandelion Wine*, twelve-year-old Douglas Spaulding, his younger brother Tom, and their father were picking fox grapes and wild strawberries, when suddenly Doug experienced a revelation. "I'm alive!" he thought.

When he expressed it to Tom, the younger boy wasn't impressed.

I

"I'm alive."

"Heck, that's old!"

"*Thinking* about it, *noticing* it, is new. You do things and don't watch. Then all of a sudden you look and see what you're doing and it's the first time, really. I'm going to divide this summer up in two parts. First part of this tablet is titled: RITES AND CEREMONIES. The first root beer pop of the year. The first time running barefoot in the grass of the year. First time almost drowning in the lake of the year. First watermelon. First mosquito. First harvest of dandelions. Those are the things we do over and over and over and never think. Now here in back, like I said, is DISCOVERIES AND REVELATIONS or maybe ILLUMINATIONS, that's a swell word, or INTUITIONS, okay? In other words you do an old familiar thing, like bottling dandelion wine, and you put that under RITES AND CEREMONIES. And then you think about it, and what you think, crazy or not, you put under DISCOVERIES AND REVELATIONS.[14]

—Ray Bradbury

With his increasing maturity, Douglas Spaulding had experienced a shift in his psychological point of view. He realized that he was no longer a child, content with just experiencing life. From that point on, he would think about life and interpret it.

Not all shifts in psychological point of view are so all-encompassing and so long lasting. Nonetheless, your particular psychological perspective at any given time can have a profound effect on the way you see things and the way you react to them.

As you tell a story from a character's psychological point of view, you must always consider how such a viewpoint makes the character look at the scene or events. By explaining any changes in that point of view you make your story more believable.

ACTIVITY 11K

Analyzing Paragraphs for Physical and Psychological Viewpoint

Read the following pairs of descriptions to see how changes in physical and psychological viewpoints can completely alter a description. Write a short paragraph discussing how the change in viewpoint changes the selection and presentation of ideas. What techniques in these examples can you use in your own writing?

PHYSICAL VIEWPOINT

1. From the back of the auditorium the stage set for the senior class play looks like the proverbial desert island on which the cast of *The Admirable Crichton* is supposed to be stranded. Tall, graceful palm trees frame the stage and their fernlike fronds meet above the center front. A row of exotic marsh plants extends across the stage front so that the viewers seem to be peering from a dense forest into a tiny clearing, in the center of which is the bamboo shelter of the castaways. To stage right of the hut, casting flickering shadows as high as its palm-thatched eaves, a cheerful fire warms the actors. Directly behind the fire, a path curves up and around behind the hut, leading, the audience knows, to the great signal fire dimly visible in the distance.

2. When viewed from the first few rows of the auditorium, the set for the senior play is theatrically fake. The second act is

supposed to occur on an island on which the Loam family, some of their friends, and their butler, Crichton, have been cast away. The palm tree trunks on each side of the stage are actually painted strips of muslin. The edges curl slightly, and when an actor walks nearby, they wave and sway in the breeze. Overhead are painted fronds cut from wrapping paper and pasted on a kind of scrim, or cheesecloth. Across the front of the stage, a row of dried cattails cut from Turkey Creek almost hides the footlights, and completely hides some of the important action. In the center of the stage, cardboard tubes collected from carpeting stores have been painted to look something like bamboo and wired together to make a two-dimensional hut. But as one looks into the windows or through the door, it is evident that only two walls have been finished. The fire to stage right of the hut quite obviously consists of piled sticks, red and yellow cellophane, a few strips of red cloth tacked to the floor at one end, a pair of light bulbs, and a small fan. Not only does the "fire" look like what it is, but the faint hum of the fan reminds the audience that civilization is not too far from this particular desert island. Behind the fire, a papier-mâché hill built on a set of narrow steps leads to a "distant" signal fire painted on the cyclorama. Unfortunately, however, as the actors reach the top of the hill which is supposed to be behind the hut, the audience can see them stoop and clamber down a little stepladder.

PSYCHOLOGICAL VIEWPOINT

1. That first day of basketball practice, the locker room had been a mass of eager, shouting, half-dressed boys chortling about the coming season. As Stan burst through the second set of swinging doors, he saw the traditional varsity benches where only letter winners sat and dressed. With its short row of taller lockers and wider, more comfortable benches, varsity row radiated dignity and security. Stan anticipated being there next season with a special heartskip. Walking past varsity row to the crowded sophomore benches, Stan saw the cheerful glassed-in office where Coaches Rice and Lopez were discussing strategy. From the shower room behind the coach's office came the pseudo-operatic, reverberating voice of a singer from the last gym class. Stan smiled confidently as he pushed his coat into an empty, khaki-colored locker, and began to undress. The faint mist from the shower room put rainbow halos around the lights.

2. After the third week of practice Coach Lopez announced who had made the traveling squad and who had been "cut." Stan could hardly believe his ears. Some of the others who were no longer on the squad elected to complete the two-hour practice session—their final session on the team—but Stan and three others moved gloomily toward the locker room. When the last boy pushed through the swinging door, it flapped mournfully slower and slower. The only sound in the locker room was a minor echo of an off-key tune from the nearby showers. Stan slowly opened the dull, scratched, khaki-painted locker door, which was stained with adhesive-tape marks where he had stored the strips he had used to bandage his sprained ankle. He could see only with difficulty; the room was half in shadows because the tall varsity lockers shut out the light. Even the light from the coach's office seemed to shine reluctantly through the smudged and steam-clouded windows. The mist from the nearby shower room caused the overhead bulbs to radiate many colored sunsets, "the same sunsets you see when your eyes are full of tears," thought Stan.

ACTIVITY 11L

Using Point of View

1. After you have discussed the examples in Activity 11K, write two similar pairs of contrasting paragraphs. Choose a single scene and describe it from two different locations. Then choose another scene and describe it from two different psychological viewpoints. Perhaps the following will suggest some possibilities:

PHYSICAL VIEWPOINT

    a. A racetrack from the point of view of a jockey and as seen from the grandstand.

    b. The deck of an aircraft carrier from the point of view of a pilot and of the deck crew.

    c. The highway as seen from a motorcycle or from inside a bus.

    d. A scene at a throughway toll booth from within the toll booth and from inside an approaching car.

PSYCHOLOGICAL VIEWPOINT

    a. A moving subway train from the viewpoint of passengers aboard the train and of a girl who has just missed it.

    b. A school election from the point of view of a winner and of a loser.

    c. A school band practice session outside in a cold, blustery wind from the point of view of a member and of an outsider.

    d. An issue of a school newspaper from the point of view of a faculty member and of a student.

2. After you have written the viewpoint paragraphs, work with them as your teacher directs. Discuss the difference that the change in point of view has made. A partial list of the differences in the physical viewpoint paragraph on page 278 follows:

FROM THE BACK OF THE AUDITORIUM	FROM THE FRONT OF THE AUDITORIUM
a. Graceful, swaying palm trees	a. Painted strips of muslin to represent tree trunks
b. Overhead fronds	b. Wrapping-paper fronds pasted on cheesecloth
c. Exotic marsh plants	c. Dried cattails that hide the action and fail to hide the footlights

Subordination of Ideas

The skill of subordinating ideas is an important one for you to use in your writing. The word "subordination" means "placing below in order or importance." A reader will follow your story more easily if you indicate the relative importance of your ideas. Here are two ideas presented as if they were of equal importance:

Steve collected old newspapers and glass for recycling and he was interested in ecology.

The writer should have provided "thought connections" for these two ideas. For example:

ADVERBIAL CLAUSE   beginning with *after, although, because, before, if, in case, provided, since, when, while, unless, until,* or several others.

Steve collected old newspapers and glass for recycling because he was interested in ecology.

or

Since Steve was interested in ecology, he collected old newspapers and glass for recycling.

PARTICIPIAL PHRASE   beginning with an -ing verb

Being interested in ecology, Steve collected old newspapers and glass for recycling.

PARTICIPIAL PHRASE   beginning with an -ed or -en verb

Steve, interested in ecology, collected old newspapers and glass for recycling.

PREPOSITIONAL PHRASE

Steve collected old newspapers and glass for recycling because of his interest in ecology.

INFINITIVE PHRASE

To show his interest in ecology, Steve collected old newspapers and glass for recycling.

RELATIVE CLAUSE   beginning with *who, which, that*

Steve, who was interested in ecology, collected old newspapers and glass for recycling.

ACTIVITY 11M

Experimenting with Subordination

Here are some sentences that might appear in your writing. Working as your teacher directs, see how many of the preceding patterns you can use to subordinate one idea to the other.

1. The little boy sat on the patch of grass, and the petunia border made a picture frame around him.

2. Kim couldn't believe the applause, and she returned to the stage for an encore.

3. The shadows of the ancient cypress trees began to lengthen, and the sun began to merge with its reflection on the water.

4. America has lost almost a foot of topsoil in the last hundred years, and farmers are beginning to make much greater use of such measures as contour plowing.

5. The sound of the television announcer's voice filled the room, and the news of the plane disaster stunned the listeners.

6. The students drifted slowly into the auditorium, and the program didn't appeal to them.

7. Congress approved the new voting age of eighteen, and young people were slow to register for voting.

8. The Florida beaches are bright and endless and beautiful, and the hills of New York State are sweeping and lush and green.

9. The little garden with the crystal pool is crowded into the apartment-house patio, and the little garden seems out of place in the middle of all that concrete.

10. Sara was concerned about the proposed legislation, and she wrote a letter to her Representative.

Eliminating Deadwood

Some writers think that lots of words, especially long words, improve a piece of writing. Actually, good narrative writing, like all good writing, uses only the words required to accomplish the task at hand. Effective writing is achieved through use of precise, expressive words. Each word should contribute to the author's intention. If your ideas are complex, or if you are aiming at a special emotional tone, you may need to use many words, but the rule still holds: Always use the fewest words that will do the job.

ACTIVITY 11N

Removing Deadwood

Read the following paragraph in class. Decide which words and phrases are repetitious. Cut the paragraph down to a minimum number of effective words. Write out your revised version and be prepared to discuss it with your classmates.

In my opinion, I think it is essential for me to recognize that my best friend is the one person whom I know who can amuse me and make me laugh and entertain me completely at the same time that she is irritating and bothering me a great deal. I can't help but smile because when she is feeling in a humorous mood and wants to make me laugh, she reminds me of a particular kind of monkey which I think is very funny, the Rhesus monkey. When I look at her and try to picture what she is like, the first thing I see at first glance is a balloon of red fuzz that when closely examined by looking intensely at it can be seen and thought of as hair. Then her sharp little nose, which is in the middle of her face struggling under a pair of huge glasses, comes into view, closely followed by her wide-open mouth which is usually open so as to show her teeth because she is talking and giggling and laughing so much. I have never gotten a good look at her body because it is always active and moving so that she is never still long enough for me to form an impression of what it is like. She darts over here and then darts over there and then whirls around to reach for something she forgot in the first place when she darted over there. While jumping up and down at a fast pace she is doing all this darting. She is so funny to watch that after a time I can't stand to look at her because she is so funny and active that as I look at her I become tired and want to stop looking out of sheer exhaustion. The thing, however, that irritates me the most is her habit of being so completely agreeable and pleasant all the time. No matter what I suggest, she agrees to do, but if I change my mind because I no longer want to do the thing I originally suggested that we do, she changes her mind just as I did and agrees immediately to the new idea by saying, "Oh, no, I wouldn't think of doing anything like that." When moments before she was gung-ho for that activity, she is still willing to change her mind just because I have changed my mind and she wants to be agreeable. But she is still my friend because, no matter how much she irritates me, I realize that her silliness is just her way of showing that she is an individual and this is her way of showing that she is a person different from all other people.

MAJOR WRITING ASSIGNMENT

A NARRATION

Refer to the "storehouse of materials" that you developed in connection with Activity 11A, page 274. Think of some specific event you experienced in one of the areas you selected. Impose a purpose or meaning on the event; give it the significance that will make it worth writing about.

You may write a personal narrative; recounting this actual experience in the first person. Or you may tell the story of an imagined event. Another choice you have is to write an account of another person's experience, using a third-person narrator.

Whether you choose to write about an actual experience or an imagined event, be sure you take into account these elements:

point, purpose or significance	emotion
structure or order	action
point of view	suspense
effective description	

Before you begin to write, try to think through this outline. If you cannot use the outline in this way, plunge ahead with your first draft and then reread the outline to see if you can add anything from it to improve your narrative.

GENERAL NARRATIVE PATTERN

I. Introduction
    A. Introduces the *who, what, when,* and *where*—with a mystery (for suspense) about the *why* and *how*.
Optional   B. Reveals any necessary background.
Optional   C. Suggests importance of the subject.
Optional   D. Provides a point, or purpose, for the narration. (This may be saved until the end, or even omitted entirely so that it is left to the reader's imagination.)

II. Body
    A. Explains and describes selected events, usually in order of time.
    B. Explains, comments on, and interprets the events, when necessary.
    C. Provides guides to time, place, sequence, and significance so reader doesn't get lost.

III. Conclusion
    A. Ends interestingly as soon as possible after the climax.
Optional   B. Comments on, reaffirms, or simply clarifies the meaning.

From what point of view would you write a character sketch of this Apache woman? The picture shows her gathering the fruit of cactus plants.

Chapter 12

The Character Sketch

When the editor of a small country newspaper was able to double the circulation of his publication after several previous editors had failed, he was asked to explain the secret of his success.

"It's easy," he said. "All I have to do is mention the name of every single person in town at least once each month. They all want to see their own names in print, and besides that, they're curious about everybody else."

Successful newspaper and magazine editors have all learned this rule for building readership: Names are news.

Perhaps you've thought of the character sketch as a classroom exercise—something that teachers assign, but that doesn't exist outside of school. Well, think again! Almost every magazine, journal, and newspaper runs character sketches of one kind or another. Is it a magazine catering to hotel managers? Then the readers are interested in outstanding, successful, and colorful people in the hotel business. Is it a magazine emphasizing science? Then the editor will present a character sketch of an outstanding scientist. Whatever the publication, it will publish character sketches of men and women who will be interesting to its particular audience. Some successful magazines consist entirely of brief character sketches of well-known people.

307

There are three things to consider in writing a character sketch: the subject, the point of view, and the method you will use to present your subject. The subject must be worth writing about for some reason. That reason will be the focus of your sketch. Do not attempt to describe every aspect of the character's life. Instead, select the traits that will make the character "live" on the page. Another pitfall to avoid is the use of stereotypes, stock characters, which lack both individuality and realism. As you write your character sketch select the details that make your subject unique among all others. The best way to avoid stereotypes is to become more sensitive to the people around you, noticing the qualities that make each person distinct and individual.

As you read the character sketches that follow, keep in mind the differences between individualized characters and stereotypes.

I

The cat Shakespeare, however, was not enough for Father. For a while he thought of getting a canary. "They look so pretty," he said. But he changed his mind. He decided that "jailing" a bird in a cage was a cruel thing. He said: "Every living thing should do as is ordained. Birds were ordained to fly, so they should fly."

Often he would take me on walks with him, and whenever we would pass a stable he would take me in and look lovingly at horses and stroke their sides and feel their necks and rub their noses. "Ah," he would exclaim, "a really aristocratic animal a horse is! So proud! Look at the way he holds his head." Father had dealt, in a very small way, in horses when he was in Russia and knew a great deal about them. One of the tales he told me I still remember. "A horse," he said, "is in many ways like a human being. They are big and strong, but they have feelings like a man, even like a woman. In Kalenkevitch, where I come from, there was a big horse, and a Russian horse I want to tell you is a horse, really. Well, we noticed that he played with a little mouse in the stable. He didn't pounce on the little thing. He just moved it here and there like he was playing with it—oh, the way you would play with a ball. Well, a stable has to be cleaned out, of course, and mice and rats were eating up our grain and causing all kinds of damage. So we killed the mouse that the horse seemed to be playing with, and we thought nothing of it. Would you believe it—the horse became morose, sick. Yes, really sick. He refused to eat, drank very little, and we could see that he was really sick. We wondered what was the trouble. We called in a peasant who knew about horses and he said he didn't know, he seemed all right. Another peasant said the same thing. And we got worried. Just about then, the grandmother of one of the peasants in our neighborhood came to see us, and we told her of our worries about the horse. She said: 'It could be that he is missing something, something you took away from him. Horses have feelings, you know.' Just at that minute it occurred to somebody that we had killed the mouse, and, to make a long story short, we got another mouse for him, and the horse began to play with it like he played with the other mouse, and he began to eat again and be himself again. So, you see, my son, horses are not just horses."

One evening, not much later, after Father had fed Shakespeare, he said to me, as he was eating his own supper, "David, you noticed that I fed the cat before I sat down to eat myself. A great rabbi once said that a good Jew first feeds his dumb animals before he feeds himself. It is God's will that we be kind, not only to human beings, but also, and especially, to those of His creatures who cannot so well take care of themselves, and who are dependent upon human beings."[1]

—Charles Angoff

II

The family had one friend who never came too close, and that was Eriksson. He would drive by in his boat, or he would think about coming but never get around to it. There were even summers when Eriksson came nowhere near the island and didn't think about it, either.

Eriksson was small and strong and the color of the landscape, except that his eyes were blue. When people talked about him or thought about him, it seemed natural to lift their heads and gaze out over the sea. He was often unlucky and was plagued by bad weather and engine trouble. His herring nets would rip or get caught in his propeller, and fish and fowl would fail to turn up where he had expected them. And if he did have a good catch, the price would go down, so it was always six of one or half a dozen of the other. But beyond all these routine troubles that can spoil a person's livelihood, there were other, unexpected possibilities.

The family had long realized, without ever discussing it, that Eriksson didn't especially like fishing and hunting and motorboats. What he did like was harder to put your finger on, but perfectly understandable. His attention and his sudden wishes raced here and there across the water like ocean breezes, and he lived in a perpetual state of quiet excitement. The sea is always subject to unusual events; things drift in or run aground or shift in the night when the wind changes, and keeping track of all this takes experience, imagination, and unflagging watchfulness. It takes a good *nose*, to put it simply. The big events always take place far out in the skerries, and time is often of the essence. Only small things happen in among the islands, but these, too—the odd jobs that arise from the whims of the summer people—have to be dealt with. One of them wants a ship's mast mounted on his roof, and another one needs a rock weighing half a ton, and it has to be round. A person can find anything if he takes the time, that is, if he can afford to look. And while he's looking, he's free, and he finds things he never expected. Sometimes people are very predictable: they want a kitten in June, for example, and come the first of September they want someone to drown their cat. So someone does. But other times, people have dreams and want things they can keep.

Eriksson was the man who fulfilled these dreams. No one knew exactly what he found for himself along the way—probably a lot less than people thought. But he went on doing it anyway, perhaps for the sake of the search.

One of the mysterious and attractive things about Eriksson was that he didn't talk about himself. He never seemed to feel the urge. Nor did he talk about other people; they didn't interest him very much. His infrequent visits might occur at any time of the day or night, and they never lasted long. Depending on when he arrived, he might have a cup of coffee or a meal or even take a drink just to be polite, but then he would turn quiet and uneasy, he would start listening, and then he would leave. But as long as he stayed, he had everyone's undivided attention. No one did anything, no one looked at anything but Eriksson. They would hang on his every word, and when he was gone and nothing had actually been said, their thoughts would dwell gravely on what he had left unspoken.[2]

—Tove Jansson

Student Composition 12A

GRANDDAD

I awoke to the clanking and rumbling of my anti-quated radiator as the frantic steam gushed from the heater through the rusty pipes. I burrowed deeper into the warm blankets and lay quietly, listening contentedly to the sounds of the winter dawn. From the hall bathroom came the gurgling of hot water as it filled the chipped, narrow basin, and I could hear a muffled voice humming like a giant bumblebee. Granddad was up already and was preparing to shave. I smiled and resisted the impulse to go and watch him. I loved to watch his leathery hands, his methodical strokes, and his steady patience, and I couldn't remember ever seeing him shave differently. And as I let my mind wander back to my childhood, I realized that Granddad's habits and moods had changed little over the years.

"Aye, lassie," Granddad said to me once, "I like things the way they are, and I canna' be changed now." Granddad was a cooper in the local brewery when the whole family lived in the Scottish village of Coldstream. He took pride in the neat, sturdy wooden ale kegs he created. His job demanded that he be up at sunrise and ready for a long day. I can still remember Granddad singing in a lusty tenor as he washed and shaved while I lay in my cot waiting for the breakfast porridge to be cooked. He would leave for work, dressed in coarse overalls and leather cap, just as I came down to the parlor, and his greeting was the same nearly every day. "Good mornin' to you wee'un," he would call, "it's a fair sight to behold at the morn, you are!"

One midday Granddad came home with a frown creasing his brown face. "Mary," he said to my grandmother, "I'll tell you directly. The other coopers have been listening to the union men from Edinburgh, and now the lads themselves want a union. It would mean better pay and less work. It would mean pay benefits during sickness." He

How does the writer tie the beginning and end of this paper together? What do they have in common?

What sensory images does the writer provide in her opening paragraph?

How does the writer communicate her emotional relationship with her subject?

What do Granddad's actual words add? Why is their flavor particularly strong and effective?

What natural connections does the writer make between life in the United States and life in Scotland? How do these connections help shape the paper?

What is the American word for "porridge"? What does this word add to the picture of Scottish life?

How does the writer get tension and suspense into her paper? What is the conflict about whose outcome you are uncertain?

Why does the writer put Granddad's absolute position on the side of individual work at the end of the paragraph, rather than earlier in it?

What adjective would you use to describe the writer's attitude toward her grandfather's lone labor?

In what ways has the writer increased the pressures on Granddad and the suspense of the reader?

How do Granddad's words and images reinforce his personality and character? What connections have they with his work?

How does the ending echo the opening paragraph?

stopped abruptly and looked from Grandmother's face to the rough flagstone floor. Then he said, slowly, "And it would mean team construction on the kegs, an end to the individual's work." He looked up again into my grandmother's startled eyes and spoke, defiance crackling in his voice. "And I'll tell you, Mary, I'll never let that happen. I'll work for my day's earnings and care for mysel' when I'm sick. And for sure I'll build the kegs alone without anyone else's advice!"

Granddad didn't even stay for his dinner that day, but returned to his work. But despite his warnings and protests, the unions did come to the Coldstream brewery. Granddad refused to join. Many times he threatened to leave altogether and move the family to Islay where the larger breweries were located, but time and again he was persuaded to stay. Soon he was the only cooper who worked alone, bending the taut fresh slats of wood into barrels and fastening them with black iron rings and seals. He remained the only cooper to brand his initials, as was tradition, onto the bottoms of the kegs.

Granddad resisted unions, but he could not stand against the waves of progress that flooded even the smallest breweries. Aluminum kegs were being cast in large Edinburgh factories for the transportation and storage of ale. The cooper no longer had a job. Gradually the Coldstream coopers left the brewery to accept jobs elsewhere. But Granddad was adamant. "Even the best stout will rot in those silver caskets." He encouraged his mates not to leave town. "These manufacturing fools will soon realize their mistakes. I, for one, will not go near the damned things. I canna' change my mind about quality, progress or no progress." Granddad never did go near the "damned things," for he retired from the brewery as other coopers were fired.

Despite the fact that the Coldstream village no longer held the promise of work for Granddad, he stubbornly refused to leave his home when my father suggested a move to America.

"I canna' change this old body to fit a new place. You don't seal new iron rings to the wood with worn and rusted clasps. So leave me here in my own home." But eventually Granddad did leave for America with us, and although he adapted to the new environment, he never really changed.

Granddad finished shaving by now; I could no longer hear water splashing or a Lowland country song being hummed. I smiled and climbed out of bed to get my breakfast, thinking of Granddad's latest problem.

The doctor had forbidden him to smoke cigarettes and to eat starchy foods. The young doctor had also warned Granddad about getting rest and dressing wisely for winter. I passed Granddad's door on the way downstairs. Everything was in order: the Bugler cigarettes, which Granddad rolled himself, were stacked neatly in a biscuit tin on the night stand; the remains of three slices of toast and jelly lay on a sticky plate atop the alarm clock.

Chuckling softly, I ran down the stairs to the kitchen. There was Granddad, sitting sweaterless in the drafty room, cheerfully reading the sports page.

Good morning, Granda."

"Mornin' to you, wee'un." He smiled. "You're a fair sight in the mornin', lassie."

—Robin Wilkening

In what way are Granddad's actions symbolic of his character? What does his disregard of the doctor's orders indicate?

How does the repetition of Granddad's words affect the reader? Why do they make an effective ending? What do they tell you about his adjustment to American life?

Student Composition 12B

MR. BRICCETTI

Mr. Briccetti raised his baton and collapsed in laughter. "I've just gotta tell you this joke about Stravinsky," he gasped. He lowered his baton and proceeded to tell the almost pointless anecdote with generous Italian gestures. The story wasn't particularly funny, but Mr. Briccetti could make anything seem hilarious.

Maestro Thomas Briccetti is short and thin, but wiry. His longish hair is coarse, straight, and black. Beneath his thick, expressive brows, his big black eyes constantly crinkle with amusement. And even though his complexion is too sallow and his nose is a bit too large, his appearance is dashing.

His flamboyance carries over into his style of conducting. He dances across the podium, stooping and leaping, his face frowning, then smiling. But his showmanship is supported by a deep knowledge and understanding and love of music. Briccetti demanded a great deal from all of us in the Youth Symphony, and we worked as hard as we could for him. Frequently he called extra rehearsals for each instrument—I played cello—so he could explain the music and help us struggle through the more tortuously constructed passages. These trials were punctuated by jokes, admonishments, reassurances, and individual workouts.

Mr. Briccetti tried to make each person feel important. He could focus all of his vast supply of charm on an individual to make even the least gifted person feel like a virtuoso. Every player had a vital part in the overall sound of the Symphony; each person had to feel necessary.

Mr. Briccetti was too wonderful to last. He lost his job with the St. Petersburg Symphony when a

In what ways is the texture of this opening thinner and less interesting than the opening of the preceding composition?
Do you think this character would use "I've just gotta. . . ."

What order does the writer use in describing Mr. Briccetti? What aditional details would you like to have?

Have you felt a need to know who Mr. Briccetti is and why he is worth writing about? How might this information have been presented earlier?

What is another form of the word "admonishments"?

How might the writer have ended her paper if Mr. Briccetti had not left town?

How do you feel—how does the writer feel—about her not playing the cello any more? Is Mr. Briccetti responsible for her quitting? Why?

bigwig conductor was flown in. Many of us in the Youth Symphony quit when he left town. I don't even play the cello any more, but I still have vivid memories of Mr. Briccetti. He was a surging, innovative, tolerant, colorful personality, and he was fantastic with young people. While so many other adults were impatient and condescending, Mr. Briccetti stressed our uniqueness and individual importance.

—Susan Hicks

Elements of a Character Sketch

As was mentioned earlier, three things to consider in writing character sketches are: the subject, the point of view, and the method.

1. The subject. Who will the subject be? The subject of a character sketch may be real or imaginary. There should be some outstanding quality, feature, accomplishment, or trait that will make the subject interesting to the reader.

2. The point of view. If the subject of your character sketch is a real person, you will probably write from your own point of view. You may, however, decide that your sketch could be more forceful or more effective if your wrote from another point of view—that of a close friend, a son or daughter, even a pet dog. In such a case, even though your subject is a real person, your viewpoint is fictional.

If the subject of your character sketch is imaginary, you may write from a third-person point of view or you may assume the point of view of a "persona," a voice other than your own. There is no limit to the possible points of view you may assume in writing a character sketch.

3. The method. There are a number of methods a writer can use to reveal character. Some of them parallel quite closely the ways we build up impressions of the people we meet in everyday life. Others are techniques that belong only to writing. The subject you have decided upon and the point of view you have chosen will help you determine what method or combination of methods you will use.

Evaluating the Character Sketches

With the three elements of a character sketch in mind, reread the professional models and the student compositions. Evaluate the choice of subject, determine the point of view, and notice the way the writer presents the character in each case. Discuss and evaluate each sketch in the light of these questions:

1. Is the subject real, interesting, and worth writing about?
2. What details selected by the writer focus the reader's attention on an important quality of the subject?
3. What method has the writer chosen to reveal or develop the character? What other method could have been used?
4. One of the methods of revealing character is the use of words, that is, dialogue (conversation) or monologue. Two people speaking to each other may shed light on a third character, or they may tell the reader something about themselves. A monologue is a convenient device for revealing character. It lets you "read the mind" and learn the inner thoughts of the character. Does the writer use dialogue or inner monologue effectively?
5. How does the setting affect your perception of the character?
6. What incidents, actions, or reactions reveal traits of the character?
7. What use is made by the author of imagery (figures of speech, vivid language) or symbolism?

As you work on the activities and as you do your regular literature assignments, be thinking of a subject for a character sketch. Students usually find it easier to write about people they have known, rather than about characters from fiction or drama. You may enjoy researching a currently popular figure, collecting information from several sources, and then writing a vivid character sketch based on the information. If you decide to write about a real person, try to choose someone who has been influential in your life or who has made a great impression upon you.

Selecting a Subject for a Character Sketch

The first thing you must do is to choose a subject—someone interesting enough to be worth your time and your readers' time. Following are several character sketches taken from various sources. Discuss the kinds of people chosen and possible reasons the writers selected them. Then begin making up lists of people about whom you might write.

I

He lay in his bed at Georgetown University Hospital, looking so drawn and tired, the intravenous needles feeding his right arm and hand. He motioned for me to come up on the left side of his bed. I went up to him and squeezed his hand, trying to say without words all the things I wanted to say, how much I had learned from him, how grateful I was, how much I loved him

"Ouch," he said. "Don't break my hand."

And Vince Lombardi grinned, that grin that could lift you or warm you or dazzle you, that grin I had seen so many times in locker rooms and on sidelines, in meeting rooms and at banquets. That grin didn't belong in a hospital room. He didn't belong in a hospital room. If anyone had ever suggested to me that there was one indestructible man in this world, I would have thought it was Vince Lombardi.[3]

—Jerry Kramer

II

She was a splendid young creature.

Oh, sure—she knew she was silly. You could tell that from her eyes: "I'm a fool!" they shouted happily. I guess that was her charm—her silliness. It was as if she knew she was beautiful. It was as if she knew she was almost perfect.

She *was* spoiled. They had spoiled her when she was very young. They were sorry sometimes—but not often. And that too was because of her eyes which, when they were not shouting "I'm a fool!", were whispering: "I am just a helpless, lovable little thing, and I love you, I am devoted to you . . . you will make me cry if you do not melt right there on the spot and caress me and act as if you love me more than anything in the world."

And they would caress her, stop whatever they were doing and caress her. And talk to her.

When one looked at her—at her splendid young body, straight, perfectly molded, eager and sure in its movements; when one watched her frolicking about of an afternoon—one could only think of youth. Watching her you dreaded even thinking of her ever getting old, ever moving slowly with caution and wisdom. It would be like the sun growing dark.

But what matter! Now she is young. And beautiful. And almost perfect . . . my "almost" collie.

And her name is Spice. . . .[4]

—Lorraine Hansberry

III

Something in the general drift now has John Kauffmann on his feet and off to the river. He assembles his trout rod, threads its eyes. Six feet three, spare, he walks, in his determination, tilted forward, ten degrees from vertical, jaws clamped. He seems to be seeking reassurance from the river. He seems not so much to want to catch what may become the last grayling in Arctic Alaska as to certify that it is there. With his bamboo rod, his lofted line, he now describes long drape folds in the air above the river. His shirt is old and red. There are holes in his felt hat and strips of spare rawhide around its crown. He agitates the settled fly. Nothing. Again he waves the line. He drops its passenger on the edge of fast water at the far side of the pool. There is a vacuum-implosive sound, a touch of violence at the surface of the river. We cheer. For two minutes, we wait it out while Kauffmann plays his fish. Adroitly, gingerly, he brings it in. With care, he picks it up. He then looks at us as if he is about to throw his tin star in the dust at our feet. Shame—for our triple-hooked lures, our nylon hawsers, our consequent stories of fished-out streams. He looks at his grayling. It is a twenty-five-ounce midget, but it will grow. He seems to feel reassured. He removes the fly, which has scarcely nicked the fish's lips. He slips the grayling back to the stream.[5]

—John McPhee

IV

John Reed was a schoolboy of fourteen years old; four years older than I, for I was but ten; large and stout for his age, with a dingy and unwholesome skin; thick lineaments in a spacious visage, heavy limbs and large extremities. He gorged himself habitually at table, which made him bilious, and gave him a dim and bleared eye and flabby cheeks. He ought now to have been at school; but his mama had taken him home for a month or two, "on account of his delicate health." Mr. Miles, the master, affirmed that he would do very well if he had fewer cakes and sweetmeats sent him from home; but the mother's heart turned from an opinion so harsh, and inclined rather to the more refined idea that John's sallowness was owing to overapplication and, perhaps, to pining after home.

John had not much affection for his mother and sisters, and an antipathy to me. He bullied and punished me; not two or three times in the week, nor once or twice in the day, but continually: every nerve I had feared him, and every morsel of flesh on my bones shrank when he came near. There were moments when I was bewildered by the terror he inspired, because I had no appeal whatever against either his menaces or his inflictions; the servants did not like to offend their young master by taking my part against him, and Mrs. Reed was blind and deaf on the subject: she never saw him strike or heard him abuse me, though he did both now and then in her very presence; more frequently, however, behind her back.

Habitually obedient to John, I came up to his chair: he spent some three minutes in thrusting out his tongue at me as far as he could without damaging the roots: I knew he would soon strike, and while dreading the blow, I mused on the disgusting and ugly appearance of him who would presently deal it. I wonder if he read that notion in my face; for, all at once, without speaking, he struck suddenly and strongly. I tottered, and on regaining my equilibrium retired back a step or two from his chair.

"That is for your impudence in answering mama awhile since," said he, "and for your sneaking way of getting behind curtains, and for the look you had in your eyes two minutes since, you rat!"[6]

—Charlotte Brontë

ACTIVITY 12A

Choosing Character Sketch Subjects

1. Put these headings either on the blackboard or on your paper: Real People I Know, Real People the Class Knows, Fictional People from Literature, Celebrities. In a group, prepare a list of five or six people for each of the last three headings, and then, by yourself, prepare a list of five or six for the first heading. Don't forget the possibilities within your own family and circle of friends.

2. After you have prepared your list of people, select five whom you find most interesting. Next to each of these five characters, jot down the reason for your interest and, in a few words, the outstanding aspect of the character.

This is a page from the only surviving manuscript of *Beowulf*, the Anglo-Saxon epic poem. It was written on sheepskin a thousand years ago.

Selecting a Dominant Impression

At every moment of every day, thousands of sense stimuli bombard your nervous system. If you perceived all of these and gave them equal consideration, you would be unable to "make sense" out of the world. From long experience you have learned to ignore thousands of these stimuli, to group others into meaningful patterns, and to concentrate on a few significant impressions.

As you describe a character, you must do the same thing. Even if you could perceive and write down every single thing about a character, your reader would expect you to single out and focus on the important, meaningful and striking aspects.

ACTIVITY 12B

Restating the Dominant Impression

Review your list of five characters and the aspect you singled out for each one in Activity 12A. Now, rewrite that characteristic in a more subtle manner as it might appear somewhere in the introduction or conclusion. The following is an example of how this is done.

BLUNT STATEMENT

The most outstanding aspect of Milton Foster's personality is his stinginess.

MORE SUBTLE STATEMENT

Milton Foster smiled happily as he realized that the homeroom clerk was not going to ask him for a United Fund contribution. He felt the change in his pocket and thought how pleasant it was not to have to part with a penny.

Be prepared to discuss your rewrites in class.

Experimenting with Point of View

The next thing to consider in writing a character sketch is point of view. Character sketches may be written from a kind of neutral, distant, third-person point of view; from the writer's own point of view; or from an imaginary point of view. If you move from nonfiction to fiction by assuming the point of view of a "persona" or character or voice other than your own, you must make up insights, events, conversations, and relationships which exist only in your imagination.

If you choose to write your character sketch from a fictional point of view, you should make full use of the special advantages such a point of view offers:

1. It enables you to report details which an outside observer could not know. For example, a politician might make comments in front of her cat that she would never make in public! An actor who is courteous and charming in public might act and speak before his family in ways no outside reporter could imagine.

2. It enables you to include judgments, explanations, emotions, attitudes, and reactions to the character. These should all be consistent and clearly recognizable as fiction, coming from your assumed persona, or voice. Such comments can be humorous, ironic, surprising, or awe-filled.

3. It enables you to experiment with a style completely different from your own. If you wrote from the point of view of the politician's cat, you are faced with the question, "How would a cat express itself?" Could you write from the point of view of a Martian? Or a doting mother? Assuming a persona, or voice, can be fun for the writer.

ACTIVITY 12C

Experimenting with Point of View in a Character Sketch

Working as your teacher directs, think of three or four different points of view you might assume if you were writing about each of three different characters. Prepare to tell a group of other students how you would make use of the three special advantages described above.

Multiple Ways of Showing Character

When you have chosen your subject and decided on your point of view, you will then consider the best way of revealing the character to your reader. Writers create characters by:

1. **Letting the characters reveal themselves.**

   a. Their own actions, words, and thoughts may reveal the kind of persons they are. (A skillful writer may heighten interest by having a character's actions contradict his or her words.)

   b. The reader may be told quite specifically what minor characters are like. Then the writer describes the main character's *reactions* to other characters, and thus reveals much about the main character.

2. **Letting other characters shed light on the main character.**

   a. They give the reader an idea of what the character is like by what they *say* to and about the main character as well as what they *think about* and how they *react to* the main character.

3. **Showing the way the writers themselves perceive the characters.**

   a. They may describe the appearance of the character.

   b. They may make interpretive comments about the thoughts, words, actions, and reactions of the character (explanations, analyses, hypotheses).

   c. They may compare the main character with other characters.

4. **Using miscellaneous techniques.**

   a. They may describe (in a way that sheds light on the character) a setting in which the character appears.

   b. They may give the character a name that reveals something to the reader (Scrooge, Becky Sharp, Apeneck Sweeney, Casper Milquetoast).

   c. They may relate the character to a symbolic object or action.

   d. They may present a series of scenes that reveals some change in the character.

ACTIVITY 12D

Analyzing Professional Techniques

Choose one character from a short story and examine all the passages in which the author develops that character's personality. Make a list of phrases that describe the character, list under each phrase the words or events that support that phrase, and then determine which of the techniques listed in the preceding section your author has used. Come to class prepared to discuss the different techniques and their relative effectiveness.

Using Action to Reveal Character

As you prepare to write your character sketch, you should observe your subject closely or else do some research to gather information. If your subject is a real person find some actual situations in which behavior communicates a dominant impression about the nature of your subject. Notice how the writer of the following selection accomplishes this.

I

Relatively few women specialize in science writing for newspapers. One of the exceptions is Nancy Hicks, by-liner of *The New York Times*. She started there in 1968 as a reporter on the Education News Desk and then became a metropolitan reporter. That same year she won the Russwurm Award of the New York Urban League, an honor given to a journalist whose work has "contributed materially to improving the plight of the unfortunate in the New York community."

In her science and medical coverage, Mrs. Hicks has reported on lead poisoning of slum children, ex-Army medics as civilian health aides, sickle-cell anemia (a disease that affects the black population almost exclusively), a black medical school and a moon walk by American astronauts. She said of her work:

"I cover general science, social science and some medicine and health. I have found it is possible to make this area meaningful to black people. Many science stories, however, are not particularly relevant to blacks, and I make no apologies for these. They are interesting and/or fun and, if done well, give me the leverage to do the stories I feel are important."

The slender young reporter has had her share of thrills in journalism. On a July morning in 1968, when she was a reporter for the *New York Post*, Mrs. Hicks was walking along Madison Avenue on her way to an assignment. Suddenly she heard the scream of sirens as two ambulances raced by her. They turned down the next cross street, and Mrs. Hicks ran toward them as they stopped a block away. She saw two policemen carrying a wounded man.

"Get down," one of the patrolmen shouted at her. "There's a sniper in the park!"

A man in a white undershirt was on the roof of a public lavatory in nearby Central Park. He had a long-barreled .45-caliber revolver with which he had killed a twenty-four-year-old woman and critically wounded an eighty-year-old man.

Instead of getting down, Nancy Hicks went into action. She bolted down the street, pounding on private doors in search of a telephone to call her paper. She finally got one, rang up her city editor and gave him the story. He then instructed her to stay with it until other reporters and photographers arrived.

There was plenty to keep her occupied until they got there. More than one hundred policemen converged on the scene as gunshots sounded through the area. Two officers, wearing bullet-proof vests, tossed tear-gas pellets onto the roof as the sniper continued firing. He was finally killed by the two policemen, who climbed ladders on the roof and shot him at close range. Mrs. Hicks had watched the action from behind a line of buses parked on Fifth Avenue. She said later in an interview for *Long Island University Magazine*:

"I had mixed feelings. As a citizen I was terrified that a man had run amok like that and shot four people. [Two officers were wounded.] As a reporter, celebrating my first anniversary in the business, I was reassured. My instinctive response to the urgency of the situation had been correct."

Nancy Hicks began "working my way into journalism" in junior high school as a reporter for its monthly newspaper. At George Washington High School in New York she was editor-in-chief of the paper, an honor that cemented her decision to major in journalism at Long Island University, where she won several honors. In her senior year, she landed a parttime job as a copygirl at the *Post* and became a reporter on that paper when she graduated.

Her advice to teen-agers weighing a news career: "Study as many different kinds of things as possible. Every young writer has to learn that you don't have to write about everything you know about. Blacks understand the black story best. But the insight into human nature they have gained by understanding that story can be applied to many other subjects as well. It sometimes is good to hold the ace and play it at a later time."[7]

—M. L. Stein

Writing imaginary incidents. In some instances, over a long period of time you may have formed a dominant impression of a person, but you may not have observed any single specific action that you can use to present your dominant impression in a dramatic and effective way. Is it acceptable, then, to make up an imaginary incident that communicates this impression of your character?

Many years ago, Parson Weems was faced with this very problem while he was writing his famous biography of George Washington. Because he wanted to reinforce his dominant impression that, even as a boy, young George was honest and truthful, the Parson made up the famous story about George, the hatchet, and the cherry tree. Today, no one thinks very much of Parson Weems' biography of Washington, but everyone is familiar with the cherry tree story. You can, if you wish, make up an incident to support your dominant impression, but in doing so you change from writing fact to writing fiction. For your character sketch, you may write either fact or fiction, but don't err as Parson Weems did by claiming fiction to be fact.

ACTIVITY 12E

Suggesting an Incident to Reveal Character

1. Working with a partner whom you know well and with whom you may have many acquaintances in common, make a list of several of the people you know and try to agree on a dominant impression for each. Consider such character-revealing adjectives as friendly, courageous, intelligent, altruistic, selfish, domineering, generous, confident, foolish, and helpful. Try to recall an incident you have observed in which the individual did something to reveal such a nature. Write a brief description of the incident to share with the class.

2. For any person for whom you could not provide an actual incident to support your dominant impression, create an incident that might have revealed the characteristic you listed for that person. Note clearly at the bottom of your page which items are fictional.

Using Conversation to Reveal Character

Almost everything people say reveals something about their characters. In the following passage, a husband and wife are discussing their daughter's future. Notice how their words and his thoughts reveal something about the character of each.

I

'Lunch isn't over,' said Nan, 'just because *you've* finished eating. And the two-fifteen bell hasn't rung yet. Don't forget we must talk to Felicity about her future.'

'*Must* we?' said Mor. This was the sort of provocative reply which he found it very hard to check, and by which Nan was unfailingly provoked. A recurring pattern. He was to blame.

'Why do you say "must we?" in that peculiar tone of voice?' said Nan. She had a knack of uttering such a question in a way which forced Mor to answer her.

'Because I don't know what I think about it,' said Mor. He felt a cold sensation which generally preluded his becoming angry.

'Well, I know what I think about it,' said Nan. 'Our finances and her talents don't leave us much choice, do they?' She looked directly at Mor. Again it was impossible not to reply.

'I suggest we wait a while,' said Mor. 'Felicity doesn't know her own mind yet.' He knew that Nan could go on in this tone for hours and keep quite calm. Arguments would not help him. His only ultimate defence was anger.

'You always pretend people don't know what they want when they don't want what you want,' said Nan. 'You are funny, Bill. Felicity certainly wants to leave school. And if she's to start on that typing course next year we ought to put her name down now.'

'I don't want Felicity to be a typist,' said Mor.

'Why not?' said Nan. 'She could have a good career. She could be secretary to some interesting man.'

'I don't want her to be secretary to some interesting man,' said Mor, 'I want her to be an interesting woman and have someone else be her secretary.'

'You live in a dream world, Bill,' said Nan. 'Neither of your children are clever, and you've already caused them both enough unhappiness by pretending that they are. You've bullied Don into taking the College exam and you ought to be satisfied with that. If you'd take our marriage more seriously you'd try to be a bit more of a realist. You must take some responsibility for the children. I know you have all sorts of fantasies about yourself. But at least try to be realistic about *them*.'

Mor winced. If there was one thing he hated to hear about, it was 'our marriage'. This entity was always mentioned in connexion with some particularly dreary project which Nan was trying to persuade him to be unavoidably necessary. He made an effort. 'You may be right,' he said, 'but I still think we ought to wait.'

'I know I'm right,' said Nan.[8]

—Iris Murdoch

ACTIVITY 12F

Analyzing Character Through Conversation

Without telling you directly about the characters in the previous selection, Iris Murdoch lets them tell you certain things about themselves. How would you describe the character and personality of Nan and Mor? Do either Nan or Mor remind you of anyone you know?

In the following passage from a short story called *Cress Delahanty*, the main character reveals something about herself in a conversation with her parents. Read the passage carefully and be prepared to discuss what it is about Cress that is revealed by the conversation.

I

"You have a perfect right to say, 'I told you so' now if you want to, Mother," Cress said. "You told me I was getting to be a character and I was, all right."

"What do you mean, Cress?" her father asked.

"I mean I'm a Character," Cress said bleakly. "I'm 'Irresponsible Delahanty.' I'm that 'Crazy Kid.' If I said I was dying, people would laugh." Water ran out of her hair and across her face and dripped off her chin, but she scorned to wipe it away.

"I made a good speech to the Student Council, and they laughed at every word I said. They laughed and held their sides and rolled in their chairs like loons."

"What speech was this, Cress?"

"The speech everybody who is a candidate for an office has to make to them. Then if they like you, they nominate you. I was a candidate for freshman editor. What they nominated me for was *Josh* editor. *Josh* editor. A two-year-old can be *Josh* editor. All you need to be *Josh* editor is a pair of scissors to cut out jokes with. I wouldn't be *Josh* editor if they shot me for not being. It's a silly job."

"Take off your coat, Cress," Mrs. Delahanty said, and Cress, not ceasing to speak, began also to unbutton.

"I would've been a good editor, and I told them the reasons—like I was responsible, knew the meaning of time, would see that the assignments were in on time, and so forth. They laughed like hyenas," she said, not bitterly but reflectively. "They said, 'This is the richest thing yet. Delahanty is a real character.' So they nominated me for *Josh* editor and I'm branded for life."

She threw her raincoat, which she had finished unbuttoning, onto the floor, said, "I have ruined my life," and walked out of the room, no longer trying to hide the fact that she was crying.[9]

—Jessamyn West

ACTIVITY 12G

Planning Conversations That Reveal Character

1. Think of several dramatic situations in which one or more characters reveal more about themselves in their words than they intended to. The following situations are possibilities for you.

   a. A girl who has just celebrated her eighteenth birthday tries to register to vote. A local election official tries to discourage her and, in doing so, reveals some attitudes about youth, politics, democracy, and change.

   b. The owner plans to sell a tract of land opposite a historic landmark. During his interviews with a manufacturer of chemicals, a minority housing official, and a representative from a foreign embassy, he reveals his own biases.

   c. Two students discuss a recent, highly-rated motion picture treating an important human theme. One student reveals either failure to understand the theme or inability to accept its values.

   d. A recruiter for a college reveals, as she interviews seniors in your school, that her values differ from those of some of the students.

2. After you have worked out several situations, write one or two pages of the conversation in rough form. If you have not thought of a better situation of your own, you may use one of those suggested in the first activity above.

3. In order to write conversations into your character sketch, you need to know the mechanics of organizing, punctuating, and capitalizing them. Refer to the Style Sheet on pages 398–410 to determine how you punctuate dialogue when:

   a. Introductory words such as *he said* or *she replied* precede the actual words of the speaker.

   b. Such words interrupt the actual words of the speaker, coming in the middle of the direct quotation.

   c. Such words follow the actual words of the speaker. You may also want to read the selection by Charles Angoff on pages 308–309. It contains all three dialogue requirements.

4. After you have checked the conventional mechanics of writing conversations, review and rewrite the pages you prepared in the second activity. Be prepared to discuss the kinds of details that make your dialogue sound natural.

Using Description to Reveal Character

Writers often use a straightforward descriptive passage to make their readers "see" the subject of a character sketch. In an article called "Under the Auchincloss Shell," C. D. B. Bryan describes the famous author this way:

I

When Louis Auchincloss chooses to be stiff and formal—which is rare—he can be imposing. He is 61 years old, looks 15 years younger, is six feet tall, weighs a trim 170 pounds, has deep-set dark brown eyes and the sort of patrician nose one associates with, say, the American eagle. There is, in fact, something quite birdlike about the way Louis can turn to look at someone: His head swivels leisurely, magisterially, as if his neck were scarved in rich plumage; his eyelids lower slowly, than rise, providing pause enough for feathers to settle, and when he speaks he *pronounces*.[10]

—C. D. B. Bryan

In his book, *Coming Into the Country*, John McPhee describes a man he met in Alaska. The author not only paints a vivid word-picture of the man, he also lets you know where he lives, how he lives, and what his philosophy of life might be.

II

With no trouble at all, Dick Cook remembers where every trap is on his lines. He uses several hundred traps. His annual food cost is somewhere under a thousand dollars. He uses less than a hundred gallons of fuel—for his chain saws, his small outboards, his gasoline lamps. The furs bring him a little more than his basic needs—about fifteen hundred dollars a year. He plants a big garden. He says, "One of the points I live by is not to make any more money than is absolutely necessary." His prospecting activity has in recent years fallen toward nil. He says he now looks for rocks not for the money but "just for the joy of it—a lot of things fall apart if you are not after money, and prospecting is one of them."

In winter on the trail, he wears a hooded cotton sweatshirt, no hat. He does use an earband. He has a low opinion of wool. First off, it's too expensive. Second off, you don't have the moisture problem up here you have in the States." He wears Sears' thermal long johns under cotton coveralls, and his feet are kept warm by Indian-made mukluks with Bean's felt insoles and a pair of wool socks. He rarely puts on his parka. "You have to worry up here more about overdressing than about under-dressing. The problem is getting overheated." Gradually, his clothes have become rags, with so many shreds, holes, and rips that they seem to cling to him only through loyalty. Everything is patched, and loose bits flap as he walks. His red chamois-cloth shirt has holes in the front, the back, and the sides. His green overalls are torn open at both knees. Half a leg is gone from his corduroy pants. His khaki down jacket is quilted with patches and has a long rip under one arm. His hooded sweatshirt hangs from him in tatters, spreads over him like the thrums of a mop. "I'll tell you one thing about this country," he says. "This country is hard on clothes."

Cook is somewhat below the threshold of slender. He is fatless. His figure is a little stooped, unprepossessing, but his legs and arms are strong beyond the mere requirements of the athlete. He looks like a scarecrow made of cables. All his features are feral—his chin, his nose, his dark eyes. His hair, which is nearly black, has gone far from his forehead. His scalp is bare all the way back to, more or less, his north pole. The growth beyond—dense, streaked with gray—cantilevers to the sides in unbarbered profusion, so that his own hair appears to be a parka ruff. His voice is soft, gentle—his words polite.[11]

—John McPhee

ACTIVITY 12H

Writing Description That Reveals Character

In Activity 12G you worked out several dramatic situations and made up conversations to reveal character. Choose one of the subjects of those sketches and write a paragraph of description. Choose details of appearance, mannerisms, facial expressions, and gestures that make your subject different from anyone else.

Finding Insights into the Characters of Real People

Travelers driving across Connecticut often encounter the Wilbur L. Cross Expressway. Sometimes people wonder who Wilbur Cross was and why the Expressway is named for him.

Dr. Cross was a professor of English at Yale University, the Dean of the Yale Graduate School, and an author and editor of many books. When Dr. Cross retired from Yale in 1930, someone, as a joke, nominated him as the Democratic candidate for governor in staunchly Republican Connecticut. No one expected him to win since he was quite old, a complete novice in politics, a Democrat, and an arch enemy of a firmly entrenched political machine. Everyone was amazed when he won. People were even more amazed when he fought politicians in his own party to keep them from making him a figurehead while they used his power. He went on to serve four terms as governor and, during the Great Depression, he instituted extensive government reforms and building programs which made him one of Connecticut's best governors. He wrote his life story in the book *Connecticut Yankee*.

There are many such fascinating people in American and world history. By looking through the reference books in your library, you can find thousands of such stories of real people in interesting situations. After skimming some of the reference books, you may have to do additional research to flesh out your character sketch.

Here are some books in which to begin your search:

Current Biography. New York: H.W. Wilson Co. (Ask your librarian to show you how to use this excellent monthly magazine, which is issued also in annual bound volumes.)

Drake, Francis S. *Dictionary of American Biography Including Men of the Time*, 2 Vols. Detroit: Gale Research Company, 1879.

Gridley, Marion E. *American Indian Women*. New York: Hawthorn, 1974.

————————— . *Contemporary American Indian Leaders*. New York: Dodd, Mead, 1972.

Howat, Gerald, editor. *Who Did What*. New York: Crown, 1974.

Ohles, John, editor. *Biographical Dictionary of American Educators*. Westport: Greenwood Press, 1978. (The information on Wilbur Cross comes from this text.)

Pappas, Martha R., editor. *Heroes of the American West*. New York: Scribner, 1969.

Walker, Greta. *Women Today: Ten Profiles*. New York: Hawthorn, 1975.

ACTIVITY 12 I

Exploring Library Resources for Your Character Sketch

Spend at least an hour browsing in your school or community library to find the kinds of resources that would be available to you if you decided to write your character sketch on a celebrity or a historical figure. Look especially at the reference section, the section on "collective biography" in which the lives of several people are presented in one volume, the vertical file, the magazine and periodical collection, and *Current Biography* magazine.

■ MAJOR WRITING ASSIGNMENT

A CHARACTER SKETCH

Reread the sample character sketches at the beginning of this chapter and review the techniques the professional and student writers used. Then choose a subject and begin to work on your character sketch. To write an effective character sketch you must:

1. Observe as many aspects of a given character as possible.
2. Decide which aspects to emphasize and which to ignore.
3. From the material selected, decide on a *dominant impression* and try to put it into words.
4. Write down the description, interpretation, dialogue, and action that seem to support the dominant impression.
5. Compare the material written down with the dominant impression you decided to focus on.
6. If necessary, revise either the dominant impression or the material.

Just as in other kinds of writing, a character sketch has a beginning, a middle, and an ending. You may wish to begin your sketch by showing your subject engaged in a significant action. Fill in the descriptive details that will make the sketch come alive for the reader. One technique is to indicate your dominant impression indirectly. Choose the most appropriate method for supporting your dominant impression and for revealing or developing your character. Be sure the setting is appropriate for the subject. If you have decided to use conversation to reveal character, write it, read it, and rewrite it. Sometimes reading a dialogue aloud helps you to spot any false or artificial notes. Provide careful transitions to make your sketch move along smoothly. One interesting way to end a character sketch is to have the subject perform an action that symbolizes or reinforces the dominant impression that was the focus of the sketch.

Diadems - drop -
And Doges - surrender
Soundless as Dots,
On A Disc of Snow

E. Dickinson

Chapter 13

Imaginative Writing

All writing is creative in the sense that it involves "the originating, the making, and the bringing into being" of a new communication. The kind of writing most people think of when they use the term "creative writing," however, differs from the kind of writing that explains, analyzes, or persuades. The creative writer is a poet in the Greek sense of the word *poietes*, "one who makes." Creative writers create or recreate an experience and stamp it indelibly with unique marks of their own personality, background, experience, and perception. When the work is successful, the reader and the writer are joined through the sharing of an experience and of a response to that experience.

Essential Aspects of Creative Writing

As you write your next major composition (and perhaps others that you will submit), you will want to emphasize these aspects of your writing:

1. Sincerity
2. Emotion

3. Originality

4. Recreation of an experience

Sincerity. An absolute essential of creative writing is sincerity. No matter how beautiful and how technically perfect a work of art is, if it lacks sincerity—and, amazingly enough, professional critics can almost always tell—it is worth little. In his poem "Andrea Del Sarto," Robert Browning emphasizes the need for sincerity. Andrea Del Sarto was a Renaissance painter whose draftsmanship was so perfect that he was called "The Faultless Painter." In the poem, Del Sarto, while boasting of his skill, acknowledges that he lacks a spiritual quality—part of which is sincerity—and without it he cannot create great art. He says:

> No sketches first, no studies, that's long past:
> I do what many dream of all their lives,
> —Dream? strive to do, and agonize to do,
> And fail in doing.
>
>   *   *   *   *   *
>
> Well, their less is more, Lucrezia! I am judged.
> There burns a truer light of God in them,
> In their vexed beating stuffed and stopped-up brain,
> Heart, or what'er else, than goes on to prompt
> This low-pulsed forthright craftsman's hand of mine.
> Their works drop groundward, but themselves, I know,
> Reach many a time a heaven that's shut to me. . . .
>
> —Robert Browning

Some students, when trying their hand at creative writing, forget that above all they must be sincere in what they are trying to express. They make the mistake of including an off-the-subject idea that will pad their paper and make it look more impressive, or they dash off a line which, though it may be nonsensical, has the desired rhythm and rhyme.

In a parody of Edgar A. Guest's poetry, Louis Untermeyer satirizes the problem of the hurried or insincere writer. Edgar Guest was for many years a popular, syndicated-newspaper "versifier" who had to write at least a poem a day to meet the ever-pressing deadlines. Mr. Guest was conscious that in writing hastily for a large audience he was at times less effective than at other times, and he insisted that he should not be called a poet. Though he was never so unconcerned with meaning as Louis Untermeyer's parody suggests, the parody nonetheless emphasizes how ridiculous verse can be if the poet lets rhythm and rhyme dictate content.

EDGAR A. GUEST

SYNDICATES THE OLD WOMAN WHO LIVED IN A SHOE[1]

It takes a heap o' children to make a home that's true,
And home can be a palace grand, or just a plain, old shoe;
But if it has a mother dear, and a good old dad or two,
Why, that's the sort of good old home for good ol' me and you.

—Louis Untermeyer

Notice how Untermeyer sacrifices logic, sense, and sincerity, simply to fill out a line and make a rhyme.

Emotion. Most of your writing this semester has been expository; that is, it has been the kind of writing that communicates facts or ideas. Creative writers, however, are usually less interested in communicating facts than they are in communicating attitudes and emotions. Expository writing is important for what it *contains*; creative writing is important for what it *is*. In his article "What Does Poetry Communicate?" Cleanth Brooks is writing specifically of poetry, but he might be speaking of all art when he says, "The poem communicates so much and communicates it so richly and with such delicate qualifications that the thing communicated is mauled and distorted if we attempt to convey it by any vehicle less subtle than that of the poem itself."[2] In other words, creative writing communicates attitudes and emotions that cannot be communicated in any other way. It's relatively easy to communicate an expository idea—you can use a hundred different methods— but in expressing an emotion or an attitude, no two pieces of writing will do it in exactly the same way. Expository writing tends to make readers think; creative writing tends to make them feel.

Originality. Every human being is unique. Nobody like you has ever existed before. No one has had your particular physical and mental makeup, your individual background, and your special experiences. Because you are unique, you have ideas and emotions that no one else has ever had, and if you respect your own uniqueness you will write sincerely and originally about what only you can write about. As Emerson said, "Envy is ignorance and imitation is suicide!"

Recreation of an experience. Of course, words can never actually recreate an experience. Words are simply symbolic sounds—sounds that stand for something. Yet they can convey the impression of an experience. Notice how D. H. Lawrence in *Sea and Sardinia* communicates, with the rhythm and sound of his sentences, the movement of a ship:

> And so we steam out. And almost at once the ship begins to take a long, slow, dizzy dip, and a fainting swoon upwards, and a long, slow, dizzy dip, slipping away from beneath one. The q-b [Mrs. Lawrence] turns pale. Up comes the deck in that fainting swoon backwards—then down it fades in that indescribable slither forwards. It is all quite gentle— quite, quite gentle. But oh, so long, and so slow, and so dizzy.[3]
>
> —D. H. Lawrence

In writing creatively, then, you create or recreate an original experience as vividly as possible. To accomplish this, you use concrete words that appeal to your reader's senses. You include actual conversations. You choose your language so that your images summon up the effect of the original experience.

Finding Ideas for Creative Writing

If a one-inch line could represent all the possible ideas and experiences suitable for expository writing, then it would take a yard-long line to represent all the possible emotions and experiences suitable for creative writing, for the range of ideas takes in all of human feeling and experience. The problem, therefore, is not in finding enough ideas but in selecting the right idea. First of all, you must recall and isolate an emotion and experience you feel strongly about; and secondly, you must figure out some way to communicate it. Ideas suitable for exposition consist of subjects which, by definition, can be expressed in words. Ideas suitable for creative writing, by definition, cannot be expressed in simple, ordinary words. Artists of all kinds—painters, dancers, composers, sculptors, poets—are always searching for new ways of communicating emotions and experiences.

As you do the activities in this chapter, think of an emotion, an attitude, or an experience from your own background, and think about the form that you will want to write it in. You may write a short story, a poem, a prose poem, an essay, or even the impressionistic description of an event, perhaps in the "stream-of-consciousness" style. This is a style in which the writer records all the thoughts flowing through the mind of a character at any given moment.

Some students will want to know: "Is it all right to write on a purely imaginary subject? How about science fiction or a war story? Or how about a poem on something that we haven't experienced yet, such as death?"

The decision will be up to your teacher. Certainly, many creative writers have never experienced some of the things they write about. It is possible to write good, honest, creative material on subjects outside of your own experience, but it is more difficult.

Student Composition 13A

THE VISIT

This poem does not rhyme or have a regular rhythm. Why can it be considered a poem?

Who is the speaker in the poem? How can you tell whether or not the poet is writing in her own voice?

What is the relationship between the speaker in the poem and the person being described? Perhaps this poem will make you think of the final scene in Willa Cather's *My Antonia*.

In what way does the speaker feel superior to the person she is describing? How does this feeling of superiority make you regard the person speaking?

Point out lines in which the poet appeals to the various senses—sight, sound, touch, taste, smell.

How would you describe the *tone* of the poem?

Poets must select carefully from objects and events in reality. Suggest some objects and events the writer hints at but leaves out.

She stares at the floor
And thinks—
Her thoughts are not in tune
With mine
As I watch her
And try to make polite conversation
While the sun fades the carpet
and the flies buzz
Around the electric fan.

Her baby cries
In the next room,
But she is used to the sound
And doesn't look up
And doesn't ask questions
About the things I tell her.

I begin to wonder
What she's thinking about—
The tragedy of living
In one town all her life
Or maybe
The days when
We would explore the valley
And climb trees and
Walk the dirt roads—
Children in a Paradise—
And how time has changed
Everything.

Does she envy me?
I like to think so . . .
I like to think
That next to her
I am richer,
I am better,
Having moved out
Into the world.
For the old ties of friendship
Have melted away
After too many days apart.

And soon I leave.
She watches me
From the screen door;
I look back
Only once.
I left my home here
Long ago
But so did she—
In another way.

—Carol Barlow

Student Composition 13B

WASTED SMILES

I was feeling so free and liberated
From the pains and sorrows of loving
    someone,
Glad to be seeing new smiles
And smiling back—
Knowing it meant more than what most
    passers-by saw.
And then I found you and now,
Everyone's smile but yours is wasted
    on me.

                —Stephen Janson

The previous poem was a kind of narrative poem. (It told a story.) What makes this a lyric poem—one expressing personal feelings or emotion?

Paraphrase the poem (put it in your own words). Which is more interesting to read, your paraphrase or the original poem?

Student Composition 13C

LONELINESS

Sometimes I feel that all the world's a
    party cake
And I am the crusty edges left stuck
    to the pan. . . .

                —Susan Rogers

This couplet depends on a single image for its impact. What other image, or picture, might you use to communicate the feeling the writer is describing?

Student Composition 13D

IN SEPTEMBER

In September when the air is
Hot and sticky with all the sounds and
Smells of summer
And the pungent smell of tar
Drifts along with the wind and the
Taxi driver sweats and curses the detour,
The sun burns down and steam
Rises off the wet pavement where dirty
Children play and flies buzz in and
Out of screen doors that bang when they close;
And gulls sit on the lampposts that line the

To what senses does this poem appeal?

What are the tone and atmosphere of the poem? Point out some specific words that create the tone and atmosphere.

What is the dominant picture, or image, in the poem?

Street that runs along the docks and
Factories belch white clouds that
Billow up and hang low over the city;
People work and play and sweat and
Drink beer in the entirely oppressive heat;
Then everyone in the city carries a
Knife in their back pockets and one day
They all take out their knives and carve
Sections of the hot, heavy air like
Pieces of juicy pie and they eat those
Slices of air and the heady aroma
Dissolves into the clear nothingness of fall.

—Doug Ryals

Student Composition 13E
TWILIGHT

Another way of saying what these first few lines say would be "The crickets clacked in the twilight after we finished doing the dishes." What makes the original version more poetic?

What is the "shaggy freight train" that "begs for table scraps?" Describe the creature in your own words. How do you know all those details about it, when they are not given in the poem?

From the porch
twilight came softly
with crickets clacking
    when dishes didn't
and fried okra smells
    that brought a shaggy freight train
      rolling
        down
          the
            hill
              to beg for table scraps.

Dying sun turned the new corn
    golden
and played like fire in
    tumbled red curls
of one
    who fell asleep
    in a soft warm lap

    Unaware.

—Allyson Fisher

Student Composition 13F

You've probably heard the word *irony*, before. Look this word up and discuss how it relates to the poem.

In Pittsburgh there is a man
Who works with steel
And punches a clock
At nine and five.
He struggles to make ends meet.
He knows that unless food prices go down
He can never send his son to college.

He does not know that

In Iowa there is a man
Who works a field
And sows or harvests
From sun to sun.
He struggles to make ends meet.
He knows that unless food prices go up
He can never send his daughter to college.

But in Pittsburgh, what matters now
Is that it's almost five.

—Pamela Taylor

This poem contains few vivid images and sensory impressions. To what extent would the poem be improved if these were added in a revision? What images might you add?

What comment do the last two lines seem to make on life in Pittsburgh as compared with life in Iowa?

Student Composition 13G

STAR

The lights hit her
trapping a pale face
in hot, white blindness.
Terror dilates the eyes
of the stage prisoner
as she searches
for an identity;
frozen shock thaws
under the intense glare
of the spotlight.

The actress laughs loudly,
safe behind her phony smile:
one frightened creature
at home
in the soul of
another.

—Allyson Fisher

What are some other titles you might suggest for this poem?

What other images would you use in describing stagefright and ways of coping with it?

How does the writer seem to feel about hiding behind a mask?

What is the voice, or point of view, of the speaker in the poem?

Student Composition 13H

WHATEVER HAPPENED TO

UNCLE MARTIN

My uncle was the most obstinate man in Vermont. If you know Vermonters, then that means he was the most obstinate man in the world, and for some reason, he had the power to disbelieve things out of existence. Let me tell you how he got that power.

Who is the narrator? How would you describe him?

It all started when I got a telegram from Aunt Edith that said, "MARTIN STRUCK BY LIGHTNING. COME AT ONCE." There was a sound of alarm in those seven words which scared me. I caught the first train to Lakeside. Zeke Hanson, who was also town constable, met me in his beat-up taxi. I asked him how Uncle Martin got hit by lightning.

"Got hit by his own stubbornness. If I told him once, I told him a thousand times, don't get under a tree during a thunderstorm. Trees draw lightning. Well he got under the oak tree. Guess he figured he could ignore that lightning. Well, lightning hit that tree, split it, knocked Martin 20 feet."

"Did it hurt him," I asked Zeke.

"No," he said, "Guess it's because he had such prime good health. Ain't been sick a day of his life, except that time he fell off that horse and thought he was a farm machinery salesman named Walt Morrison from Gary, Indiana. Actually I think it helped him. He walks like he's on springs and he seems to give off electricity from every pore."

From the train station, we passed through town, and I noticed a group of people standing and staring at something. The something they were staring at was an empty marble pedestal that had formerly held a large bronze statue of a local statesman named Arnold J. Quantly, an individual whom Uncle Martin had always held in the utmost contempt.

Uncle Martin absolutely refused to admit that anyone would erect a statue to anybody like Quantly. He actually refused to admit there was any such statue in the village square, but there had been, and now it was gone.

I leaned forward and asked Zeke what had happened.

"Stole," he replied, "Yestiddy afternoon, 'bout five. Yessir, in plain view, took between two winks of an eye. We was all in Charlie's store—me 'n' Charlie 'n' your Uncle 'n' your Aunt Edith 'n' some others. Somebody said as how somebody ought to clean that statue, 'come plumb pigeonfied past few years.

" 'What statue?' Martin wanted to know. 'There ain't no such thing as a statue to a blubbery-mouthed fool nincompoop like Quantly in this town!'

"So I knowed it wasn't any use, he wouldn't believe in that statue if he walked into it an' broke his leg. Never met as obstinate a man as Martin Carabiener for not believing in something he don't like—anyway, I turned to point at it and it was gone. Minute before it was there, now it wasn't. Stolen between one look an' the next."

I asked him if maybe being struck by lightning had softened Uncle Martin's obstinacy.

Sometimes writers use *flashbacks* to provide background information in dramatic form. Point out some flashbacks in this story. Why are they effective?

"Made it worse," he said. "Most obstinate man in Vermont, your Uncle Martin. Dad blast it, when he says a thing ain't, even though it's right in front of him, blamed if he don't say it so positive you almost believe him.

Zeke dropped me off at Uncle Martin's gate. Uncle Martin wasn't in sight, but I headed around back and Aunt Edith came scurrying out of the kitchen.

"Oh, Joseph!" she cried. "I'm so glad you're here. I don't know what to do, I simply don't. The most dreadful thing has happened to Martin and . . ."

"If you didn't know the truth, you'd think it actually did him good to be hit by lightning, but here he comes. I'll tell you more after dinner. Oh I hope nothing dreadful happens before we can stop it."

Uncle Martin walked over and shook my hand, and my arm tingled as if from an electric shock. We strolled over and sat on the front porch and started looking at the old rotting barn which spoiled the view.

Looking for something to talk about, I mentioned it was too bad the storm two days before hadn't knocked down the barn and finished it.

"Barn? What barn? No barn there, boy!" said Uncle Martin. "Nothing but the view—finest view in Vermont. If you can see a barn there, better get to a doctor as fast as you can hike."

Like Zeke said, he spoke so convincingly that I looked again to be sure. I stood looking for a long time, because Uncle Martin was telling the truth. There wasn't any barn—NOW.

Aunt Edith only sighed when I told her about the barn.

"Yes," she whispered, "I knew yesterday when the statue went. Yesterday, we were in Charlie's store. I was looking at the statue when Martin said what he did, and then it was gone, right from under my eyes. That's when I sent you the telegram."

"You mean," I asked, "that since Uncle Martin was struck by lightning his stubbornness has taken a new turn, that before he just didn't believe in things; and now because of a huge heightening of his stubbornness, that now he can just disbelieve things right out of existence?"

Aunt Edith nodded. "They just go!" she cried almost wildly. "When he says a thing's not, now it's not."

Suddenly Uncle Martin came in, "Listen to this," he said, and read us a short item that told about Martin's step-brother, Seth Youngman, who owned Marble Hill. Seth somehow got Marble Hill away from Martin and since then Martin refused to believe in it. When he finished, he said, "What are

Many writers begin stories in the midst of the action, rather than near the climax. They then provide the background through flashbacks. Put the events in this story in chronological order—in the order of the time in which they happened. How near to the climax does the writer begin the story?

they talking about? There's no hill around here by that name."

Then we heard a far distant rumble, like stones being displaced. Aunt Edith and I both looked out the window and looked at Marble Hill, or where it had been.

Uncle Martin turned and walked away. As he passed the doorway, he caught his foot in the turned-up linoleum and fell the full length of the hall and hit his head on the table. He was unconscious when we reached him. We picked him up and put him on the sofa. Soon he opened his eyes and blinked at us without recognition.

"Who're you?" he asked. "What happened to me?"

"Martin," Aunt Edith cried, "I'm your sister. You fell and hit your head. You've been knocked out."

Uncle Martin stared at us with deep suspicion. "Martin?" he repeated, "My name's not Martin. Who do you think I am anyway?"

"But it is Martin!" Aunt Edith wailed. "You're Martin Carabiener, my brother, and you live in Lakeside, Vermont. You've lived here all your life!"

Uncle Martin's lip stuck out obstinately. "My name's not Martin," he declared rising, "I'm Walt Morrison. I sell farm machinery. I'm from Gary, Indiana. I'm not your brother. I've never seen you before, either of you. I've got a headache and I'm tired of talking."

Uncle Martin's amnesia had come back, just like twenty years ago when he fell off the horse and thought he was Walt Morrison from Gary, Indiana, for a whole week.

He turned and stomped up the stairs.

Aunt Edith and I followed him up and watched him slam the door. We heard the bedsprings squeak as he sat down and the sound of a match being struck, then the smell of cigar smoke. He always allowed himself one cigar before bed.

"Martin Carabiener," we heard him mutter to himself and one shoe dropped to the floor. "Nobody's got such a name. It's a trick of some kind. Don't believe there is such a person."

Then he was silent. The silence continued. We waited for him to drop the other shoe. When a full minute had passed, we gave each other a horrified look and then slammed open the door. The window was locked from the inside. A cigar in the ashtray was sending a curl of smoke upwards. There was a hollow in the bed covers slowly smoothing out where someone might have been sitting. One shoe was on the floor where Uncle Martin had dropped it.

But Uncle Martin, of course, was gone. He had disbelieved himself out of existence.

—Paul Soukup

The writer knows that a reader enjoys recognizing events, incidents, and even phrases from earlier in a story. Point out some of the repetitions from the early part of the story.

One editor thought the last two lines of Paul's story should be cut. Do you think they are necessary? Would removing them provide more impact—or less?

Student Composition 13 I

It's all in the . . .

POINT OF VIEW

Bernie sat stiffly on the edge of the bed, his finger poised over the telephone dial.

I just know she won't go, he thought. She's probably not home and her mother won't like me. He clenched his fist and watched the knuckles whiten. No, wait—it's now or never. If she says "No," it won't be the end of the world. So let's get on with it! It was a steady finger that dialed the seven digits.

Oh, no, it's ringing! His confidence vanished in a flash. Maybe if I hang up now, she'll never . . .

"Hello?"

Calm now. Just take it easy, he mouthed silently. "Julie?"

"Yes?"

"This is Bernie Potter. There's a great movie on at the Palace and I thought maybe if you weren't doing anything . . ."

Boy, you're dumb, he thought. You sounded too eager. Make her think you don't care. Oh well. Too late now.

"Sure, Bernie, that'd be great."

He let out a great sigh of relief and leaned back on the flowered bedspread. No sweat, he thought. I knew I'd knock her dead.

"I'll pick you up at eight, then," he said, tapping casually on the clock radio beside his bed.

"All right. 'Bye."

"So long."

He stood up and strode from the room, a broad smile on his face. Never any doubt in my mind, he muttered. I knew she'd go. I *knew* it."

Julie slumped into the green beanbag chair, her eyes staring blankly in the general area of the television set. She absent-mindedly twirled a lock of auburn hair with her right hand and thought, What's wrong with me? I haven't been out for three weeks and I'm bored. Lonely. I try to be nice to everybody, but . . .

The phone jangled, and she shuffled over to answer it.

"Hello?"

There was a slight pause on the other end, then, "Julie?"

What's this all about? she thought. C'mon, now, Babe, don't blow it.

"Yes?"

"This is Bernie Potter. There's a great movie on at the Palace and I thought maybe if you weren't doing anything . . ."

She thought, Wow, this is like something out of a grade-B movie, me lying around thinking about it and . . .

"Sure, Bernie," she said. "That would be great."

How dumb, she thought. Make him think it's all the same to you. Oh well, it's done now.

"I'll pick you up at eight then."

"Sure. 'Bye."

"Okay. So long."

Julie gently set the phone on the hook, turned slowly and did a forward flip on the green and orange shag carpet.

—Bill Post

ACTIVITY 13A

Critiquing *It's All in the POINT OF VIEW*

1. This story narrates only a simple and almost universal experience shared by most young people. In a brief paragraph, explain what makes it worth reading.

2. Writers used to be advised to write short stories from one point of view only. What do you think of such advice? Explain when it would be appropriate.

3. Writers often capitalize on the fact that there is pleasure in recognizing parallels in the experiences of different people. Using two columns, jot down the parallels in this selection and compare them. To what extent has the writer been very careful to make them identical?

4. Discuss how irony contributes to your enjoyment of this story. Can you identify with either speaker in the selection?

5. Notice the way the writer handles the dialogue in the story. How has he saved words and yet kept the identity of his speakers clear? Rewrite some of the dialogue yourself to reveal more about the speakers.

6. In several places the writer *shows* the emotions of the speakers. What are some of the ways he communicates the emotions without simply stating what they are? Go through the selection and *state* the emotion being shown in each case.

Discussing the Student Creative Writing

1. To what extent do the examples measure up to the four criteria for creative writing given in the introduction to this chapter (sincerity, emotion, originality, and recreation of an experience)?

2. Do the selections appeal to your senses, present vivid images, and use special techniques to help you experience the actual emotion the writer wishes to communicate?

3. What is the emotion expressed in "The Visit"? How do you react to the viewpoint it projects?

4. Poetry often tries to deal with attitudes and emotions in terms of things and events. How effective are the figures of speech in "Loneliness" and "In September" in revealing the writer's inner feelings? What do they communicate to you?

5. "In Pittsburgh . . ." is a "protest" poem. Can it be considered literature, or is it only propaganda on behalf of a certain point of view? What does it protest?

6. Do the stories have point or purpose, meaningful structure and order, and carefully selected details that support the intended effect or meaning? Do they express emotion? Provide concrete details? Contain suspense? Deal with action (external or internal)?

7. Is the tone of the stories maintained throughout? Do they succeed in presenting a mood or character consistently? What is the attitude of the writer in each case toward the characters?

Collecting Materials for Your Writing

When you read an absorbing short story or an emotion-filled poem, you become aware of the wealth of experience the writer has packed into the language. Poets, particularly, seem to be more perceptive and to react more deeply than other people. It may be true that poets are more sensitive, but you too can increase your awareness and begin to collect and store the raw materials that will enrich your own writing.

Throughout his entire life, James Joyce, one of the greatest Irish writers, collected and stored away details, information, and sensory impressions to use in his books. One of his friends observed the way he worked in preparing to write *Ulysses*.

I

I have seen him collect in the space of a few hours the oddest assortment of material: a parody on "The House that Jack Built," the name and action of a poison, the method of caning boys on training ships, the wobbly cessation of a tired unfinished sentence, the nervous trick of a convive [one who eats and drinks in festive fellowship] turning his glass in inward-turning circles, a Swiss music-hall joke turning on a pun in Swiss dialect, a description of the Fitzsimmons shift.

In one of the richest pages of *Ulysses*, Stephen, on the seashore, communing with himself and tentatively building with words, calls for his tablets. . . . [Like his character, Stephen] Joyce was never without them. And they were not library slips, but little writing blocks specially made for the waistcoat pocket. At intervals, alone or in conversation, seated or walking, one of these tablets was produced, and a word or two scribbled on it at lightning speed as ear or memory served his turn. No one knew how all this material was given place in the completed pattern of his work, but from time to time in Joyce's flat one caught glimpses of a few of those big orange-colored envelopes that are one of the glories of Switzerland, and these I always took to be storehouses of building material. The method of making a multitude of criss-cross notes in pencil was a strange one for a man whose sight was never good. A necessary adjunct to the method was a huge oblong magnifying glass.[4]

—Frank Budgen

Like Joyce, many writers use notebooks, journals, or diaries to record fragments of experience from which to build their work.

ACTIVITY 13B

Building a Storehouse of Ideas for Writing

Create a list of the different kinds of ideas, emotions, and information you might collect from your daily experiences to help you with your writing. Then decide on a way to record and store this material. Spend three days making an intensive effort to build a storehouse of materials to use in your writing. Include your experiences, impressions, and reactions, as well as images, passages you read, or phrases you hear. If you are finding the recording and storing process helpful, continue it indefinitely beyond the three days.

Thinking in Pictures

Several of the student models that you read earlier include vivid pictures to reflect the meaning, feeling, or psychological situation the writers are describing:

In "The Visit" a screen door separates the speaker and the young woman, just as they are separated psychologically.

In "Loneliness" the speaker pictures her feelings of despondency as the crusty edges that stick to a pan after a party cake has been removed.

In "In September" the speaker compares the hot, heavy summer air of a city to a juicy pie.

In "Twilight" the speaker pictures the shaggy dog as a freight train.

Sometimes a poet will build an entire poem around a single image such as each of these. Here are some examples by professional writers of such single-image poems.

I

Serve me a slice of moon
on a hot summer day.
A
nice
ice
slice
that rustles like taffeta
against my teeth—
and trickles winter through me
drop by drop.
Serve me a slice of moon
on a hot summer day—
with just a dab
of deep,
dark
shivery shadows
on top.

II

Rain
polished the night—
then,
over patent-leather streets,
cars moved
on narrow stilts
of
light.

III

I saw a man
murdering flowers—
a long parade of marching flowers
in giddy-bright happy-hats.
He pushed into the parade
with a steel mower.
The blades bit.
The flowers shrieked
and fell,
their giddy-bright happy-hats
askew.
And as their green life
trickled out
the
murderer
sang. [5]

—Marcie Hans

IV

THE TOASTER [6]

A silver-scaled Dragon with jaws flaming red
Sits at my elbow and toasts my bread.
I hand him fat slices, and then, one by one,
He hands them back when he sees they are done.

—William Jay Smith

In your reading of poetry you will find many images. Poets have compared a train crawling across the countryside to a dragon puffing smoke and flames, the headlights of two cars passing at night to the lances of two duelling knights, and traffic lights to glowing emeralds and rubies.

ACTIVITY 13C

Looking for Metaphors (Implied Comparisons)

1. Both in poetry and in prose, writers create vivid pictures by imaginatively comparing one thing with another. Think of metaphors (comparisons), images, or pictures for each of the following:

typewriter	frightened deer	long, boring class
night light	dog in a car	feeling of triumph
garbage disposal	unjust scolding	class bell
bridge game	a disappointment	sound of a crowd
concert	flat tire	vicious grin
soiled wallpaper	lightning flash	unforgettable melody
unexpected cry	bashfulness	conflict

2. This time, begin by making a list of objects, events, and emotions that most students will have experienced. Then create word pictures to represent them.

Letting Sound Reinforce Meaning

Early in this chapter you saw how D. H. Lawrence let the sound of his language reinforce the motion of the waves he was describing. The poetry in Chapter 14 demonstrates how emotion and tone can be conveyed through the choice of words, the length of lines, the selection of details, all uniting to transmit meaning through sound.

There are two useful techniques for letting sound echo sense. First is the use of *onomatopoeia*—the use of words that sound like what they mean. Examples of onomatopoeic words are "swish," "murmur," "crackle," "whiz," "zip," "trudge," "buzz," "drizzle." These words are very expressive. The second technique is the arrangement of words (as in the passage from D. H. Lawrence) to recreate the mood and experience.

ACTIVITY 13D

Creating Mood Through Sound

1. Choose a situation in which a certain mood, emotion, or kind of activity is dominant. Then write a brief paragraph or a poem in which you reinforce the sense with the sounds you use. (Your poem does not have to rhyme.) Remember that the primary requirements of creative writing are sincerity, emotion, and originality. Above all, do not write nonsense sentences in which the words, chosen for their sounds alone, are meaningless or inappropriate. Perhaps the following subjects will suggest some ideas to you:

a **storm**	an empty church	a roller coaster	a locker room
a **seashore**	a waterfall	a street corner	a kite in flight
a **cave**	a concert	a cafeteria	a mountaintop
a **cemetery**	a zoo	a pep rally	a typing room

2. After you have written your paragraph or poem, prepare to read it to the class. As each person reads, note where sound has been used with particular appropriateness. Be prepared to discuss changes or additions you might make.

Borrowing from Your Reader's Experiences

In Chapter 5 (page 109), you reviewed several common figures of speech. When writers wish to convey many impressions in few words, as in poetry, they often use figures of speech—they "borrow" from impressions that are stored in the reader's mind. For example, in the sentence "The guard sullenly *croaked* his refusal," the reader immediately transfers to the guard all his impressions of a frog: unpleasant, stupid, dull-eyed, slimy.

With figures of speech, the writer draws the reader into an experience. The reader's own background and conditioned emotional responses fuse with those of the writer.

ACTIVITY 13E

Using Figures of Speech

Rewrite each of the following sentences to include a figure of speech that borrows from your reader's storehouse of experiences. Try to use several different figures of speech and to vary your sentences. After you have rewritten each sentence to include at least one figure of speech, list beneath each the major sensory impressions that you intended to borrow from your reader's previous experience. Avoid sensory impressions that seem inappropriate.

1. The car went by.
2. Charley was surprised.
3. The ball went into the stands.
4. The team ate supper.
5. The college gave him the diploma reluctantly.
6. Frightened, the boy used his sister as a shield.
7. Everyone seemed ready.
8. The pencil was the prize.

Developing Expressive Forms

In addition to using figures of speech and onomatopoeia, some writers try to make the *form* of their selection express the meaning they wish to communicate. Here is an anecdote that makes the concept of "expressive forms" clear.

In *The Sacred River*, L. A. G. Strong tells of a revealing conversation between James Joyce and Frank O'Connor. The scene is Joyce's flat: O'Connor has just touched the frame of a picture on the wall.

I

> "What's this?"
> "Cork." (The city of Cork in Ireland)
> "Yes, I see it's Cork. I was born there. But what's the frame?"
> "Cork."
> This anecdote illuminates one of Joyce's major artistic techniques. . . . The technique—to which I have given the name "expressive form" [borrowed from Yvor Winters]—seeks to establish a direct correspondence between substance and style. The form "expresses" or imitates qualities of its subject. . . . Thus an episode which takes place in a newspaper office is cast in the form of a newspaper, or a section on sentimental girlhood is written in a "namby-pamby . . . style."[7]

In short, to emphasize the fact that the name of the pictured city was Cork, Joyce framed the picture with a cork frame! To emphasize the fact that an episode took place in a newspaper office, he wrote the passage as though it were a newspaper article. Here are some examples from Joyce and others in which the writers have used expressive form to reinforce their content.

In *A Portrait of the Artist as a Young Man*, James Joyce begins at the beginning—when he was a baby. Notice how his style in this passage is mostly baby talk to reinforce the subject he is writing about. (As the artist matures in the story, the style, too, "grows up.")

II

> Once upon a time and a very good time it was there was a moocow coming down along the road and this moocow that was coming down along the road met a nicens little boy named baby tuckoo. . . .
> His father told him that story: his father looked at him through a glass: he had a hairy face.
> He was baby tuckoo. The moocow came down the road where Betty Byrne lived: she sold lemon platt.
>
> > *O, the wild rose blossoms*
> > *On the little green place.*
> He sang that song. That was his song.[8]
>
> —James Joyce

In *The Sound and the Fury*, William Faulkner uses expressive form to emphasize his theme—that life is meaningless. To make the point, he tells the story through Benjy, a young man who is retarded. This is the way Benjy sees a golf game. The caddy, Luster, removes the flag from the cup and searches for lost balls in the rough. Benjy, of course, doesn't understand what is going on.

III

Through the fence, between the curling flower spaces, I could see them hitting. They were coming toward where the flag was and I went along the fence. Luster was hunting in the grass by the flower tree. They took the flag out, and they were hitting. Then they put the flag back and they went to the table, and he hit and the other hit. Then they went on, and I went along the fence. Luster came away from the flower tree and we went along the fence and they stopped and we stopped and I looked through the fence while Luster was hunting in the grass.

"Here, caddie." He hit. They went away across the pasture. I held to the fence and watched them going away.[9]

—William Faulkner

In poetry, too, writers sometimes use expressive forms to reinforce the content. The poet e e cummings is well known for his unusual forms and his departure from customary spelling, punctuation, and sentence structure. (Notice the way his name is printed.) In this poem, cummings uses expressive form to represent the ugly skyline of suburbia. (The word *ecco* is the Latin word for "behold" and the spelling *ts* is sometimes used to express the sound of disapproval.)

IV

e
cco the uglies
t

s
ub
sub

urba
n skyline on earth between whose d
owdy

hou
se
s

l
ooms an eggyellow smear of wintry sunse
t[10]

—e e cummings

ACTIVITY 13F

Experimenting with Expressive Forms

In most of the writing you do, especially in college and in the business world, you will be communicating ideas and information in a straightforward way. Consequently, in most of your writing, the use of expressive forms would not be appropriate. By experimenting with expressive forms, however, you will become sensitive to possibilities of the language that can enrich all of your writing. In addition, for your own enjoyment of effective self-expression and for the occasions when you want to communicate feelings and attitudes and atmosphere in your writing, experience with expressive forms will help you.

1. List words which can be written or printed so that the form expresses the meaning. Here are some examples.

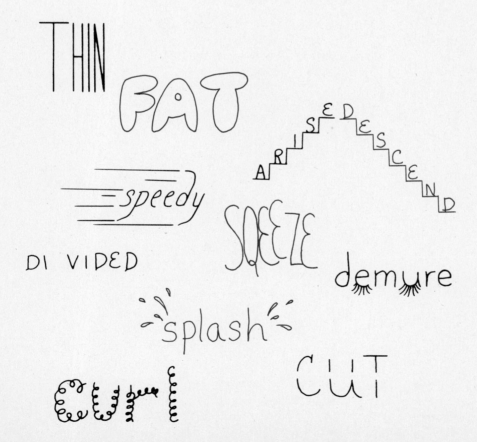

2. Write a concrete poem in which the words actually form the shape of the object you write about, as in the mouse's tale (tail) from *Alice in Wonderland*.

<pre>
          "Fury
      said to a mouse, That
          he met in the house,
                'Let us both go
          to law: *I* will prose-
          cute *you.*—Come,
      I'll take no denial:
      We must have the
      trial; for really
    this morning I've
    nothing to do.'
        Said the mouse
            to the cur,
                'Such a trial,
                    dear sir,
                        with no
                          jury
                      or judge,
                  would be
              wasting our
          breath.' 'I'll be
          judge, I'll
          be jury.'
              said cun-
              ning old
                  Fury: I'll
                try the
                whole
                cause,
                and
              con-
              demn
              you
                  to death'."
</pre>

—Lewis Carroll

Here are some possible subjects for which you might try matching meanings, impressions, sounds, or feelings to the shape:

a question   a bouncing ball
a geyser erupting   a river (or a waterfall)
a religious symbol   a bird in flight

3. Write a brief passage in which you use words that imitate the language or atmosphere of the place you are describing.

a kindergarten classroom   a submarine
a jetport in the future   a church
a gymnasium   a cave
a mountaintop   a subway station

4. Write a brief passage or a poem in which the sound of the words, the rhythm of the language, and the form you use all combine to reinforce the content.

the sound of an echo in a deep, rounded cave
the sound of the sea battering a rocky coast
the sound of a jet taking off

Various Poetic Forms

Over the years, poets have developed many different patterns for expressing ideas and emotions. You can find whole volumes describing these patterns and the uses to which they can be put.

Many poets today create their own forms, but few of the best poets ignore the patterns developed in the past. Often, as they work toward developing their own patterns, they have already internalized earlier forms. The word "internalize" here means that the poets have become so familiar with the forms that they have incorporated them into their own patterns of thinking. Following are explanations of some poetic forms.

Couplet—A couplet is simply two related lines of poetry. Often they rhyme, but they need not. They may be of any length and rhythm. Here are two examples.

I

ON THE ANTIQUITY OF MICROBES

Adam
Had 'em.

—Strickland Gillilan

II

THE QUARREL

The clouds and the wind in
heated debate
Argued on whether to rain
or wait.

Haiku—Haiku is a Japanese form consisting of a total of seventeen syllables, with five in the first and third lines and seven in the second. The subject matter is nature, and the lines should contain an image of permanence and an image of change. Usually the haiku makes an indirect comment on life.

III

THE TEMPTER[11]

Plum blossoms swaying:
Here! Here! Steal this one!—is that
What the moon's saying?

—Issa

IV

SILENCE

The sound of the moth
Wings folded on the clapper
Of the temple bell.

—Nishi

Tanka—Tanka is another Japanese form that begins with exactly the same pattern as the haiku and moves into the *ageku.* The ageku consists of two additional lines of seven syllables each, for a total of thirty-one syllables in the complete tanka.

V

THE FISH

The fish feels water
Squish along his scaly back
And doesn't know it.
He feels the sudden hook yank
And his water world is gone.

—Catherine Clint

VI

MY TRIUMPH

The conversation
Wasted through the dawdling hour.
Subjects like blind worms
Turned upon themselves and nipped
Their tails. I sat in silence.

—Fred Prince

The Chain Haiku (or Chain Tanka)—A series of related verses following the same form—is used to tell a kind of story by revealing little pictures of a sequence of events. For example, how might you develop a series of events around the conversation in the foregoing tanka? Another use is for two writers to write and respond to each other in a series of haiku or tanka.

Cinquain—The cinquain is an American form invented by Adelaide Crapsey of Rochester, New York. It has five lines of two, four, six, and eight syllables respectively. The double cinquain may have twice as many syllables in each line. A good way to develop a cinquain is to use a noun in the first line to provide a subject and title; to use two adjectives in the second line describing the subject; to use an —ing phrase in the third line expressing an action; to use a sentence fragment in the fourth line communicating a feeling; to use another noun, a synonym for the title, or a symbol for the object named by the title as the fifth line.

VII

Homework
Heavy, pushing,
Pulling deep breaths from me
Marathon runner charging home
Hard grind.

—Leonard Van

VIII

Gamble
Sweating, hoping,
Wishing she would miss me
The grinding force of ancient Rome
Latin.

—Barbara Auchey

Limerick—Limericks have been used for hundreds of years for light subjects and word games. Though some people think they were invented by Edward Lear or first developed in Limerick, Ireland, no one knows for sure where and when they originated. They consist of five lines, with the first, second, and fifth rhyming, and with the third and fourth lines either not rhyming or having a different rhyme. Limericks do not use the traditional rhythms of most poetry written in English. Instead, they use a system of counting only the primary (very heavy) accents. Lines one, two, and five have three primary accents each, whereas lines three and four have only two. Often such surprise elements as puns, allusions, or plays on English spelling make the verses humorous. The limerick below has been marked to show the typical pattern of syllables and rhymes.

IX

There was a young girl in the choir (a)

Whose voice rose up higher and higher (a)

Till it reached such a height (b)

It was clear out of sight (b)

And they found it next day in the spire. (a)

Sonnet—All sonnets consist of fourteen lines of iambic pentameter; that is, lines such as the following with a ten-syllable accent pattern:

O par|don me,|thou blee|ding piece|of earth,|

—William Shakespeare

Beyond the common elements of fourteen lines and iambic pentameter, there are other characteristics that divide sonnets into two groups. The English (or Shakespearean) sonnet consists of three quatrains (four-line groups) and a couplet. The Italian (or Petrarchan) sonnet is organized into an octave (eight-line group) and a sestet (six-line group). Both types display a structured elegance and demand great discipline and skill on the part of the poet. When well handled, the rigid form of the sonnet is submerged in the poem's meaning and goes almost unobserved by the reader. In the examples below, however, the organization and rhyme pattern of both types have been highlighted for purposes of comparison.

X

SONNET 29

(an English sonnet)

quatrain	When, in disgrace with Fortune and men's eyes,	(a)
	I all alone beweep my outcast state,	(b)
	And trouble deaf heaven with my bootless cries	(a)
	And look upon myself and curse my fate,	(b)
quatrain	Wishing me like to one more rich in hope,	(c)
	Featured like him, like him with friends possessed,	(d)
	Desiring this man's art and that man's scope,	(c)
	With what I most enjoy contented least;	(d)
quatrain	Yet in these thoughts myself almost despising,	(e)
	Haply I think on thee, and then my state,	(f)
	Like to the lark at break of day arising	(e)
	From sullen earth, sings hymns at heaven's gate;	(f)
couplet	For thy sweet love rememb'red such wealth brings	(g)
	That then I scorn to change my state with kings.	(g)

—William Shakespeare

XI

ON THE GRASSHOPPER AND THE CRICKET

(an Italian sonnet)

octave	The poetry of earth is never dead:	(a)
	When all the birds are faint with the hot sun,	(b)
	And hide in cooling trees, a voice will run	(b)
	From hedge to hedge about the new-mown mead;	(a)
	That is the grasshopper's—he takes the lead	(a)
	In summer luxury—he has never done	(b)
	With his delights; for when tired out with fun	(b)
	He rests at ease beneath some pleasant weed.	(a)

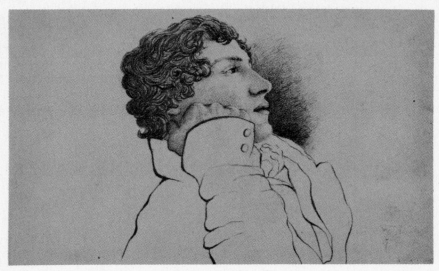

Just two years after this drawing was made, in 1819, Keats died at the age of twenty-five.

	The poetry of earth is ceasing never:	(c)
	On a lone winter evening, when the frost	(d)
sestet	Has wrought a silence, from the stove there shrills	(e)
	The cricket's song, in warmth increasing ever,	(c)
	And seems to one in drowsiness half lost,	(d)
	The grasshopper's among some grassy hills.	(e)

—John Keats

Triolet—The triolet is rarely used today. It is a French form that is delicate and dancing, consisting of eight lines, with the first line repeated as the fourth and the seventh and the second line repeated as the eighth. Although any kind of rhythm is acceptable, the triolet uses only two end rhymes.

XII

THE TRIOLET[12]

Easy is the Triolet,
    If you really learn to make it!
Once a neat refrain you get,
Easy is the Triolet.
As you see!—I pay my debt
With another rhyme. Deuce take it,
Easy is the Triolet,
    If you really learn to make it!

—William Ernest Henley

Blank Verse—Blank verse consists of unrhymed lines of iambic pentameter. Of course, departures from the rigid pattern are necessary to express ideas naturally, and sentences frequently continue from line to line rather than ending at the end of a line. Shakespeare's plays are in blank verse, except for occasional passages. As a matter of fact, ordinary conversation is spoken, and can often be written in the form of blank verse. Here are some lines from *Hamlet*:

> But look, the morn in russet mantle clad
> Walks o'er the dew of yon high eastward hill.
> Break we our watch up, and by my advice
> Let us impart what we have seen tonight
> Unto young Hamlet, for upon my life
> This spirit, dumb to us, will speak to him.

> —William Shakespeare

Free Verse—Many of the student poems near the beginning of this chapter are in free verse, a form that has no specific requirements for syllables, lines, rhymes, meters or rhythms. But a free verse poem *does* have form, usually a form that matches its content, mood, and meaning. As professional poets know, good free verse is as demanding as any other form and can be written successfully only when the poet has become familiar with other forms and is willing to work hard at polishing each phrase in the poem.

These are only a few of the many, many forms that poets have developed over the centuries. Others are the rondeau, rondel, villanelle, ode, ballade, ballad (two different forms), and epic. If you are interested in these and other forms, go to your library and get a book on "prosody," which will explain and illustrate them.

Various Prose Forms

The usual form most students choose for creative writing in prose is the short story. A short story can be read at one sitting and aims at a single effect. It often begins with an event which leads to complications; these complications increase and intensify the suspense until there is a crisis. After the crisis comes the climax, the point of highest interest in the story. At this time some decision is made that influences the ending of the story. After the climax comes the "falling action," or denouement (which means "the untying of the knot"), and the writer concludes the story quickly.

Many short stories do not follow the "classical pattern" just described. In fact, the only requirements are that short stories be fiction, that they be interesting, and that they have a purpose of some kind—even if that purpose is simply to describe "a slice of life."

You need not be limited to the short story to be inventive and creative in prose. Here are only a few of the forms you might use in writing imaginatively in prose:

1. Tell a story in a series of letters.
2. Tell a story in a series of journal or diary entries.
3. Create a tall tale, a joke, or a legend.
4. Develop a dream or a daydream into a story.
5. Write a fantasy, letting ideas come to you as you listen to music or view a painting or sculpture.
6. Dramatize an event, real or imagined.
7. Tell a story using a series of newspaper clippings.
8. Write a film, radio, or television script.
9. Recreate fictionally an historical event.
10. Extend a short story or an historical event by imagining a sequel.
11. Write a dramatic monologue in which one person recounts and reacts to action as it is taking place.
12. Describe a single incident from various points of view using thoughts that each of several characters would have during the event.
13. Write a serial consisting of several parts, each ending with a "cliffhanger"—an event creating unusual suspense and causing the reader to want to know what happens next.
14. Make up an interview with a real or imaginary person.
15. Write a *pourquoi* (which means "why") story, a fable explaining why something exists ("How the elephant got its tail" or "How the Finger Lakes were created," for example).

Avoiding Clichés

One of the four requirements of creative writing stressed in the introduction to this chapter is originality. You might agree with the writer of Ecclesiastes that "There is nothing new under the sun," and you would, in a sense, be correct. For thousands of years people have been writing on the same themes: *carpe diem* (live for the day), salvation through suffering, ambition and its effect, loyalties, the place of human beings in the universe, among many others. But though they write on age-old themes, they handle them in individual and original ways. Originality, then, may be a new expression of an old idea.

One of the great obstacles to originality is the use of clichés. A cliché is an expression or idea that has been used so often that it has lost its effectiveness. Imagine getting set to take a delicious bite from a savory hamburger—only to discover you have a mouthful of sawdust! Clichés in writing have the same effect. A reader gets all set to savor an incisive new expression, only to discover a worn-out cliché.

One must also avoid the other extreme, using expressions that are too new or unusual or ridiculous. A great creative writing teacher, Hughes Mearns, published these verses written by one of his students.

XIII

B.C. (BEFORE CLICHÉS)
MORNING

I watched a fluffy cloud drift by
Across the boundless blue of sky
And saw the sun's rays, molten gold,
Upon the dewy earth unfold.

EVENING

I felt my fettered soul uplift
Before the rosy sunset drift
And in the hazy blue afar
I saw the gleaming evening star.

XIV

A.D. (AFTER DISCOVERING 'EM)
MORNING

I saw the sun with battered face
Trying to warm the human race;
I watched a sodden cloud limp by
Like some discouraged custard pie.

EVENING

The sleepy sun in flannels red
Went yawning to its Western bed;
I saw one shivering small star
No brighter than our dishpans are.[13]

—Jewel Martin

Do not be surprised if an expression that sounds new and exciting to you turns out to be a cliché that you have not heard. In a way, earlier writers had an advantage over you since they have already used the images that you might like to use now. Because these expressions were so appealing and vivid, they were used again and again and so became clichés. Robert Burns' "My love is like a red, red rose that's newly sprung in June," and Shakespeare's "All the world's a stage and all the men and women merely players," were fresh, vital lines when they were written. You, however, must go on to create new and equally effective images of your own.

ACTIVITY 13G

Creating New Expressions

1. The following expressions are the beginnings of common clichés. See if you can fill in the standard expression and then see if you can create a new image or a new comparison to replace the old one:

   a. crazy as a _____
   b. dead as a _____
   c. happy as a _____
   d. white as _____
   e. strong as an _____
   f. it rained _____
   g. mad as a _____
   h. clever as a _____
   i. skinny as a _____
   j. eyes like _____

   k. red as _____
   l. cold as _____
   m. black as _____
   n. modest as a _____
   o. full as _____
   p. sings like _____
   q. writes like _____
   r. whimpers like _____
   s. wet as a _____
   t. blind as a _____

2. After you have identified the clichés and created new comparisons, see whether the class can list any additional clichés. Go through both processes with your own list.

▬▬▬▬▬▬▬ MAJOR WRITING ASSIGNMENT

CREATIVE WRITING

Write a short story, an essay, or a poem, keeping in mind that your creative writing must have sincerity, emotion, and originality, and that you should try to recreate an experience. Refer to the storehouse of ideas you gathered in Activity 13B. Make use of the suggestions in this chapter: try to think in pictures, use sound to reinforce your meaning, use images that your reader will respond to, use expressive forms and avoid clichés. After you have written a rough draft, go over your work to look for ways to improve it. (See Chapter 2, Polishing and Perfecting.)

Chapter 14

Criticism of Prose and Poetry

In the eighteenth century when almost every boy went into an apprenticeship to learn a trade, it was the master's job to criticize whatever the apprentice produced. "Here now," a shoemaker might say, "you've got to leave a little more welt, or you won't have anything to stitch."

Of course, the wise and skillful master knew that criticism should be positive as well as negative, rewarding as well as corrective. "That's a fine window!" the glazier (glass worker) might shout. "The sun will come like fire through those bright colors."

Criticism has always been an important activity in almost every human endeavor. It is, in a sense, a gift of insight from the past to enlighten the future.

In some areas, where the standards are clear and absolute, criticism is very easy. "Water won't flow uphill, unless it's under pressure. You've got to change the angle of that pipe!" There is no room for opinion here. The plumber has based his criticism on a clear and absolute set of standards.

In literature, standards are neither absolute nor so widely accepted as to be clear and uniform. As a result, some writers and critics adhere to one set of standards while other groups accept another. In short, there is no universally accepted, conventional set of literary values. Read, for example, this discussion of Tolstoy's evaluation of Shakespeare.

> Tolstoy felt that Shakespeare was a minor literary figure. Truly dramatic situations, Tolstoy said, do not require easy props like earthquakes, floods, or famines. Nor should they lean on black-and-white characterizations in which absolute good is juxtaposed against absolute evil. The authentic literary product finds its raw materials in everyday situations and in the struggle that goes on inside a man's soul. And it was precisely in these respects, Tolstoy believed, that Shakespeare was most deficient. . . .
>
> Tolstoy's evaluation of Shakespeare . . . emphasized three principles:
>
> 1. The subject had to be significant. It had to be important in the life of the people.
> 2. The treatment had to be authentic. Characters had to speak as people do in real life. The scenes had to be realistic. The plot had to be natural and had to engage the emotions of the audience. Emotion had to be delicately handled.
> 3. The sincerity of the enterprise had to be clearly manifest. The author had to feel deeply about what he was writing.
>
> Measured by this yardstick, Shakespeare was "inconsequential" and his characters "contrived." Pervading the whole of his work was a "premeditated artificiality" in which the author "juggles words." Tolstoy's conclusion: The sooner people free themselves from the false adulation of Shakespeare, the better it will be." This liberation, he said, would enable them to understand that the "trivial and immoral productions of Shakespeare and of his imitators . . . can never be the teacher of life."
>
> It should be apparent by now that Tolstoy's standing in world literature did not rest on the acuity [keenness] of his critical abilities.[1]

That one of the greatest of the Russian writers could so misjudge another great writer proves that criticism is a complex, difficult, and somewhat subjective activity.

Elements of Criticism

Several years ago UNESCO, the United Nations Educational, Social, and Cultural Organization, funded a study to determine a classification system of literary criticism.[2] After reading hundreds of examples of such criticism, the researchers found that when people write about literature, they follow some standard patterns.

1. They explain their own *involvement* in the work. That is, they explain what they felt, how they reacted, how the work related to their lives and the lives of others. In short, they tried to show how the work influenced them, with emphasis on its emotional impact.

2. They discuss their *perception* of the work. They explain its basic pattern, its use of language, literary devices, structure, tone, and techniques for communicating its theme. They classify it with relationship to other works and explain the significance of the classification.

3. They discuss their *interpretation* of the work. They explain the meaning of the work, giving their interpretation of any difficult passages, symbols, inferences, implications. They show what the author seems to be saying about people, about the world, about society, and about the divine.

4. They explain their *evaluation* of the work. They show what they thought the work was worth. Because values are so complex and various, the critics often set forth and explain their standards and then show how the work measures up. Critics differ in the emphasis they place on these elements: the emotion the work generates; the form or structure of the work; the unity and coherence of the work; the theme of the work and the way it comments on life; the tradition it follows; its believability.

This list of "what people say when they write about literature" gives you an idea of the subjects you can use when you write about a poem, a short story, a play, a novel, or any other literary selection. The list can be condensed into a series of questions:

1. How do I feel about the work?
2. What do I think the work means?
3. How did the writer communicate meaning? (What literary techniques, devices, customs, conventions, are used?)
4. How effective is the work? How does it compare with other works?

Sometimes a critic may go beyond the province of art into the areas of ethics, morality, and religion to answer an additional question:

5. Is the message of the work worthwhile?

Some Examples of Literary Criticism

The following excerpts from reviews of literature demonstrate how professional writers approach the criticism of fiction, nonfiction, and poetry. Study the technique of each and decide whether or not you would employ similar methods.

Consider these questions as you read the reviews:

Which of the five questions above does each reviewer answer?

Which question or questions does each reviewer emphasize?

Are all the questions equally important in criticizing poetry, fiction, and nonfiction?

I

FAIRY TALES AND AFTER: FROM SNOW WHITE TO E. B. WHITE
BY ROGER SALE
REVIEWED BY CLARA CLAIBORNE PARK

"Children's literature," writes Roger Sale, "is one of the glories of our recent literary heritage." Therefore he takes it seriously, as he takes any literature that is precious to him—the works of George Eliot, William Empson, or Spenser, for instance, the authors who are for him irreplaceable. So *Fairy Tales and After* is not a casual series of remarks and judgments, of interest to librarians and professors of education who preside over a ghetto called "children's literature," but considered literary criticism, useful to all of us who remember the books of our childhood. "Useful," of course, should be taken to mean "enjoyable"; "seriously" is not at all the same thing as "heavily."

Sale begins with one of the oldest definitions of the function of literature: that it give profit and delight, a definition these days honored chiefly in the breach. He writes—on fairy tales and talking animals, on Lewis Carroll, Beatrix Potter, Kenneth Grahame, L. Frank Baum, *Kim,* and *Charlotte's Web*—in the genial spirit of one wanting to write about very good books that nobody else has been writing about.

For Sale, children's literature is literature, make no mistake. *The Wind in the Willows* is, quite simply, "part of the ongoing emotional equipment of all who love it," and "The River Bank," its first chapter, is "one of the great opening chapters of any reader's reading life.[3]

II

THE NIGHT COUNTRY
BY LOREN EISELEY
REVIEWED BY RAY BRADBURY

Let's clear away dead fact and dry description first. *The Night Country* by Loren Eiseley, professor of anthropology and the history of science, University of Pennsylvania, is 240 pages long. It is a book about rats, birds, bones, spiders, shadows, and time. It can be read, one would imagine, in about three hours.

The vibrations from those three hours, however, might well last the rest of your life.

Because to read Loren Eiseley is to fall instantly in love.

* * * * *

"The Night Country" is the summation of Eiseley's life of turning over rocks, submerging himself in caves, visiting spider dens, ducking bats, and puzzling over fossil apeman's bones.

Eiseley is a haunted man, haunted by the shadow of himself on hotel walls, which will be replaced by yet other men's shadows tomorrow. But his heart beats and his hand moves to record past history, gaze steadily at the present which buries itself by the instant, and look to a future where Man, with his odd machines, can hope to toss further, brighter shadows.[4]

III

THE FOLLOWED MAN
BY THOMAS WILLIAMS
REVIEWED BY RICHARD MAREK

The "followed man" of Thomas Williams's new novel is Luke Carr, a hero in the old style: strong, brave, intelligent, a man of conviction. Bereft of his much-loved family by a plane crash, he cannot help looking over his shoulder to see what new disasters might be stalking him. Plenty of dangers are there. An anonymous Avenger sends him threatening notes that accuse him of murdering his wife. Scheming women, merely unhappy or actually suicidal, lay traps to lure him away from his happy memories. His friends have become "flawed, dangerous, too interested or needful." The world is suddenly all violence; survival is the only imperative.

Luke retreats to the New Hampshire woods, where the process of building a cabin provides him with the soothing feeling that he is in control. But, human nature is unavoidable even in this rural paradise, and although he survives the "bashings and dismemberments, plots and betrayals" that seem to define his life, he does so with the sense that he will always be followed by them.

The attentive, detail-laden prose of this somber tale shares many of the virtues of Luke's hand-built cabin: it is sturdy, attractive, and provides warmth in a chilly environment. But faults in the construction—frequent coincidences, occurrences that lead nowhere—point out the ordinariness of a plot full of sex and violence, and despite the cast of cowed and snarling characters, it is never quite possible to believe in Luke's paranoia. Disappointingly, *The Followed Man* lacks the depth as well as the complexity of Williams's award winning *The Hair of Harold Roux*.[5]

IV

A REVIEW OF MARGE PIERCY'S "THE TWELVE-SPOKED WHEEL FLASHING"
BY HAYDEN CARRUTH

Marge Piercy's book *The Twelve-spoked Wheel Flashing* contains much wit, moral concern, close observation, valuable thought and feeling, and it is well-written; yet it misses excellence, if by only a little. I open to a random page:

> My grandmother used to drink
>   tea holding a sugar cube
> between her teeth: hot boiling

> strong black tea
> from a glass. A gleaming
> silver spoon stood up.
> Before we make a fire of
> our bodies I braid my black
> hair and I am Grandmother braiding
> her greystreaked chestnut hair
> rippling to her waist before
> she got into bed with me
> to sleep. . . .

. . . and so on and so on. You see? The substance is there, but the poetry is the same lineless, tuneless, stressless stuff, with the same expectable enjambments, that thousands of others are writing. The common American style, in other words. I cannot find Piercy in her book, though I find abundant information about her. Is this what we want, this anonymity? I have heard people say that we live in an age of collectivism, which can become only more and more collectivized, and that consequently art should speak in a collective voice. Well, this is just what we have. Myself, I rebel. I cannot imagine a real art that lacks the presence of an authentic, authorial person, which alone can combine and integrate the other components. The common American style is interesting, but it is not moving, and hence, to my mind at least, it is not real art.[6]

V

"LÉON DAMAS: PIGMENTS AND THE COLONIZED PERSONALITY"
REVIEWED BY ELLEN CONROY KENNEDY

Pigments is an attack, a cry of pain, an anguished inventory of the personal loss of Africa, of Black identity, of discomfort and revolt at the inauthenticity of being "whitewashed." It does not go further, and did not need to.

In a blunt, dry, vivid style, marked by fresh images, unashamedly plain language, staccato rhythms and acridly witty puns, Damas' short poems lay bare their author's often violent rejection of white European "ci-vi-li-za-tion." "They did their thing so well," he writes (co-lo-ni-za-tion? as-si-mi-la-tion?) "that one day we let all/all that was once ours go/we threw it all away." Damas' language is always informal, close to the spoken word. The poems are built on the repetition of key phrases, images, rhythms and word-play. These were similar to the techniques of other French Surrealists of the time—Damas' friend, Desnos, for example, and the popular Jacques Prévert. Damas absorbed, hammered and perfected them until they were his own style, perfectly fused with what he had to say.[7]

Examining the Professional Criticism

In each of the preceding criticisms, the writer seems to begin by suggesting the contents and value of the work being discussed. The first review begins with a quotation, whereas the third review begins with a reference to the title of the book. Look at each of the examples and try to discover where the intention of the writer is defined by the reviewer. Are the writers' intentions, summarized below, stated or implied by the reviewers?

1. *Fairy Tales and After* presents serious criticism of children's literature, which is valuable to all who remember the books of their childhood.
2. *The Night Country* pursues the history of man, recording the past, observing the present, and looking ahead to the future.
3. *The Followed Man* tells the story of a threatened man in a violent world, whose only job is to survive.
4. *The Twelve-spoked Wheel Flashing* uses a kind of neutral collective voice to speak of varied subjects.
5. *Pigments* presents in colloquial, informal, appropriate language a cry of anguish at the Blacks' loss of their identity and their sham "whitewashing."

In these reviews, most of the reviewers considered all five critical questions. They differed, however, in their choice of which question to begin with. Look again at the reviews to see which of the questions each reviewer treated initially. If one of the reviewers introduced other information, how do you justify the extra inclusion?

As you read the following student reviews, look at the different ways the reviewers answered the five critical questions.

STUDENT COMPOSITION 14A

A REVIEW OF *REUNION* BY FRED UHLMAN

Discuss the wisdom of Laura's openness in specifying her reason for choosing *Reunion*.

How effective is the "outer structure" in arousing interest?

Which of the critical questions does this section answer?

How do you feel about this generalized and opinionated description?

How necessary is this almost complete summary of the book's action?

The thing that attracted me to the book *Reunion* was its length. With a busy weekend scheduled, and my six-weeks' book report due on Monday morning, I had to get something short, and *Reunion* is very short. It's so short, in fact, that it could be called a novelette or novella or short story, instead of a novel. But it's printed as a book so it meets our school requirement for a book report.

The story is told by Hans Schwarz, the schoolboy son of a Jewish doctor just as Naziism is becoming important in Germany. Hans goes to a funny, old-fashioned school, but he is lonely and shy until a new boy comes. Konradin is the son of a wealthy German nobleman and a beautiful, noble Polish wife. Though the two boys become close friends, Konradin never takes Hans to his home while his parents are there, and at the opera one evening Konradin pretends not to know Hans at all. During all this time, Naziism is becoming stronger and the pressures against Hans and his family are very great. A poignant scene describes how a storm trooper stands before Dr. Schwarz's office to drive patients away from the "Jewish doctor"—but Dr. Schwarz dresses up in his German uniform from World War I, complete with a medal for bravery, and the crowd jeers at the Nazi.

Finally, Hans is sent out of Germany for safety; but before he goes, Konradin writes him that though their friendship was very important, Hitler is a great man and Naziism will help Germany regain its former glory. That letter makes Hans realize that his friendship with Konradin is over and that Konradin is an enemy.

Thirty years later, Hans is living in the United States, when he receives a request to contribute to a memorial for former classmates killed in the war. What he learns from the request provides the climax of this little book. I almost cried when I read it.

The reason I liked *Reunion* was that it moved so swiftly. Although the two boys were a little quaint and would have even been considered peculiar in our school, I liked the way the author described their friendship, and I felt the pain of their separation. The story moved right straight through, with no flashbacks or subplots or excessive decoration. The language was simple with a little bit of a different rhythm, because it was a foreign story. Sometimes there was a strange contrast between the evil social events in Germany and the peaceful, almost sentimental description of the country: "the soft, serene bluish hills of Swabia . . . covered with vineyard and orchards and crowned with castles."

The title of the book is *Reunion,* and I think that is the theme of the book as well. I don't want to spoil the story by telling the climax, but it seems to me that the author is presenting his belief that the evil impulses of a person or a society may get temporary control, but that eventually, there will be a "reunion of the good."

I think the message of this book is very important. It's easy enough to go over the horrors of Naziism and World War II, as the television play *Holocaust* did, and we ought to do that so we won't forget. But it's even more important to emphasize that there can be this reunion, even though one person, or group, went crazy for a while.

—Laura Stephens

Why does Laura choose one definite scene for longer treatment? How does her summary differ from the way you would treat such scenes in a short story or character sketch?

If this is the climax, why doesn't Laura tell what happened?

Which critical question does this section answer?

Which critical question does this section answer?

How effective are the direct quotations? Should Laura include more of them?

Which critical question does this section answer?

How do you feel about the "outer structure" ending at this point?

STUDENT COMPOSITION 14B

REVIEW OF *ODE TO A NIGHTINGALE* BY JOHN KEATS

This limited critical selection does not attempt to answer all of the critical questions. Which one does it focus on?

The three parallel words in the first sentence lose effect because they are not recognizably parallel. How would you change "longing," "heartache," and "yearning" to make them truly parallel?

The word "this" ordinarily should refer to complete subjects, rather than to whole sentences. To what does the word "this" in the second sentence refer? How might the sentence be improved?

How does the writer keep the reader "on the track" as she progresses through the poem? What is the order of arrangement of the selection?

Again, notice the misuse of the word "this." How would you improve this sentence? How might you avoid the passive voice in the same sentence? Why is the passive not desirable?

How could the writer *show* that Keats makes "good use of imagery" rather than just *telling* that he does?

One problem with interpreting and explaining a poem is that readers differ in their interpretations. Unless you include exact quotations and reasons for making certain inferences, readers may not accept your ideas. What ideas really need support from the poem?

Look at the poem itself and then suggest an ending for this review that uses a short, telling quotation. Why would such a conclusion be more effective than the present ending?

The "Ode to a Nightingale" is a poem of longing, heartache, and yearning for a better existence. This is shown in the first stanza, where Keats is obviously envious of the nightingale as he listens to its song. Yet he claims not to be envious of the bird's happiness, but speaks of himself as "being too happy in thine happiness." He longs for the simple, free, and happy existence of the bird.

Keats speaks in the second stanza of leaving his cruel, hard world completely, perhaps by means of getting drunk and joining the bird in his mind. Reality crushes Keats as he recalls in the third stanza the "weariness, the fever, and the fret" that make up his existence on earth. Keats falls deeper into sorrow as he yearns for a release from this anguish. He wishes to "fade, far away, dissolve. . . ."

A burst of energy causes him to release his sorrow and decide he can join the free bird after all. This is to be done through his poetry, his writings, not through a fuzzy, foggy, dreary-eyed drunken state. The fourth stanza shows the joy he felt as he made his decision. It was as if a great weight (of death, perhaps?) had been lifted from his shoulders.

In the fifth stanza, drunk on poetry, he uses his imagination to describe his death, "in embalmed darkness" and his rebirth into the joyous world of the nightingale. Keats makes good use of imagery to show the transition of the imagination to this new environment.

The nightingale sings on in the sixth stanza. Keats has called on death to release him from his tortuous life. He longs for death, true death, as he listens to the songs. An easing of pain and sorrow is what is signified by death, the bird representing a rebirth and carefree new life.

The bird again captures Keats' attention in the seventh stanza, and the poet realizes that his bird is immortal and not born for death, but for eternal life. Sadness fills Keats' heart as he comprehends his inability to join the free flight of the bird, perhaps symbolizing God and eternal life, because he is bound to earth with his forlorn, lethargic life. He refers to Ruth whose story reflects the sadness and yearning for home which he felt. One could almost feel his heart breaking.

The reader feels a release of tension as Keats falls back to his sorrowful life in the eighth stanza. A dazed existence awaits him, in a world where there is no hope, no music.

—Mary Lutgen

Discussing the Student Criticism

Whether you study the student compositions individually at home or in class as a group, you should be able to agree on answers to the following questions:

1. To what extent have the writers followed the composition pattern that you learned in Chapter 3? As you recall, that pattern consisted of an outside structure and an inside structure, with the outside structure "wrapping up" the main body of the paper.

2. To what extent have the writers been aware of their audience, their situation, and their purpose?

3. Some beginning critics tell either so little about the work that the comments are meaningless or so much that the review practically repeats the whole story or poem. How effective have the student reviews been in this respect?

4. Have the writers made generalizations, interpretations, or evaluations without supporting them? How have they supported such statements? Some students write concretely about their own experiences but become very abstract when writing about literature. To what degree are the reviews concrete or abstract? What contributes to this quality?

5. When critics say, "This story is excellent" or "This story fails to hold the reader's interest," often they are not talking about the story at all. They are describing their personal reactions to the story. Our language—or at least our use of language—seems somewhat faulty for criticism. The sentences seem to mean, "In absolute terms on which everyone can agree, this story is excellent" or "According to standards established and agreed upon by everyone, this story fails to hold the reader's interest." Actually, they mean, "*I* like this story" or "This story fails to hold *my* interest." How do the reviewers indicate that they realize the difference between their opinions and absolute facts? What expressions do they use to avoid stating their judgments as absolutes?

6. In most cases, high-school students will do a more competent job of writing criticism if they handle a shorter work rather than a novel or another longer work. Is the treatment of these works complete and successful? Why?

7. Criticism has many different purposes, depending upon the individual writer's approach. It may explain a work; interpret the meaning; place the work in relation to a particular school of ideas, form, or historical development; analyze the artistic techniques used; relate to other works; connect with other works; or evaluate and judge the work. A single criticism

rarely includes all these functions. Which of these functions does each of the student compositions perform?

8. Look back at the five questions in the checklist for literary criticism on page 365. How well do the students deal with each question in their reviews?

Examining the Critical Questions

The five questions listed on page 365 can provide a convenient framework for organizing a review. As you have seen in the reviews you have read so far, not all critics use the questions in the same order or give them the same emphasis. Before you can use these questions effectively in your own writing of reviews or criticism, you must become more familiar with the possible implications and development of each.

The First Critical Question: How Do I Feel About the Work?

You probably won't begin your review by answering this question, although that is one possibility for an opening. It is a good idea, however, to begin your analysis of your subject by thinking carefully about your personal reaction to it.

Ask yourself the following questions: Did I like it? Did I not like it? How did I respond to it? Did it make any connections with my past experience? Does it suggest to me any application in my own life? Does it remind me of any other idea or presentation?

Since there is no "right" or "wrong" answer to the question, "How Do I Feel about the Work?" you should certainly be honest with yourself and refuse to deny your own impressions in order to follow those of either another student or of a professional critic. Later, after you are sure of your own reactions, you may want to check them against those of others, but unless you can clearly see a reason to change, trust yourself.

ACTIVITY 14A

Determining Your Response

Read thoughtfully each of the poems that follow. When you have finished each, jot down your initial response to the work. (Do not be afraid to say you didn't like one or more.) Then reread each one and note your answers to these questions:

How did the poem make you feel (happy, sad, amused, depressed, nervous, etc.)?

How, if at all, did the poem relate to your own life—to past experiences or to present or future situations?

Did the poem remind you of another idea, emotion, or situation? If possible, compare your responses with those of several other students to see how varied and personal each person's response was.

I

The golf links lie so near the mill
That almost every day
The laboring children can look out
And see the men at play.[8]

—Sarah N. Cleghorn

II

SYMPATHY[9]

I know what the caged bird feels, alas!
When the sun is bright on the upland slopes;
When the wind stirs soft through the springing grass
And the river flows like a stream of glass;
When the first bird sings and the first bud opes,
And the faint perfume from its chalice steals—
I know what the caged bird feels!

I know why he beats his wing!
Till its blood is red on the cruel bars;
For he must fly back to his perch and cling
When he fain would be on the bough a-swing;
And a pain still throbs in the old, old scars
And they pulse again with a keener sting—
I know why he beats his wing!

I know why the caged bird sings, ah me,
When his wing is bruised and his bosom sore,
When he beats his bars and would be free;
It is not a carol of joy or glee,
But a prayer that he sends from his heart's deep core,
But a plea, that upward to Heaven he flings—
I know why the caged bird sings!

—Paul Laurence Dunbar

III

PETIT, THE POET

Seeds in a dry pod, tick, tick, tick,
Tick, tick, tick, like mites in a quarrel—
Faint iambics that the full breeze wakens—
But the pine tree makes a symphony thereof.
Triolets, villanelles, rondels, rondeaus,
Ballades by the score with the same old thought:
The snows and the roses of yesterday are vanished;
And what is love but a rose that fades?
Life all around me here in the village
Tragedy, comedy, valor and truth,
Courage, constancy, heroism, failure—
All in the loom, and Oh, what patterns!
Woodlands, meadows, streams and rivers—
Blind to all of it all my life long.
Triolets, villanelles, rondels, rondeaus,
Seeds in a dry pod, tick, tick, tick,
Tick, tick, tick, what little iambics,
While Homer and Whitman roared in the pines!

—Edgar Lee Masters

IV

EX-BASKETBALL PLAYER[10]

Pearl Avenue runs past the high school lot,
Bends with the trolley tracks, and stops, cut off
Before it has a chance to go two blocks,
At Colonel McComsky Plaza. Berth's Garage
Is on the corner facing west, and there,
Most days, you'll find Flick Webb, who helps Berth out.

Flick stands tall among the idiot pumps—
Five on a side, the old bubble-head style,
Their rubber elbows hanging loose and low.
One's nostrils are two S's, and his eyes
An E and O. And one is squat, without
A head at all—more of a football type.
Once, Flick played for the high school team, the Wizards.
He was good; in fact, the best. In '46,
He bucketed three hundred ninety points,
A county record still. The ball loved Flick.
I saw him rack up thirty-eight or forty
In one home game. His hands were like wild birds.

He never learned a trade; he just sells gas,
Checks oil, and changes flats. Once in a while,
As a gag, he dribbles an inner tube,
But most of us remember anyway.
His hands are fine and nervous on the lug wrench.
It makes no difference to the lug wrench, though.

Off work, he hangs around Mae's Luncheonette,
Grease-grey and kind of coiled, he plays pinball,
Sips lemon cokes, and smokes those thin cigars;
Flick seldom speaks to Mae, just sits and nods
Beyond her face towards the bright applauding tiers
Of Necco Wafers, Nibs, and Juju Beads.

—John Updike

The Second Critical Question: What Do I Think The Work Means?

Answering the question, "What does the work say?" only partially affords an understanding of what a piece of writing *means*. Often what it seems to be saying is not what it really means. For example, in *A Modest Proposal*, written in the eighteenth century, Jonathan Swift advocated that Irish children be fattened and sold for food. Swift didn't really propose that Irish children be eaten; he wanted to say to the English, "You are so brutal and callous to the poverty-stricken Irish that you might as well be eating their children!" In 1932, Aldous Huxley described in *Brave New World* a frighteningly amoral, scientific, controlled society of the future. Huxley was not in favor of the society he described; he wanted to show that if the world continued in the direction in which it was then moving, such a society might result.

When authors intend to convey the opposite of what the words seem to be saying, they are using the literary device called *irony*. Irony, if effectively written, can be very powerful, but it requires that readers recognize the author's intention. If they are not aware of what is going on, readers may think the writer is saying the very opposite of what he or she actually means. In all writing, not only in ironic writing, the reader must be alert to subtle meanings and nuances. Indeed, recognizing and understanding subtle shades of meaning give skillful readers the greatest pleasure.

Tentative interpretations. Because critics cannot read an author's mind and discover exactly what the author intended, they can only read the work very carefully and then say, "I believe that what the author means is. . . ." Note that critics do not say, "The author means. . . ." They can only report what the work seems to mean.

Themes in literature. When critics present a view of what a work of art seems to mean, they are presenting the theme of the work. A theme in literature is the main idea, the interpretation of life, or the truth about human experience that a writer expresses. Everything in a literary work should contribute to the theme. The theme may consist of either a specific idea, which can be phrased in words, or a "general area of exploration," which may be inseparable from the total work of art. (In other words, sometimes you can legitimately say, "I can't put the idea into words.") Only with long experience in reading literature do you acquire the ability to recognize the theme easily; therefore, your initial efforts may be somewhat frustrating. Remember that even highly trained literary scholars may be baffled by a work or may disagree on its meaning. Finally, remember that a work is often richer because it may have many meanings or interpretations.

Interestingly enough, sometimes a work may have more meanings than the author consciously intended. What people derive from a work depends partly on the background they bring to it. Moreover, the same person may find more meaning in a work by reading it again later in life.

Four types of "meaning." Many works of poetry and prose are difficult in language, in ideas, and in style. Such works, however, are frequently rewarding because they yield greater insight and deeper satisfaction than do works that are easier to grasp.

The meaning of poetry can be especially elusive. Since poetry tends to compress a great deal within a comparatively small space, it often requires rereading and concentration before all of its emotion and its ideas come through to the reader. The meter and the rhyme of much poetry give it a special quality that appeals to the reader but sometimes make the inner meaning more difficult to find.

This special difficulty of poetry was investigated some years ago by Professor I. A. Richards, a literary critic, who found that many of his students disliked poetry and claimed they could not understand it. To discover the reasons for their difficulty, he distributed copies of various poems and asked students to write down the meaning of each poem. He then carefully analyzed the responses and presented his findings in the book *Practical Criticism*. Among other things, he stressed two important factors:

1. Many people fail to understand poetry because they concentrate on *one* kind of meaning in a poem, rather than on the *total meaning*.
2. Before people can understand and appreciate the total meaning of a poem, they must understand its *paraphrasable content*. That is, they must be able to put into their own words the physical event described in the poem.

But a prose statement of a poem is not the poem. (Some critics object to the making of prose paraphrases; but others, like Richards, see the prose paraphrase as simply a first step in getting closer to the poem's total meaning.) Richards says that a poem has at least four different kinds of meaning, and only when readers can recognize all four can they begin to understand and appreciate the poem.

Many modern critics extend Richards' ideas to prose. Both prose and poetry can have four different kinds of meaning.

First meaning. Richards' first meaning is the physical event in the poem—its *paraphrasable content.* Although Robert Frost once defined poetry as "that which gets lost in translation," Richards said that the paraphrasable content leads to an understanding of the other meanings of the work. In other words, it is the *who, what, when, where, why,* and *how.*

Second meaning. The second meaning is the *feeling* of the work—its appeal to the *senses,* rather than to the intelligence and understanding. Through its language, its style, its imagery, it stimulates an emotional reaction in the reader.

Third meaning. The third meaning is the *tone*—the attitudes shown by the writer toward the material, and the audience as expressed in choice of words, phrasing, and selection of details. It is not enough, says Richards, to understand the "sense" of the poem and to experience its feeling; one must also understand the tone, and the spirit in which the situation is described. Tone will vary according to the effect the writer wishes to produce.

Fourth meaning. Finally, Richards emphasizes *intention.* This is closely related to tone. The subject of the poem (first meaning) is expressed sensually (second meaning) with a certain tone (third meaning) in order to achieve a certain end or intention (fourth meaning). One must always be subjective in discussing intention. A poem or a piece of prose will not have the same intention for each reader.

Most poems attempt to create for the reader an experience that selects certain vivid details from life and intensifies them through rhythm, imagery, and other poetic devices. In this way, the poet increases the readers' awareness by giving them a more vivid glimpse of life than they could ever experience outside of art.

What One Poem "Means"

To see how the four meanings of a poem relate to one another, read the following poem by John Crowe Ransom and discuss one reader's interpretation of the meanings.

V

PIAZZA PIECE[11]

—I am a gentleman in a dust coat trying
To make you hear. Your ears are soft and small
And listen to an old man not at all,
They want the young men's whispering and sighing.
But see the roses on your trellis dying
And hear the spectral singing of the moon;
For I must have my lovely lady soon,
I am a gentleman in a dust coat trying.

—I am a lady young in beauty waiting
Until my truelove comes, and then we kiss.
But what gray man among the vines is this
Whose words are dry and faint as in a dream?
Back from my trellis, sir, before I scream!
I am a lady young in beauty waiting.

—John Crowe Ransom

First meaning: Paraphrasable content. The speaker in the poem is an old man, or perhaps Death himself. He is struck by the beauty of a young lady seated alone before a trellis of roses on a piazza. He tells her to enjoy life, to live it to the fullest before she gets too old. The line, "For I must have my lovely lady soon," suggests—if he is simply an older man—that he would like to court her. If he is Death personified, he has come to warn her that she has not long to live, for ". . . the roses on your trellis . . . [are] dying. . . ."

In either case, the lady is impatient and will not listen. She wants (desires) "the young men's whispering and sighing." She considers the speaker a threat and wants him gone.

Second meaning: Feeling. The poem is rich in feeling and emotion. Readers can feel the desire of an old man to talk to the young beauty and perhaps to enjoy her beauty even while encouraging her to live her life fully. Readers can also feel the radiance and confidence and impatience of the young lady as she waits for her truelove. They can even sympathize with her uneasiness as the old gentleman approaches her. Underlying the whole poem are feelings of sadness and regret. The man has something the lady should hear; she refuses to listen. She waits confidently for her truelove; he will not arrive in time. The roses are dying, and she refuses to see that so is she.

Notice the images in the poem. Dust coats were worn by fashionable gentlemen driving open touring cars, or convertibles. Here, the term suggests both a rich, antique fashion and, in addition, the fact that all human beings return to dust. The lady's soft, small ears suggest beauty and refinement. The dying roses and the spectral (ghostlike) singing of the moon make the reader feel the melancholy of a summer night.

Third meaning: Tone. The events described in the poem might really have happened to the poet, but whether or not they are real or fictional, he has a definite attitude toward them. He communicates a tender appreciation of the lady and a sad regret that she will not listen. For the speaker—probably not the poet himself—there is the attitude of quiet acceptance of the inevitable. If she will not listen, it does not matter. The course of the world continues, and the speaker will not be appreciably affected by her actions. The attitude communicated by the entire poem is likewise a quiet acceptance. It is as though the poet were saying, "This is the way life has always been. We are young, beautiful, impatient for a short time. It is understandable that we do not live to the fullest because we look to the future and ignore the wisdom of those who have lived longer. It does not matter much that the end of our dreams—through death—comes all too soon."

Fourth meaning: Intention. We can never be sure that we have truly received the author's intended comment about life. But the finished poem seems to develop a life of its own and an intention of its own—regardless of what the poet intended. This poem, then, seems to advise the reader: Live now; enjoy life; don't wait. At the same time as the speaker gives this advice, the poet seems to be shaking his head a bit sadly about the brevity and shallowness—the blindness—of human life.

ACTIVITY 14B

Finding Paraphrasable Content

1. The following brief selections are relatively easy to understand. Read each carefully and answer the following questions:

   a. What is the physical situation described?

   b. Who is speaking? (Be careful. As in "Piazza Piece," there may be a speaker other than the poet.)

   c. What is happening?

   d. Where is the event taking place?

   e. What is the speaker's relationship to the event?

Who are the speakers in this poem? How can you tell?

Many dialects omit linking verbs. What would the title be if the linking verb were included?

How do you know that the poet is not the person speaking?

What is her attitude toward the speakers? Does the fact that she is Black make any difference in her attitude? Should it?

What final sounds are left off words in the third stanza?

What is the effect of the final sentence?

Who are the speakers in this poem? How do you account for the fact that you accept them as speakers?

Translate these "actions" or "events" into what is really happening. Why is the poetic form more interesting than your paraphrase?

What "mushrooms" in people's minds insist on pushing their way into consciousness? What is the figure of speech in which you talk about one thing, but are really commenting on another? What is the figure of speech in which a long narrative about one subject really refers to parallel actions on another subject?

What is the irony of the meekness of the mushrooms? How does it parallel the meekness of another subject?

I

WE REAL COOL[12]

THE POOL PLAYERS.
SEVEN AT THE GOLDEN SHOVEL.

We real cool. We
Left school. We

Lurk late. We
Strike straight. We

Sing sin. We
Thin gin. We

Jazz June. We
Die soon.

—Gwendolyn Brooks

II

MUSHROOMS[13]

Overnight, very
Whitely, discreetly,
Very quietly

Our toes, our noses
Take hold on the loam,
Acquire the air.

Nobody sees us,
Stops us, betrays us;
The small grains make room.

Soft fists insist on
Heaving the needles,
The leafy bedding,

Even the paving.
Our hammers, our rams,
Earless and eyeless,

Perfectly voiceless,
Widen the crannies,
Shoulder through holes. We

Diet on water,
On crumbs of shadow,
Bland-mannered, asking

Little or nothing.
So many of us.
So many of us!

We are shelves, we are
Tables, we are meek,
We are edible,

Nudgers and shovers
In spite of ourselves.
Our kind multiplies:

We shall by morning
Inherit the earth.
Our foot's in the door.

—Sylvia Plath

If you know anything of Sylvia Plath's life, comment on her sensitivity as revealed in this poem.

III

"Is my team ploughing
    That I was used to drive
And hear the harness jingle
    When I was man alive?"

Ay, the horses trample
    The harness jingles now;
No change though you lie under
    The land you used to plough.

"Is football playing
    Along the river shore,
With lads to chase the leather,
    Now I stand up no more?"

Ay, the ball is flying,
    The lads play heart and soul;
The goal stands up, the keeper
    Stands up to keep the goal.

"Is my girl happy
    That I thought hard to leave,
And has she tired of weeping
    As she lies down at eve?"

Ay, she lies down lightly.
    She lies not down to weep
Your girl is well contented
    Be still, my lad, and sleep.

"Is my friend hearty;
    Now I am thin and pine,
And has he found to sleep in
    A better bed than mine?"

Yes, lad, I lie easy
    I lie as lads would choose;
I cheer a dead man's sweetheart.
    Never ask me whose.

—A. E. Housman

Who is speaking in this first stanza? What do you know about him or her? What details give you information about the sex, work, and present condition of the speaker?

Who is speaking in the second stanza? Is it the same as the person speaking in the first stanza? How do you know?

Who is speaking in the third stanza? What more does this stanza add to your knowledge of the speaker? What is the significance of the implied past tense of the action?

By this point you have the basic pattern of the poem. What is it?

Are the events, content, and questions arranged in ascending or descending order of importance? Why?

What is the double meaning of the words "thin" and "pine"?

What is the irony in the final stanza?

2. When you have completed the first part of Activity 14B, write a short paragraph explaining the first level of meaning. You may have to mention feeling, tone, and intention, but try to concentrate on paraphrasable content. If possible, try to connect the writer's experience with some experience of your

own. Bring your paragraphs to class for group consideration and discussion.

3. After you have written your paragraphs and discussed them in class, try to come to some conclusions about the following questions:

a. Is it necessary to understand the meaning of every word in a work in order to understand the work? Should one attempt to guess at word meanings from context and only afterwards use a dictionary?

b. How do writers appeal to your senses of sight, sound, touch, taste, and smell? What words, allusions, or comparisons in the foregoing selections make you "think" a certain sound or smell?

ACTIVITY 14C

Understanding Feeling in Literature

You may have understood a work on the first level of meaning, the paraphrasable content, but you must still react to the underlying emotion and feeling that the writer has evoked. The following poems are easy to understand on the first level of meaning, but much depends upon the reader's understanding of the emotional aspect. After reading the poems, choose two and write brief papers in which you 1. explain the paraphrasable content (the first level of meaning) and 2. explain the feeling (the second level of meaning) in each poem. Bring your papers to class for discussion and class evaluation.

I

PORTRAIT BY A NEIGHBOUR[14]

Who is the speaker in this poem? When do you suppose this poem was written, or what time period was it written about? Do you know anyone like the woman in the poem?

What image do you have of both the neighbor and the woman being described?

Before she has her floor swept
Or her dishes done,
Any day you'll find her
A-sunning in the sun!

It's long after midnight
Her key's in the lock,
And you never see her chimney smoke
Till past ten o'clock!

She digs in her garden
With a shovel and a spoon,
She weeds her lazy lettuce
By the light of the moon.

She walks up the walk
    Like a woman in a dream,
She forgets she borrowed butter
   And pays you back cream!

Her lawn looks like a meadow,
    And if she mows the place
She leaves the clover standing
    And the Queen Anne's lace!

—Edna St. Vincent Millay

What tells you the speaker doesn't quite understand the neighbor? How are the speaker's life and schedule different from the neighbor's?

What do the details of the last two lines tell you about the neighbor? How does the speaker feel about the neighbor's actions? How do you feel about them? How do you think the poet wants you to feel?

II

THE UNKNOWN CITIZEN[15]

(To JS/07/M/378 This Marble Monument

Is Erected by the State)

He was found by the Bureau of Statistics to be
One against whom there was no official complaint,
And all the reports on his conduct agree
That, in the modern sense of an old-fashioned word,
    he was a saint,
For in everything he did he served the Greater
    Community.
Except for the War till the day he retired
He worked in a factory and never got fired
But satisfied his employers, Fudge Motors Inc.
Yet he wasn't a scab or odd in his views,
For his Union reports that he paid his dues,
(Our report on his Union shows it was sound)
And our Social Psychology workers found
That he was popular with his mates and liked a drink.
The Press are convinced that he bought a paper every
    day
And that his reactions to advertisements were normal
    in every way.
Policies taken out in his name prove that he was fully
    insured,
And his Health-card shows he was once in hospital but
    left it cured.
Both Producers Research and High-Grade Living
    declare
He was fully sensible to the advantages of the
    Installment Plan
And had everything necessary to the Modern Man,
A phonograph, a radio, a car and a frigidaire.
Our researchers into Public Opinion are content
That he held the proper opinions for the time of year;
When there was peace, he was for peace; when there
    was war, he went.
He was married and added five children to the
    population,

What questions do you have about *why* a nation would build a monument "To an Unknown Citizen"?

The poem seems to describe the "ideal" person of this nation. What details of his life do you object to? What things that were a part of his life would you not want as part of yours?

How do you react to the words "saint," "Fudge Motors," "scab," "Greater Community"?

What seem to be the values of the nation? Are they your values? Are they the values the poet holds?

Why is there so much emphasis on "belonging"—on fitting in smoothly with the Greater Community, the job, the Union?

The words and sentences in this poem are very simple and easy to understand. What background must you bring to the poem to understand its feeling?

Which our Eugenist says was the right number for a
    parent of his generation.
And our teachers report that he never interfered with
    their education.

Was he free? Was he happy? The question is absurd:
Had anything been wrong, we should certainly have
    heard.

—W. H. Auden

III

BASE DETAILS[16]

"Base" can have two meanings
here: a military base and "low or
disgraceful."

How does the poet make you
feel about officers who stay far
behind the lines?

What is the poet's attitude
toward the situation he describes?

If I were fierce and bald and short of breath,
    I'd live with scarlet Majors at the Base,
And speed glum heroes up the line to death.
    You'd see me with my puffy petulant face,
Guzzling and gulping in the best hotel,
    Reading the Roll of Honor. "Poor young chap,"
I'd say—"I used to know his father well.
    Yes, we've lost heavily in this last scrap."
And when the war is done and youth stone dead,
I'd toddle safely home and die—in bed.

—Siegfried Sassoon

ACTIVITY 14D

Understanding Tone in Literature

After you have written your papers for Activity 14C and discussed them in class, write a brief paper discussing each of the
following questions.

1. Every *image*, or picture, a poet puts into a poem should
   "work," not only in contributing to the meaning of the poem,
   but also in contributing to the emotion communicated. How
   does each of these images contribute to the feeling of the
   poem?

   "Portrait by a Neighbour"—she weeds her lazy lettuce, the
light of the moon, like a woman in a dream, she leaves the
clover standing and the Queen Anne's lace.
   "The Unknown Citizen"—he paid his dues, he was popular
with his mates, his reactions to advertisements were normal in
every way, he had everything necessary to the Modern Man, he
held the proper opinions for the time of year.

"Base Details"—fierce and bald and short of breath, glum heroes, guzzling and gulping in the best hotel, youth stone dead, toddle safely home, die—in bed.

2. Each of the preceding poems involves a change of mood, emotion, or attitude. Discuss the change in each and try to determine how the poet brings about the change.

ACTIVITY 14E

Understanding Intention in Literature

The following selections mean more than they seem to mean. Read them carefully and try to find a meaning in addition to the surface story. Then write a short paper interpreting one of the selections and describing the "clues" that led you to your interpretation of its intention. After you finish, work in a group with students who wrote on the same passage, and criticize one another's interpretations.

I

SOUTHBOUND ON THE FREEWAY[17]

A tourist came in from Orbitville,
parked in the air, and said:

The creatures of this star
are made of metal and glass.

Through the transparent parts
you can see their guts.

Their feet are round and roll
on diagrams—or long

measuring tapes—dark
with white lines.

They have four eyes.
The two in the back are red.

Sometimes you can see a five-eyed
one, with a red eye turning

on the top of his head.
He must be special—

the others respect him,
and go slow,

when he passes, winding
among them from behind.

They all hiss as they glide,
like inches, down the marked

tapes. Those soft shapes,
shadowy inside

the hard bodies—are they
their guts or their brains?

—May Swenson

II

In one of the most famous passages in all philosophy, Plato records Socrates'
"Allegory of the Cave." Chapter XXV of *The Republic* is concerned with the nature
of our perception of the world around us. The following version is considerably
abridged and simplified.

Imagine a group of people living in a great cave where no daylight
reaches them. Here they have been chained from childhood to face the
wall. They cannot even turn their heads to look directly at a fire that is
glowing behind them. Between their backs and the fire, puppeteers
crouch and manipulate puppets. When the dolls are held up their shadows are cast by the fire upon the wall which the prisoners are facing.

Having never seen anything else but the shadows on the wall, the
prisoners believe that the shadows are real. They know nothing of the
puppets that cast the shadows. If the puppeteers speak, the prisoners
think that the echo coming from the wall is the real sound. Imagine what
it would be like if the prisoners, after looking at shadows all their lives,
were forced to stand up, turn around, and walk toward the fire. They
would probably be so dazzled that they would not even be able to
distinguish the puppets whose shadows they had always watched. If
they finally did see them, they might think them less real than the
shadows they were used to seeing. They would turn from the light and
long to return to the shadows.

Suppose someone were to drag some of the prisoners out of the
cave into the sunlight. They would be so completely blinded that they
would suffer pain and frustration at not being able to see their accustomed shadows.

And suppose, after long adjustment, they finally accepted the reality of the puppets and the light of the sun. What would the other
prisoners think if one returned to the cave and tried to tell them that their
reality consisted only of shadows?

The Third Critical Question: How Did the Writer Communicate Meaning?

You have now examined a number of literary works in the light
of the first two critical questions. You have asked:

How do I feel about the work?
What do I think the work means?

The third major consideration in criticizing a literary work
refers to the techniques employed by writers to achieve the

Criticism should praise as well as instruct. This page from a Gutenberg Bible, printed about 1453, gives a commentary on the Proverbs of Solomon.

desired response. These techniques include the use of expressive words, the flow of sentences, rhythm, emotion, and appeals to the senses. All are common to both prose and poetry. In poetry, however, the ideas and the emotion are frequently compressed, the pattern is more defined, the rhythm is developed in a special, noticeable meter, and the sensuous appeal is frequently heightened by rhyme and poetic imagery. Prose, on the other hand, has its own unique qualities, such as variety in sentence and paragraph length, in-depth analysis of character, exciting or suspenseful action, and extended description. Sometimes a work has the qualities of both genres and might fit into either category. A literary composition of this type may be called a prose poem or poetic prose.

Communicating the theme of a work. Every piece of prose or poetry has a theme—the core of its thought. Through this theme writers convey their reactions to the world around them, their view of humanity, or their insights into the meaning of what they have experienced.

The methods writers use to convey their themes vary, of course, with their personality, training, experience, and talents. Following is a list of some methods authors have used to communicate themes. Read the list carefully and try to recall short stories, novels, narrative poems, and films that use these techniques.

1. A situation in which a limited number of characters in a simplified setting encounter problems that parallel those in the world. (In *Lord of the Flies*, William Golding shows how a band of British boys marooned on an island turn a paradise into a land of horror. He suggests that this parallels what adults have done to the world.)

2. A situation exaggerated until it becomes ridiculous. (In *Catch-22*, Joseph Heller exaggerates the absurdities of war.)

3. One character created to be the author's spokesman. (In *Our Town*, the Stage Manager presents many of Wilder's ideas.)

4. A description of what will happen if current trends continue. (In *1984*, George Orwell suggests what the world of the future may be like if today's trends continue.)

5. The reader identifies with one of the main characters and thus absorbs that character's ideas. (Most readers tend to identify with Huck Finn and thus to learn from the problems Huck faces, particularly his treatment of Jim.)

6. Newspaper articles, letters, telegrams, diaries, or even the author's own comments are used to reveal a position. (In *Cry, the Beloved Country*, Alan Paton uses a newspaper article and a diary entry to comment on the murder of Arthur Jarvis.)

7. Different types of people representing different positions are caricatured. (In *Elmer Gantry* by Sinclair Lewis, the characters are caricatures rather than real people.)

8. Basic ideas or moral principles are presented through a story (called allegory) in which people or things have a hidden or symbolic meaning. (In *Animal Farm*, George Orwell comments on totalitarianism—such as Russian communism—by describing a farm on which the animals revolt and take command.)

9. A significant event, symbol, or scene is repeated at various points in the story. (Three times in *The Scarlet Letter*, Nathaniel Hawthorne has his three main characters stand on the scaffold in Boston.)

ACTIVITY 14F

Working with Theme Techniques

List and discuss in class ten themes about which an author might wish to write. Then select one theme and write a paragraph describing how you would try to convey it in a story. Use not less than three techniques, including, if you wish, techniques not listed.

Other students have suggested the following themes for this activity:

1. The sins of the father are visited on the children.
2. Conflict between generations is inevitable, but it can be advantageous.
3. The bad sport hurts only himself.
4. Every person is a bundle of contradictions.
5. Responsibility brings maturity.

The following paragraph is an example of how a theme might be developed in a story.

> If I were attempting to explore the theme that "Responsibility brings maturity," I would set up a microcosm in which various people act in different ways when given a responsibility. I might, for example, borrow the Biblical parable of the rich man who gave each of his servants some talents and charged them to use them well in his absence. With this as the framework of the story, I could use caricature in making clear my dislike of the actions of certain of my characters. In the final scene, I might have the rich man return and deliver a lecture on responsibility. His words would be my words, and they would drive home my message.

ACTIVITY 14G

Analyzing Techniques for Communicating

In criticizing a piece of literature, a reader should try to be sensitive to the various technical aspects of that work—the tools with which the writer achieves his or her purpose. Unless readers are aware of and appreciate these techniques, they cannot fully understand or evaluate the work.

Reread the selections in Activities 14C and 14E and write a brief paper (several paragraphs) analyzing the techniques employed in one of these selections. Bring your paper to class and be prepared to take part in a discussion on the various methods by which the writers communicate ideas and emotions.

ACTIVITY 14H

Understanding Special Effects

One requirement of good style is that it achieve an intended end simply and economically. Each of the following short passages uses a noticeable technique to achieve some kind of special effect. Examine the technique defined in the question following each passage and write a brief paragraph explaining what the writer may have been attempting to do by using that particular technique.

I

Jack be nimble.
Jack be quick.
Jack jump over
The candlestick.

1. Each of the first two short lines is a complete sentence and ends with a period. Why may the unknown writer have chosen to have the third line continue right into the fourth with no pause?

II

UPON A CHILD

Here a pretty baby lies
Lulled asleep with lullabies.
Tread softly that you do not stir
The easy earth that covers her.

—Robert Herrick

2. Why does the poem not reveal until the last line that the child is dead?

III

FROM ESSAY ON CRITICISM

True ease in writing comes from art, not chance,
As those move easiest who have learned to dance.
'Tis not enough no harshness gives offence,
The sound must seem as Echo to the sense:
Soft is the strain when Zephyr* gently blows,
And the smooth stream in smoother numbers flows;
But when loud surges lash the sounding shore,
The hoarse, rough verse should like the torrent roar:
When Ajax** strives some rock's vast weight to throw,
The line too labours, and the words move slow;
Not so, when swift Camilla† scours the plain,
Flies o'er th' unbending corn, and skims along the main.

—Alexander Pope

*the west wind

**legendary Greek hero famous for his strength

†legendary woman warrior

3. In four lines of this extract, Alexander Pope demonstrates what he means by making the sound "an Echo to the sense." Choose any two of these lines and explain how Pope matches the sound of the line to the meaning it expresses.

IV

SONNET 130

My mistress' eyes are nothing like the sun;
Coral is far more red than her lips' red;
If snow be white, why then her breasts are dun;
If hairs be wires, black wires grow on her head.
I have seen roses damask'd, red and white,
But no such roses see I in her cheeks;
And in some perfumes is there more delight
Than in the breath that from my mistress reeks.
I love to hear her speak, yet well I know
That music hath a far more pleasing sound;
I grant I never saw a goddess go;
My mistress, when she walks, treads on the ground:
    And yet, by heaven, I think my love as rare
    As any she belied with false compare.

—William Shakespeare

4. Although most poets of his time compared their beloveds' eyes with the sun, their lips with coral, their breasts with

snow, their cheeks with roses, their breath with perfume, their voices with music, and their walk with the floating of goddesses, Shakespeare specifically says that these comparisons would be false if applied to his beloved. Why may he be doing so?

The Fourth Critical Question: How Effective Is the Work?

Only by painstaking inquiry into the first three critical questions can you arrive at a balanced and sound critical evaluation of a literary work. Certainly you must recognize the elements of style and understand why the various artistic devices are used before you can judge how successful and effective the work is.

Such judgments are largely subjective; that is, they reflect the reader's personal response to the work of art. But opinions and emotional reactions are not valuable unless they are based on features within the work itself. You must examine the piece of prose or poetry carefully, note what effect it has had on you as an individual, and demonstrate how that effect is produced. Then you can arrive at an appraisal of the effectiveness of the work, frequently by comparing it with other works with which you are familiar.

Supporting opinions in criticism. Some students do not realize that when they write about literature they must support any generalizations they make. General statements like "This writer's work is very difficult to understand" or "That writer captures the flavor of life in New York" may or may not be true. If such assertions are made, the reader wants to know what evidence the writer has as the basis for these statements. In creative writing, a writer deals primarily in concretes—descriptions and accounts of events from which the reader draws generalizations. In critical writing, as in most other expository writing, the writer makes generalizations which require support. Critics supply the strongest support possible when they quote from the work itself.

ACTIVITY 14 I

Supporting Generalizations in a Critical Review

Following are some generalizations that might appear in a critical review. Read them carefully. Be prepared to discuss in class the kinds of support a reader would expect for each statement.

Then read again a piece of prose or poetry your class has read recently. Review it and then write five generalizations similar to those listed below. List under each generalization some specific quotations or examples which would help demonstrate or prove your assertion.

1. In John Steinbeck's books, women do not seem to be real people.
2. Ernest Hemingway often wrote in a nervous, staccato style.
3. The poetry of Kenneth Fearing captures the flavor of modern popular music.
4. The reader often feels that a descriptive passage is not quite finished.
5. Shelley often wrote very bad poems.

The Final Critical Question: Is the Message or Meaning Worthwhile?

You have examined the work of art to determine what it says, what it really means, what literary techniques were used, and how effective the work is. But you still do not have a complete analysis of that work. What remains is to determine whether that work has value, whether it was worth the writer's trouble to produce it.

Writers may be very skilled in their art. They may be adept at using writing devices that pique curiosity. They may be very ingenious in inventing situations or arousing emotions. But if their works have no genuine worth, if they are superficial or frivolous in conception, they might just as well never have been written. On the other hand, many literary works have been condemned for various reasons (moral judgments, use of language, story line, for example) but have survived because they had special qualities that made them worth reading and rereading.

Special qualities in literature. One of the most common misconceptions about literature is that only the story—the plot—is important. Everyone, of course, enjoys a good story, but perceptive critics read a work on many levels. For example, students today are reading the following books and finding, among others, the values indicated.

Lorraine Hansberry, *To Be Young, Gifted and Black*—literature as philosophy and social criticism.
John F. Kennedy, *To Turn the Tide*—literature as eyewitness history, practical wisdom, idealism, and social comment.
Ray Bradbury, *Farenheit 451*—literature as a picture of human life, and social comment.
Alvin Toffler, *Future Shock*—literature as social criticism, projection of the future, and invitation to involvement.
Erich Maria Remarque, *All Quiet on the Western Front*—literature as social criticism, eyewitness history, and condemnation of war.

Literature can bring pleasure, expand knowledge, provide new insights, inspire positive action, and promote a more informed approach to life.

ACTIVITY 14J

Finding Values in Literature

Look up (or review in your mind) two books you have studied in school or read on your own this year. Then list the different values in each that have made it worthwhile. Be prepared to take part in a class discussion of your list. Be careful not to confine yourself to a consideration of the plot alone.

Tone in a Critical Review

Although some popular professional critics and reviewers have established their reputations by being opinionated, sarcastic, and even cruel, most critics feel that they best serve both the artist and the reader if they try to maintain a positive approach and an open, searching, encouraging tone. Their job, as they see it, is to help readers by revealing to them what the writer has been trying to do and by describing the techniques the writer has used. They also feel that they help writers by showing them where they have succeeded or failed.

Of course, the critic and reviewer approach any work of art from a personal point of view, but they try to remember that any single point of view is limited. They are inclined to qualify their judgments, to define the point of view from which they are speaking, and to indicate possible additional values for others. They rarely take an omniscient and authoritarian stand.

ACTIVITY 14K

Examining Tone in a Review

Look up a number of periodicals noted for book reviews, play reviews, and film reviews, such as *Time, New Republic, New York Times* Book Review Section, *Atlantic Monthly, Saturday Review,* and *Harper's.* From these, choose two reviews and read them carefully, noting particularly the *tone* the writer has used. Then prepare a two- or three-minute talk for presentation to the class. After arousing class interest in your subject, follow this order:

1. Indicate the title and author of the work being reviewed and the author of the review, if it is signed, as well as the source. (Which is preferable, a signed or unsigned review? Why?)
2. Tell enough about the work (either from reading it or from information given in the review) to enable your audience to understand your later comments.
3. Discuss the general tone of the review—the reviewer's general opinion, the emphasis with which it is presented, and any qualifications that are made.
4. Discuss how the reviewer sets the tone of the review: word choice, comparisons, suggestions, judgments, irony, sarcasm.
5. Make a judgment as to how helpful the review would be to a reader as well as to the author of the work being reviewed.

■ MAJOR WRITING ASSIGNMENT

A CRITICISM OF PROSE AND POETRY

Reread the reviews in this chapter and note the organization of each. Select a short story or poem. Try to choose a selection you know well and feel strongly about. Prepare a critical paper based on the information you have learned in this chapter.

Remember that you will be trying to answer the critical questions listed on page 365. The organization of your paper will probably be as follows:

1. Introduction.
2. Enough description of the subject of the review to enable the reader to understand your comments.
3. Statement of what you think the theme or purpose is. Give evidence to support your interpretation.

4. Some of the outstanding techniques the author uses (citing examples).

5. Your opinion of how successful the story or poem is.

6. Your opinion of its value.

If you choose your literary selection with care, writing a review should give you little difficulty. Remember from Chapter 13 that when a work is successful the reader and writer are joined through the sharing of an experience. Try to communicate your response to this experience honestly. Approach your review as an opportunity both to express your opinion on a work that is important to you and to learn a major writing skill.

Appendix

Style Sheet

A Style Sheet is a form or pattern which the members of a certain group or institution (school, college, publishing house, office staff) work out and agree to follow whenever possible. It is entirely possible that your school has its own Style Sheet or that your group will prefer to establish one. If you do not have an accepted Style Sheet, this one will serve.

I. MANUSCRIPT FORM

A. Whenever possible, type your work. For typed papers, use standard 8½ by 11-inch white paper. Do not use "erasable" paper or onionskin. Always doublespace between lines. For handwritten papers, use standard, full-sized, wide-lined notebook paper.

B. Write or type on one side of the page only. Use wide margins: at least one inch on the left and bottom and one-half inch on the right.

C. Place your name, the course and period or section number, the name of your teacher, and the date of your paper in the upper right-hand corner of the first page.

Jo Ellen Perez
English 103, Period 2
Ms. Clark
November 4, 1980

D. Center the title on the first line. Skip a line and begin the actual paper on the third line.

E. Do not use the term *English* as a title. Use a specific title instead, such as, *Inserting Transitions*. Do not use quotation marks around the title even though you use quotation marks when you refer to the title within a paragraph.

II. CAPITALIZATION

A. Capitalize the first word and all other important words in a title. Do not capitalize prepositions, conjunctions, articles, and unimportant words with fewer than five letters.

B. Capitalize the first word in a sentence.

Capitalize the first word of a quoted sentence following such introductory words as *he said, she replied, Jane wondered,* when the quoted sentence immediately preceding the explanatory words is complete.

> Preceding quoted sentence is complete: *"Vacation is over," she said. "School starts next Monday."*
> Preceding quoted sentence is incomplete: *"Vacation," she said, "is over."*

C. Capitalize proper nouns and abbreviations of proper nouns.
Buildings: the Graybar Building, the Flatiron Building
Business Firms: Prentice-Hall, Inc., General Electric
Churches, religious groups, and their members: First Methodist Church; Mormons, Muslims, Hindus
Days, months, holidays, holy days: Monday, August, Thanksgiving, All Soul's Day, Yom Kippur
Historical documents, events, periods: the Constitution, the Hegira, the Renaissance
Institutions: Heidelburg College, Art Institute of Chicago
Organizations: Kiwanis Club, Campfire Girls
People: Paul Anka, Betsy Howkins, Rachel Carson
Places: Indiana, Syracuse, Gambia, South America
Planets, except when *earth* and *moon* are used with *the*: Mars, Saturn; the earth, the moon
Political Parties and their members: Labor Party, Laborite; Democratic Party, Democrat

> Races, languages: Chinese, Thai, French
> Sacred figures, Bible, portions of holy books: Jehovah, Allah, Krishna; Koran, Pentateuch
> Names of ships, planes, trains: S.S. Titanic, Concorde, Orient Express
> Trade Names: Coca-Cola, Lifebuoy, Xerox, Cheerios

D. Capitalize adjectives formed from proper nouns, but not the words they modify unless they would be capitalized written alone: the French language, Iranian oil, Dutch colonial; *but* Japanese Empire, English Bible

E. Capitalize such words as avenue, building, school, park, river, and so on when used as a part of a name, but not when used alone: First National Bank, Fourth Street, Lee High School, Kirkwood Hotel; *but* the bank, a hotel, our school

F. Capitalize personal titles showing office, profession, or rank when using them either before a person's name or as a substitute for the name:

Senator Davis	"Won't the senator reconsider?"
Mayor Rice	She is the mayor.
Commander Lewis	The commander spoke.
Doctor Higgins	The doctor is very competent.
"Send me in, Coach!"	The coach is fair.

The title of the nation's highest executive is always capitalized:

In 1789, Washington became the first President.

G. Capitalize words showing family relationships when they appear before a personal name or in place of one:

Uncle Jasper and Aunt Faye live in Kansas City.
I heard Mother coming down the steps.
I like to visit my uncle and aunt in Kansas City when my mother takes me.

H. Capitalize such one-letter words as *I* and *O*, which would otherwise tend to disappear.

I. Do not capitalize the following types of words:
- adjectives which no longer remind the reader of the proper noun from which they come: parliamentary law, the china dishes, macadamized road
- school subjects (except for languages and specific, numbered courses): geometry, economics, psychology; *but* Geometry I, Economics II, English, and French
- names of directions (except when they name sections of

the country): north, south, east, west; *but* I live in *the* North. *The* West is quite scenic.

- names of seasons (except when personified): The autumn is beautiful; *but* Winter walks in magnificence.

III. PUNCTUATION

A. Period. In addition to some conventional uses (after numbers and in abbreviations), a period marks a pause at the end of a complete thought.

1. Use a period after declarative or imperative sentences and after mild exclamations.

   The sun is very bright today.
   Be careful of your tan.
   How nice the weather is.

2. Use a period after abbreviations and initials.
   Inc. Ltd. Co. N. Y. L.C. Smith
   (Use few abbreviations in formal written work.)

3. Use a period between dollars and cents when a dollar sign is used and to indicate a decimal point between whole numbers and decimals.
   $3.42 $9.98 $.14 3.1416 19.2%

4. Use three periods (these are called *ellipses*) to indicate you have left words out of a quotation. Use a fourth period to indicate the end of your sentence.

   I remembered, "Yea, though I walk in the valley . . . I shall fear no evil."
   He urged us, "Ask not what your country can do for you. . . ."

5. Place periods within quotation marks when the two come together.
   Place periods within parentheses when a complete sentence surrounded by parentheses appears between complete sentences. Do not use periods when such a sentence appears in the middle of another sentence.

   He ate syrup on his roast beef. (He was a little strange.) I soon got used to him.
   He ate syrup (I can hardly believe it) on his roast beef.

B. Exclamation Mark. Use an exclamation mark after any word, phrase, or sentence to show strong emphasis or emotion.

   Help!
   What a day!
   She became a star!

C. **Question Mark.** A question mark indicates an inquiry, un-certainty, or lack of information.

1. Use a question mark to indicate requests for information.

   Where are they going?
   Were they working this morning?

2. Use a question mark after each element in a series of interrogative words for special emphasis.

   What did the Aldermen say? and the city manager? and the mayor?

3. Use a question mark, usually in parentheses, to indicate doubt or inexactness.

   Toussaint L'Ouverture (1743?–1803) led a slave revolt and liber-ated Haiti.
   Theodore Brady, an inventor, was born in Waterloo (?), Iowa.

4. When using a question mark with other marks follow these general procedures:

   • If the question mark pertains to the entire sentence, place it outside the other marks.

     Quotation marks: Did she repeat the words, "I do solemnly swear"?
     Parentheses: How often have you seen Richard Harris (I mean in person)?

   • If the question mark pertains only to the enclosed part of the sentence, place it inside the other marks.

     Quotation marks: Dad asked patiently, "Are we finally ready?"
     Parentheses: I've seen five whales (can you believe it?) in less than an hour.

D. **Comma.** Use a comma both in conventional uses and where a pause is needed to prevent confusion, uncertainty, or unin-tended humor.

1. Use a comma before, but not after, the coordinating con-junction (*and, but, for, or, nor, so, yet*) joining independ-ent clauses, unless the clauses are quite short or easily distinguishable.

   We climbed Mt. Washington, but the wind and weather kept us from enjoying the view.
   I studied hard but she got the *A*.
   Perseus had to save Andromeda, or the monster would kill her.
   (How might this be read without the comma?)

2. Use a comma to set off interrupting elements. (*I hope, I suppose, do you think, don't they, of course, after all*)

unless they are closely connected with the meaning of the sentence. Use a comma to set off introductory words, such as *yes, no, well, oh,* and tag questions such as *isn't it, don't we, aren't they.*

> The cost, of course, is passed on to the consumer.
> Yes, what you see is what you get.
> That's the tragedy, isn't it.
> I suppose you know what you want. (no comma)

Treat conjunctive adverbs, such as *nevertheless, consequently, therefore,* and *however,* as interrupters.

> The investigation, nevertheless, had it humorous sides.

3. Use a comma to set off words, phrases, or clauses in a series. When there is no danger of misreading, a comma before the last item of a series is often omitted.

> That charge is ridiculous, preposterous, and absurd.
> We looked in the basement, in the living room, in the bedrooms, and in the attic.
> Mao came to New York City, he worked at a menial task, and he returned to China.

Do not use a comma at the end of a series.

> Arthur insisted on asking how geometry, algebra, and trigonometry ( ) would help him become a florist.

4. Use a comma after introductory phrases and clauses.

> Participial phrase: Inspired by the art exhibit, Mussorgsky composed *Pictures at an Exhibition.*
> Gerund phrase: By swimming with the Gulf Stream, Gastón almost escaped from Cuba to Florida.
> Prepositional phrase: With little to distract them from their purpose, the Vandals sacked all of Europe.
> Adverbial clause: Whenever I hear that magnificent song, I remember our first date.

5. Use a comma to set off nonrestrictive modifiers. Nonrestrictive modifiers can be omitted from the sentence and the subject will still be clear. Restrictive modifiers, which are required to identify the subject, cannot be omitted and must not be set off by commas.

> My brother, who lives in Kansas City, loves the Midwest.

I have only one brother. The words "who lives in Kansas City" are nonrestrictive and nonessential, for you would know which brother is intended without them. In this nonrestrictive use, commas are required.

> My brother who lives in Kansas City loves the Midwest.

I have more than one brother. The words "who lives in Kansas City" are needed to indicate which brother I am talking about. They are essential (restrictive) and commas must not be used.

6. Use a comma to set off nonrestrictive appositives. An appositive is a noun or a noun equivalent that follows another noun construction and means the same as the first. It is nonrestrictive if it is not needed to identify what the first noun refers to.

   Nonrestrictive: The shoemaker down the street, Ivan, is a gentle man.
   Restrictive: The czar Ivan the Terrible killed his own son.

7. Use a comma to set off direct quotations from the introductory words, such as *he said, he replied, she insisted.*

   He said, "I shall see you very soon."
   "I shall see you," he said, "very soon."
   "I shall see you very soon," he said.
   "I shall see you very soon," he said. "It should be tomorrow."

8. Use a comma for various routine purposes.

   a. Use a comma to set off items in dates and addresses.

      London, England
      December 7, 1941
      Georgetown, Great Exuma, The Bahamas
      Nancy Dee West, 5516 Walton Way, Waterloo, Iowa 55164

   b. Use a comma after the salutation in personal letters and after the complimentary close in all letters.

      Dear Liz,   Sincerely,
      My dear Mrs. Jacobs,   Gratefully,

   c. Use a comma to set off thousands, millions, and so on in large figures: $6,000,000   14,323 applications

   d. Use a comma to set off degrees and titles following a name:

      Ralph B. Tennant, D.D.S.
      James Froseth, Jr.
      The Honorable Booth R. Desmond, Mayor.

9. Avoid unnecessary commas. The parentheses in the examples below indicate the absence of commas.

   a. Do not use a comma between a subject and verb. (It is proper, of course, to set off an interrupting element between the subject and verb with a *pair* of commas.)

That school is requiring more of students these days ( ) is hard to dispute.

b. Do not use a comma between the parts of either a compound subject or a compound predicate.

> Compound subject: Many of the people elected to Boy's State ( ) and many of the people chosen for Girl's State were good friends.
> Compound predicate: We read *A Tale of Two Cities* ( ) and then saw the movie starring Ronald Colman.

c. Do not use a comma between a verb and its object or complement.

> The restriction on entering the contest was ( ) that no one related to the judges could enter.

d. Do not use a comma between an adjective and the noun phrase it modifies.

> The entire industry is now the target of a thorough ( ) congressional investigation.

e. Do not use a comma between two complete sentences. Such a comma fault, as it is called, results in a run-on sentence, which may confuse readers.

> Comma fault: Few volunteers answered the call, the house burned to the ground.
> Preferable: Few volunteers answered the call; the house burned to the ground.
> Few volunteers answered the call. The house burned to the ground.
> Because few volunteers answered the call, the house burned to the ground.

E. Semicolon. A semicolon signals a pause that is longer than that of a comma but shorter than that of a period. When used between two sentences it indicates a closer relationship between them than a period would.

1. Use a semicolon to join clauses of a compound sentence which do not have one of the coordinating conjunctions between them.

> Grace did not attend the lecture; she went to the museum instead.

2. Use a semicolon to join clauses connected by such conjunctive adverbs as *however, moreover, nevertheless, consequently, still,* and *then.*

> Scientists will have to tackle the energy problem head on; still, it will be many years before we have an answer.

F. **Colon.** The colon designates a pause and points ahead to what follows.

1. Use a colon to introduce a long or formal quotation.

> Benjamin Franklin wrote: "Experience keeps a dear School, but Fools will learn in no other, and scarce in that; for it is true, we may give Advice, but we cannot give Conduct. . . . They that won't be counselled, can't be helped . . . if you will not hear Reason, she'll surely rap your knuckles."

2. Use a colon to introduce and emphasize a list of appositives at the end of a sentence:

> He prefers any of four fruits for dessert: strawberries, grapes, pears, or melon.
> Jill Paton Walsh has written three excellent books: *Goldengrove, Fireweed,* and *Unleaving.*

3. Use a colon for several conventional uses.

After a formal business letter salutation:

> Dear Sir:
> Dear Madam:

Between hours and minutes written in numbers:

> 12:32 a.m.
> 1:18 a.m.

G. **Quotation Marks.** In general, quotation marks enclose words the writer has borrowed *exactly* from another source. In addition, they identify titles of short works or portions of longer works.

1. Use quotation marks to enclose the exact words of speakers. Note that whether introductory words such as *he said* or *she replied* come before or after or in the middle of the quotation, they are excluded from the quotation marks.

> Before: Josh Billings said, "The ant takes no holidays and doesn't go on strike."
> After: "They have no loafers among them," he continued.
> Middle: "They get up early," he emphasized, "and work all the time."

- Use only one pair of quotation marks to enclose a direct quotation, even if the quoted material goes on for several sentences. (If the quoted material includes several paragraphs, put a quotation mark at the *beginning* of each new paragraph to remind the reader that the material he or she is reading is still part of a quotation. Do not put quotation marks at the ends of the paragraphs—except for the last one.)

- Put periods and commas inside closing quotation marks and semicolons outside them.

> "That's my favorite book," she said, "but you can borrow it."
> Woody replied, "Thanks, but I've already read it."
> She snapped, "I suppose you didn't like it"; then she rushed off without waiting for an answer.

- Put a question mark or an exclamation mark inside the quotation mark if it applies only to the material being quoted. Place it after the quotation mark if it applies to the whole sentence.

> Helen heard Jerry ask, "Is it really as bad as they say?"
> Did you hear her reply, "I really don't think so"?
> Neal tried to outshout her, "Of course, it is. It's worse!"
> How strange that Helen calmly said, "You're wrong"!

- Use the single appropriate mark inside the quotation marks when both the sentence and the quotation ending the sentence are either questions or exclamations.

> Was Lynn being funny when she responded, "Who knows?"
> How frightening when the charging soldiers yelled, "Banzai!"

- Use new-paragraph indention, along with pairs of quotes, to indicate in a narrative the change of speakers in a conversation.

> It's hard to believe that dirt could overcome hunger, but it did.
>   "Ma, I'm hungry."
>   "Wash your hands; I'll give you a piece of bread and butter."
>   "I'm not hungry."[1]
>
> —Sam Levenson

- Use single quotation marks (' ') to enclose quotations within quotations.

> Maynard said, "Our teacher is constantly quoting Patrick Henry's 'Give me liberty or give me death!' "

(Note that both pairs of quotation marks—both single and double—must be complete.)

2. Use quotation marks to indicate titles of materials shorter than book length.

> Longfellow's poem, "The Wreck of the Hesperus"
> Your story, "Beware the Ides"

3. Use quotation marks to call attention to technical words, words that need explanation, or words you are defining.

The "ampersand" (&) used to be considered the twenty-seventh letter of the alphabet.

H. Apostrophe. The apostrophe is used to form a possessive or to signal that one or more letters have been left out of a word. It is also used in a few specialized cases.

1. Follow these rules for forming the possessive:

- Add an apostrophe and an *s* to any singular noun to show possession.

boy	boy's pencil
Ross	Ross's idea
Mabel	Mabel's victory

- Add an apostrophe and an *s* to form the possessive of a plural word not ending in *s*:

  The children's toys
  the mice's tracks

- Add only an apostrophe to a plural noun ending in *s*.

  the two boys' projects
  the Burnses' home
  the three lawyers' offices

- Generally, to show joint ownership, make only the last noun possessive.

  Uncle Ernest and Aunt Daisy's plans were quite different from ours.
  The principal and teacher's decisions were final.

  Note how making both nouns possessive changes the meaning from shared, or joint ownership to individual ownership:

  Uncle Ernest's and Aunt Daisy's plans were quite different.
  Both the principal's and teacher's decisions were final.

- Do not use an apostrophe with relative and interrogative and personal pronouns which are already in a possessive form:

my	our	yours
your	their	hers
his	whose	ours
her	mine	theirs
its		

2. Use an apostrophe to show the omission of one or more letters in contractions, such as: doesn't   shouldn't wouldn't   they're   it's (it is).

3. Use an apostrophe and *s* to show plurals of numbers, signs, letters, and words discussed as words. (In some cases writers use the *s* alone, when leaving out the apostrophe will not cause confusion.

    How many TV's do you have? (or TVs)
    too many &'s (or too many &s)
    a number of confusing *therefore*'s

I. Brackets [ ]. Brackets are used to enclose comments, explanations, queries, corrections, or directions inserted in quoted material by someone other than the original author.

    1. Use brackets to enclose words you insert in material you are quoting.

        Kuhn reported, "The hawk [an emblem of the soul in ancient Egypt] was pictured throughout the temple."

J. Dash. The dash is an emphatic and attention-demanding mark. Use it sparingly.

    1. Use the dash to show an abrupt change in a sentence.

        We started for the restaurant at ten—why, no, I'm thinking of Thursday night.
        Now, Shakespeare frequently says—yes, here's an example on page thirty-three.

    2. Use the dash to emphasize interpolations or interrupters. Both commas and parentheses perform this function, but the dash makes the interrupter stand out emphatically and dramatically. Be sure not to waste such emphasis on something that isn't worth the attention.

        Pliny the younger—he was actually there—wrote about the eruption of Vesuvius.

    3. Use the dash to attract attention to appositives, important modifiers, and emphatic conditional phrases.

    4. Use a dash after a list or series before you summarize or comment on it.

        Democrats, Republicans, Independents—the whole House voted against him.

K. Hyphen. Used between words, the hyphen has the effect of unifying the words and making them act as a single word.

    1. Use a hyphen to join words placed before a noun as a single modifier.

        up-to-date almanac   a so-what attitude

2. Use a hyphen between elements of a compound noun and between the prefix and root of various words.

> post-World War II   anti-American   half-truth
> pre-Columbian   self-pity   fourth-grader

Usage is so varied in this area that the surest solution to the problem of hyphenation is to consult a dictionary.

3. Use a hyphen to divide a word at the end of a line. Consult your dictionary to be sure you divide between syllables.

4. Use a hyphen in compound numbers from twenty-one to ninety-nine and within fractions used as modifiers: seventy-eight, five-eighths finished, one hundred forty-nine.

L. **Parentheses.** Use parentheses to set off and deemphasize nonessential explanatory material. If the material in parentheses appears *within* a sentence, no capital letter or period is used, although other marks, such as a comma, semicolon, or question mark are used as usual.

> The space probe of Venus (it was only last year) revolutionized theories of the origin of the Universe.

M. **Figures.** In deciding whether to use numerals or spell out numbers, the nature of the writing should be considered as well as consistent style.

1. Spell out all numbers at the beginning of a sentence and all other figures that require only one or two words.

> *Three* people decided not to come. The other *345* indicated that they would come. Perhaps *twenty-seven* were undecided.

2. Use figures for all numbers in a technical or scientific report or in any paper including an unusual number of figures.

> The gross national product was $980.5 billion that year.
> Annie Jump Cannon, an American astronomer, analyzed 286,000 stars.

Acknowledgments

Chapter 3 **1** Based on Chapter 1, "The Computerized Society," *Elements of Computer Careers*, Northwest Regional Laboratory, © 1978, Fearon-Pitman Publishers, Belmont, California. **2** "House-Hunting As Easy As Watching TV", Tampa *Tribune*, Oct. 1, 1978. Reprinted by permission of United Press International. **3** From "The Land Palimpsest" by Roderick Nash, Sierra Club Calendar, 1979. **4** Letter to the Editor by Frank Baltar, Tampa *Tribune*, Sept. 3, 1978. **5** From "Good Sports" by Nash Stublen, Florida *Accent*, August 27, 1978. **6** Harriet Webster, Christian Science Monitor Service, Tampa *Tribune-Times*, Sept. 17, 1978. **7** From "Miracle Plant/Anyone for Winged Beans?" *Time* Magazine, April 17, 1978. Reprinted by permission from TIME, The Weekly Newsmagazine; © Time, Inc. 1978. **8** From "It's Called 'Sweat Equity' and It Saves You Money" by Paula Span, Parade Magazine, Oct. 1, 1978. **9** From "What Price Victory?/Why Winning is Everything in Big-Time College Sports," Nutshell Tenth Anniversary Issue by Janice Kaplan. **10** From promotional material of *The American Spectator*, Bloomington, Indiana. **11** By Jak Miner, Christian Science Monitor Service, Tampa *Tribune-Times*, August 13, 1978. **12** From "Moneypower: How to Beat Inflation," by Benjamin Stein with Herbert Stein, *St. Petersburg Times*, Florida, September 17, 1978. **13** From *The Great Gatsby* by F. Scott Fitzgerald, Charles Scribner's Sons, New York. © 1953 by Frances Scott Lanahan. **14** From *Across The Bridge* by Graham Greene. Reprinted from *Twenty One Stories* by Graham Greene. © 1947 by Graham Greene. By permission of The Viking Press, Inc. **15** From "Flying the Crowded Skies," *Time* magazine, August 14, 1978, p. 55. **16** From *National Geographic*, August 1968, Volume 134, No. 2, p. 219. **17** From *Parade*, August 13, 1978, p. 12.

Chapter 4 **1** From *Writing Skills*, Department of Command, U.S. Army and General Staff College, Fort Leavenworth, Kans. **2** From "Is Advertising Losing Its Creative Touch?" by H.D. Quigg, Middletown, New York *Record*, August 13, 1978. **3** From A NEW ENGLAND GIRLHOOD by Nancy Hale. Reprinted by permission of Little, Brown and Company, Boston. Copyright 1936, 1937, 1940, 1941, 1942, 1954, © 1955, 1956, 1957, 1958 by Nancy Hale. **4** From *The World Book Encyclopedia*, Vol. 1, World Book, Childcraft International, Inc., Chicago, © 1979. **5** From *The Little Locksmith* by Katherine Butler Hathaway, Coward McCann, Inc., New York, 1943. **6** From NOTES TOWARD A NEW RHETORIC: *Six Essays for Teachers* by Francis Christensen. © 1967 by Francis Christensen. Reprinted by permission of Harper & Row, Publishers, Inc. **7** From "Back to America/The Hurricane Highway," by Dale Wittner, *Adventure Road*, Vol. 14, No. 4, Winter 1978. **8** From *A Civil Tongue* by Edwin Newman. Copyright © 1975, 1976 by The Bobbs-Merrill Co. Inc. Reprinted by permission of The Bobbs-Merrill, Co. Inc. **9** From *Navajo Slave* by Lynne Gessner, New American Library (A Signet Book). Copyright © 1976 by Lynne Gessner. **10** From *Wipeout* by Pete Pomeroy, Scholastic Book Services, Four Winds Press, New York. Copyright © 1968 by Pete Pomeroy. **11** From *Are You in the House Alone*, Dell Publishing Company, New York. Copyright © 1976 by Richard Peck. **12** From *Born Innocent* by Bernhardt J. Hurwood, Ace Books Novelization © 1975. Copyright © 1974 by Tomorrow Entertainment, Inc., New York. **13** From *Farewell the Tranquil Mind* by R.F. Delderfield. Pocket Books, New York, © 1973. Pocket Book edition is published by arrangement with the Estate of R.F. Delderfield. Copyright © 1950 by R.F. Delderfield. All rights reserved.

Chapter 5 **1** From HOW MONEY WORKS/THE FEDERAL RESERVE SYSTEM by Adrian A. Paradis. © 1972 by Adrian A.

Paradis. Reprinted by permission of Hawthorn Books, Inc., New York. **2** From *Wonders of the World* by Joseph Gies. © 1966 by Joseph Gies. Reprinted by permission of Thomas Y. Crowell Company—Division of Harper & Row, Publishers, Inc. **3** By Art Buchwald. *New York Post*, December 14, 1968. Reprinted by permission of Art Buchwald as adapted and edited. **4** "How to Avoid Shark Bite" from HOW TO by Peter Passell. © 1976 by Peter Passell. Reprinted with the permission of Farrar, Straus and Giroux, Inc. as adapted and edited. **5** From *Reminiscences* by Douglas MacArthur, McGraw-Hill, New York © 1964. **6** From *Time* Magazine, September 11, 1978. Reprinted by permission of TIME, The Weekly Newsmagazine; © Time, Inc. 1978. **7** From " 'Rip Van' Pasco Awakens to Meet Problems of Growth" by Jan Glidewell, *St. Petersburg Times*, October 16, 1978. **8** From *The Story of Mankind* by Hendrik Van Loon, Boni and Liverwright, Inc., © 1921. **9** Article by Ellen Goodman in the Tampa *Tribune*, September 12, 1978. © 1978, The Boston Globe Newspaper Company/Washington Post Writers Group. Reprinted by permission of The Boston Globe Newspaper Company/Washington Post Writers Group. **10** From *The Invisible Pyramid* by Loren Eiseley. Reprinted by permission of Charles Scribner's Sons, New York. Copyright © 1970 by Loren Eiseley. **11** *Ibid.* **12** From "The Management Team—Its Selection and Development" by Robert K. Burns, Year Book of American Iron and Steel Institute, 1955. **13** From "Folklore, Fakelore, and Poplore" by Marshall Fishwick, *Saturday Review*, August 26, 1967. Reprinted by permission of Saturday Review, Inc. **14** From "Synthetic Perfumes and Flavors" by Edwin E. Slosson, *Creative Chemistry*, Appleton-Century-Crofts, Inc., New York. Reprinted by permission of the publisher.

Chapter 6 **1** From *Ford's Insider*. Reprinted by permission of 13-30 Corporation, Knoxville, TN, © 1978, as adapted. **2** By Jack R. Hunt, from *Lighter Than Air Flight: The Watts Aerospace Library*, ed. Lt. Col. C.V. Glines, U.S.A.F., Franklin Watts, Inc., New York, © 1965. **3** "Beef Prices: Why So High?" from Everybody's Money/A Guide to Family Finance and Consumer Action, Winter 1978, Volume 18, Number 4. Copyright © 1978, Credit Union National Association, Madison, Wisconsin. Reprinted as adapted. **4** By Mark Stevens, *St. Petersburg Times*, October 16, 1978. **5** By Philip S. Callahan and R.W. Mankin, *Time*, Magazine, November 20, 1978. Photo courtesy of Philip S. Callahan.

Chapter 7 **1** Adapted from "Preface" in *The Mysterious West*, World Publishing Company, by Brad Williams and Choral Pepper. © 1967 by Brad Williams and Choral Pepper. By permission of Harper & Row, Publishers, Inc. **2** From *Maine Times*, Topsham, Maine, December 1, 1978. **3** "State Corrupts With Gambling" by George Will, *The Hartford Courant*, October 15, 1978. © 1978, The Washington Post Company, Washington, D.C. **4** From *A Civil Tongue* by Edwin Newman. Copyright © 1975, 1976 by The Bobbs-Merrill, Co., Inc. Reprinted by permission of the publisher, as edited. **5** By Russell Baker, Tampa *Tribune*, August 16, 1975. © 1975/79 by The New York Times Company. Reprinted by permission. **6** "A History of Western Philosophy" by Bertrand Russell, Simon & Schuster, Inc., New York. © 1945. **7** From *A Study in Scarlet* by A. Conan Doyle from *The Complete Sherlock Holmes* by Sir Arthur Conan Doyle, Doubleday and Company, Inc., New York. © 1953. **8** Based on *The Teaching of English Usage* by Robert C. Pooley. Copyright © 1974 by the National Council of Teachers of English, Urbana, Illinois. Reprinted by permission of the National Council of Teachers of English.

Chapter 8 **1** Caterpillar Tractor Company advertisement, *Time* magazine, April 17, 1979. **2** Advertisement "There Are Answers", National Rural Electric Cooperative Association, Washington, D.C., *Smithsonian Magazine*, May 1978, Vol. 9, No. 2, p. 137. **3** "What You Should Know About the Hazards of Nuclear Power", brochure, Union of Concerned Scientists, Cambridge, Massachusetts. **4** Promotion letter, The Whale Protection Fund, 1925 K Street, N.W., Washington, D.C. 20006, as edited. © Center for Environmental Education. **5** Adapted from the referendum, Common Cause, Washington, D.C., Spring 1977. **6** From '*The Husband of Xanthippe' and Other Short Plays* by Conrad Seiler, Walter H. Baker Company, Boston. ©1929. **7** "Candidates Meet Match in Vocal Carrollwood Audience", story by Kim I. Eisler, The Tampa *Tribune*, August 29, 1978. Reprinted by permission of The Tampa *Tribune*. **8** Letter and reply from Ann Landers' column, New Orleans *Times-Picayune*, August 13, 1978. © Field Newspaper Syndicate, reprinted by permission of Ann Landers. **9** From "Cop-Out Realism" by Norman Cousins, *Saturday Review*, September 2, 1978. **10** "Catch 22 Incident" by Joseph Heller. © 1955, 1961 by Joseph Heller. Reprinted by permission of Simon & Schuster, a Division of Gulf & Western Corporation, New York. **11** " 'Tax Reform Crusader' Should Get the Facts Straight" by Clyde A. Benedex. The Tampa *Tribune*, August 14, 1978.

Chapter 9 **1** Excerpt from article by Karl Meyer, *Saturday Review*, October 14, 1978, p. 56. © *Saturday Review*, 1978. All rights reserved. **2** From *The Scientific Approach* by J.T. Davies, Academic Press, Inc., New York, 1965. **3** From *Letters from Pompeii* by Wilhelmina Feemster Jashemski, © Copyright 1963 by Ginn & Company (Xerox Corporation). Used with permission.

Chapter 10 **1** Section on solar energy from *Readers' Guide to Periodical Literature*, August 1978, Vol. 78, No. 10, p. 350. © 1978 by the H.W. Wilson Company. Material reproduced by permission of the publisher.

Chapter 11 **1** Edited excerpt from *To Race the Wind/An Autobiography* by Harold Krents. © 1972 by Harold Krents. Reprinted by permission of G.P. Putnam's Sons, New York. **2** From *Nigger/An Autobiography* by Dick Gregory (with Robert Lipsyte). © 1964 by Dick Gregory Enterprises, Inc. Reprinted by permission of E.P. Dutton & Company, Inc., New York. **3** From *The Women's Room* by Marilyn French. © 1977 by Harcourt Brace Jovanovich (Jove), New York. **4** From "When Mount Vesuvius Erupted . . ." by M.W. Newman, Chicago Sun-Times, August 1978. **5** From *The Great Railway Bazaar* by Paul Theroux, Ballantine Books, New York, © 1975. **6** From "Remembering Betsy of the Evil Eye" by Gene Plowden, *Parade*, September 20, 1978. **7** From *Richard Halliburton His Life's Adventures* by Richard Halliburton, © 1940 renewed 1968 by The Bobbs-Merrill Co., Inc. Reprinted by permission of the publisher. **8** From "The Pompidolium" by Horace Sutton, *Saturday Review*, September 2, 1978, p. 44. © 1978, *Saturday Review*. All rights reserved. **9** From "What Can the Technical Writer of the Past Teach the Technical Writer of Today?" by Walter James Miller from *The Teaching of Technical Writing*, edited by Donald H. Cunningham and Herman A. Estrin, National Council of Teachers of English, Urbana, Illinois, 1975. **10** From "Repent, Harlequin!" Said the Ticktockman by Harlan Ellison, © 1965, Galaxy Publishing Corp. Copyright assigned 1969 to Harlan Ellison. All rights reserved. **11** From *Crime and Punishment* by Fyodor Dostoyevsky. **12** From *Cane* by Jean Toomer, Liveright, Publishers, New York. Copyright © 1951 by Jean Toomer. **13** From *How to Survive in Your Native Land* by

James Herndon, Simon & Schuster, Inc., New York. Copyright © 1971 by James Herndon. **14** From *Dandelion Wine* by Ray Bradbury, Copyright © 1953 by Ray Bradbury. Reprinted by permission of Harold Matson Co., Inc.

Chapter 12 **1** From *Something About My Father/and Other People* by Charles Angoff, Thomas Yoseloff, Inc., Cranbury, N.J. Copyright © 1956 by Charles Angoff. Reprinted by permission of the publisher. **2** From *The Summer Book* by Tove Jansson, translated by Thomas Teal. Copyright © 1975 by Random House, Inc. Reprinted by permission of Random House, Inc. **3** From "We Played for Lombardi" by Jerry Kramer, *Life*, Vol. 69, No. 11, September 11, 1970. Reprinted by permission of the author. **4** From *To Be Young, Gifted, and Black* by Lorraine Hansberry, Prentice-Hall, Inc., Englewood Cliffs, N.J. © 1969 by Robert Nemiroff and Robert Nemiroff as Executor of the Estate of Lorraine Hansberry. **5** From *Coming Into the Country* by John McPhee, Farrar, Straus and Giroux, New York. © 1976, 1977 by John McPhee. **6** From *Jane Eyre* by Charlotte Brontë, © 1943 by Random House, Inc., New York. **7** From "Blacks in Communications: Journalism, Public Relations and Advertising" by M.L. Stein, © 1972 by M.L. Stein. Reprinted as adapted and edited by permission of Julian Messner, a Simon & Shuster division of Gulf & Western Corporation. **8** Excerpt from "The Sandcastle" by Iris Murdoch. © 1957 by Iris Murdoch. All rights reserved. Reprinted by permission of Viking Penguin, Inc. and Chatto & Windus, London. **9** Excerpt from "Cress Delahanty" by Jessamyn West, © 1951 by The Curtis Publishing Company. Reprinted from "Cress Delahanty" by Jessamyn West by permission of Harcourt Brace Jovanovich, Inc. **10** From "Under the Auchincloss Shell" by C.D.B Bryan, *The New York Times Magazine*, February 11, 1979. **11** McPhee, op.cit.

Chapter 13 **1** From *Selected Poems and Parodies* by Louis Untermeyer. © 1916 by Harcourt Brace Jovanovich, Inc., New York. Copyright © 1944 by Louis Untermeyer. Reprinted by permission of Harcourt Brace Jovanovich, Inc. **2** From *The Well-Wrought Urn* by Cleanth Brooks. Published by Harcourt Brace Jovanovich, Inc., New York, 1947. **3** From *Sea and Sardinia* by D.H. Lawrence, © 1921 by Thomas Seltzer, Inc. Copyright © 1949 by Frida Lawrence. All rights reserved. Reprinted by permission of The Viking Press, Inc. **4** From Frank Budgen, *James Joyce: Two Decades of Criticism*, in "The Art of James Joyce/Method and Design in *Ulysses* and *Finnegan's Wake*." by A. Walton Litz. Oxford University Press, London, © 1960. **5** From *Serve Me a Slice of Moon* by Marcie Hans. © 1965 by Marcie Hans. Reprinted by permission of Harcourt Brace Jovanovich, Inc. **6** From *Laughing Time* by William Jay Smith, © 1955, Little Brown and Company, Boston, and *The Atlantic Monthly*. **7** From "The Art of James Joyce/Method and Design in *Ulysses* and *Finnegan's Wake* by A. Walton Litz, Oxford University Press, London, © 1961. **8** From *A Portrait of the Artist as a Young Man* by James Joyce. © 1972 by Viking Penguin, Inc. Reprinted by permission of the publisher. **9** From *The Sound and the Fury* by William Faulkner, copyright © 1929 and renewed 1957 by William Faulkner. Copyright © 1946 by Random House, Inc., New York. Reprinted by permission of Random House, Inc. **10** From *73 Poems* by e. e. cummings. © 1963 by Marion Morehouse Cummings. Reprinted from *COMPLETE POEMS 1913-1962* by e. e. cummings by permission of Harcourt Brace Jovanovich, Inc. **11** From AN *INTRODUCTION TO HAIKU* by Harold G. Henderson. © 1958 by Harold G. Henderson. Reprinted by permission of Doubleday & Company, Inc. **12** From *The Book of Humorous Verse* compiled by Carolyn Wills, © 1920 by Doubleday & Company, Inc., Garden City, N.Y. Reprinted by permission of Maurice O'Connell,

Jr. **13** From "Method in Certain Cases" by Jewel Martin in *Creative Youth*, edited by Hughes Mearns, © 1925 by Doubleday & Company, Inc., Garden City, N.Y. Reprinted by permission of the publisher.

Chapter 14 **1** From "Outlooks/Editorial: The Paradoxes of Lyof Tolstoy", *Saturday Review*, October 28, 1978, p. 54. © *Saturday Review* 1978. All rights reserved. **2** Based on *Elements of Writing About a Literary Work: A Study of Responses to Literature* by Alan C. Purves and Victoria Reppere, NCTE Research Report #9, National Council of Teachers of English, 1968. **3** From "A Review of FAIRY TALES AND AFTER: FROM SNOW WHITE TO E.B. WHITE by Roger Sale" by Clara Claiborne Park, *Saturday Review*, December 12, 1978, p. 53. © *Saturday Review* 1978. All rights reserved. **4** From "Of Rats, Bones, Shadows and Time by Ray Bradbury", a critique of *The Night Country* by Loren Eiseley, in *The Sunday Record*, Hackensack, N.J., January 23, 1972. © 1972 by Times Mirror Company. Reprinted by permission of Harold Matson Company, Inc. **5** "Review of The Followed Man by Thomas Williams" by Richard Marek, *Atlantic Monthly*, December 1978, Vol. 242, No. 6. © 1978 by The Atlantic Monthly Company, Boston, Mass. Reprinted by permission of The Atlantic Monthly Company. **6** From "Excellence in Poetry" by Hayden Carruth, *Harper's Magazine*, November 1978, Vol. 257, No. 1542. © 1978 by *Harper's Magazine*, all rights reserved. Reprinted by special permission of *Harper's Magazine*, as edited. **7** "Pigments and the Colonized Personality by Léon Damas" by Ellen Conroy Kennedy, *Black World*, Vol. XXI, No. 3, January 1972, p. 10. Copyright © 1972 by Ellen Conroy Kennedy. Reprinted by permission of the author. **8** From *Portraits and Protests* by Sarah N. Cleghorn. All rights reserved. Reprinted by permission of Holt, Rinehart and Winston, Inc. **9** From *The Complete Poems of Paul Laurence Dunbar*. Reprinted by permission of Dodd, Mead & Company, Inc. **10** "Ex-Basketball Player" from *The Carpentered Hen and Other Tame Creatures* by John Updike. Copyright © 1957 by John Updike. Originally appeared in *The New Yorker*. Reprinted by permission of Harper & Row, Publishers, Inc. **11** From *Selected Poems*, Third Edition, revised and enlarged, by John Crowe Ransom. Copyright © 1927 by Alfred A. Knopf, Inc. and renewed 1955 by John Crowe Ransom. Reprinted by permission of Alfred A. Knopf, Inc. **12** "We Real Cool"—The Pool Players. Seven at the Golden Shovel from *THE WORLD OF GWENDOLYN BROOKS* by Gwendolyn Brooks. © 1959 by Gwendolyn Brooks. Reprinted by permission of Harper & Row, Publishers, Inc. **13** "Mushrooms" from *THE COLOSSUS AND OTHER POEMS* by Sylvia Plath. © 1960 by Sylvia Plath. Published by Faber & Faber, London, © 1971 by Ted Hughes. Reprinted by permission of Alfred A. Knopf, Inc. **14** "Portrait by a Neighbor" from *COLLECTED POEMS* by Edna St. Vincent Millay. Harper & Row, Publishers, Inc., New York. Copyright © 1922, 1950 by Edna St. Vincent Millay. **15** From *Collected Shorter Poems 1927-1957* by W.H. Auden. Copyright © 1940, 1968 by W.H. Auden. Reprinted by permission of Random House, Inc. and Faber and Faber, Limited, London. **16** From *Collected Poems* by Siegfried Sassoon, © 1918 by E.P. Dutton and Company, 1946 by Siegfried Sassoon. Reprinted by permission of The Viking Press, Inc. and Mr. G.T. Sassoon. **17** Poem, *Southbound to the Freeway* from *New and Selected Things Taking Place* by May Swenson. Copyright © 1963 by May Swenson. Originally appeared in *The New Yorker*. Reprinted by permission of Little, Brown and Co. in association with The Atlantic Monthly Press.

Style Sheet **1** From *Everything but Money* by Sam Levinson, Simon & Schuster, 1966.

Index